Artificial Intelligence, Simulation and Society

Series Editor

Petra Ahrweiler, TISSS Lab, Institute for Sociology, Johannes Gutenberg University of Mainz, Mainz, Germany

This book series brings into its fold key and emerging topics on the interactions between growing artificial intelligence technologies and their social impacts. It addresses various aspects of the relationship between AI, simulation, and society and provides insights into their intersections and stimulates discussions on the opportunities and challenges they present. The series is multi- and transdisciplinary in scope, and dynamic. It invites academic contributed volumes and monographs, but also more popular work suitable for lay readership, and innovatively includes some science fiction to initiate readers into the scope and aims of this novel series.

The specific themes and topics covered under the series are:

- **The ethical and societal implications of AI**: The series delves into the ethical considerations and societal impacts of AI technologies. It explores topics such as privacy, bias, job displacement, and the role of AI in shaping social structures from a social science point of view (sociological, political, economic, cultural, legal).
- **Simulation and modeling of social systems**: The series explores how simulation techniques are used to model and understand complex social systems and create artificial societies in silico. It covers topics such as social network analysis, agent-based modelling (ABM), and the simulation of collective behaviour.
- **AI and social simulation**: The series explores how AI technologies are used in social simulation, for example, modelling intelligent agents in agent architectures of ABM, or calibrating and validating models using intelligent data mining and analysis techniques.
- **AI and simulation in social philosophy**: It looks at how AI and simulation are depicted in social philosophy, for example, the role of AI and simulation in socio-technical evolution, the position of AI and simulation in Western rationalism, philosophical counter-designs of current developments, ontological and epistemological limitations and barriers of AI and simulation.
- **AI, simulation and society in fiction**: The series also innovatively examines the portrayal of AI and simulation in and as fiction, demonstrating how these themes reflect societal fears, aspirations, and ethical dilemmas. The series contains both original fiction and second-order analyses.
- **AI and simulation in entertainment:**It covers simulation techniques, combined with AI, that are used to create virtual worlds and characters that mimic human behaviour. Such simulations are used, for example, in video games, virtual reality experiences, and entertainment applications.
- **AI and simulation in various disciplines**: The series discusses the applications of AI and simulations that are/will be transforming various disciplines and domains such as healthcare (e.g. in medical diagnosis, drug discovery, and patient care), work (e.g. automation, Industry 4.0, workforce dynamics), or education (e.g. virtual reality, personalised learning systems, intelligent tutoring systems). It discusses the potential benefits and challenges of integrating these technologies into the conventional space.
- **AI, simulation, and policy**: The series analyses how AI and simulation techniques can inform the policy cycles. It discusses the use of predictive modelling, analysis of what-if scenarios, and decision support systems in shaping policies in various policy domains such as public policy, technology policy or environmental policy.

Petra Ahrweiler

Angels and Other Cows

A Celestial Adventure into AI Worlds, the Social Good, and Unknown Connections

Petra Ahrweiler
TISSS Lab
Johannes Gutenberg University Mainz
Mainz, Rheinland-Pfalz, Germany

ISSN 3004-9822   ISSN 3004-9830 (electronic)
Artificial Intelligence, Simulation and Society
ISBN 978-3-031-60400-3   ISBN 978-3-031-60401-0 (eBook)
https://doi.org/10.1007/978-3-031-60401-0

© The Editor(s) (if applicable) and The Author(s) 2024. This book is an open access publication.
Open Access This book is licensed under the terms of the Creative Commons Attribution 4.0 International License (http://creativecommons.org/licenses/by/4.0/), which permits use, sharing, adaptation, distribution and reproduction in any medium or format, as long as you give appropriate credit to the original author(s) and the source, provide a link to the Creative Commons license and indicate if changes were made.

The images or other third party material in this book are included in the book's Creative Commons license, unless indicated otherwise in a credit line to the material. If material is not included in the book's Creative Commons license and your intended use is not permitted by statutory regulation or exceeds the permitted use, you will need to obtain permission directly from the copyright holder.

The use of general descriptive names, registered names, trademarks, service marks, etc. in this publication does not imply, even in the absence of a specific statement, that such names are exempt from the relevant protective laws and regulations and therefore free for general use.

The publisher, the authors and the editors are safe to assume that the advice and information in this book are believed to be true and accurate at the date of publication. Neither the publisher nor the authors or the editors give a warranty, expressed or implied, with respect to the material contained herein or for any errors or omissions that may have been made. The publisher remains neutral with regard to jurisdictional claims in published maps and institutional affiliations.

This Springer imprint is published by the registered company Springer Nature Switzerland AG
The registered company address is: Gewerbestrasse 11, 6330 Cham, Switzerland

If disposing of this product, please recycle the paper.

Prologue

Angels' Play

Location:
Colibri Wharf, Headquarter Docks, Office Cloud Block, Gamma Hydra, Sector 14, Coordinates 22,83,7. Heaven with billowing clouds.

Time:
Real-time CET, 15 August 2018, 04:35

Players:
Two operating angels have golden wings—one in an orange robe and the other in a green one. The orange one is obviously from St. Gabriel's team, as can be deduced from its outfit.

It has androgynous, even female, features. Its hair boasts a beautiful Madonna lily. Gabrielite angels always have a musical accessory with them to play proper music; the orange one carries a big golden trumpet around its shoulders. The green one is a quite macho-looking seraph from St. Michael's team, with a visible robotic implant on its right biceps. Although these are supposed to be peaceful angels, members of this team habitually carry weapons with them: The green one's outfit for this day includes a big endrispec, which is a futuristic machinegun-type firearm with some slight allusion to the armour of Arnold Schwarzenegger in Terminator.

Setting:
The two guardian angels simultaneously apparate with their travel kits in front of a Shared-Office Cloud. Both have their marching orders and cloud transponders in their hands to open the workspace and unlock functions. They nod their greetings a little suspiciously because angels from the same team usually work together on assignments. This does not seem to apply here. They assess each other's outfits with disapprovingly raised eyebrows.

TA (*smartly saluting, with the endrispec to its new colleague and with its fingers dangerously close to the trigger*):

Peace and bliss. I am Tilda's angel. You can just call me TA. Nice to meet you!

GA (*anxiously pointing to the firearm*): You are not allowed to fire on clouds. This can lead to decommissioning—you know that. (*getting back its countenance, graciously bowing and curtsying*) Gabriel's guardian angel. GA, if you like. Fifty-four years of work experience. Delighted to be with you on this travel assignment. Seems to be a dangerous one if the TRINI-T Personnel Section has called for a Michaelite. Shall we go in?

TA uses its transponder, and the cloud pops open. Both angels enter and freeze in surprise. It is not the standard twin-office interior that they're used to, but a comparatively huge workspace with all the amenities of a top work environment has been divided into two generous areas.

On the left is the usual twin-seat cockpit bridge of a standard office cloud with two big commanding chairs full of consoles, screens and buttons; between the two commanding chairs is a huge round looking-glass with a direct view of earth—at the moment blinded because the cloud is docked.

On the right is a fully equipped conference space, the size of a cinema: large interactive computer screens on the walls, all types of virtual- and augmented-reality equipment, open planetary glass ceilings, a large meeting table with a 3D server for holograms in the middle, two high-performance laptops for machine-learning and XAI applications, seven multipurpose chairs, flipcharts, pinboards, sticky notes in all colours, storage space with all sorts of toolkits and even a smart kitchenette with a fridge and a coffee machine that immediately starts to brew when they enter.

TA (*admiringly*): Blimey. This is what it looks like when you are assigned to headquarter business. Pure luxury. My last assignment took place in what amounts to a broom closet compared to this. What's our assignment about?

GA (*scanning its marching order*): My marching order says that our two charges will travel the world together "to put together an international aid project." The project is about repairing technology (*wrinkling its little nose because it heartily dislikes technology*). Artificial intelligence. Machine learning.

TA (*looking at the blinking computers on the conference facility*): We use that technology ourselves. What's wrong with it?

GA (*no expert on technology but happy to see that it is explained in simple words*):
Repair down on earth is planned for a specific application. AI that is used worldwide for distributing social services such as unemployment benefits, pensions and kindergarten placements. (*looking up incredulously*) Did you know that a computer decides whether you get a kindergarten placement if you apply for one? And that this is already the way they do it in many countries?

TA (*shaking its head*) No, I did not. I do not need a kindergarten placement anyway. (*thinking hard what it could apply for instead*) But I could do with some official job training as a musician if I had such a nice golden trumpet (*enviously looking at the shiny instrument around the shoulders of its colleague*).

GA (*protectively clutching its trumpet*):
AI would never give you one. Only Gabrielites can apply for job training as musicians. I mean, you can apply of course, but you will never get it. Michaelites are not famous for their musicality. You simply do not fulfil the criteria. Statistically, you are crap at music.

TA (*insulted*):
Unfair. You don't know me. I'm very good on the triangle. I deserve training. (*stomping with its little foot*) Terribly unfair.

GA (*reprovingly shaking its head and reading on*):
Seems that earthly AI is accused of making unfair decisions concerning kindergarten placements, pensions and unemployment benefits. Our two charges shall repair the mess. Making AI fairer.

TA (*a little rebelliously*):
Why is this angel business anyway? Repairing technology doesn't exactly suit our job description, does it?

GA (*matter of fact*):
Being guardians to people no matter what they do is our job description. Furthermore, (*reading again from the marching order*) in this case, repairing technology is connected to all sorts of ethical issues that touch on central angel business. Building a machine that can make a fair decision on whether you get or do not get something from the state seems to be a big challenge. If you don't get this right, it will endanger peace and justice.

TA (*trying again*):
Yes, I'm already angry and don't feel peaceful. I want to have a golden trumpet from whoever decides—AI or no. (*seeing that its colleague will not react to this, the angel searchingly looks around*) Where's the Script for our next steps? It should be here somewhere.

They soon discover the usual smart tablet with the instruction manual in the middle of the conference table. The device is available for every assignment and is called the Script. Both angels take a chair before reading the first sentences.

TA (*leafing through the first pages of the Script*): Here is a little editorial telling us how to get started. First thing is a mutual assessment of our charges. You go first.

GA presses a few buttons on the console, and a hologram of Gabriel appears on the table. He is handsome, tall and slim, blond with much hair for a middle-aged man, blue-eyed with a face both clear-cut and candid, cleanly shaven. He smiles at the two angels and winks amiably for a greeting. With an elegant swing, he turns around to let the angels see him from all sides.

GA (*doing the social assessment in its professional reporting voice*): Gabriel David. Male. Age: fifty-four. White. Heterosexual. Married to a medical doctor with two grown-up kids. Family person. German nationality. Hobbies: reading, singing and playing piano. Catholic convert. Helper syndrome. A complete Westerner. Romantic. Womaniser. Raised with a golden spoon in his mouth. Anthropologist with a strong focus on justice issues. High-school degree from a Jesuit school. Baby boomer. Professional career with international welfare organisations as a manager of social development projects across the globe. High intercultural competence and social skills. Now working at an international aid company in Berlin called B1. (*laughing*) Funny name: 'Be One.' Experienced in leading large teams. Strong management skills. Entrepreneurial and active.

TA (*scanning Gabriel's profile and disapprovingly watching the still-smiling hologram*): Bit full of himself if you ask me. This guy will be scoring high in the category of terrible softie. Pretty useless. Why has he been assigned?

GA (*explaining*): Gabriel was chosen by the TRINI-T Saints Section as a subject for revelation because he is religiously receptive. Furthermore, he is a good moderator. As you can imagine, there is a lot of conflict around the topic of the project. (*hastily going on before its colleague can start trying to claim a golden trumpet again*) Gabriel is supposed to bring people together to discuss fair solutions (*waving away the sceptical face of its colleague*). He *can* do that. Baby Boomers are good at integration, cooperation and communication; they love negotiation.

TA (*still doubtfully looking at the benevolently smiling hologram on the table*): Hm. (*then hitting a few keys on the machine-learning laptops on the conference table*) How do our AI machines score the guy?

TA uses the search term "subject for revelation + bringing people together to help with better AI." The laptop screen shows how the computer algorithm scans the world population database to score individuals. Only milliseconds elapse before the scoring shows the five top-ranked living individuals in the world who come closest to the profile searched for thanks to their personal attributes. Gabriel comes out as the highest score among the top-ranked individuals.

GA (*triumphantly*): See? Now, what about Tilda? What about your charge?

TA produces the hologram of Tilda on the conference table. GA can't suppress a surprised little noise, which alerts the virtual Tilda, who then looks up from her mobile phone, which she is typing on, and scowls at the angel. Tilda is small, wiry and full of muscles. She has dark mouse-like hair with a few blue highlights in between. She has shoulder-length hair on one side of her head, and on the other side is shaved above her ear. Her ears, nose and lips are pierced. On her right bicep is an elaborate text tattoo that GA can't decipher at this distance.

TA (*apologetically shrugging its shoulders, then standing to attention for the social assessment report*): Tilda. Female. Age: twenty-eight. White. Single. Lives with her boyfriend in Berlin Kreuzberg. German nationality. Low income.

Kickboxing champion in the international martial arts league in 2013. The unwieldy type. Hobbies: Fitness, weight training and obviously her smartphone. No religious affiliation but some ideological convictions. Dedicated vegan and antivaccinationist. Animal rights activist. Has studied political science. Strong presence on alternative social media. Disappointed by public institutions; does not believe in "the state." Has worked as a junior project operator in Gabriel's team for a few months.

GA (*squinting, discouraged by Tilda*): No travel experience. No intercultural competence. How can TRINI-T Personnel Section think that she can create better AI? I wonder. Tilda does not sound like the usual suspect for a religious revelation either. Are you sure you're on the correct person? Why are you here?

TA (*defensively*): Martial arts. Tilda is an athlete. She can endure all hardships that can be expected during a world-travel project. And she is intelligent. Gabriel has appointed her to his team because of her proficiency with social media.

Tilda was the best choice anyway—believe me. It's incredibly hard to find somebody with both brains and athleticism. Furthermore, TRINI-T Personnel Section wanted somebody with the strong discipline of an athlete. How many people do you think fit that bill?

GA (*still doubtful*): My marching order says that Tilda can't fully fight, because she sustained a combat injury on her ankle, and she sometimes can't even walk properly. And she is female. Last but not least, she is much too young and inexperienced. She and Gabriel are totally mismatched. They'll kill each other. Was she really the first choice for this assignment with such a dreadful profile? What does AI say about her social assessment score?

GA tries to start the profile search string on the machine-learning laptop again, but TA unexpectedly pushes the laptop away.

TA (*pleadingly*):
You know that this old-fashioned AI algorithm is full of discrimination and bias! It's trained on old data from the past. It just reproduces statistical evidence from the past and extrapolates it into the future. If the training data show that mostly rich old white farts like Gabriel have been recruited for revelation in the past, people like Tilda will never get a chance, no matter how good they would be on the job.

Just because people like Tilda are not the usual suspects does not mean that she can't do it. There's no causality behind AI, only correlation. Scores don't say anything about the exact future behaviour or performance of a concrete individual. Give Tilda a chance!

GA does not look very convinced. In the meantime, the Tilda hologram has started her gym exercise with some round kicks against an invisible antagonist. The woman tries to give the impression of a very dangerous person, but she limps sometimes when she lands on her foot, obviously hurt. GA shakes its head and fumbles for the hotline number to TRINI-T Complaints Department.

TA: (*threateningly*): If you do that, I'll report you for sexism and ableism. Any assignment has to prefer disabled people and women. And there is also a rule to recruit early-career candidates. Tilda is perfect.

GA (*giving in*):
OK. Let's try with her. Starting place is Sussex, UK, according to the Script. Do you have the coordinates?

TA (*walking over to its cockpit seat, starting the WX drive and checking all navigation instruments*):
I will bring us out of here with WX 5.

As acting pilot, the angel pushes a few buttons, and the cloud slowly billows out of the docks in the direction of Workspace Galaxy in real time.

Location:
The cloud stops above a tiny train station in southern England. In the middle of nowhere. The station sign reads 'Stonegate.' No village, no dwellings to be seen far and wide—only rolling Sussex hills. A warm, sunny October afternoon.

Time:
Real-time CET, 1 October 2018, 16:35

Two people have just disembarked from the little local train already disappearing in the distance. Gabriel and Tilda are seemingly as mismatched as the two angels before. The well-groomed gentleman is in his fifties, wearing an orange long-sleeved shirt, elegant white chinos and cool orange reflective sunglasses. He has only a small office rucksack on his back and is giving warm smiles to the few fellow passengers that have disembarked with them. He seems to hope that somebody will offer them a lift. However, everybody is quickly leaving the little car park of the train station without paying him any mind.

Sunset in Sussex

After Gabriel and Tilda checked their mobile phones, which had no signal, and scanned the sparse information on the station display board of the train station in vain for any hint of what people who end up here should do for transportation, they decided to set off on foot, following the small winding country road in search of a village. It helped that Gabriel had lost his luggage when changing flights in Frankfurt: no trolley to drag behind and hands free—at least for him. The sun shone golden on the Sussex fields, the birds were singing and the wind breathed lightly through the hawthorn hedges.

Gabriel was embarrassed. He anxiously watched his new employee, Tilda, who seemed completely out of place in this idyllic Sussex landscape. Her attire looked as if she came directly from a battlefield. She was clad in dark-green camouflage khakis and hoodie; on her feet were Bovver boots. She had a heavy military rucksack on her back and a small black office rucksack on her front. Her brows were furrowed. She was obviously in quite a bad temper, scowling at the final cars as they disappeared into the solitary countryside. "Shall I carry one of your rucksacks?" Gabriel asked. Tilda only shook her head disdainfully.

Slightly abashed to have led her to such a lonely place on their first business trip together, he said encouragingly, "I think I can see Stonegate. It'll be a lovely walk, and we'll get to see the sunset." Tilda responded unpleasantly: "I don't care about the sunset. Stupid idea of your colleagues to rent a manor for a one-week workshop in the middle of nowhere. Why can't we meet at a proper place in the city?" Gabriel felt defensive when he responded: "Nature is good for increasing work performance. Everybody knows that. English country life!" Tilda looked at him mockingly. "Including a nice hiccup where we switch locations at the very last minute from Kent to Sussex. We had to change our train tickets and lost money because of it. A water leakage in Kent, believe it or not."

Gabriel shrugged his shoulders. "This here is pure nature, indeed," she continued sullenly, kicking away some leaves in her way. "Really great for my work performance. I already feel it coming." "There will be a swimming pool and a jacuzzi on the terrace, I've heard," Gabriel said soothingly and innocently. Tilda scowled. "Dirty old man" was clearly written on her face. Instead, she said, frustrated, "And I've heard that we'll be making our own food. I'm strictly vegan, as you know. I do hope your colleagues will at least do some adequate shopping."

Angels' Play

Location:
Heaven above Stonegate. Shared-Office Cloud.

Time:
Real-time GMT, Monday, 1 October 2018, 17:39

Players:
The two angels as before.

Setting:
Both angels are sitting at the VR simulation table. They're on duty, as their gear clearly shows: They wear headphones to stay connected to the world communication network; each has a tablet console with blinking lights, buttons and switches on its lap; and each has a huge suitcase with equipment, gadgets and devices at its side. They can look directly down on earth through a big round looking-glass between them.

TA (*leafing through one of the books beside its seat*):
Here is a Jesuit guy named Pierre Teilhard de Chardin. In his book *Heart of Matter*, he describes a sunset-in-Sussex experience. Listen (*citing*):

"All that I can remember is the extraordinary solidity and intensity I found then in the English countryside, particularly at sunset, when the Sussex woods were charged with all that 'fossil' life which I was then hunting for, from cliff to quarry, in the Wealden clay. There were moments, indeed, when it seemed to me that a sort of universal being was about to take shape suddenly in nature before my very eyes."

That sounds like it, right?

GA (*checking the Script*):

It is indeed similar, but we have to follow a different author. Author's birth name is Alan Richard Griffiths. He is Benedictine, not Jesuit. His order name as a monk is Bede, which means "eternal, living, immortal." Bede Griffiths, the guy is called. "Sunset in Sussex—a vision of nature" is his text, the one that we're supposed to follow. You're the simulation expert. Can you simulate the Griffiths text? We have all the relevant data, right?

TA types on its tablet and starts TRINIT-Logo, the multiagent, programmable modelling environment for general-purpose simulation.

TA (*programming a Sussex landscape that slowly appears as a VR environment on the simulation table*):

Not so easy to manage the immersive reality effect. It will only be a substitute for the real thing. Just a model of a Sussex landscape. Don't be disappointed. The advantage is that as a computer simulation, the model is not static but instead displays behaviour. It will be a landscape with a sinking sun, flying birds and billowing clouds.

GA (*drily*):

This is not about convincing me. *Simulacrum*, the word that *simulation* stems from, means "similarity" not "sameness." The main purpose of the simulation is to give a nature experience to Gabriel and Tilda.

TA (*in a complaining voice*):

This last-minute change from Kent to Sussex was pretty difficult to operate, by the way. I could hardly manage to facilitate the booking change to Sussex. How could you make such a mistake? It should be in your files where Bede Griffiths went to school and had his first mystical experience. Not in Kent, right? This is hopefully the only mistake in your preparation!

GA (*defensively*):

At least it was a splendid idea of mine to hold on to Gabriel's luggage. Lost luggage, good thinking. (*contently looking at the little rucksack on Gabriel's shoulders*) No point in walking with two suitcases on a lonely country road.

TA (*nearly done with the simulation, which is displayed on the simulation table secretly admired by GA*):

Anyway, I will increase probabilities in my statistical modelling that his bags will arrive tomorrow in time for dinner. Otherwise, Gabriel won't have his swimwear for the pool.

TA pressing buttons on its tablet for downloading the finished simulation to earth.

Prologue

GA (*excitedly peeping down at the scenery*):
Are you ready? They're coming! What next? Sunset, alright? You know we need a real one *(watching TA meticulously follow the Script with its programming)*.

TA (*clenching its teeth*): Blimey, I can't do a lark. It's simply too late in the season. They've all left to go to Spain. I don't have a specimen to copy. I can't possibly ask one to return just for this purpose.

GA (*soothingly*): I think we can do without. Look at them. They've been telling each other stories on their way. They wouldn't hear your lark anyway. If they backtrack later, they'll notice the missing lark, but for the time being, we'll be OK.

TA (*enthusiastically finishing its little hackathon*):
OK, then. Count down. Three, two, one… Hush!
Both angels silently and admiringly watch the red-gold sunset below.

Preface

"Angels and Other Cows" is a novel in literary fiction blending genres such as sci-fi, romance, adventure, mystery and comedy. The novel precedes two scientific publications on the use of artificial intelligence (AI) for the distribution of public social services,[1] which are forthcoming in this series. Its task is inclusive science communication, making available the research topics, results and consequences of AI use in the public sector to a broad readership and also attracting nonscientists to academic research.

In more and more countries, public administrations increasingly use AI algorithms to decide on social service provisions among their citizens, hoping to achieve greater efficiency and objectivity. The topic is important for the future of our societies, and research results should be accessible by and available to all citizens. The question of who gets what from the state concerns everybody—be it a policymaker hoping for efficiency and objectivity in allocation, a recipient hoping for support and wellbeing, a service provider, a taxpayer or a member of a vulnerable group confronted with barriers. Whether AI makes things better or worse is of actual interest to all. This makes all people living in welfare systems stakeholders of research. Thus, science communication needs to be open, inclusive, accessible and participatory. Research, however, is often available only to experts, is shaped by their interests and is framed by their language. These conditions act as barriers that exclude the general public, especially those people particularly affected, i.e. in need of better methods for social service provision. Hence, science communication requires inclusive formats that are accessible to nonscientific audiences.

In AI-based social service provision, citizen profiles are automatically assessed for their scores to receive—or not to receive—scarce public goods. Everywhere, delegating distributive justice to machines exacerbates important questions about bias and discrimination. Systems are challenged for using "unfair AI," i.e. their potential

---

[1] The author gratefully acknowledges funding for open access publication by the German VolkswagenStiftung related to grant agreement number 98 560, and matching open access funding by Johannes Gutenberg University, Mainz in Germany. Both funders support the four books approach of the inclusive science communication strategy.

to increase and cement existing inequalities and injustices via technology. However, this does not mean the same thing across the globe. For example, in India, social service provision is related to membership in religious castes; in China, to political attitudes and desired social behaviour; and in Ukraine, to places of residence because of the current war situation. Also in countries seemingly alike in welfare approaches, such as European Union countries, differences related to cultural values are huge, as will be revealed by the research results of the two scientific volumes following this novel. There is no one-size-fits-all approach to social justice that would be perceived as fair everywhere. Decision-making on social welfare questions is highly contingent and dependent on values, culture and context. "Better AI" technically that supports fair welfare decisions has different meanings to different people in different places.

The story of "Angels and Other Cows" unfolds both in heaven and on earth. The real-world part narrates the adventure of Gabriel and Tilda, who work for an international aid company called B1. Their mission is to recruit case study partners for a project on AI-based social assessment. Collaborating with partners from diverse countries and societal backgrounds, they delve into the impact of values and culture on social assessment, highlighting issues of bias and discrimination in different systems that categorise humans for the purpose of receiving social welfare. The novel terms this *autoethnographic learning*. Gabriel and Tilda grapple with defining their own relationship, which is fraught with bias, mutual assessments, generational power struggles and milieu-specific world-view clashes.

Their personal journey is intertwined with a global plea for unity in a world marked by dystopian conditions, such as limited public resources, economic crises and disparities in life opportunities across different countries. The world seems divided into antagonistic societies with unique religious and sociocultural belief systems that perpetuate social injustice. The reader gains a comprehensive understanding of these complex themes and embarks on a quest with Gabriel and Tilda to explore whether AI can exacerbate or alleviate these issues. Readers also gain insights into AI and its workings, building a rudimentary understanding of machine learning for AI-based social assessment. Furthermore, they discover the potential benefits and risks, as well as the importance, of involving society in designing technology.

The celestial part of the story is dedicated to reflection. As Gabriel and Tilda grapple with their intellectual and emotional connection, they are aided by two guardian angels, GA and TA, tasked with saving the planet through interpersonal and intercultural integration. These angels mirror their protégés' struggles and provide comic relief, reminiscent of characters Statler and Waldorf from *The Muppet Show*. The "voice of wisdom" is represented by English Benedictine monk Bede Griffiths, who enthusiastically supports Tilda and Gabriel in their unlikely love story.[2] Here, the novel introduces, discusses and negotiates the "deep questions" of the

---

[2] The novel contains longer quotes by Bede Griffiths, who died in 1993. The author gratefully acknowledges these invaluable resources. Quotes are cited and paraphrased from the following books:
Griffiths, B. (1976): Return to the Center. Templegate Publishers: Springfield, Illinois.
Griffiths, B. (1982): The Marriage of East & West. Templegate Publishers: Springfield, Illinois.
Griffiths, B. (2004): Essential Writings. Selected with an Introduction by Thomas Matus. Orbis Books: Maryknoll, New York.

earthly project, and the celestial characters represent various perspectives on the theme. GA aligns with Gabriel's views, whereas TA aligns with Tilda's. This section also reflects on epistemological and ethical limitations and the barriers of AI. By integrating the perspective of Bede Griffiths, a former contemporary mystic of interreligious thought, into cultural studies, the novel presents a counter-design of an alternative society that challenges technocratic pessimism and posthuman evolution, mediating between radical positions.

The fictional story of the novel introduces, reflects and discusses the main epistemological, sociological and technical concepts of the research area. The author of the novel, a social scientist, fictionalises the concepts of AI research to familiarise the reader with the scope of the problems and the "deep questions" of the topic:

- Why is the perpetual categorical differentiation by and of humans a fundamental cultural and social phenomenon?
- How does social assessment, categorisation and differentiation in society work?
- What roles do values, religions, cultures and contexts play in social assessment?
- What roles do bias and discrimination play in social assessment?
- How is social assessment used in public social service provision?
- What is AI-based social assessment, and how does it work? What are the benefits and risks of using that technology for social assessment?
- What questions are asked by technology assessment, in particular in assessing AI when as AI assesses people and people assess AI?
- Is AI the crown of sociotechnical evolution?
- Is AI connected to a specific approach to knowledge, e.g. rationalistic and dualistic concepts, in the wake of digitalisation?
- What might alternative approaches, e.g. intuitionalist and nondualistic concepts, look like?
- What are the epistemological and ethical limitations and barriers of AI?
- Why is involving vulnerable groups important in developing AI?
- Why is involving vulnerable groups in codesigning technology difficult?
- What is a participatory approach in technology production, assessment and governance?
- What would be needed to develop "better AI"?

Given the novel's theme, potential sensitivities in the context of discrimination and cultural appropriation might arise. Because the novel revolves around culture, values, religion, social context and potential bias or discrimination in AI-based social assessment, some readers might be sensitive to some of the topics discussed. While the novel addresses issues from various perspectives, it is centred on inclusivity, justice, equality and nondiscriminatory practices. Sensitivity may arise in how these issues are presented, which cannot always be foreseen. The title, for example, is not meant to be offensive to people in Western religious belief traditions who might wonder why angels and cows are presented on the same level. On the contrary, it stems from a discussion by Gabriel and Tilda at the end of chapter 1 on the isomorphism of cultural concepts—an isomorphism that can serve as a bridge to understanding by following the thoughts of Bede Griffiths on interreligious dialogue. The author is a white female sociologist from the Global North in a nonprecarious job situation who is well aware of the particularity of perspectives that arise from such a position. As a social scientist, she wants to emphasise that discriminatory wording and cultural appropriation have been avoided to the best of her knowledge and ability. However, readers can get in touch if they have other opinions; the fourth and concluding book of the series, which will be another novel evaluating the scientific volumes, will publish all input, discussion and feedback.

The author is very much indebted to her family and friends for patiently bearing the long times when there was no distinction, and consequentially no balance, between work and life. She is especially grateful for the many constructive and sometimes-controversial discussions with fantastic academic colleagues and project partners, who helped to shape the novel's content: among others, Demian Frank, Dale Harwin, Hans Martin Lorentzen, Nigel Gilbert, Sumathi Srinivasalu, Ebin Deni Raj, Albert Sabater Coll, Beatriz Lopez, Roger del Campepadros, Emmanuel Ejim-Eze, Hassan Bashiri, Hui Li, Erik Johnston, Margaret Hinrichs, Chelsea Dickson, Steven Popper, Elina Treyger, Jesús Siqueiros Garcia, Martin Neumann, Elisabeth Späth, Blanca Luque Capellas, David Wurster, Jennifer Abe, Gerhard Kruip, George Kampis, Elisabeth André, Ruben Schlagowski, Katharina Weitz, Bei Gao, Aoibheann Gibbons, Markus Knauff, Zsolt Juranyi and Dario Brockschmidt.

Special thanks for great contributions to the deep questions of the book, open-mindedness and generous hospitality go to the "safe spacers," i.e. the monastic leads and coordinators of the project's safe spaces for technological codesign with vulnerable groups—namely M. Maire Hickey OSB, Sr. Josephine Yator OSB, Fr. Cyprian Consiglio OSB Cam, Fr. Dorathick OSB Cam, P. Manel Gasch OSB, Br. Johannes Tebbe OSB, Br. Elija Pott OSB and P. Jeremias Marseille OSB Cam—together with their communities.

Last but not least, the author is grateful for the entrepreneurial spirit of Springer Nature Publishers, first of all to senior publishing editor (social sciences and positive psychology; Springer Nature Women internal commissioner) Shinjini Chatterjee for finding methods and formats that support our challenging, inclusive science communication strategy of combining fiction and science books. Because these two domains and markets are usually completely separated, combining them into one series for a broad readership with diverse backgrounds is novel and innovative.

The author takes full responsibility for all content in the novel. "Angels and Other Cows" is a work of fiction, and any similarity to actual persons, living or dead (with the exception of biographical details about Bede Griffiths, which he provided in his autobiographical writings), or actual events is purely coincidental.

Mainz, Germany Petra Ahrweiler
06.01.2024

Contents

1	**A Vision of Nature**	1
	The Red Corvette	2
	Telepathy Works	6
	Telepathy with Cows	10
	Taxi to Heathrow	14
	The First Google Maps Miracle	18
	Angels and Other Cows	20
	Dualities Fight Back	23
2	**The Perpetual Allegory**	27
	The Spanish Case	27
	Angels' Play	29
	Experiencing Hardships	30
	Angels' Play	32
	On a Miracle Tour	34
	The Birth of a Project	36
	Thinking About India	38
3	**Dreams and Consciousness**	43
	Angels' Play	45
	A Tika on the Forehead	47
	The Intuitive Mind	49
	Angels' Play	49
	What Men and Machines Cannot Do	53
4	**An Alternative Society**	57
	Are You Going with Me?	57
	Methods at Safe Spaces	58
	Angels' Play	60
	Pita Jungle Detours	62
	The USA Case	63
	Elopement	65

	Angels' Play	66
	"We" and "them"	68
	Not Going Anywhere	70
	Freedom and Determination	70
	The Serpent in the Wilderness	72
	Angels' Play	72
	The Rattlesnake	73
5	**Chinese Walls**	77
	The Chinese Case	77
	Society and Technology on Eye Level	79
	The Second Google Maps Miracle	81
	Tilda in China	82
	Angels' Play	84
6	**What Machines Cannot Do**	87
	California Greening	87
	Angels' Play	88
	Green Shots	89
	Green Food	91
	Angels' Play	94
	The Green Flash	98
	Venice Beach	101
	The Third Google Maps Miracle	103
	Angels' Play	105
	Safe Spaces	106
	The German Case	107
	The Birth of a Concept	109
	Sophia and San Albertino	110
	On the Beach and in the Library	112
	Angels' Play	113
	The Green Ray	116
	Angels' Play	118
	The Divine Dance	118
	Angels' Play	120
	Participation is a Sham	122
	Repairs and Amendments	126
	Angels' Play	128
	Mt. 11:29	130
	And Mt. 10:9-15	131
	The Estonian Case	132
7	**A Visitation from India**	135
	Angels' Play	136
	That All May Be One	138
	Angels' Play	139

	Indian Anthropology	140
	Angels' Play	140
	The Serpent in the Lecture Room	141
	Angels' Play	142
	The Proverbial Meaning of *Terribly Unfair*	142
	Angels' Play	143
	Ayurveda for all	143
	Angels' Play	144
	Outrageous	144
	Angels' Play	146
	Sex with Machines	149
	Angels' Play	151
	Antipasti	153
	Angels' Play	153
	Initial Conditions	156
	Angels' Play	157
	First-level Dialectics in a Sandbox	158
	Angels' Play	159
	Second-level Dialectics in a Sandbox	159
	Angels' Play	160
	Third-level Dialectics in a Sandbox	161
	The Individual, Interactive and Systems Level	161
	Angels' Play	163
	Risks	166
	An Auto-ethnographic Promotion Course	167
	Angels' Play	167
8	**The Heart Shape of India**	**173**
	Angels' Play	173
	Passage to India	175
	Angels' Play	177
	The First Hours in India	178
	Bouribi, the Singing Tuktuk Driver	181
	Angels' Play	183
	The Elephant Son of Shiva and Parvati	184
	Angels' Play	186
	Going to Kerala	187
	Angels' Play	189
	Eating from Banana Leaves	192
	Angels' Play	193
	The India Case	198
	The River Kaveri	201
	Angels' Play	205

9 Final Unity ... 207

- The Heart of Everything ... 208
- Angels' Play ... 209
- Toilet Paper and Salvation ... 211
- Angels' Play ... 212
- Mortal Fear ... 213
- Miraculous Salvation ... 215
- Angels' Play ... 217
- Evolution Starts from the Waters ... 219
- Angels' Play ... 220
- Meeting Shiva and Parvati Again ... 224
- On the "Undoing Differences" Interface Again ... 227
- The Limits of Artificial Intelligence ... 228
  - Angels' Play ... 228
- Where the Three Oceans Meet ... 231
- Angels' Play ... 235
- Mortal Fear Again ... 237
- Infanta ... 239
- A Narrow Escape ... 240
- Angels' Play ... 242
- In the Fair ... 243
- Cooperation, Evolution and Safe Spaces ... 245
- No Sunrise and a Black Swan ... 246
- Angels' Play ... 248
- Summary of Project Definition ... 249
- Healing ... 251
- The Sage of Pondicherry ... 252

10 Land's End ... 255

- Angels' Play ... 255
- Video Nearly Killed the Radio Star ... 259
- Angels' Play ... 262

Chapter 1
A Vision of Nature

Gabriel and Tilda walked side by side in deep conversation. Suddenly they stopped together in the middle of the road and looked around, awestruck. The birds were singing the chorus of creation. The hawthorn trees greeted them in sweet harmony in a garden of paradise. And the golden sun spread its warm embracing red glow as a unifying symphony over the playing fields. A big show. It was like watching how the curtain in a huge theatre slowly raised upwards. It was a spectacular moment. Like a dream in colour, sound and brightness. "Hush!" Gabriel exclaimed at Tilda.

Angels' Play

Location:
Heaven above Stonegate. Shared-Office Cloud.

Time:
Real-time GMT, Monday, 1 October 2018, 17:53

Players:
The two angels as before.

Setting:
Both angels are still sitting at the virtual reality (VR) simulation table discussing their next steps.

GA (*coughing modestly to break the spell while knocking on the Script*):
  Hey, now, "the veil of dusk will begin to cover the earth," you know. End of show.
  What is the plan for bringing them from Stonegate to the meeting venue as quickly as possible? It is no good letting them hang around down there forever. What was to be seen, they have seen. What we can add are some nice pointers for hinting to them that this was a special experience. Any ideas?

TA (*giggles and hits a few keys on its tablet to programme a red cabrio sports car, which triumphantly display it on the simulation table in front of GA's puzzled face*):

How about this? Red Corvette with the chauffeur driving them to the next pub, then two ice-cold draught beers, then their project partners driving by to fetch them by car with some Indian vegan food and red wine... (*seeing the shocked face of its colleague*)

Indian food, you understand? Bede Griffiths will like that as well. The meal should be vegan for my girl. No more hardship. Let us give them a rest.

GA (*warningly shaking its head*):

This red sports-car business is much too obvious! You must be joking. You have no discretion, no taste, no feeling for tact. I only say, "Objective One." Any blackmail, miracle or brute force is strictly out of the question for angels like us. It is a red-line TRINI-T directive not to be crossed. If you start to spoil them this way, they will become lazy. They need to engage! You know that. Humans need to get engaged, not delegate everything to fate or to machines.

TA (*pleadingly admiring the simulated red Corvette*):

Only tonight, OK? Gabriel is used to being spoiled. He will not be suspicious about it. Promise. It will even encourage him. And think about dinner.

The Red Corvette

Arriving at the village of Stonegate with the last arrays of the sinking sun, where dusk and darkness would soon take over, quickly revealed that there would be no hope for a shop, a pub, a phone booth, a taxi or anything else helpful in Gabriel and Tilda's situation. This was just a little hamlet in the middle of nowhere. Not a single soul in the street, no lights behind the curtained windows of the few houses. After aimlessly wandering around for help, Gabriel and Tilda found a middle-aged man in a backyard fetching something from his garden shed whom they could at least ask for the way to Ticehurst.

The man started laughing. "I regret to inform you that we are still about two miles away from Ticehurst, with no public transport and no taxi service if not pre-ordered one day ahead." Despite the recent sunset experience and its glorious inspiration, they felt quite exhausted by then and must have looked very unhappy with the outlook, too unhappy to continue their solitary walk—Tilda tiredly bending under her heavy rucksack.

The man looked at them compassionately and took initiative. "Can I offer you a lift in my car?" "This is very kind of you, sir" Gabriel gratefully answered. The man smiled. "I have just a coupé and can only take one of you at a time if that's OK." Gabriel anxiously looked at his companion for consent, which she silently granted by nodding at him. What the man then fetched from his garage, however, was simply breathtaking: a red Corvette, a cool sports car, which nobody would have ever associated with him and which was obviously his personal pride and joy.

"What's going on?" Gabriel murmured. "This is totally out of place. It seems indicate that something very special is happening here." It also made the man a little suspicious in Gabriel's eyes. He gallantly told Tilda that he, as her boss, would take the first turn to try the red Corvette, to see whether this transfer would be safe for a woman. The man pointed to his house behind and advised Tilda, "Just knock at the door and ask my lady for some hospitality while waiting." Tilda was usually a little shy with these things. However, as she told Gabriel later, that lady, not his wife as she immediately explained to Tilda, was surprised but not unhappy to find an unknown visitor at her doorstep, taking her away from her telly routine.

The two of them had a nice chat about this and that in the surprisingly modern middle-class sitting room. "Amazing that a group of international development managers visits our modest part of the county," the hostess said. "I have never heard of the place you are supposed to go to at Ticehurst." That, indeed, was not such a good message, but maybe she and her boyfriend just lived too remote to know much about what's around them.

Anyway, the ride in the top-opened car through the twilit Sussex countryside was brilliant with its—rolling fields of gold. Gabriel talked with his driver about football. "I am a big fan of Icke Häßler," the man at the wheel confessed. He knew everything that was to be known about the German football league. Soon, they arrived at Ticehurst, which was not much bigger than Stonegate. The man dropped Gabriel off in the village centre, where he patiently waited for Tilda Toelz on a public bench. The red sports-car driver brought his companion half an hour later through the quickly approaching night. After receiving Gabriel's and Tilda's profound thanks, the kind driver left for good. Gabriel and Tilda decided to go to the village pub for a drink and maybe something to eat, as well as to ask the landlord about their final destination. It was pretty dark by then.

Scanning the menu of the cosy old English pub was a disappointment to Tilda, though: Nothing vegan, only meat-heavy pub food, plus fish and chips. They each ordered a well-deserved beer at the bar and brought it outside to one of the few tables facing the high street. There was not really anything to look at but an Indian takeaway across the street, the only place with a little life. They were happy to see it, though, because it ensured that they would both get something to eat tonight. Otherwise, the village held a handful of shops that were already closed, maybe one or two solitary strollers and a passing car every now and again. However, Gabriel and Tilda were very comfortable with their beers. A small group of people quietly talked at the next table, the only guests of the pub except them.

They were not even into the very first sips of their beer when Dorothy drove by in her car, already on the lookout for them. The evening turned splendid. Tilda and Gabriel got two rooms side by side in the souterrain of the house, both with large windows because the building was constructed on hilly grounds where each level had a window to the outside. In the darkness, they could see that tomorrow they would have a great view on a small lake and the Sussex countryside. Gabriel smiled when he realised that he was supposed to share the bathroom with his new colleague, though at least they had washing basins in their own rooms. Seeing Tilda

Toelz's little toothbrush in the bathroom was quite pathetic, and Gabriel decided to leave his own shaving gear next to it.

What he did first on arrival was use the Jacuzzi on the terrace after this long and eventful day. Of course, he had to do it in his underwear in lieu of his swimwear, which was probably still hanging around at the Berlin airport. Albert joined him. First, Gabriel thought he would have preferred to be alone under the dark night sky full of blinking stars, but Albert told him great stories. "I have just returned from a meeting in Oregon," he said. "I was invited because I once belonged to the inner circle of Osho." Amazing. Gabriel would never have guessed this, though the English colleague sometimes wore Indian clothes. They talked pleasantly about Osho in the hot Jacuzzi and had a great time.

Over the course of that conversation, Albert called Gabriel various times a "favourite child of the universe"—whatever that was supposed to mean in guru language. After a good and nourishing Indian dinner with the others, Gabriel dressed in a white Lufthansa XXL T-shirt from in the kit of lost luggage, which he used as pyjamas, and went to bed highly satisfied with his day.

Next door, Tilda contemplated her day in her bed while talking to her boyfriend Ken on her mobile. "Honestly," she said, "I don't know whether this can work out. What a laugh. I have to put a stop to the illusions that Mr David seemed to have about me. Probably, he considers me as his new companion, maybe even as a friend or something." She shuddered. Her true feelings might give her boss some unpleasant surprises; he had no idea. He had ruminated about the fact that they now shared a great nature experience. From her side, there had never been any sharing between them. "Tell him that your talk about nature had just been information exchange," Ken advised sternly and gave her his usual two cents about communication philosophy. "People regularly update each other with what they think is their life. Only if two are prepared to dig deeper, not resigning themselves to scratching the surface, can deep friendship emerge after a kind of 'archaeology of the individual.' I say 'can' because it might be possible to come across artefacts while digging which are displeasing."

Tilda shuddered. Yes, like in her case. Her new boss had not even caught a glimpse of her mental-archaeological excavation site. None of her own precious artefacts had been excavated by Mr David; it had been just 'updating' what he had heard from her. Friendship between her and him was impossible. "You're right," Tilda said to Ken. "Take his stance on vegan eating, for instance. And he eats animals." Tilda shook her head. She could not imagine why somebody educated such as Gabriel David could take the important issue of conscientious food choice so light-heartedly. It was fundamental to her identity, her health, her values and morals, to the environment and to the wellbeing of her fellow creatures.

Her boyfriend Ken was working as an executive manager at the Berlin central animal shelter. Ken knew everything because he had to nurse the poor creatures that were thrown away by the worst bio-trash that this planet had ever produced: humankind. "I could never be together with a person who eats animals. In fact, I cannot even really like such a person," she said as she got excited. "Eating animals is worse than experimenting on them. And I could never trust a person who supports animal experiments, regardless of what type of animals are involved—except human beings." Ken agreed. "Yes, do people think animals do not feel pain as they do? And if they agree that animals feel it, what is their excuse to administer this pain to creatures slaughtered for them?"

Tilda nodded against the phone. "What we forget about animals, we begin to forget about ourselves" was a sentence that had stayed on her mind. She had been very impressed when reading a book written by Jonathan Safran Foer—*Eating Animals*, in 2011—who wrote this sentence. For him, the decision to eat meat was a decision to agree to animal suffering in factory farms. Meat consumption was pure cruelty. The same applied to the products of industrial farming, such as eggs and milk, and to those of industrial fishing. Having read that book, Tilda became a vegetarian.

And then becoming vegan was only the next logical consequence of this reasoning. And she felt in good company with this choice: *Annihilation* actor Natalie Portman claimed that reading the Foer book changed her from a twenty-year vegetarian into a vegan activist; she made a documentary movie from Foer's book in June 2018 that Tilda greatly admired. "Some people realise that meat eating is unethical, and they are rightfully ashamed of themselves. However, they are too weak and inconsequential to adapt their food choice behaviour." Ken showed why he was her boyfriend. "These people are slaves to their desires and to other people's marketing tactics," he said. "The meat industry makes you believe that they are processing happy animals, keeping consumers in the dark of what is really happening on factory farms." Tilda frowned into her bed sheets: Meat eaters like Mr David were bad people, full stop. Whether their moral choice was conscious or unconscious did not matter: Consequences were always real. Tilda was convinced that people were used to being cruel to animals anyway. Even if they would call them their "pets" and their "friends." People like Mr David. There were some who ate animals and some who did not. This was the division that mattered.

Angels' Play

Location:
Heaven above Ticehurst. Shared-Office Cloud.

Time:
Real-time GMT, Tuesday, 2 October 2018, 10:04.

Players:
The two angels as before.

Setting:
Both angels are at work in their cockpit seats. Business as usual. There, Tilda and Gabriel are working again on their project publications.

TA (*caressingly playing with the telepathy board in its lap*):
Shall we start the flow and synchronise them to get them more effective so that they can make the deadline?

GA (*cautiously*):
Yes, but not like last time—nice and slow, please. You always connect people too quickly. Their sparrow brains cannot take it.

TA slowly moves the slider of the telepathy board to the power position, and both angels smilingly observe the effects on their charges.

Telepathy Works

The Allen curve was a mathematical equation developed by Professor Tom Allen from the Massachusetts Institute of Technology. It said that geographical proximity was conducive to cooperation. At Ticehurst, Tilda and Gabriel started to use telepathic collaboration via the Allen curve. This interesting telepathy connection between them was very handy and effective for their cooperation at work but also quite spooky. So far, they had not discussed it openly. But they were using it all the time and sometimes played around with it. For example, they could call on each other to look up from their computer screens or make the other turn round when they wanted to pass something over in the kitchen while cooking. It worked best when they locked eyes. Then it could get so strong that Gabriel sometimes had to block his glance with his arm. But it even worked when they were far apart. Fascinating.

For Tilda, it was a matter of course that this was working, even if the scientific mainstream was totally set against it. She loved the book by Rupert Sheldrake about dogs that instinctively knew who was approaching the house door, wagging their tails when it was their owner. In fact, she owned that book. Sheldrake was one of her favourite science authors: She had watched numerous YouTube videos featuring him ever since she read the dog book. Sheldrake was a biologist talking about morphic fields structuring human perceptions of what was called reality. For her, the "scientific mainstream fascists," as she called them, tried to suppress findings such as Sheldrake's that did not fit into their world view. He thought that the brain could do many things, such as telepathy, that were still under-researched. This had nothing to do with anything supernatural. It was just that people did not yet know everything that could be known. Sheldrake considered telepathy as an empirical fact. However, Tilda admitted to herself that some people were more receptive to telepathy than others. It was very easy for her to reach out to Gabriel. Probably, their brains shared some neural architectures, creating an isomorphic field.

This had already started in her job interview with him. He had come across as a reasonable boss who was about double her age and height – quite good-looking if she went for the classical gentleman type. He looked a little bit like this Robert Redford guy, who was so fashionable in the old days. Gabriel had interesting deep-blue eyes and could hold her gaze for a long time. She had been quite fascinated by his habit of looking unblinkingly and permanently into the eyes of the person he was talking to. They had stared at each other during the job interview because she'd also had this habit since she was a little kid. She stared others down until they had to lower their eyes, or she connected to them. It was their choice. For Tilda, the telepathy connection to Gabriel was established between them from the very first minute, and it happened naturally. Gabriel would have never thought that this telepathy stuff worked, but it did. It was like mechanics: They could switch it on and go to that place in tele-space where they connected their brains for exponential use. It was easy to accept when seeing it work so successfully. Of course, it was spooky but also quite comforting and straightforward. Why not, if it worked? The problem, of course, was that it was highly seductive and addictive: Normal communication with other people became really shallow and cumbersome when this was possible.

These days, Gabriel pondered a lot about Tilda and his relationship with her. It was of course very different from the usual relationship that he had with his team members, though he had always been on good terms with them. Tilda amazed him with her intellectual capacity. She was a really smart person. When he was explaining something logically complex to Dorothy without any hope that anybody else would have even the slightest idea what they were talking about, suddenly Tilda would step into the discussion and not only show her complete understanding of the issue at hand but also provide some interesting comments that were helpful for our considerations and the progress of ongoing work. He was surprised because he was usually alone in these areas, and suddenly, somebody else with that capacity was around. He looked at her with new eyes.

Of course, he thought her to be a strange little creature: very small and thin, quite muscular for a woman. Probably doing a lot of sports. Otherwise, he found that she looked like everybody else in her age group, trying to appear "radical" or "not mainstream." Starting with her half-shaven hairdo. He found seeing the skin of a woman's head quite unfavourable. Both her ears were heavily pierced. He took a closer look while she stood near him in the kitchen. He had to smile. It was quite sweet because every single piercing was in the form of a heart, each in different style and colour. This mediated a bit the martial aspect of being so heavily pierced, in her case.

In telepathy, not only strictly work-related stuff was transmitted, by the way. Feelings such as gratitude, anger, anxiety or sorrow could easily be distinguished from one another. He learnt much about Tilda that way. What he learnt was that thinking and talking were two different things with her. He discovered that Tilda tried to hide many things from him. She had secrets she did not want him to see. He felt a certain darkness in her: It was a kind of pettiness, parochialism and insularity, full of gloom and sombreness. Gabriel shook his head: He realised that this sounded rather obscure if not also unfriendly. Maybe one could just say Tilda was composed, a little shy, withdrawn and serious. However, to him, she sometimes came across as cagey, secretive and guarded.

Gabriel wondered whether it was just him realising that something very strange was going on. What he got through the "telepathy channels" was that Tilda was suspicious, cautious and reserved about all this. And he completely understood. To be honest, it was not so very different with himself. What was this about? Your usual love story would not work like this. It would be too much ado about nothing. Furthermore, he did not go for kids, and she was that to him: She wasn't even thirty, goodness gracious! Last but not least, he reminded himself, she was small, dark haired and wiry – not his favourite type of woman. But she had nice eyes and a sweet laugh. On Tuesday, another colleague arrived to join the little group of eight for the writing retreat: Now they were six women and two men. Gabriel had met the new arrival, Simone, at a couple of former project meetings and always found her a good-looking blond, though a little too full of herself. She confirmed that impression this time too. Tuesday night, they all went out to the Ticehurst village pub for dinner, where Simone wanted to show off as a vampire. "I like my steak really raw," she told the waiter. "Meat is best when the blood still drips red out of it." Gabriel was sitting opposite of vegan Tilda, who looked so disgusted that he had to laugh out loud.

However, the most interesting story that was told in that pub after dinner came from Tilda: She told the group about the end of her semi-professional sports career, which took place in 2012. She was heavily injured in a fight at a kickboxing tournament, where she broke her left ankle. The injury never completely healed, so she could not return to her sports. "This is why I see you limping sometimes!" Gabriel exclaimed, the words escaping his lips before he could prevent it. In fact, he had been too much of a gentleman to remark on her gait so far. He had also wondered about why her face had contorted with pain sometimes. When she talked about the accident, he could see how difficult this was for her. He looked her up on the Internet later, when they were back at the cottage, and found out that she had been pretty good at her sports. He found an outdated public fighter profile for her on the Internet for international league tournaments that ended the day of her last fight. It proved that she had been one of Germany's best female kickboxers in her time.

In the daytime, Simone sat around talking a lot of nonsense and trying to keep the others from work. Gabriel found her quite annoying. However, it became even worse the evening before the group's departure. While everybody was sitting at the dinner table chatting after dinner, Gabriel was bored and went to the terrace Jacuzzi, hoping for Tilda to join him: They had such a nice time working together, jogging in the mornings, cooking dinner for everybody after having volunteered for that out of fun, and chatting in the evenings. Lying lazily in the Jacuzzi, he could see the people at the dinner table through the terrace windows. However, who came after him, having heard that the Jacuzzi had been switched on, while he was sitting in the hot bubbles was Simone. "It will only take me a minute to undress and join you," she whispered with a promising smile. Gabriel could not get out of the Jacuzzi quickly enough once she had left to undress in her room. Good thing he had left his bedroom window open. So he ran around the house in the dark night and scrambled in through the window with his dripping wet boxer shorts to avoid Simone on the stairs.

He went to bed early because Tilda and he had decided to do some London sightseeing before catching their return flight to Berlin. They had agreed to start at 6:00 am, using the early-morning village bus to the next, bigger town with railway transportation.

Angels' Play

Location:
Heaven above Ticehurst bus stop. Shared-Office Cloud.

Time:
Real-time GMT, Friday, 5 October 2018, 05:57.

Players:
The two angels as before.

Setting:
Both angels are in their cockpit seats as before.

GA (*wildly turning sliders on the telepathy board, which answers only with weak beeps*):
Why is it not working? She is totally pissed off with him without any reason.

TA (*laughs at its colleague*):
She thinks he did it with Simone in the pool. Don't you think this is an appropriate reason to freak out?

GA (*indignantly*):
But he did not, as you very well know. And Tilda should know as well if the gear were working properly, as it is supposed to do (*shaking its telepathy board*). Unreliable integration technology. I hate that. Look at her sullen face. That is totally stupid. Can we not do anything?

TA (*shrugging its shoulders*):
No, Objective One applies. And this objective forbids any unnecessary meddling from our side. You know what TRINI-T Board says about "stepping down from the cross" and the like. Our charges need to find their own way. (*sarcastically*) How about talking to each other? Empathy? Communication helps.

Both angels silently watch the bus coming, the two people entering and taking seats in separate rows and then looking out of their windows. The same happens inside the train to London. Both charges stare out of the window into the misty early morning, where it now even starts raining.

TA (*annoyed*):
Please contact somebody in charge of the weather. Otherwise, the London trip will be a wet experience, and they do not have good raincoats with them. Plus, we will need the sun for the cows.

GA (*talking to the saints section, asking for support from St. Peter, then turning to its colleague watching the charges*):
Gabriel no longer wants to go sightseeing around London with Tilda, as you can see. Now he is pissed off as well. A whole working day lost for an unworthy girl like her to look at a city he has seen a thousand times before. (*listening to the cackle in its earphones*) OK, weather should improve by now.

TA (*eagerly reading the Script for guidance*):
We should start our descent soon and should manipulate the train timetables to get them over to Horsham.

BG is eager for them to see the place where he went to school and where his own sunset experience took place. This will give them something to think about, and it is good for an exegesis on playing-field vision.

GA: OK, let's go (*sighing*). Otherwise, your girl will never talk about cows, the mood she is in right now.

Both angels step down from the cloud and elegantly slide downwards to earth on two rays of sunshine. During the last 300 metres, they apparate as two beautiful cows softly landing on the green grass of the Sussex meadows in the middle of an only mildly surprised cow herd.

Telepathy with Cows

Thinking that he would enjoy a day out with Tilda for London sightseeing. How could he have been so stupid? Gabriel was furious with himself. Already, when they left Ticehurst early this morning, Tilda had looked at him as if he had tortured a little puppy. The journey to London had been awful—both on the bus and on the train: two strangers travelling through foggy and rainy England heartily disliking each other.

Shortly before reaching London Waterloo (Waterloo station), the weather improved a little when the sun looked through the clouds again. As travel information had revealed, Waterloo had no luggage storage, because of terrorist warnings, so Gabriel and Tilda jumped aboard the next train to Farnham, which was already ready and waiting for departure, leaving their luggage with Dorothy, who lived close to the train station. This would at least give them free hands for sightseeing, and they could use the Heathrow airport shuttlebus from Woking later. However, when sitting on the already moving train, Gabriel read from the information screen that it would be taking a tremendously long detour owing to construction sites on the route—travelling through all the countryside of West Sussex before actually going into Surrey again, taking more than double the time that the quick hourly train would have needed for the short distance from Waterloo to Farnham. They were travelling back to where they had just come from! What was wrong with this day?

Adding to this misfortune, the train even came to a complete standstill in a little town called Horsham because something was wrong with the engine. Gabriel could not believe it. Tilda was quite desperate, pressing her little face against the fogged train window. They both stared at the station nameplate "Horsham" on the platform for what they felt were ages without speaking a word. When they finally arrived at Dorothy's place out of breath, Dorothy told them that they would have to hurry back to the station for the quick train returning them to Waterloo if they wanted to stick to their sightseeing plans. At least the sun was back now in full force, and their mood was a little better, with conversations starting again. Back in London, Gabriel and Tilda wanted first to have a look at Buckingham Palace but missed the entry gate and had to go around the whole place to find it. It was a long distance, but while walking and thus having time for extensive conversation, the reason for Tilda's bad temper was revealed: "At Ticehurst, there were some nice people. We had a good time. Especially you with Simone." Gabriel could not believe his ears. "When did I have a good time with Simone?" "Yesterday night, when you amused yourselves in the Jacuzzi." "Blimey! Obviously, I am not known for my good taste. How can you think that I would be interested in such a shallow person?" Tilda scowled. "I saw her going after you."

After having clarified this bit of worried half-knowledge, her temper immediately subsided and her mood improved. They chatted away about this and that. For example, they talked about different habits of crossing a street, which vary among cultures of course but also among people. Tilda compared Gabriel to her boyfriend. "Ken would never cross a red light as pedestrian." Gabriel, on the contrary, would go whenever traffic allowed. Tilda confessed, "I quarrel a lot with Ken about his law-abiding behaviour." Gabriel did not get a very favourable impression of this boyfriend from her revelations.

"He is not such a nutter as he comes across," Tilda protested. "Quite the opposite: He is the nicest person I know. He is a family person who likes to stay at home—especially, he does not like air travel, due to the global CO_2 footprint. Of course, he's vegan. Ken and me both live outside the mainstream. Ken dislikes all injustice and exploitation. For example, he supports Anonymous for the Voiceless, an animal rights organisation. At university, we always sat together in the lecture theatre critically appraising everything we were 'taught' by our ridiculous professors. Ken joined me in making fun of these so-called experts who were very often pathetically helpless in the intellectual domain. It was good to distance ourselves from the mainstream standard knowledge we were presented with and to join forces to earn our degrees as a purpose for an end. Kennie, who can be quite manipulative when he chooses to, was good at liaising with the professors, massaging their egos and preparing them for goodwill, while I was working on sound reasoning and explanatory powers backstage." Gabriel raised his eyebrows. He was not convinced that he liked "Kennie" any better now.

Later, Tilda bought Asian seafood for Gabriel, and they had a nice street dinner while watching some kids laugh about a puppet player's skeleton string puppet, which danced to some music. Gabriel said to Tilda "With music, you can let even the most horrible and frightening thing look harmless and funny." Unfortunately, they enjoyed the rest of the time so much that they missed the quick train to Farnham. The next quick one was cancelled, and what were they supposed to do as the only solution? Yes, take the snail train again with the endless detour owing to track construction sites to see their luggage again. At that time, first doubts arose in Gabriel about whether they would make their return flight home to Berlin.

These doubts were affirmed when the train stopped again for a long wait owing to construction in the middle of the sunny Sussex hills. Tilda, who had decided to trust Gabriel again, happily chatted away, pointing to things to see from the train windows. While discovering some cows lying lazily in the sun under the Sussex trees in high green grass, she even told Gabriel private things about a walk with her boyfriend: "We have 'talked' to some cows, with Ken mooing to them, me using silent telepathy." She was totally convinced that the cow-to-Tilda telepathy had worked, and Gabriel could only second this view given what they were doing at work all the time without talking about it. Building integral relationships was probably possible across different species.

Though agreeing that telepathy worked, they did not refer to their own telepathy connection but stuck to the cow topic, dreamily meditating about the sleeping cows in the sunshine outside of the train window. However, discussing telepathy with cows proved to be a brilliant trigger to start talking about stuff that really mattered.

Tilda told Gabriel about Rupert Sheldrake. "He is a biologist working on the topic of telepathy. He is a scientist to be taken quite seriously. However, the mainstream scientific community rejects his theories as esoteric." They talked a lot about the sense and nonsense of glorifying the mechanistic world view of modern science and technology and of discarding everything not immediately complying with the current scientific consensus. Gabriel got interested, and Tilda promised, "I will send you some links to Sheldrake's YouTube videos." Then, the train slowly moved away from the cows in the sun—only to get stuck shortly afterwards, completely irrationally, at Horsham again. They endlessly stood there, again staring at the town's name on the station sign but this time with even more desperation because the chance to get their flights on time diminished by the minute. When they finally reached Dorothy's place again to fetch their luggage, Dorothy announced that they would never make it in time to Heathrow. She would have provided a lift with her car but was scheduled for an important meeting in London city. So Gabriel and Tilda ran to the station to get the train to Woking, where the airport shuttle would leave. What else could they do but try their luck?

At least, Gabriel was able buy a small bottle of water before jumping aboard the waiting train. They had not drunk anything since the lunch at London and were dried out. It was such a challenge, as everything on this trip. Tilda and Gabriel shared the bottled water amiably, but with the foreboding of the last supper. They bought airport shuttlebus tickets right on arrival at Woking station and joined the crowd of waiting people. Unfortunately, there was an issue with the bus company, and the next bus was cancelled, with about forty people angrily waiting. The bus after was supposed to come in an hour. "Catastrophe!" Gabriel mouthed to Tilda.

Angels' Play

Location:
Heaven above Woking train station. Shared-Office Cloud.

Time:
Real-time GMT, Friday, 5 October 2018, 16:51

Players:
The two angels as before. Bede Griffiths (BG).

Setting:
Both angels are in their cockpit seats as before. Bede Griffiths has not yet arrived but should be there any minute. The angels have called for him as an emergency contact.

TA (*curiously whispering*):
Say again: Why is the guy a member of the saint section? An English monk who went to India to live with the Hindus? He has not even been beatified by Rome! Why is he a saint?

GA (*patiently explaining*):
Because he is the great lover.

TA (*surprised*): I beg your pardon? He is a monk!

GA (*confirming*):
Exactly. A monk should really know what love is. Father Bede loves others to tears, like St. Romuald.

TA (*puzzled*):
And who now is St. Romuald when he is home?

GA (*knowledgeably*):
Another monk and saint. Same order as Bede Griffiths. It is said of him that he cried out of love all the time because he felt it so strongly.

TA (*slightly appalled and starting to prepare itself for a weird encounter*):
Does Father Bede also cry out of love all the time?

GA (*mildly*):
No idea. But there is a nice story from the Benedictine ashram where Father Bede lived in India. They regularly received guests for retreats following the hospitality rule of St. Benedict, and Father Bede was the guest master of the place. Sometimes weird guests arrived. Among them was a guy who was mentally deranged and sang opera arias day and night with a full voice. It was a terrible noise in the retreat place dedicated to perfect silence, and it did not cease. After a few days, everybody was fed up with the guy and wanted to get rid of him.

TA (*very supportive of that*):
Sure, I would have killed him right away.

GA (*dismayed*):
Tut, tut. The monks and the other guests asked Father Bede to tell the guy to leave. Instead, Father Bede started to cry and told them to love the singer and receive him as they would receive Christ himself. The guy was safe with him, like in the womb of his mother.

TA (*foolishly*):
Like in the womb of whose mother?

GA (*explaining*):
There are only few human places that are good metaphors for safe spaces. The womb of the mother is one, the loving heart of a friend is another. And Father Bede's heart was an icon of a safe space for others. He loved others completely and wholeheartedly.

TA (*amazed*):
Everybody the same way? Is that possible?

GA (*carefully*):
Same approach to everybody, yes. But of course, Father Bede was a human being, with some people being closer to him than others. You could break his heart like that of any other person.

TA (*shaking its head in doubt*):
Hmm, that concept of love sounds a bit risky for my taste.

GA (*warningly*):
He is coming. Get up from your cloud!
Both angels reverently stand to attention for greeting a saint with a long white beard and amazing blue eyes, an Indian monk sannyasin outfit and a red tika on his forehead. It is Bede Griffiths who has just apparated. He is in emergency mode.

BG (*in a hurry without further introductions and with friendly authority*):
Hello, dearies, nice to meet you. I will take over from here. When Gabriel and Tilda miss their flight, this trip will count as a "bad experience." We do not want that.

TA (*embarrassed*):
Father, pleased to meet you. We regret that we could not cope, ourselves, and had to call for you.

BG (*turning into his forty-year-old self of Alan Richard Griffiths exchanging his Indian monk outfit for an Englishman's casual attire*):
No problem. One of you with me. TA is the better driver. Can you maybe look a little more Indian, dear? Indians are excellent car drivers. Will give you more credibility.

BG and TA evaporate, leaving GA behind on the now solitary cloud. GA switches on some music, switches its dashboard to "default monitoring," lies back in the softness of the white cloud and is soon fast asleep.

Taxi to Heathrow

While Gabriel and Tilda were standing in this huge crowd of waiting people, they felt solidarity and companionship because everybody was in the same horrible situation. Complete foreigners related what the delay would mean to them. For example, there was an elderly lady who was about to miss her daughter's wedding, and there were many other sad stories.

But then a miracle occurred in the middle of all this gloom and frustration. A very good-looking man of about forty with blazingly water-blue eyes walked through the waiting crowd. Everybody made space while staring at him because he had a kind of friendly but demanding authority.

He directly approached Gabriel of all people, locking eyes as if they had met before. Probably homosexual, Gabriel thought. This impression strengthened when he addressed Gabriel with a voice of loving care: "Nice to meet you, my dear. Are you OK?" Strange question. Far from OK, just like everybody else desperately clutching their bus tickets. The man said, "Please leave it to me and trust me. You are going with me." He was obviously soft on Gabriel, or else it was a mystery why he had singled him out from the big crowd of people. Tilda raised her eyebrows and grinned. She was slightly jealous while watching Gabriel ask the stranger, "What would it help us going with you? There is no other connection to Heathrow airport." "Oh, yes, there is," the man complacently replied, "by car." "Cars will be too slow on the jammed motorway to reach our scheduled flight time," Gabriel said but the man just shook this off. "Even if these station officers are not known for reimbursing once-sold bus tickets," Gabriel tried to convince him, but the stranger only waved away all these considerations with an elegant hand. "Please accompany me to the bus ticket counter."

Gabriel shrugged his shoulders at Tilda, let chance happen and complied. Inside the station then, he witnessed an amazing scene: The blue-eyed man had their money back from the ticket office in no time, doing it with his mere personality. People simply did what he wanted. Outside again, the man waved to a waiting car where a martialist-looking Indian with tattoos sat in the driver seat and begged Gabriel to fetch Tilda. They also asked the elderly lady with the marrying daughter whether she wanted to join them, but she refused: "Thank you, I will wait for the bus. You will never make it to the airport in time." Probably, she thought them a bit phony—if not totally mad. They jumped into the car, where the three of them sat in the backseat, and the driver immediately took off.

The blue-eyed man bowed to Gabriel and Tilda and introduced himself: "My name is Richard. I am an Englishman from the North." Politely, Gabriel answered: "We are coming from a workshop in Sussex and are employees of an international aid organisation." "Delighted, delighted!" the saintly Richard replied, beaming. He was a bit strange, though. The conversation that he had with the Indian taxi driver was the strangest thing he did : Drives was the name that he called the driver, as if the man were a Latourian actant rather than a human being. "Latourian actant" was Gabriel's description. Bruno Latour was a French sociologist who thought that not only human beings but all entities in our world should be perceived as acting and as important in understanding the complex network of relationships of everything and everybody with everything and everybody else. Drives was just a neutral way to address an entity as acting—be it a human, an angel or anything else. And Richard gave Drives strict directions about the proper way—even though he, an Englishman from the North, had no idea about traffic hereabouts. Drives, a professional taxi driver from the London area, obediently followed Richard's directions without discussion.

And the result was stunning: They arrived at Heathrow airport just in time to drop their luggage off at the counter, running to the gate and jumping aboard their flight home. But before that, they thanked Richard, their patron saint, profusely. He was gone with the car—as was Drives— as quickly as he had appeared, probably to make his own flight at another terminal.

"Without this smart blue-eyed Englishman," Gabriel commented, sitting on the plane next to Tilda with his beer in front of him, "we would never have made it. Everything worked out the best it could have in the end." Tilda ridiculed Gabriel: "You have problems—an English saint is singularly sent to save you. That is what you believe. I do not know whether I should envy or despise you for this. Mr David, get a grip on the facts! All of this was pure coincidence. You are a naïve man."

"I am not Dr. Pangloss!" Gabriel grinned. "And who is that when he is home?" Tilda grimaced. "He is a person in French philosophy coming close to your description of a naïve man. In Voltaire's *Candide* Dr. Pangloss teaches his innocent pupil Candide unreasonable optimism against all empirical evidence of vice and misery in the world." Tilda nodded. "The world is a dangerous place. There are no saints, angels or any god coming down, performing miracles, and saving you. Otherwise, why is there all this crap? Either God allows it, in which case he is not good; or, if he must let this happen and cannot help it, then he is not almighty. Pessimism and fear are the only reasonable responses to shit happening all the time. They are preventing you from tumbling into your doom immediately. In fact, fear is the only good thing to rely on. For all the rest, you must rely on your own devices. There is just you. Better be strong. If you are, you will get the upper hand on this world. If you do not take great care and precaution—which you can only do by following your fear—you will soon be the garbage of history. If you do not empower yourself to strong will and perseverance, the others will win and you will be the loser. Simple as that."

Gabriel was shocked. He had not heard her talking so wildly before. She was right of course: The empirical evidence for vice and misery in this world was overwhelming. How could he argue for the possibility of "everything turning out for the best"? It had proved to be true in their story with blue-eyed Richard, but would it hold against pessimist world views firmly grounded in cruel reality? Tilda shook her head: "How can you seriously argue for the possibility of the world turning out to be good when you actually see how bad everything is?" Gabriel did not give up; the rescue work of blue-eyed Richard was still too vivid in his mind. "This is not a purely academic question," he said as he scolded Tilda. "In fact, the whole success of our work, for international social development, for a better life on this planet, depends on the answer to that question. Is a better world possible? We need to answer this question affirmatively, or our international aid projects will not make any sense!" "Dreamer," Tilda said to Gabriel. It didn't even sound unfriendly. "Think of all the other people probably still standing at the bus stop in Woking waiting for the airport shuttle. Think of that poor mother missing her daughter's wedding. Why make us of all people happy and leave the rest in the dark? Think of the millions of much-more-miserable, painful fates and experiences of all people stricken with pain and misfortune. Where is your Richard over there?" The options for an integrated world society in future, for the participation of the many voiceless people, for equality, and for justice seemed to be nil, as far as Tilda was concerned.

She ended the conversation here and turned away from Gabriel to look out of the window for the rest of the flight. The whole trip seemed somehow surreal to her and left her a bit overwhelmed.

She had the feeling of having been thrown into a saccharine US TV soap opera full of candy, cake and popcorn, where Mary Poppins and Alice from *Alice in Wonderland* would be strolling around the corner anytime. Thus, she felt quite content and sobered when the plane finally approached rainy Berlin-Tegel. It was lovely to return to the everyday chatter of Ken, who fetched her from the airport, and to go home on the X9 shuttle bus.

Ken had been among the protesters against the festivities for the third October celebrating the German reunification where French street-art activist JR had shown a 25-metre-high photo collage. Sitting on the bus home, Ken eagerly told her that he had fought against politicians who had tried to capture the show for their personal bravado. Tilda was quite proud of Ken, who had dared to join the protest group protecting the collage. This was finally something real and hands-on after the terrifying mysteries that had happened in England. She smacked herself on the head: Why had she ever started rambling on about cows and telepathy?

Gabriel, however, felt completely different about their journey. He was happy and composed. The journey had been like a story in a novel, full of mystery, miracles and funny adventures. As soon as he reached home, he first took a bath and then took a curious look at the YouTube links that Tilda had sent on Rupert Sheldrake. He was not so convinced when he first watched the videos, though: too much strange talk about morphic fields and the like, for his taste. However, it at least got him interested enough to search for Sheldrake on Wikipedia. He had to find out more about the meaning of the journey. He had to read. His academic training asked for exegesis: *Exegesis* means an interpretation of a text—not an arbitrary, subjective interpretation but rather a careful excavation and examination of its meaning that is deeply rooted in knowledge and evidence. You could read any situation, any experience, indeed your whole life as text. Everything could turn into a text, becoming subject to exegesis. Maybe the Sussex story was an experience for exegesis.

Gabriel fetched a glass of red wine from the kitchen and settled down comfortably on the sofa in his sitting room, with his laptop next to the wine. Rupert Sheldrake. Here was his Wikipedia entry. And here was the comment on the morphic field book, including the reasons why telepathy works. Gabriel's eyes widened. The paragraph mentioned the venue where Sheldrake wrote that book. In a Benedictine monastery. Finally, here was something that Gabriel was most familiar with: The Benedictines were a monastic congregation in which he had some friends. That afforded Sheldrake some credit in his eyes—enough at least to read on and give Sheldrake some credibility.

Gabriel learnt that Sheldrake had "an interest in Indian philosophy, Hinduism and transcendental meditation," that he went to India to work as a plant physiologist at a research institute and that he then focused "on writing *A New Science of Life*, during which time he spent a year and a half in the Sacchidananda ashram of Bede Griffiths, a Benedictine monk active in interfaith dialogue with Hinduism. Published in 1981, the book outlines his concept of morphic resonance." Gabriel curiously clicked on the hyperlink leading to Bede Griffiths. He had never heard that name before. The Wikipedia entry showed an old man with blazingly blue eyes, a long white beard and an Indian sign on his forehead.

The text revealed that Father Bede was an English Benedictine monk who died in 1993, who was raised in Sussex/UK, who converted to Catholicism and who emigrated to India to lead the abovementioned ecumenical Sacchidananda ashram. Raised in Sussex. "Interesting," Gabriel thought. He read on: "His mother took the children and established residence in a smaller home which she maintained, though she had to find work to support herself and the children. At the age of twelve, Griffiths was sent to Christ's Hospital, a school for poor boys." Gabriel shook his head. Went to school in a place called Christ's Hospital. Strange name for a school. He clicked on the Wikipedia link for Christ's Hospital.

"Christ's Hospital is a public school (English independent boarding school for pupils aged 11–18) with a Royal Charter located to the south of Horsham in West Sussex," Wikipedia reported. Magically, Gabriel's eyes were caught by a single word: Horsham. Horsham in Sussex. This was the small town that the slow train with the extra route had to take twice to Farnham yesterday, stopping on its way from Waterloo both times for an overly long time.

The First Google Maps Miracle

Now, Gabriel was curious like a detective. Why had the train taken the detour through Sussex anyway instead of going right from London into Surrey? He opened Google Maps and searched for the train route from Waterloo to Farnham. It was pretty clear: Horsham was way out of the direct train connection between these two places. In fact, Horsham was nearly as far away from Farnham as Waterloo itself, located in a completely different county. Why had the train ended up there twice? It seemed impossible that a train from London Waterloo to Farnham should go through Horsham of all places.

Amazingly, this was the town where Father Bede went to high school and where his spiritual foundations were planted, as Wikipedia reported. "Who has ears shall hear," Gabriel murmured following a Bible quote that St. Benedict had loved so much. Next, he looked up the maps and timetables of UK train company webpages, looking for an explanation for the detours that they experienced during their train ride. While looking at the UK train services, he found information on the disruptions that had taken place over the past few days. Network Rail called it the Brighton Mainline Improvement Project. "The work will be carried out on several weekends between September 2018 & May 2019," the webpage said. "Brighton and stations to the west will have trains to and from London, but these will be diverted via Littlehampton and Horsham."

"There you have it," Gabriel murmured. He clicked on a further link, this time from the *Brighton and Hove Independent*, where he found an online article by the newsroom titled "These are the weekends a major Sussex to London railway route will be closed." Here, the detour through Horsham was announced exactly for the day that he travelled with Tilda. Handy that the train did not break down completely at Horsham, because at that point in time, they could not have yet deciphered why. That evening, Gabriel wrote a strange email to Tilda describing what he had found out:

"It ended with the words 'world communication,' so it obviously wants us to go to India for some reason: I have never been there before. It must be loud and confusing. Far too many people. Furthermore, I do not want to go into an ashram." Gabriel scanned what he had written. "Blimey, the girl must think I am totally daft! Or that I am getting muddy in the brain due to old age. Maybe that's even true. What am I doing here? 'Remystification of the world' following a word from famous German sociologist Max Weber? I need to get a grip and stop this." However, he could not deny evidence. The lovely London day, which had only started to become lovely when Tilda discovered that he had not muddied their relationship with somebody else, had been a prerequisite of building enough trust between them that she could muster enough courage to talk to him about her telepathy experience with the cows at home in Germany.

The English cows on their train journey that triggered her confession would have gone unrecognised if the train hadn't stopped for ages just in front of these animals, providing ample opportunity for long-term conversation. Talking about cows and telepathy had been prerequisites for Tilda to mention Rupert Sheldrake and then send these Wikipedia links and for Gabriel to find out that Sheldrake wrote his telepathy book in an ecumenical ashram in India named Shantivanam, hosted by Benedictine monk Bede Griffiths.

Gabriel would just have marvelled about this discovery of a Benedictine connection for a few minutes if he hadn't stumbled across the town name of Horsham. Remembering that name from twice staring at it for endless periods when the train got stuck at the station of that town twice. These periods were enabled by a most unlikely incident caused by British Railways. On that very day, they had travelled to Southern England, where their two trains were detoured so much out of the usual way by rail construction sites that they travelled to Horsham, a desperate tiny town in the middle of nowhere, where this Bede Griffiths had obviously gone to school in a place called Christ's Hospital.

"What else can I say but 'Hello, Mr Griffiths! Nice to meet you'?" Gabriel was stunned.

Maybe it was just his feeble attempt to make himself interesting and attractive to Tilda by pointing at hidden secrets of the spiritual world that only he has access to. How embarrassing could he get? Very strange things happened. The whole journey was a strange experience and had made him really curious as well. Therefore, the last thing he did before closing Wikipedia for the night was scroll down to the reference list and literature recommendations for the Bede Griffiths entry. The monk was obviously a famous mystic, having written an enormous body of religious literature on spiritual life. Gabriel copied and pasted the first literature recommendation into

Amazon and ordered *Essential Writings*, by Bede Griffiths. If Tilda hadn't talked about telepathic cows, nothing would have ever happened.

Angels and Other Cows

A few days later, Gabriel and Tilda sat in B1's company cafeteria and stared at the two pages lying before them on the table. Gabriel had copied them for Tilda immediately after *Essential Writings* arrived. The shock still was deep.

"I opened the book randomly when it came," Gabriel reported tonelessly. "It fell open on page twenty-seven, where *Essential Writings* starts with Bede Griffiths' autobiography, *The Golden String*." He knocked on the page. "Please read it out to me." Hesitantly, Tilda drew the page closer to herself and began to read the words of Bede Griffiths, audibly but under her breath so that the other guests at the cafeteria would not overhear. The opening passage from *The Golden String* was titled "Sunset in Sussex" and started with a poem by William Blake. Tilda read from page 27:

> *I give you the end of a golden string;*
> * Only wind it into a ball,*
> * It will lead you in at Heaven's gate,*
> * Built in Jerusalem's wall.*

"Nice poem," scowled Tilda prickly, "if you go for poems." She read on:

> *One day during my last term at school, I walked out alone in the evening and heard the birds singing in that full chorus of song which can only be heard at that time of the year at dawn or at sunset. I remember now the shock of surprise with which the sound broke on my ears. It seemed to me that I had never heard the birds singing before, and I wondered whether they sang like this all year round and I had never noticed it. As I walked on, I came upon some hawthorn trees in full bloom, and again I thought that I had never seen such a sight or experienced such sweetness before. If I had been brought suddenly among the trees of the Garden of Paradise and heard a choir of angels singing, I could not have been more surprised. I came then to where the sun was setting over the playing fields. A lark rose suddenly from the ground beside the tree where I was standing and poured out its song above my head, and then it sank still singing to rest. Everything then grew still as the sunset faded and the veil of dusk began to cover the earth. I remember now the feeling of awe which came over me. I felt inclined to kneel on the ground, as though I had been standing in the presence of an angel; and I hardly dared to look on the face of the sky, because it seemed as though it was but a veil before the face of God.*
>
> *These are the words with which I tried many years later to express what I had experienced that evening, but no words can do more than suggest what it meant to me. It came to me quite suddenly, as if it were out of the blue, and now that I look back on it, it seems to me that it was one of the decisive events of my life. Up to that time, I had lived the life of a normal schoolboy, quite content with the world as I found it. Now I was suddenly made aware of another world of beauty and mystery such as I had never imagined to exist, except in poetry.*
>
> *It was as though I had begun to see and smell and hear for the first time. The world appeared to me as Wordsworth describes it with "the glory and freshness of a dream." The sight of a wild rose growing on a hedge. The scent of lime tree blossoms, caught suddenly*

> as I rode down a hill on a bicycle, came to me like visitations from another world. But it was not only that my senses were awakened. I experienced an overwhelming emotion in the presence of nature, especially at evening. It began to wear a kind of sacramental character for me. I approached it with a sense of almost religious awe, and in the hush which comes before sunset, I felt again the presence of an unfathomable mystery. The song of the birds, the shapes of the trees, the colors of the sunset, were so many signs of this presence, which seemed to be drawing me to itself.

Tilda looked up and met Gabriel's excited gaze. "A very familiar visual impression, indeed. We have seen that sunset in Sussex," she slowly said. "Yes, only without lark, and the red cabrio is not mentioned," Gabriel eagerly agreed. "It must have been where he saw it or, at least, very close to the place where he saw it, right?" Tilda asked.

"Yes," Gabriel confirmed, scanning the GPS app on his mobile, "forty miles between Christ's Hospital and Stonegate, three hours on his bicycle."

Tilda drew the other page closer. "The editorial remarks, called *A Vision of Nature*, by Thomas Matus, introducing the sunset scene are also interesting because they use the ideas we are using at work all the time—such as a network model of reality, the world as a complex web of interdependent relationships and so on. Exactly the concepts our work is based upon. And this is definitely not mainstream. Have you ever seen such a perfect fit to our professional approach? Furthermore, the Matus introduction talks about India. Shall I read the passage out, too?" Gabriel nodded. "Go on," he said.

Tilda read from page 26:

> As for scientific thought, Bede Griffiths distinguished between the traditional mechanistic paradigm, on which the edifice of industrial society is based, and the newer vision of reality, the "network" model propounded by such thinkers as David Bohm, Rupert Sheldrake, and Fritjof Capra. The metaphor of the universe as a complex web of interdependent relationships enabled the scientist to think of the universe as a whole, with many hidden dimensions, and not just as an assemblage of parts, which could be examined separately and then exploited without concern for their place in the whole. ... Finally, half a century after his playing-field vision, he once more saw the same light of the setting sun, heard the same bird songs and the same voice of the soft wind in the trees, and smelled the same fragrances, but now he was in India, at the ashram he had inherited from Monchanin and Le Saux, by the banks of the river Kaveri. He saw nature in its beauty and in its fragile contingency, and above all, he saw his own contingent being both within the cosmic body of the universe and within the Word, the ground of nature, in which he had existed from all eternity.

"From sunset in Sussex to an ashram at border of the river Kaveri: It seems to indicate that we have to go to India. What do you think?" Gabriel slowly concluded. Tilda held his gaze. "What I think is more stunning is that this passage provides the context for the sunset scene with reference to scientific concepts such as complexity and network models. This is your dedicated conceptual approach at work. You have used and developed these concepts throughout your whole life. All your publications are about them. From our own Sussex experience, only the cows do not make much sense. What do they have to do with a sunset in Sussex leading to India of all places? Whatever. I would love to go to India. If literature recommends, this is what we should do. And cows are holy in India. No idea why, though. Cows are not like angels, right?"

"Angels and cows are indeed the same thing!" Gabriel laughed. Enjoying Tilda's bewilderment, he fetched another scanned page from his bag and placed it in front of her. He had marked a few words with a yellow highlighter for her better understanding: "See what I learnt from Bede Griffiths' main book *The Marriage of East and West*, which I got today. It is about the role of cows in the Vedas, one of the main religious reference texts from India." Tilda groaned but curiously started to read.

> The Vedic understanding of the mystery of existence is revealed in the Vedic myth. This myth centres on the Sun as the source of light. But the Sun in the Vedas is not merely a physical body which gives light to the eyes. It is a cosmic power which gives light also to the mind.
> The gods (devas) of the Vedas are the "cosmic powers" of St. Paul. ... In the theology of St Thomas Aquinas, these are conceived as the angels through whose agency the order of the world is maintained. ... The Sun therefore is a god in this sense, the source of intellectual no less than of sensible light. ... In the Vedic myth, there is a constant conflict between the light and the darkness. The darkness is represented by Vritra, the primeval monster, who holds back the waters of life and hides the light of the Sun. He represents the primeval darkness of the unconscious, conceived as a rocky cavern in which the cows of the Sun are concealed. The cows themselves, strange as it may seem to us, are symbols of light. They are called the Cows of the Dawn and represent the rays of the Sun, so that the dawn can be described as the releasing of the cows from their pen. But these rays of light are not merely earthly light, they are the light of the mind, and the search of the rishis (enlightened people) in the Vedas is a search for illumination of mind.

"Moo," Gabriel said to Tilda.

Angels' Play

Location:
Heaven above Berlin. Shared-Office Cloud.

Time:
Real-time GMT, Monday, 8 October 2018, 22:21

Players:
The two angels as before.

Setting:
Both angels are sprawling in their cockpit seats. They are still working overtime.

TA (*yawning and stretching its cracking golden wings, which were today decorated with sharp knifes at the feather tips*):
OK, I think we can call it a day and go home. They have now got to the basic literature and are on track. Anything else from your side, or should we have an after-work drink now?

GA (*stemming its fists in its angelic hips*):
According to the Script, we have all sorts of catastrophes coming up. We need to get prepared!

TA (*unconvinced, longing for its evening beer*):
What is it?

GA (*reciting from the Script*):
Your girl will interpret Gabriel's spiritual insights in terms of realpolitik.

TA now definitely looks a little alarmed.

GA (*puzzling over the next catastrophe item*):
Have you ever heard of the postmodern critique of cultural colonialism and identity politics?

Hearing these words, TA groaningly wobbles back to its workplace.

Dualities Fight Back

Tilda had done a terrible thing, in Gabriel's eyes. She formally claimed overtime at the HR system of B1. Gabriel was furious. "This is a 'don't' in our kind of job. Overtime is actually part of the job description!" he shouted. "We are not factory workers or petty Babbitts but working for the social good. We do not count hours." Angrily, Tilda demanded, "I want to know what is wrong with you!" She stood her ground in his office, quarrelling with him about it; nobody could say that she shied away from conflict or could not communicate difficult topics. "I have just applied for a day off. This is an unimportant, formal thing, Mr David."

He told her that he had never seen any formal overtime notice from any of his staff except the part-time admin people. "Otherwise, our work mission to help people cannot work out—at least if everybody is law abiding. All these nice achievements of modern labour-union regulations are not for us. They only keep you from your mission that you fulfil with your work. Some of us—including me—would even pay money to do their job. What a shame. Have you never heard about dedication to your professional vocation?"

"Sorry, but such an idiotic statement can only stem from a person born with a golden spoon in his mouth. It is an interesting specimen of human stupidity and misinterpretation," Tilda heatedly answered. "For you, Mr David, it is all very well to relinquish your legal rights as employee and speak of dedication and vocation instead. You earn about five times what I earn, and you can take holidays whenever and as long as you want, in contrast to me." "That is not true," Gabriel protested. But Tilda was in full gear: "You are the last person in this world to give me this shit about morals. You are the last person who can speak about these things. You may say nothing about my work ethics. You are privileged. And with this, you have to relinquish any right to be in a position to tell me off like that!" Gabriel could not believe his ears.

"I am your boss, Mrs Toelz. Of course, I can assess your performance. And I see and understand your situation. Why have I 'relinquished any right to talk to you just due to my so-called privileged position,' as you say? I do not understand." Tilda got fundamentalist now: "I could only accept to be told off by a person of my own kind: young, female, dependent, in precarious work conditions. From you, this is inacceptable and even unethical. Indeed, it is annexation of the worst kind. It is hubristic, colonialist and invasive."

This seemed to go political. Gabriel's suspicion was confirmed by Tilda's next words: "If you want to talk about white people, be a white person, Mr David. Otherwise, your statement will be compromised by your outsider perspective. It will be invalid by source. If you want to talk to me about work ethics for people in precarious work situations, be in that position yourself. Otherwise, get lost!"

Identity politics. Gabriel was gobsmacked. He had read about cultural appropriation that white authors were accused of when trying to write about POC characters, or "crippling up," writing as an able-bodied person about disabled people and somehow unjustly benefiting from it.

He looked at Tilda. "Mrs Toelz, please think about your viewpoint. If our access to the world is principally corrupted—be it by elites, dark powers or any other antagonists that stand between us and the world—how then can we say anything at all? That is bad philosophy."

She went to his bookshelves, fetched a book and waved it at him. It was Immanuel Kant's *Critique of Pure Reason*. "Here. This guy is of the same opinion I am, and he is famous. The baseline is, whoever is human will recognize the world under the condition of a human being. The fly will recognize the world with the cognitive and epistemic apparatus of a fly. Human beings will recognize the world with the apparatus that makes us human beings. Nobody shares exactly my constitution and apparatus, namely being Tilda. Therefore, the appearance of the world for me is totally different from yours. This means if we do not see the same thing, we cannot share knowledge, we cannot talk to each other."

"This is called relativism," Gabriel patiently explained, "but you totally misconstrue Kant." He looked for a second book and gave it to Tilda. "Kant searched for the basic apparatus that all human beings share and that distinguish us—let's say—from the apparatus of the flies. For Kant, this shared *conditio humana* is not only cognitive and epistemic; it also has a moral component, as shown in his *Critique of Practical Reason*. That we share this basic access to the world with all other people is the grounding for emancipatory equality concepts and social justice."

Tilda looked stubborn. "Read that second book beside the first," Gabriel said as she pointed to Tilda's hands, "then you can see what you are doing when you maintain that only Black people can recognise anything about Black people, only disabled people can say anything about the disabled and so on. You do just the opposite of what you want. You rob us of exactly what you want to shelter – the *conditio humana*: the condition for our equality, our dignity as fellow humans." Tilda felt that she could not argue anymore with two books of Kant in her hands, which made her the more furious: "Elites invade what normal people think and say. These elites are corrupt, and you are a representative of the elite, Mr David. You are doing wrong everywhere: in epistemology, life objectives and morals!" With this, she stormed out of his office.

Open Access This chapter is licensed under the terms of the Creative Commons Attribution 4.0 International License (http://creativecommons.org/licenses/by/4.0/), which permits use, sharing, adaptation, distribution and reproduction in any medium or format, as long as you give appropriate credit to the original author(s) and the source, provide a link to the Creative Commons license and indicate if changes were made.

The images or other third party material in this chapter are included in the chapter's Creative Commons license, unless indicated otherwise in a credit line to the material. If material is not included in the chapter's Creative Commons license and your intended use is not permitted by statutory regulation or exceeds the permitted use, you will need to obtain permission directly from the copyright holder.

Chapter 2
The Perpetual Allegory

Gabriel was sorry. He had not meant to provoke Tilda. As indemnification, he wrote an email, apologised and offered her an opportunity to accompany him to the Barcelona symposium, which he was scheduled for next month, along with some sightseeing like they had done in London. This symposium had the strange name Post-Normal Science Symposium, and he was interested in what it would be about. Tilda obviously shared his curiosity because she gracefully accepted his apologies and even helped him to create the poster that he was to present there on a panel. Shortly before the day of their departure, Gabriel watched telly and switched to ARTE, the European public service channel dedicated to culture "Association Relative à la Télévision Européenne", because nothing else was on the usual channels. There, he got lucky: He watched a fantastic personality feature of Freddie Mercury. He thought it was very moving and nicely put together. The loveliest part was about the piece that Freddie did with Montserrat Caballé.

For Gabriel, it came right on time because the album was titled *Barcelona*. The city was the hometown of Montserrat Caballé, and "Barcelona" was the name of the first great song they produced together. Such talented singers—and both dead already. It was a pity. However, Gabriel suddenly knew exactly where to go with Tilda for sightseeing: He would show her Montserrat Abbey, which was close to Barcelona. He knew that there was a local express train from Barcelona to Montserrat going every hour. The next day, he bought the album.

The Spanish Case

Adsila Idrissi had missed the coastal Vinolas bus connecting the little holiday village Canyelles Petites to Roses in the North of Catalonia where the Pyrenees fall into the Mediterranean Sea. Her kids would not get their supper in time. Probably, Aisha Maria had not done her homework yet and would fall back in school. Little Vaclar was probably asleep already despite his grumbling tummy.

Adsila sighed sadly and started her solitary walk along the rocky coastal path. It had been her last day as kitchen helper in the little beach bar. They closed in September but would open again in May. What to do in between? How to survive? There were no jobs once the tourists were gone, not even in Barcelona. She had already been to the agencies over there. However, since her husband has left her last winter, she was the only worker in her family. And she did not have any education. Nor could she speak Spanish. Nor did she have official refugee status. Nor anything she could count on as helpful. Except the priest. He was now in jeopardy with his dioceses because he had helped too many single, unemployed mothers with non-Spanish backgrounds, like her. She had an appointment with him this evening. But she knew that he could not do very much for her any longer. Shiveringly, she drew her Dschellaba close around her, fighting her way against the strong coastal wind called Tramontana. The few people passing her on the coastal path certainly had her down as Muslima, though she was a Christian, which was why her government had thrown her out of Morocco.

Her husband had worked on an orphan project near Fez. They had to leave their foster children behind when they left the country. So much the better because now they would have only shared poverty and mobbing at school from racism with their kids. When she reached the priest's house in Castello d'Empuries two hours later, having finally caught the Moventis bus from Roses to Figueres, she was exhausted. "Did you eat?" the priest asked compassionately. She shook her head, not having eaten even though she had spent the whole day close to the oven where tons of food had been processed. But she was not allowed to take something away. He brought some bread, olive oil and tomatoes with a glass of red wine, Tres Fincas, from the local Cooperativa at Palau-Saverdera. Then, he put some money on the table between them. "This is some of what I got from last Sunday's church collection in our basilica. You know that we do not have regular income through that. But last Sunday was good. You can buy Aisha new sports clothes at Decathlon. Her old ones are torn, and she is mobbed by her classmates because of it." Adsila took the money gratefully.

The priest was the only one helping her. And now, her only friend and supporter was transferred to Germany by his bishop because of financial irregularities. A joke. He was the only one daring to help out. He was her one and only support. But today, he had another message for her, which took her by surprise: "Artificial intelligence might help you to get support from the agencies," he said. Adsila looked at him questioningly. He had not come across as a techie or even technologically knowledgeable. AI she only knew through Hollywood. Wasn't Arnold Schwarzenegger, the terminator, an AI machine? "They are introducing social assessment systems where machines decide on your eligibility for certain services," the priest explained. "I fall through all nets," Adsila said. "Do not you remember? I have applied many times over the past years. They are done with me. They have me down as permanently unemployed, not employable, not fitting any standard categories for people they can support. I am both a nobody and a singular kettle of fish. I am out. I won't fit any of their standard cases. The only thing I can hope for is every now and again a temporary employer taking compassion on my specific circumstances. Machines work for standard cases, not for my specific case. Where I am standing, I am alone. How could AI make things better?"

"It is just a plan in Barcelona," the priest said. "They work on novelty. The Spanish social assessment algorithm will not work with standard profiles. It is supposed to be a case-based system where the algorithm assesses your whole life trajectory, your history and your biography and analyses the complex situation you are in at the moment, how you have come there. Then, it looks at the options and resources of the state, whatever social service can be possibly applied, and tries to find the best match for what the state in its current situation can do for you." Adsila looked at him. "Do you think it can work?" she asked. "No idea," replied the priest. Adsila nodded. "If I am assessed by an AI algorithm, I want to be heard. Who am I? Where do I want to go, me and my kids? Who do I want to be? How important is culture and tradition for me, both Moroccan and Spanish? What society do I want to live in? So far, I cannot see that government taking any of this into account. Individual people are not really considered." The priest had some crema catalana for her as desert. "What will you do?" he asked, wanting to know. Adsila smiled. "I will challenge the algorithm to really mean me. Would be the first guy doing that."

Angels' Play

Location:
Heaven between Barcelona and Monistrol de Montserrat. Shared-Office Cloud.

Time:
Real-time GMT, Friday, 16 November 2018, 07:45

Players:
The two angels as before.

Setting:
The cloud is flying in slow motion on automatic control above the train from Placa Espanya to Monistrol de Montserrat.

Both angels are sitting relaxed in their cockpit seats reading the Script and from time to time checking on Gabriel and Tilda, who are aboard the train after having bought some proviant in a little supermarket in Placa Espanya.

TA (*giggling delightedly*):
Showtime! Happy to demonstrate that this Spanish trip is a Bede Griffiths intervention. Gabriel and Tilda are not here for fun and sightseeing. They need to realise that Spain is on the agenda for the AI project. Have you read Adsila Idrissi's case?

GA (*very worried*): Yes, sad story, but I am really concerned that Gabriel and Tilda will not survive this trip. Gabriel has severe vertigo. He has never free climbed before.
Is it really necessary to put their lives in danger to make them understand that they follow the chapters of Father Bede's *Essential Writings* in their travels?

The worst of the three climbing trails is up to the monastery in this wet and misty weather. They don't even have proper shoes, only trainers… (*shaking its head in dismay*)

TA (*regretfully and also a little anxious*):
It is in the Script, and I already configured Tilda's GPS so that it will point them to the steep climb. Climbing vertically up, and nothing else. That is the cave experience. Otherwise, no chance for revelation afterwards (*encouragingly*). They are tough. It will be super hard, but then *da da-da*! Divine mystery! Your boy has to see sense, that this is not only about going to India, and all is fine. Think of Adsila!

GA (*consenting*): Yes, and by the way, we need to get vulnerable people like Adsila involved in the project. They need to have a voice because they know exactly what is wrong with their current situation and can advise on improvements for the AI.

The two of them harmoniously bend their angelic heads over the Script to reread the next passage of Pater Bed's Essential Writings.

Experiencing Hardships

Montserrat is a mountain with an abbey for the Order of Saint Benedict at the top of it, just about fifty kilometres away from Barcelona. *Montserrat* means 'serrated mountain' in Catalan. Gabriel and Tilda had bought tickets from Placa Espanya to Monistrol de Montserrat, the little town with a train station at the foot of the mountain.

On the train, which was running through the early morning dew, they had a heated discussion about machines and humans. "I am a bit stuck with the best image for a better society. One favourite dystopia of literature is that we will be bossed around by big brains, superhuman creatures or artificial intelligence that knows better than we do. I think this is crap," Tilda confessed. "Why is that, Mrs Toelz?" Gabriel asked curiously. "Do you want to be bossed around by a machine?"

"Could we not we learn as much as possible from the temporary leadership of the machines so that we could become more intelligent and powerful ourselves? Look at all these causal processes here, which we only half understand. Maybe machines are better at that. With machines leading, our societies could become better organised than they currently are," Tilda argued. "Knowledge of those dominating us today could be preserved for our everyday knowledge of tomorrow." "You must be joking," Gabriel said. "Your image of a better society should keep the very central idea of liberal democracies where vulnerable groups also have voices and participate in decision-making. There is no need to develop such a control-freak approach with machines taking over."

Tilda scowled at him maliciously. "Mr David, do you really think that your ideas of involving everybody under your generous guidance and your brilliant mind is better than the far more neutral guidance of a probably even more clever algorithm?" Gabriel looked at her gobsmacked. She had never been so cheeky before.

He was insulted and spent the rest of the journey looking sullenly out of the window. Then, Montserrat came in sight. Gabriel had been at the abbey before. This time, unlike on the other occasions, his plan was not to use the cable car from the train station up to the abbey on the top of the mountain. Most people did that to pilgrimage to the so-called sanctuary of the basilica, Mare de Déu de Montserrat, next to the Benedictine monastery that enshrined the image of the Virgin of Montserrat, one of the famous Black Madonnas of Catalonia.

This time, with Tilda, Gabriel wanted to hike up. He was only a bit worried because they had only a half day for the tour because their schedule had an afternoon poster session at the Barcelona symposium. It was already ten o'clock, and they were still on the train. The hike would start from the train station at Monistrol de Montserrat, covering an altitude difference of about 650 metres while climbing up the steep rock. All tour guides described the Montserrat hikes as difficult and technically challenging. Gabriel had to confess that he was a little concerned: not only distrusting his fitness and footwear, which were just his running shoes, but also his ability to fight vertigo. He had been afraid of heights, especially in the mountains, all his life.

Even Tilda, who dreamily followed with her eyes two big mountain birds flying for some time in parallel with the train, looked a bit awestruck when the Montserrat summits came into view through the mist of the morning for the first time. It was like the Uluru in Australia—a solitary giant stone massif with fantastic shapes and spikes unexpectedly rising up out of nowhere. "We will hike all the way up there," Gabriel told Tilda. "Fantastic!" she exclaimed with a grin. She was of course delighted, being such a sports person.

At the train station, the Internet on their mobiles showed them a few trail options. Gabriel selected the easiest one and started to hike up. However, they wandered around for about half an hour without finding access to the chosen trail. They met a man with his dog, the only others far and wide. He looked at the two of them doubtfully and said, "Unfortunately, only the most difficult hike is accessible from here if you do not want to go back to Monistrol." Gabriel sighed and said, "Please show us; we will try to make it before we get completely lost." The man looked as if he thought he would never see them again alive.

The first thing that Gabriel did on that difficult trail was put his left foot into a pulpy sand puddle and get soaked to the socks with red-yellow water, which coloured his trainers nicely. Tilda just shook her head in dismay. Hiking some time on a plateau while talking to each other about their families brought them to the feet of the rocks, and then it was just climbing straight up for 600 metres to the 1300-metre heights of the abbey. It felt as if they were the first and only human beings in this world.

There was not a single soul around them but some butterflies. It was like Adam and Eve in paradise. Tilda was very considerate and careful after Gabriel told her about his vertigo. Only once did he have to tell her off. She said "Good that it is so misty and shadowy dim, Mr David; otherwise, you would be aware of the many hundred metres of mountain steeps sloping right under your feet." "Be silent!" Gabriel told her a little rudely, but it was just mortal fear. It was only with a shaky balance that he could fight terror and blind panic. The merciful mist, however, made the rocks a little slippery. He was indeed grateful just to see what was immediately in front of his eyes and could not care less about missing the view.

Amazingly, the mist disappeared immediately when they reached the last via ferrata to the abbey where all trails came together, and many people again joined them. Climbing around the last rock corner, they stepped into the full bright light of the sun. Gabriel felt as if reborn coming out of the dark womb of a cave full of trial and physical labour.

However, he and Tilda also shared some ambiguous feelings about returning to civilisation and populated dwellings. Though it was kind of nice because the church bells from the basilica started chiming. Tilda looked at him strangely when he spoke to the bells a little breathlessly: "Yes, we hear you. And we are coming. But slowly, slowly. First we have to eat." He remembered that song where Freddie Mercury and Montserrat Caballé sing together—"Barcelona." "The bells are ringing out; they're calling us together, guiding us forever."

They found a nice place in the sunshine on the sightseeing balcony of the monastery with perfect mountain views to have their picknick, eating the food that they had bought in the little supermarket in Barcelona. They quietly sat there in surprisingly warm weather for mid November, wearing only T-shirts under the sun.

It was good that happy Gabriel could not read Tilda's thoughts. She still mused about his fitness level. She went for a run each morning and engaged in weight training in her local studio three times a week, the days in between for endurance sports and aerobiosis. Only Sundays were free. On Saturdays, she had an additional pseudo-kickboxing session with a former coach who was now well over eighty and retired. One day without sports is a bad day for her. Wherever she was, the first thing she looked for was a gym. What she deplored deeply were the training discipline and the body consciousness lacking in most people.

"He thinks that because he hiked up the Montserrat, he is a fitness hero. Hilarious," Tilda thought. "He has nearly no muscles; the few he has are not well defined. Amazing how one can be so slow and not topple over. And he had gasped for air like bellows. OK, he is over sixty. But still. I have my ankle as a handicap, and he is a man. What is wrong with these people is that they do not take sports seriously. They think it is a kind of voluntary leisure time activity rather than a necessity. No ambition." She sighed and decided to leave him to his illusions.

Angels' Play

Location:
Heaven above Black Madonna Sanctuary, Montserrat Abbey. Shared-Office Cloud.

Time:
Real-time GMT, Friday, 16 November 2018, 12:45

Angels' Play

Players:
The two angels as before.

Setting:
Both angels silently watch their charges make the last hundred metres to the sanctuary, where the goal of the Montserrat pilgrimage for all people is situated: the statue that was fetched from the mountain cave—the Black Madonna of Montserrat. Gabriel had purposeful stride thanks to his familiarity with the surroundings; Tilda, not without apprehension and considerable hesitation, looked appalled at the pilgrim streams flooding the stairs in front of the Madonna high above the church altar.

Then, Gabriel and Tilda sit in the dark church in front of the Black Madonna. Both angels are eagerly checking the scene below for similarity to the chapter 'The Perpetual Allegory' in Bede Griffiths' Essential Writings. Further books of reference, such as travel guides and religious literature, cover the floor around their cockpit seats. The angels are working hard.

GA: Now they are in the inner sanctuary to finish the chapter. Right in time for them to listen to the Escolania. By the way, this is the music choice of today (*it lets its colleague listen to 'Salve Regina' with its earphones; TA approvingly nods. The Escolania is the famous boys' choir of Montserrat Abbey, one of the best boys' choirs in the world. It will soon be time for their regular singing at midday prayer*).

TA (*proudly looking at Gabriel and Tilda, who are utterly exhausted*):
I think I managed very well in giving them a hard time and testing them to their limits: rock climbing 650 metres high with long winding passages and then sitting in the dark inner sanctuary in front of the divine mystery. Father Bede will be satisfied. Listen (*reads aloud to its colleague from page 31 of Essential Writings, with emphasis*)

> "In the Paleolithic caves which have been discovered in the south of France, it has been found that there are long winding passages leading from the front of the cave by a difficult and often dangerous path into the inmost recesses of the rock, and there in the darkness of the interior are to be found those drawings of animals which astonish us with their power and beauty.
>
> Why was it that these pictures were drawn in the darkness of the interior where they could only be seen by the light of a torch of moss dipped in animal fat? Miss Rachel Levy in her *Gate of Horn* has given us the answer. The pictures on the wall were the sacred images by means of which it was believed that human beings could enter into communion with divine powers, and the long, winding, difficult passage to the interior represented the dark and difficult approach to the divine mystery. We find this symbolism continued all through Neolithic times, in the megalithic temples and in the ritual dances of primitive peoples today; always there is the laborious approach to the sacred place where the encounter with the divine mystery is to take place. ...
>
> Thus, from the earliest times of which we have any knowledge, it seems to have been understood that our life in this world is a journey toward God. ... It is the passage from the outer to the inner world. ... All these stories are symbols of the same mystery of the search for God which is at the same time the return to our true home. It is represented sometimes as a new birth. ... Always it has been understood that our life in this world, as Keats said, is a 'perpetual allegory'; everything has meaning only in reference to something beyond."

GA (*a little piqued on behalf of Mother Mary*):

Do not you think that "drawings of animals" is something other than the Black Madonna? Look, this is Our Lady of Montserrat, La Jerosolimitana. St. Luke himself carved this statue with Mother Mary sitting as his model and him using the carpentry tools of St. Joseph. Later, St. Peter brought it from Jerusalem to Barcelona.

TA (*looking doubtfully at the text in its lap*):

OK. But it is a sacred image, nevertheless. What happened to the statue next, by the way?

GA:

When Barcelona was under attack by the Muslims in the eighth century, Our Lady was taken to the nearby mountains, hidden in a cave and forgotten until two young shepherds saw a strange light and heard angelic singing in the mountains. They alerted some church guys, and entering a cave on the serrated mountain, they found the source to be the Black Madonna. The Santa Cova, her holy cave, is just below the sanctuary.

TA (*suddenly feeling huge compassion with Tilda, who looks around shyly*):

Blimey. Did it really have to be a Black Madonna as a sacred image? This is so Catholic! Could not anything more interreligious be used? I would have thought that Father Bede with all his Indian background would have chosen something else instead.

GA (*shaking its heard and fetching a book by Matthew Fox from the floor, citing*):

> "Every archetype has its seasons. They come and go according to the deepest, often unconscious, needs of the psyche both personal and collective. Today the Black Madonna is returning. The Black Madonna is the transcendent Kali-Mother, the black womb of light out of which all of the worlds are always arising and into which they fall, the presence behind all things, the darkness of love and the loving unknowing into which the child of the Mother goes when his or her illumination is perfect."

TA (*again satisfied*):

OK. Right. There you have it. But Tilda will still have a hard time digesting this.

On a Miracle Tour

Tilda's sitting in a church was just too funny. She felt so awkward. "This is my first time in years sitting in a church," she whispered uncomfortably. Gabriel soothed her: "My regular and very frequent attendance suffices for the two of us. You're OK." Tilda's opinion of Black Madonnas was written clearly on her face: How could an academically trained man such as Gabriel be so superstitious? Seeing all these poor, misguided people crawling on their knees up the last steep passages to spend a few individual seconds in front of this ugly little statue with a totally dark female face. She hissed into his ear: "Pure idolatry writ large! To think that staring at an odd sculpture or, better, even touching it—disgusting—will help them in their sorrows and heal their medical diseases. Can it get worse? Do not these Catholics have this thing with the golden calf and the commandment not to dance around it? And we right in the middle of it." They were all sitting in front of St. Mary's shrine with pilgrims crawling up there by the minute when the light suddenly first faded entirely and then came on with full brightness on the shrine. Obviously, a power outage: The whole church full of people sighed in holy shuddering. Gabriel mockingly whispered into the ear of Tilda: "A miracle! Mary!" He felt joking was just necessary to break the spell of awe. Tilda relaxed a bit after that.

She was not the only funny thing in church. There was a man in uniform who was supposed to get the pilgrim crowd under control. He constantly hissed at people with a sharp "shhhsssst!" He must have been especially trained for that because not even Gabriel with his cantor education could have produced such a penetrating sound. However, the man achieved at least a reduction in the noise that these hundreds of people were making, who had come to hear the boys' choir for its daily Angelus singing at one o'clock. Then, the choir filed in. They sang just awesomely. It was a rendition of 'Salve Regina' that Gabriel had never heard before. The quality was perfect. Gabriel held up his mobile high to record them.

While they went back to Monistrol, this time by cable car, Gabriel, who was very tired by then and wanted to have some peace and quiet, opened the Bede Griffiths book, which was in his rucksack.

However, after having read the few pages after where he had stopped reading last time, he went white and gave the book to Tilda. She read the two pages on the "perpetual allegory." "Very obvious," she said. "We have again 'lived it through,' right? This is what we did." Gabriel agreed. "No wonder that we had missed all the easier-to-hike trails, because this is what the book had advised. It had to be the hardest way up. We have made a three-step breakthrough: From obscure, misty subconscious being through hard work, pain and endurance to full light, deep insights and finally to unity."

For Gabriel, it was crystal clear: Tilda and he were somehow following the path in *Essential Writings*, by Bede Griffiths. This had various implications. For example, he was pretty sure that they would have to go to India at a certain point. Furthermore, unfortunately, it was not only following that book as in reading. He said to Tilda, "It is 'autoethnography,' Mrs Toelz. We have to live through it to get a real understanding." "What?" she asked. "It is a social science research method," Gabriel explained. "You know what *ethnography* is, right?" Tilda nodded and answered, "An ethnographer investigates the behaviours of foreign people. For data collection, he or she, for example, goes to a little Indonesian island to observe the native population in their daily activities, sometimes sharing their life for some time to get familiar with everything, returns home and writes a scientific treatise about them telling stories about their life." "Correct," Gabriel agreed, "in autoethnography, data for your research is coming from yourself: from your thinking and from your writing. You are the foreign creature under investigation. You use self-reflection to explore your personal behaviour and experience in a chosen context, and you tell a story to explain it to others."

"And this is why I have to crawl up mountains with you, nearly dying?" Tilda asked indignantly. "We are carrying our skin to market. I am sure I can make myself understandable. I am not very happy with that. The whole approach is preposterous. Much too personal. And to prove exactly what point? These autoethnographers must be joking. We were overdoing it a little for my tastes sitting in this dark overheated church like in a cave surrounded by tons of medieval rocks. Suffocating. And the hike was much too dangerous. We should be happy just to have survived this, Mr David."

She was warming to her fury and got louder and louder. "And, finally, it is a weird idea that we have to undergo many hardships, even a death experience, to move from darkness to light. Even a bit cynical," she observed. "It seems as if the bad is necessary to come up with the good. What about the current bad state the world is in? Is it only a transitional stage to a better one? How can we reach the good life? Is it only through hardships that we can achieve any improvement? Can we honestly tell people that suffering is a necessary part of a generally sense-making and positive process? When does this become merely cynical in the face of evil, pain and suffering? People really suffering might find that cynical." "Yes, me, for example." A woman with two children sitting next to them unexpectedly joined their conversation. "My name is Adsila," the woman continued, introducing herself. "I heard you talking, and I must agree with this young lady. I have no money and no job. I am a foreigner, and I am a single mother. I am completely in the hands of social services. But they refuse me basic provisions. My life is a constant hardship. Do not tell me that this is good for anything."

The Birth of a Project

The woman told them that she was on her way to Barcelona to speak to a social service agent about her needs. "Maybe for the last time, a human agent," Adsila laughed. "They have a pilot project running in that agency to let the case history be done by artificial intelligence." Tilda got very interested and took down the woman's contact details. "We are from an international aid organisation," she explained, "always on the lookout for interesting topics. We might put together a research project about this AI-based social welfare approach and speak to you again. We need your expertise. You seem to be quite in favour of the machine approach." "A machine cannot be more unfair than anybody I've had to deal with so far. But nobody would do science with marginalised people like me. I'm nobody. Me and my concerns have no voice. There is no safe space where I could even speak my mind," Adsila muttered. Gabriel eagerly looked at Tilda. A project idea was just born in his mind.

Tilda, however, was not responsive. She was very silent, very thoughtful and completely exhausted, both in body and in soul. She leant in her corner of the train seat and dreamt while looking out the window. For her, that they were somehow living out the chapters of *Essential Writings* one by one was hard to swallow. When she suddenly asked Gabriel for the next chapter, he refused: "I do not read the book as a whole, having strong feelings of reservation against that. Instead, I carry the book with me at times only to open it at special occasions." "What makes these situations special?" Tilda wanted to know. He could not explain but assured her: "I know whenever it is time to read a few more pages." She was not satisfied with that answer and, against his resistance, fetched the book out of his rucksack. "Let's see," she said. "What's next? Oh, boring. Chapter called 'Science and Wisdom.'" "Put it back," Gabriel demanded, trying to retrieve the book from her, but she started to read out loud to him. "It is not dangerous. Here, listen to page 102."

> "Modern science … is intrinsically defective both in its principles and in its methods. It is defective in principle because it looks upon the material world as an independent reality, and it is defective in its methods because it treats the material world as though it obeyed mechanical laws which are independent of the law of the Spirit. But in reality, the material world is a part—and an inferior part—of a greater whole. According to ancient tradition, there are three 'worlds'—the physical, the psychic, and the spiritual—and these worlds are interdependent as an integrated whole.
>
> This is the root cause of the 'disease' of modern civilization. … The present state of the world is not due to some defect in the use of science and technology which can be corrected. Western science and technology are based on a false philosophy which has undermined the whole of Western civilization. … There can be little hope therefore that Western science and technology will change their basic character. The only hope lies in a deliberate break with the whole system and an attempt to reconstruct science and technology on a new basis.
>
> This will only come when the Western world has undergone a radical change of consciousness—a change which will probably be accompanied by a breakdown of the present system—and has recovered the wisdom of the ancient world, the world not only of Christian Europe but of India and China and Islam. Unfortunately, India and China and the Arab world are now exposed to the full force of Western science and technology with all its devastating effects. The new world must therefore be the creation of East and West together, seeking to recover the wisdom which has been lost and to advance into the new age now beginning."

She stopped reading and looked at him, asking, "So what? No consequences from here, right? Nothing we have to do following from this. Do not get your knickers in a twist about that book." Gabriel groaned. "My dear Mrs Toelz, cannot you see how it all connects?" he asked her. "Bede Griffiths obviously wants us to put together a project around this 'new science' he speaks of. Even our Post-Normal Science Symposium is about it." He cited from the conference flyer in his rucksack: "It says something like 'escaping mainstream practices of science and look for inspiring new styles of research practice.' The new science has to be transparent, integrative and inclusive in the sense that it seeks the upstream engagement of vulnerable groups. Values should be at the centre moving into a direction of the democratisation of expertise. The symposium aims at developing support tools for informed multiactor dialogues and empowering marginalised actors."

He stopped quoting and looked at Tilda. "What this chapter of the Griffiths book tells us to do is apply for a project that will bring forward the idea of reflexivity, inclusion and societal evolution to contribute to the advent of new science and technology. And it was you who was already saying what this project will be about." Gabriel stopped talking and looked at Adsila, who had listened fascinated.

"Don't you know that in more and more countries, public administrations are increasingly using artificial intelligence algorithms to decide on the provision of public services such as unemployment benefits, pension entitlements, kindergarten places or social assistance to their citizens?" Gabriel went on: "It is not only in Spain that they are doing it; it is everywhere! Governments hope for greater efficiency and objectivity in applying AI. Data profiles of all of us are thereby analysed and evaluated by machines for decision-making. Profiles are checked by machines to determine whether the people in the profiles are 'worthy' of receiving public services. The issue affects us all: whether as recipients, as service providers, as taxpayers, or as members of vulnerable groups excluded from benefits. Social services are government benefits that address people's vital needs from cradle to grave to alleviate poverty and inequality: Most people will use them (or be rejected from receiving benefits) at some point in their lives. Whether the machine distribution of services works, whether it improves or worsens the situation, is of interest not only to national policymakers but also to all people living in national welfare systems. Can a machine do social justice, and can it do that in all cultures? It is a fascinating topic for an international aid project."

"And what has this to do with India?" Tilda watched him strangely. She saw that he was determined to kick this off immediately. He would certainly follow up the India plans and all the clues that they had got lately from this Bede Griffiths. He would try to translate all these theoretical insights that they had got over the past period by putting them into practice and try to implement the ideas of Bede Griffiths to help people around the globe. Why not have a project for saving the world? She sighed and stuffed the book back into his rucksack without looking at it again.

Thinking About India

For Gabriel, the Montserrat excursion had been most enlightening. It had been more than helpful for discovering that all their travels seemed to be connected to the exegesis of Bede Griffiths' *Essential Writings*. What remained clear to him was the fact that the two of them had to go to India. The new chapter had again confirmed this. There was also the following passage from the editor of *Essential Writings*, Thomas Matus, which definitely pointed in that direction:

> "The parabola of his (Bede Griffiths') life linked these places—India, Rome and Britain, Subiaco and Camaldoli, Saint Gregory's Monastery and Shantivanam—like points on a star map, forming a strange constellation, and countless numbers of persons gravitated like wandering asteroids into his own far-ranging orbit, centered on God and on God's eternal Wisdom, which enters history 'at many times and in many ways' (Heb. 1:1). For those who wonder whether there was any symmetry between Bede's Roman Catholic monkhood and his Indian san-nyasa ("renunciation"), let me summarize the story enfolded in his midlife autobiography, *The Golden String*, and spun out in his writings from India."

India should be part of the new project they were obviously supposed to create. And clearly this ashram place of Bede Griffiths', which was in the south of India.

Strange. He had never been there before, and nothing had drawn him to it. India was supposed to be hot, humid and full of very poor people being unfair to each other in their believing in this weird caste system. For Gabriel, India was no place to find happiness.

He was convinced that the so-called holistic or polycentric Eastern societies had not better preserved nature or, with all their community focus, improved living conditions but were often suffering from poverty, inequality and violence, partly due to convictions in underlying ideologies, or were promoting totalitarian approaches enabled by collective-centred policies. Gabriel felt that he was a total Westerner, in spirit and action, in science and religion. He had been educated by Jesuits—or, to be more precise, by Sacré Coeur sisters (that means 'Holy Heart' in French), who constitute the female branch of the Jesuits and who also follow the rule of St. Ignatius of Loyola. The most sober, rational and hands-on people that Christian orders have on offer. And now he was supposed to go to India of all places.

Other people his age would have some clue about Upanishads, yoga, Buddhism and stuff because they would have fled to Poona or other ashrams in their midlife crisis to go on perm-meditation with some gurus. The problem was that he did not know anybody over there. If it could have been Delhi, this would have been less of a problem. As a social aid company, B1 would have many connections that he could use. They might even have a cooperation partner over there and a nice, air-conditioned office for him, where his presence would be fully justified by some kind of company secondment work. But a remote location in the middle of Tamil Nadu, South India, at the borders of the river Kaveri, as *Essential Writings* already relates on its first pages? A place with a few huts called Saccidananda Ashram Shantivanam?

In the evening after the conference had finished, Gabriel and Tilda sat in a little restaurant talking about India and the new project. Even Tilda asked for a glass of white wine. They were in good spirits, having survived their cave adventure. "Mr David, do you have any personal connections to India or to this ashram?" Tilda's first question hit right on the most sensitive spot. "Erhh," Gabriel cleared his throat, "there are two striking coincidences. 'Ananda,' as in Sac-cid-ananda, is the name of the young organ player with Indian origins who sometimes accompanies my singing in church." Tilda looked at him disbelievingly. "Probably many male Indians are named Ananda. It means 'bliss.' What else?" Gabriel mused. "Then there is Kaveri, the river where Pater Bede's ashram is close to. Kaveri is also the name of my Indian 'goddaughter,' whose schooling I've supported for years through the charity organisation of our parish." Tilda looked even more unconvinced. "Probably many female Indians are named Kaveri," she said. "Do Ananda and Kaveri, as the only two Indians you know by name, bring you any closer to India? Maybe in your dreams, but I doubt that this is any help."

"And what is with you, Mrs Toelz?" Gabriel asked rebelliously. "Any personal connections to India?" Seeing Tilda shaking her head, he continues: "Or to the new project idea?" Tilda thought for a long time. Then she replied, "I've come across the term *safe space* before." Gabriel looked at her curiously. "Once I helped rescue animals from medical experiments, though I was a police trainee at that time myself," she continued. "One of the activists with a whimpering puppy under her arm just snatched a bleeding rabbit out of my hands when we were persecuted by the police. "I will bring it to a safe space," she said before disappearing into the dark. "Stop her! Catch her!" the commanding officer shouted, but she was gone. I do hope she reached this safe space for the animals. I got heavily disciplined after that night for my refusal to obey orders. That was it for my career with the police. I lost my status as a public servant, my salary, and I got an entry in the police records. Last but not least, I got a dishonourable discharge. However, I did not care. I did not want to obey orders from a state that shelters torturers and not the powerless. I only hope that this activist managed to bring the rabbit and the dog that night to this safe space." Gabriel looked at her aghast. That had been one of the longest speeches he had heard from Tilda so far. And she had got really personal.

This provoked some little confessions from his side. "I am not overly happy with this plea to go to India," Gabriel related to Tilda. "Why is that, Mr David?" Tilda asked, then continued: "What is it precisely that you are not happy with?" Giving it some consideration, he replied, "My biggest problem is that, of course, all these revelations will not come for free. As far as I know about these epiphany stories, they all end with a so-called mission and a call for responsive action. I seriously—and anxiously—wonder what I am supposed to do as a mandate in exchange for all this spiritual apparentness."

Seeing Tilda's questioning glances, Gabriel also confessed, "And of course, Mrs Toelz, whether I have to do it with you or whether you just happen to be at the right place at the right time." Things were definitely getting difficult. "What can this mission be about?" he asked. "The only sure thing is that this is about relationship." "What makes you think so?" Tilda asked. "You have totally lost me."

Gabriel swallowed and moved away from theology and towards a more painful subject, more painful because it was more personal: "In the moment, I am mistrusting the message. All this spiritual stuff could well be just flirting with you behind the veils of a big lie about the greater common good." Tilda started to laugh. "I would not totally discard this possibility," she said. The next bit of laughter that she had happened after Gabriel confessed: "And I do not like the idea of going to an ashram, because the Bede Griffiths book seems to suggest it as next thing to do. I do not care to belong to these middle-aged people spiritually awakening and serving themselves on the world market of pseudo-religious offers, doing yoga day and night and permanently rhapsodising about Buddhism and Eastern holism without having a clue what they're talking about." She was already laughing with tears in her eyes when he continued to honestly speak his mind: "This mostly concerns women anyway, and it all disagreeably reminds me of the Julia Roberts movie *Eat, Pray, Love*, which is nothing but a great gift of idiocy and disgust!"

"Holy shit," Tilda said. Still suspiciously giggling, she more or less convincingly said, "Mr David, I do not expect you to go Julia Roberts–like," which was kind of nice of her. However, the next revelation about Gabriel's idea of an Indian ashram sent her into another fit of uproarious laughter. "You know, people there are constantly having sex with one another for spiritual reasons. I really do not feel like that. And should I not comply with their sexual inclinations all the time, they might complain that I do not fully support the unity of humankind," Gabriel revealed, desperately sharing his worst fears.

When she had finally stopped laughing, which Gabriel fretfully observed, she soberly recommended a novel to him to get a little more relaxed about issues like this. "Read D.H. Lawrence," she advised. "*Mr Noon* is an autobiographical novel detailing D.H.'s relationship to a girl named Frieda von Richthofen, related to the famous Red Baron. Frieda escaped with D.H. Lawrence in an illegitimate relationship to the North American town of Taos, New Mexico, which is just a few miles away from Santa Fe, to found a kind of new order, with Frieda as the main priestess. This is real. An ashram is nothing compared to that." "Maybe," Gabriel opined a little sheepishly, "but why must I read D.H. Lawrence when I actually just want to put together a project about AI-based social service provision?"

This time, they went back home in more unison than last time, when they came back from Sussex. At home in Berlin, Gabriel did two things: First, he watched a YouTube video about Christian ashrams in India recorded by a Jesuit named Sebastian Painadath. This cured him of most of his prejudices. Then, he tried to strengthen his connection to India by buying a little Indian elephant from the fair-trade shop in his parish. It came from a whole collection that they had on sale, where each handmade elephant looked different in the patterns of their little blankets and in colour. His was mostly orange. He also bought an elephant for Tilda. It was mainly green, and he left it on her office desk for Christmas. It was good that he had not seen her when he found it, so that he could not read her mind. Turning the green elephant in her hand, Tilda successfully fought against the impulse to throw it in the wastepaper bin immediately.

Open Access This chapter is licensed under the terms of the Creative Commons Attribution 4.0 International License (http://creativecommons.org/licenses/by/4.0/), which permits use, sharing, adaptation, distribution and reproduction in any medium or format, as long as you give appropriate credit to the original author(s) and the source, provide a link to the Creative Commons license and indicate if changes were made.

The images or other third party material in this chapter are included in the chapter's Creative Commons license, unless indicated otherwise in a credit line to the material. If material is not included in the chapter's Creative Commons license and your intended use is not permitted by statutory regulation or exceeds the permitted use, you will need to obtain permission directly from the copyright holder.

Chapter 3
Dreams and Consciousness

Gabriel and Tilda's first business trip in the new year brought them to Budapest in Hungary, one of Gabriel's favourite cities. From the Liszt Ferenc airport, they went to the Science Academy's Guest House by taxi. For Gabriel, it was a pleasure to help the academy do business because it was under heavy pressure from the Orbán government's stupid antiscience policy, which was bleeding it out by denying it funding. When he told this Tilda, she accused him of having naïve views on politics. "Why is Orbán such a bad guy to use his state apparatus and violence? Are the others any better? Nobody can tell me that it is justice when the Americans simply kill a persona-non-grata like Al Badawi," she said. Gabriel winced at that but said nothing. After work, Tilda and Gabriel walked around Fisherman's Bastion for some basic Budapest sightseeing. They had a nice vegetarian/pescetarian meal in a little Italian restaurant sitting outside in the streets of Buda with some heaters above and a candle between them. Gabriel had black spaghetti with shrimp. However, most interesting, indeed, was the dinner talk.

"Please tell me about your sports, Mrs Toelz," Gabriel requested, and Tilda looked willing to provide information. "Why has such a gentle girl such as you chosen one of the most—if not *the* most—brutal martial arts and excelled at it?" he asked. She replied, "It feels good to never have to be afraid of anybody anymore." And then she said, "I like showing off." The latter Gabriel did not really get. "You do not come across as extroverted." But she just smiled. "My boyfriend says the opposite. Do you actually want to hear me talk about my boyfriend? Do you care to know?" Gabriel answered: "I find this perfectly normal, and I am not bothered." This was actually a half-truth: In his eyes, she should concentrate on her job. Furthermore, he would have preferred that she concentrated on him while they were travelling together and would not constantly refer to her bloody boyfriend.

Then, the conversation got really heated. They tried to speak about the Spanish experience. "You were a sight for sour eyes in the church," Gabriel laughed. Tilda looked at him insulted. "I am not a believer. Leave me alone," she said. "Yes, but you need to be a little more tolerant if we want to go to India together," Gabriel demanded. "You went shut like a clam in that church in Spain! You must be a spiritual virgin or a long-suffering victim of the Catholic Church. You were shell-shocked by the whole environment. This can get interesting when we start journeying on the path of Bede Griffiths, going to the ashram in India and suchlike places. Will you then patiently wait in front of the ashram doors with the car engine running until I am done with the spiritual stuff? That is not the plan!"

Tilda shook her head. "Only because people do not share your standard Catholic spirituality, Mr David, you accuse them of having none at all. That is typically elitist behaviour." Gabriel answered: "You are spiritually closed. You are like a machine. Only a special type of rationality and logic works with you. You are not open to any new insights. You will never appreciate a very important part of the human knowledge space. The whole Bede Griffiths story seems to leave you totally untouched!"

Then he used quite imaginative language: "I really wish you would accept getting hit by experience. What does not immediately compute on an abstract logical level does not get processed by your brain. Do not always shy away and keep your forehead out of the spiritual jet stream, Mrs Toelz!" Afterwards, he was afraid that he had overdone it with his imaginative metaphors. But Tilda had not even reacted to his accusations: "You are jailed in your celestial world view" was the only comment she gave him.

She did not want to argue: Dispute was nothing but a suppression instrument. She had her own spirituality, which she reflected on once she was alone in her hotel bed. "My first axiom is, do not blame others for your misfortune," she angrily thought. "I am the only person I can change; when I change, my world changes. If Mr David feels unhappy with me, he should change his attitude. Do not put the blame on me. The second axiom of my spirituality is, identify your goals and develop your strategies to reach them. If he wants this Bede Griffiths stuff, he should follow it, but leave me alone. My third axiom is, shake off any idea of foreign determination or constraint—be it a 'god,' or circumstances such as birth, parents, whatever, or other people who think of themselves as rulers of your world. Replace it with your self-determination. This way, you are automatically becoming more powerful and happy. And more successful. You can live your true life." Gabriel should leave her alone. Thinking about Gabriel made her sick. "Mr David obviously wants to change me. That is the best reason to keep him at bay: This evening, he just tried to make me an object that should better comply to his world views. However, my life is only about me, not about him. My own spirituality starts with living outside the hamster wheel, knowing myself and understanding what this life is really about." She turned restlessly in her bed when she contemplated his request that she should let herself be hit by experience. "Does he not know? This world is nothing but a mere illusion. Experience tries to condition me. However, everything is false. My consciousness was manipulated and deluded by the people who rule. To become aware of this was very difficult. We have to work on ourselves. I am a creator. I can bring ideas to this world through my spirit. That is called creativity. I am a gatekeeper. Because all the other people permanently create this field of ideas with me, I can reaffirm certain ideas and filter out others. I am powerful. Therefore, everything here is about my advancement, about my creative mind and about my spiritual growth. Experience is not important. Mr David is not important in my world. He is in his world; I am in my world. That's it. My spiritual mission is to keep my world going. Never give up on the idea of your life, why you want to stay alive. I will keep my forehead out of his spiritual jet stream."

Angels' Play

Location:
Heaven above Budapest, Buda side, Fisherman's Bastion. Shared-Office Cloud.

Time:
Real-time GMT, Tuesday, 9 April 2019, 20:34

Players:
The two angels as before and Bede Griffiths.

Setting:
Both angels are in deep discussion with Bede Griffiths, who is in a fully orange sannyasin outfit and has a small travel backpack on his shoulders. But he seems to be rather unfit. He sits in a wheelchair, where he constantly tries to get out of being softly pushed back by the angels.

GA (*anxiously*):
Please, father, stay seated. You will get a stroke again. You are not well. Another stroke will make you worse.

BG (*patting GA's little hand*):
Tut, tut, my dear. I will tell you of my experience when I had a stroke. It was in January 1990. I was meditating at six o'clock one morning, and something came and hit me on the head. It felt like a sledgehammer. Everything went blurry.

A terrible force was pushing me out of my chair, and I did not know what was happening. I managed to crawl onto the bed, and I was found there after about an hour. Apparently, I had been unconscious for a week.

GA (*accusingly*):
There you go. Unconscious! Stay in that wheelchair.

BG (*soothingly*):
No, as I said, *apparently*, I was conscious. I did not speak, and I have no memory of it at all. But there were some wonderful people in the ashram, and they arranged everything for me each day. At the end of a week, I began to come round to normal consciousness, and there was a profound change...

TA (*knowingly*):
Yes, you became disabled. You were on the mercy of others.

BG (*explaining*):

I had died to the ego... The ego—the mind, and also... the discriminative mind that separates and divides, all seem to have gone. Everything was flowing into everything else, and I had a sense of unity behind it all. Then this began to open up. I thought I was going to die, and I... let go of the soul and body into the hands of God...

TA (*convinced*):

And then you nearly died.

BG (*feeling totally misunderstood*):

No, then somebody came and massaged me, and I came back to normal. A very important experience then happened. I felt rather restless and uncertain, and an urge came over me to 'surrender to the mother.' I surrendered, and an overwhelming experience of love came over me. They were like waves of love.

GA (*compassionately*):

Some call it a post-traumatic experience.

BG (*wildly shaking his head*):

I called out to someone who was watching there: "I am being overwhelmed by love!" I think what happened was a psychological breakthrough to the feminine. In each person is both masculine and feminine, and most men repress the feminine. I have done that to a very considerable extent, and I think it was the woman in me who came and hit me on the head! But then she came back to me as a loving mother.

TA (*repelled but somehow fascinated*):

A woman? Goodness gracious! What type of woman? Was she good-looking?

BG (*fighting angelic ignorance*):

When you let the feminine open and your unconscious lets her come up, then she is the loving mother, and in coming back to you, she transforms you. Because God is mother, we have to balance the masculine and the feminine in our nature. We must be aware of how we are repressing one aspect of our nature; by allowing it to come forth, we become whole.

TA (*not convinced and bristling*):

But the stroke made you weaker!

BG (*shaking his head*):

On the contrary! The stroke was a wonderful experience and the greatest grace I have ever had in my life.

GA (*reverently*):

Father, are you really wanting to go down, yourself, with your arthrosis in the knees? We could do it for you. TA has Gotcha painting in its armour set and can fire the colour cartridges with its precision gun (*TA proudly presenting a monstrous firearm for confirmation*).

BG (*firmly*):
Put that away, dear. This girl needs a revelation all for herself. I will go into her dreams and apparate without stressing my knees at all (*with this, he evaporates downwards, wheelchair and all*).

A Tika on the Forehead

On Wednesday, Gabriel and Tilda left Budapest. It had been a really short stay after all. The preordered taxi came very early, at 5:30 am, to fetch them to take them to the airport. They were quite tired and at first sat in total silence, each in their corner of the backseat. Then, Tilda began to talk. She sounded exhausted and upset. "I had a dream last night, Mr David," she revealed, "a strange nightmare." "What was it about?" Gabriel was curious. "I dreamt about a big hall full of people—like a huge train station with many people moving around," she said.

"Like the megacity scenes in the movie *Koyannisquatsi*? Such a place was shown there to demonstrate overpopulation and fast-moving, anonymous crowds. You might have seen the movie." He thought that explaining her bad dream with a past visual experience would soothe her, but she did not respond to that. "Then I stood in this hall among floating people, waiting for something or somebody," she quietly continued. "The next thing that happened was that I felt that something had hit my forehead with impact." She winced in memory. "When I touched my forehead with my hand, I felt something wet. Looking down at my hand, there was a yellow fluid, which spilled from my forehead." Gabriel looked at her with compassion. "I felt afraid, was badly injured and fell down to the ground." "Did you wake up then?" Gabriel asked, wanting to know because this is what often happens in dreams. "No," she replied. "People helped me to reach a kind of ambulance car, which stood in front of the big hall." "Could you get in?" Again, he wanted to know. "Yes," she answered, "but while doing this, I touched my forehead again and looked at my hand: The colour of the fluid had changed from yellow to red. I felt awfully scared."

She looked silently out of the car window for a long time. Then she continued: "In the ambulance, there was an old man with a long white beard waiting in a wheel chair. He tried to get up to his legs to greet me but could not do so quickly—obviously he had bad knees, which might have been why he was in that ambulance car. When he finally approached me with a smile, he touched my forehead, and I woke up. I was so scared."

She was really shaken. In a way, Gabriel's conscience suffered because the dream was obviously inspired by his stupidly talking the evening before about how she should herself let be hit and so on. All this had given her was a nightmare. However, then he thought about some pictures he had seen of Bede Griffiths with an Indian blessing sign on his forehead—the tika: sometimes yellow, sometimes red. And suddenly, he could see who had visited Tilda at night and who the old man was in the car singling her out from the masses in the big hall. Of course, for Tilda, this was just a bad dream, but it could very well have been something totally different. Tilda saw the sign on her forehead as an injury inflicting pain, but it could have actually been a blessing. "There might be a positive interpretation of your dream," Gabriel said cautiously, but she was still too flustered to pay much notice. However, he felt relieved. Tilda was finally subject to individual revelations as well. She had got a tika as a blessing from Bede Griffiths.

"Your brain will not run out," he told her quietly. "The good message is that our key author did not lose his wits with such a forehead mark." He showed her some pictures of Bede Griffiths on his mobile where Father Bede had yellow and red tikas, and he let her listen to a YouTube interview where Bede Griffiths wore a tika as well. "Look, this interview was taken after he had two strokes when he was over ninety. You can see and hear that despite visible exhaustion at the start of the interview, all his brain cells are working. He is trying to connect to his partner in conversation, with full concentration. I am further sure that Rupert Sheldrake probably wore such a forehead tika every now and again too, because he lived together in this ashram with Pater Bede while writing—and you think he is quite clever despite what I think about these morphic fields." Tilda did not laugh at the weak joke. "A nice example how to turn a frightening, painful experience into a revelation from heaven. I was hit on the head with a near-death infliction of pain, and you see it as a blessing 'tika.' Great."

Despite her exhaustion, she wanted him to understand. "I will not go on endlessly about it," she said, "but what do you know about pain? I've been living with pain every day since 2013. This has been going on now for seven years. My ankle is sometimes very bad. Nobody can do anything. I have consulted with many specialists. They all did their X-rays and spent expensive hours on diagnosis, ending with the same results. Unfortunately, I completed my fight before going to hospital when my ankle broke. It was a displaced fracture. Then, it was a Saturday, and no specialist was around at the hospital. My ankle blew up like a balloon. I spent a week in hospital, heavily drugged, just desperately staring at my ankle, which was secured in a strange iron cage called a *fixateur externe*, for stabilisation. It lasted for days before the swelling went down again and they could have a go at it with screws, metal plates and wiring. The operation did not go well. If my ankle had been corrected immediately after the fracture, things could have worked out. Blood vessels, nerves and soft tissues would not have been harmed so much. As it was, the bones never healed correctly either. Nobody dared to undertake a second operation in the years between 2013 and now, because it could have meant that I would lose my foot. The harmed structures were not safe to approach without ruining the functional parts. There was not one single surgeon in all of Germany who felt confident to operate again. This meant that there was no relief for my pain. I have to live with it for the rest of my life. I did as much physiotherapy as possible, but it did not really help. There were probably constant inflammations and instabilities that caused the pain I felt. All that I could do if it got too bad was take drugs against the pain. Anybody who tells me not to take drugs because you can become addicted, I am ready to kill. People have no idea."

Gabriel was deeply shocked. He had not known this. Tilda continued with her story: "Do you know the fairytale of the little mermaid? Where every step for her is as if she were walking on knives and scissors? Of course, in the fairytale, this has a symbolic meaning. For me, it was just matter-of-fact experience. Walking, hiking, running: For me, these were things I could do sometimes but not on bad days. If I overdid it, like on a longer hiking tour, I was heavily punished for stressing my ankle afterwards. Sometimes it lasted for days before I could tread normally again after overstraining. I have made an art out of not to letting other people see how much pain I have to endure. I could smile in the face of pain. This was how I sometimes felt. I was walking on knives and scissors, and my task was to not let anybody know. So, please Mr David, do not play around lightly with me on the issue of pain. You have no idea. And I won't have it that my bad dreams about inflicted pain are turned into something useful and nice. This is pure cynicism, and I hereby reject it. This is nothing to make fun of."

The Intuitive Mind

Angels' Play

Location:
Heaven above Berlin. Shared-Office Cloud.

Time:
Real-time GMT, Friday, 19 April 2019, 10:45

Players:
The two angels as before and Bede Griffiths. He wears his orange sannyasin outfit and has a red tika on his forehead. Around his neck is a floral wreath with flowers in all colours.

Setting: *Angels and BG are meditating, sitting cross-legged on the floor on a cushion. Many books are scattered around them. The air is full of incense.*

TA (*half-opening its right eye to check on the other two*):
Can we stop now?

GA (*trying to silence its colleague*):
Shhhh…

BG (*still deep in meditation*):
Ohm…

TA (*sighing unhappily*):
It is boring. Nothing happens.

BG (*now opening one eye*):

Of course something happens. Can you not feel it? But that is just what your rational mind cannot endure. You want to control everything. You are not prepared to be silent, to be still, to allow things to happen.

TA (*complaining*):

I have been silent and still now for nearly ten minutes. I have allowed things to happen, but things did not take their chance. I cannot sit here forever doing nothing.

BG (*explaining*):

This is 'active passivity.' It is what the Chinese call *wu wei*, action in inaction. It is a state of receptivity.

(*nestling with his necklace*) "Let us open our leaves like a flower," said Keats, "and be passive and receptive." These words inspired me at the very beginning of my journey, but it is only now that I realise their full significance.

There is an activity of the mind that is grasping, achieving, dominating like yours. But there is also an activity that is receptive, attentive, open to others.

This is what you have to learn.

TA (*defiantly*):

Be open and attentive to whom, for example? And what would I gain from that?

BG (*fixating GA with his glance*):

Open and receptive to GA, for a start. What is GA feeling about you right in the moment?

GA (*reddening*):

No, please....

TA (*getting angry with its colleague without really knowing why*):

What is wrong with you, you bloody cow.... (*stopping at seeing the shocked face of BG*)

BG (*quickly recovering his composure*):

Yes, try to find out what GA feels. I speak of intuitive knowledge.

It is an integral knowledge embracing the whole, starting from the 'blood,' the physical being, passing through the heart, the seat of the affections, the psychic being, and finally reaching the 'purer mind,' not the reason but the intellect, the intuitive mind.

Thus, intuition exists at every level of our being.

TA (*sceptically*):

Of your being maybe. Obviously, you need blood, a heart, a psyche. It seems you have to be a human being. Can angels and machines have intuitive knowledge?

GA (*eagerly*):

Machines no, I suppose. Angels yes! (*triumphantly reaching out and citing page 2 from a book by Rupert Sheldrake and Matthew Fox titled The Physics of Angels*):

Listen, angels are even called experts.

(*reading out loud*)

The Intuitive Mind

> "Angels are essentially understanding beings. They think deeply. They are experts at understanding—at standing under. The primal thoughts that uphold all our other thoughts, angels know through intuition, according to Aquinas and other teachers on angels. Angels don't have to go to school to learn the essence of things. They don't need discursive reasoning and experimentation to learn. They get it all intuitively, immediately. They are experts at intuition, and they can assist our intuition. This is one reason that angels and artists befriend one another so profoundly.
>
> When we look at the wonderful, amazing images of angels that artists have given us, we are dealing not just with a rich subject of painting but with a relationship going on between angels and artists. Intuition is the highway in which angels roam."

Isn't that very sweet? And it is very true. (*proudly*) Some of my best friends are artists.

TA (*matter-of-factly*):

But we have no body. Remember: Intuition starts with the 'blood,' with bodily awareness. (*turning to Bede Griffiths*) Right, Father?

BG (*confirming*):

Yes. However, dear, angels can jump this level with their astral body, because even at this level, the intellect, the self, is present.

By the bye, my good friend from the Saints Section, D. H. Lawrence, who was the prophet of this kind of knowledge, has expressed it well (*reaching out and taking another book from the floor*).

> "We have lost almost entirely the great intrinsically developed sensual awareness or sense-awareness and sense-knowledge of the ancients. It was a great depth of knowledge, arrived at direct by instinct and intuition as we say, not by reason. It was a knowledge based not on words but on images. The abstraction was not into generalizations or into qualities but into symbols, and the connection was not logical but emotional."

TA (*rebelliously*):

But that is not knowledge! I would call it just 'feeling.' (*under its breath*) Or nonsense.

BG (*authoritative*):

No, it is real knowledge: It is not merely sensual or emotional experience. It is sense awareness, emotional experience reflected in the mind—not in the rational mind, the abstract intelligence, but in the intuitive mind, the passive intellect.

(*gets up, dancing a few waltz steps, to the utter amazement of both angels*)

It finds expression not in abstract concepts but in concrete gestures, in images and symbols, in dance and song, in ritual sacrifice, in prayer and ecstasy.

(*gets more ecstatic in dancing, to the growing embarrassment of the angels*)

This is the sphere of imaginative intuition. It is here that the intuitive power of the mind is most clearly manifest.

(*sitting down again, to the relief of both angels, and pointing to another book on the floor*). It is the sphere of what the famous psychoanalyst Jung called the archetypes.

GA (*retrieving again the book of D.H. Lawrence*):

Yes, and artists bring these archetypes into the light of consciousness. They write stories about images and symbols; they compose music and perform imaginations. They transform images from the ground up.

BG (*now becoming very flowery and poetic but only in language*):

To be precise, the passive intellect receives these images from the depths of its physical and emotional experience and sheds the light of intelligence on them.

This is when the intuition begins to emerge from the darkness of physical and emotional experience into the clear light of knowledge.

TA (*soberly*):

That sounds like machines cannot do it. And for me, I have serious doubts as well. Where does all this intuition come from and go to, and what exactly is it good for?

BG (*radiantly smiling*):

There is a point where intuition, having passed through the realms of darkness and of twilight into the sun, now passes beyond.

It carries with it all the deep experience of the body and the blood and all that the emotions and the imagination have impressed upon it, and now, passing beyond images and thoughts, it 'returns upon itself' in a pure act of self-reflection, of self-knowledge.

TA (*looking enviously at GA, who has gone back to cross-legged silence*):

This is why angels have intuition, and why I should meditate to get closer?

BG (*resuming his lotus seat position and lecturing the angels about meditation*):

Indeed. This is the experience of the mystic, who, set free from all the limitations both of body and of soul, enters into the pure joy of the spirit. The spirit is the culminating point of body and of soul, where a man transcends himself and awakens to the eternal ground of his being.

(*GA slightly shuddering at the gender bias and successfully trying to hide it; TA grinning*)

The obscure intuition of physical being, the broadening intuition of emotional and imaginative experience, the light of reason discovering the laws and principles of nature and of man (*again a nearly invisible shudder from GA, followed by an even deeper grin from TA*)—all these are reflections of the pure light of intuition, in which the soul knows itself, not merely in its living relation with the world around or with other human beings but also in its eternal ground, the source of its being.

You can learn that in meditation. Marry intuition to reason. Overcome dualities!

TA (*obediently closing its eyes but investing not much hope in achieving anything by it*):

OK. One, two, om....

What Men and Machines Cannot Do

Gabriel had spent a restless weekend puzzling over Tilda. He started to feel really bad about her. Why was he having this strange, intuitive relationship with Tilda of all women? Why had she been present every time something interesting had happened in the past months in what he started to call the Bede Griffiths project? What was her role in that exactly? He wanted to push her out of the game. Very strange things had happened since he started the Bede Griffiths readings. For him, life would have been easier if all this had had nothing to do with Tilda. If she just had been in the right place and the right time as a prompter. Having talked about cows and having said 'Rupert Sheldrake' and been done with it. Then he could shake her off and go on all by himself. But if the objective was to save the world, she might be much more than just a prompter. It was time to find out. He had to talk to her about their strange connection.

"What is intuition for you, Mrs Toelz?" he asked her the next day when they walked together to the B1 cafeteria for lunch. "Is it the same as empathy or telepathy?" Tilda looked at him strangely. He continued without responding to her gaze: "For me, intuition is having a sudden, deep and direct understanding of a person or a situation without having factual knowledge. It might lead to telepathy, yes. And intuition is doubtlessly and *per definitionem* right. Otherwise, it would not be called intuition." "Aha," Tilda said. She looked at him uncomfortably. She felt that he had started to talk about their relationship and the meaning behind their telepathic connection. "Do you think that one should always follow one's intuitions and that intuitions are always good?" she asked hesitantly. Gabriel blinked. She was certainly on the right trail. "Whether following it will always result in the best for the world as a whole—that is, whether the consequences of following intuitions are right in terms of morals—is a very interesting issue. I have no idea. Maybe my intuition is not as good as it could be," he answered cautiously. "Who do you think is better in intuition?" she asked next, turning again a little back to her prickly self. "You, Mr David, or me?" He was puzzled. He had never thought about this. For him, it had seemed as if the capacity for intuitive knowledge of each other had been evenly distributed. "People say that women are more intuitive than men," Tilda said triumphantly.

"I thought you were so proud of your rational mind and your computer literacy," Gabriel said amazed. "Why do you suddenly claim female intuition against male rationality?" She looked at him furiously. Gabriel evasively answered his own question: "I apologise. I bet Bede Griffiths has some ideas on this issue." Tilda looked sceptical. A monk having ideas about women and intuition? "Let us have a look at the contents table of *Essential Writings*," she suggested. From his rucksack, he fetched the book that was always on him. They both bent over it. Tilda's eyes widened. "The Masculine and Feminine," she read loud. "Page 77, let us see what he writes." "Woman represents the intuitive power in human nature, while man represents the rational mind. These are two complementary aspects of human nature, and a human being is only complete when these two functions of human nature have been 'married,'" Gabriel read loud. "There you go. What bullshit," Tilda said disgustedly. "This is nothing but prejudice from old white men." Gabriel grinned. "You might be right, but let's see what Father Bede makes of it." He continued reading but under his breath because he was already expecting to read something that not all the staff of B1 in the cafeteria should overhear. Maybe it was not gendered enough or politically incorrect in other ways.

> "It is important to recognize that these functions are complementary; both are equally necessary. Man and woman are equal and opposite. A woman does not become more equal to man by seeking to become like a man but by revealing his opposite character. Yet it must be recognized that every man and woman is both male and female; reason and intuition exist alike in every human being, but in the man, reason is dominant and intuition is subordinate. In a perfect man or woman, the 'marriage' of opposites takes place, and in fact, the very purpose of an exterior marriage is to enable the man and the woman to complete one another by an interior marriage. On the other hand, when reason and intuition, the man and woman, are separated, then disaster follows. Reason without intuition is intelligent but sterile; intuition without reason is fertile but blind. The woman who seduces man is the blind intuition which listens to the voice of the serpent, the animal intelligence, or sexuality. This is the normal course of sin. The feminine mind, instead of being guided by reason so as to open itself to the Spirit, and so to achieve the marriage of intuition and reason and the integration of the personality, surrenders to animal instinct and drags down the reason with it."

"Oh, bloody hell," Tilda stopped him. "That is awful. The woman as the voice of the serpent. This is so idiotic." She was totally embarrassed. So was Gabriel because things took a turn that he had not expected. They had started to talk about intuition and telepathy. Now they seemed to shift into a discussion of sex. How did this happen? Was Father Bede mad? What had the serpent to do with everything? He haltingly read on. "The serpent certainly has a sexual significance, but it is not that sex is evil," he desperately read aloud as he read on. "Hallelujah, I am so happy to hear that. Sex is not evil, per se. Good to know," Tilda burst out. "Shhh," Gabriel replied, trying to calm her down. People around were starting to look at them. "Let us see where this goes. What about the snake?" Tilda asked curiously. She had obviously mastered her embarrassment. They both read the next passage but silently:

> "Sex is an animal instinct which, when the woman surrenders to the man and the man to the woman, becomes the means of their communion in the Spirit. Thus the serpent becomes the Savior, as it was said in Saint John's Gospel, 'As Moses lifted up the serpent in the wilderness, so must the Son of Man be lifted up, that whoever believes in him may have eternal life.' It is the separation of sex from intuition or feeling and from reason and understanding which is the cause of sin, while the integration of the sexual instinct with feeling and imagination—that is, the intuitive mind—and with reason and will—that is, the rational mind—brings about fulfillment of both man and woman in the life of the Spirit."

"Aha," Tilda said mockingly, "now the snake is suddenly the saviour. How weird can it get? All this talking about men and women, sex and snakes in the desert! What is it good for exactly, Mr David?" Gabriel had scanned the rest of the text. His face went pale, and he said tonelessly, "It is good for saving the world from destruction. At least in the opinion of Bede Griffiths. And it has to do with India." "What?" Tilda impolitely asked in disbelief. He read the last passage, out loud again:

> "In the West today the masculine aspect, the rational, active, aggressive power of the mind, is dominant, while in the East the feminine aspect, the intuitive, passive, sympathetic power of the mind, is dominant. The future of the world depends on the 'marriage' of these two minds, the conscious and the unconscious, the rational and the intuitive, the active and the

passive. In India and all over the world today these two minds are meeting, but often the impact of the West on the East is that of a violent aggression, whether by armed power, as in the past, or by the much more subtle aggression of science and technology… Yet it still remains possible to conceive of a development of science and technology which would not seek to dominate nature in the style of the West but to work with nature, building up from the basis of the village economy, as Mahatma Gandhi sought to do, and so create a new culture, in which humankind and nature, reason and intuition, the Yang and the Yin in Chinese terms, would be brought into harmony."

"Bloody hell," Tilda said again, "what has this serpent thing between man and woman to do with justice in the world and Mahatma Ghandi? What are we supposed to do now? Is life not complicated enough?" Gabriel pointed to the editorial remarks of Thomas Matus on this section of *Essential Writings* and said, "Look, here is a kind of answer to your question." She read:

> "The experience of his first stroke in 1990 … raised Father Bede's consciousness of the feminine in general and of the feminine dimension of his own personality. Although he admitted to having repressed his sexual instincts as a young adult, his fondness then and later for the erotic themes in D. H. Lawrence's fiction and poetry betrayed his fascination with the male–female archetype.
>
> Bede Griffiths' attitude toward sex was quite close to the paradoxical attitude of Indians, who on the one hand observe a sort of exterior 'Puritanism' while on the other they deal with sex as a purely natural need, with few ethical implications. Father Bede's sexual ethics were quite traditional, although when counseling persons he used great pastoral tact and discretion, respecting always the individual's conscience. Always a contemplative, Father Bede peered into the archetypal depths of the male–female dyad and saw there the key to the complementary relationship of peoples, cultures, and religions."

"Anyway," Tilda resolutely resumed, "so far, my intuition says that we should go to India to find out more about it. Maybe Indian people know more about intuition than we do, and maybe we will get better when we're there. Let's do some autoethnography and try it out!" "This from your mouth, Mrs Toelz," Gabriel replied, not disguising his surprise. "Before India, though, we will be going to the US next week, remember." Then he had an idea. "We can maybe visit the place where D.H. Lawrence lived. Taos it's called. We will pass by the area when we are over there." "To do exactly what?" Tilda asked suspiciously. "Reconcile the male and the female?" Gabriel did not answer.

Open Access This chapter is licensed under the terms of the Creative Commons Attribution 4.0 International License (http://creativecommons.org/licenses/by/4.0/), which permits use, sharing, adaptation, distribution and reproduction in any medium or format, as long as you give appropriate credit to the original author(s) and the source, provide a link to the Creative Commons license and indicate if changes were made.

The images or other third party material in this chapter are included in the chapter's Creative Commons license, unless indicated otherwise in a credit line to the material. If material is not included in the chapter's Creative Commons license and your intended use is not permitted by statutory regulation or exceeds the permitted use, you will need to obtain permission directly from the copyright holder.

Chapter 4
An Alternative Society

Arriving at Tucson, Arizona, USA, Gabriel and Tilda fetched their rental car. They had meetings both in Tucson and in Phoenix and had decided to establish Tucson as their base for flying in and out of Germany. Already in the morning after their arrival, they went off to Phoenix. It was a nice day. Tilda was driving. Sitting in the passenger seat, Gabriel was in high spirits while preparing some PowerPoint slides for their Phoenix partners. "The Phoenix workshop will use participatory formats and 'energisers' to get everybody going. I will teach you some dances," he said eagerly. Tilda scowled. "Please don't. I can do without," she said.

Are You Going with Me?

While driving through the sunny Arizona landscape, they listened to some music coming from their smartphones, connected to the car's sound system. "I like to listen to my rap and hip-hop stuff," Tilda said, "but what else do we have for later?" Gabriel hastily searched his files. He thought Pat Metheny's "Are you going with me?" from the album *Travels* was the perfect choice, especially to match the situation they were in. After arriving, they first checked into their motel, which was quite far away from the meeting venue, which they learnt the hard way after having decided to walk there. They had a lovely workshop day. Their hosts had a huge virtual and augmented reality facility. It was a kind of stage where people could walk around changing things with their body presence. For example, there was a kind of "heat map" where they could virtually take a stroll on the property and where the temperature would change in accordance with where their shadows shifted on the ground.

Their hosts applied these techniques to their projects on heat-management policy in hot and dry Arizona. Fascinating! They also had some fun participating in and interacting with the VR environments. Gabriel taught people a group dance with a pairwise choreography. "Men stand in a row opposite a row of women," he advised.

"Each one has somebody to pair up with directly before him or her." It was a kind of hide-and-seek dance, quite sensual. Irritatingly, Gabriel ended up forming a pair with their main male host, while Tilda danced with some student assistant. What a waste. They danced around with many red and white balloons in the augmented reality environment, pushing virtual and real balloons up again whenever one came by on its way to the floor. The next day, the group went out for adventure. They were scheduled to visit "Biosphere 2" in a small Arizona town called Oracle.

Methods at Safe Spaces

The drive from Phoenix to Oracle was long, but Gabriel and Tilda were used to long periods of silence in the car and enjoyed it. They drove through the lonely desert of Arizona, admiring the huge cacti. "We should definitely have a dedicated desert walk before returning home," Tilda said, and Gabriel wholeheartedly agreed. "But that'll have to wait because today is solely for teaching us to love the nature of our green-blue planet, right?" "Right. But might I still ask about yesterday, Mr David?" Tilda inquired. "Why did we spend our days at workshops where we sang, danced, meditated, played with balloons and engaged in further nonsense? What was this actually good for?"

Gabriel had expected these questions. He said, "Remember the Post-Normal Science Symposium at Barcelona. One of the specific objectives of new science and technology is to empower and engage the expertise of marginalised communities, minorities and other vulnerable populations, right?" Tilda nodded. "How happy, do you think these latter people will be to meet professionals they think to be intellectually highbrow, politicians-in-charge that they see as responsible for their disadvantages, other groups they conceive as competitors for social services, people from industry they distrust because they are considered—probably rightfully—as exploiting their work and so on? And how happy are all those people to talk to any of the other groups?" Tilda shook her head. "Not very happy," she responded.

Gabriel nodded. "Exactly," he said, "'a participatory multistakeholder approach' sounds nice and easy. In reality, this is one of the most conflict-prone, difficult arenas you can imagine, where different interests and high emotions crash into each other. If we want to create *safe spaces* for vulnerable people, we need a method to make this a fruitful and successful experience for everybody. You can imagine: At the beginning of such a project, distrust, suspicion, bad moods, depression, low energy, anxiety and hate will be at the forefront of people's feelings. Not a good atmosphere for discussion." "Yes, but how can we make this a safe space for everybody?" Tilda asked curiously. "The first approach that needs to constantly accompany any 'serious method' is for people to befriend each other," Gabriel answered. "People need to become friends," he continued. "This will enable them to listen to each other, to stay patient in cases of dissent and to seek solutions. The best fundament for cooperation is to like others."

"And why all this dancing and stuff?" Tilda asked. Gabriel laughed before replying: "There is a very serious *basso continuo* in all of these 'playing fields,' Mrs Toelz: This is where we stiffy professionals learn and experience participative and interactive formats that can quickly engage people with each other. It's autoethnography again. People who dare to move dare to speak. People who dare to move with each other dare to speak to each other." "Yes, but why are we dancing all the time?" Tilda asked insistently. She was obviously very uncomfortable with that component. "During workshops, as this one here in Arizona, we can test out specific formats: Is this dance low threshold enough to get people into contact with each other? Is another dance doing the trick in a better way? Does it make people feel good and competent? Is it soothing, exhausting or activating? Is it enjoyable to join forces in playful dance? Does it encourage you to be really 'here in space and time'? Do you feel energised enough to engage in serious discussion afterwards? Are you feeling courageous to speak up in the company of your dance partners? Can you not see?" "Hm," said Tilda, "what I see is that, so far, we are experimenting with these bedrock elements while pre-empting a safe space method. We do not consider these questions explicitly in all our 'energising' methods. We experience the effects and keep them as body knowledge for further use." She was certainly right. Gabriel agreed. "OK, let's say that one objective of our India project could be to develop a systematic approach including tested and approved bedrock elements that empower people to become friends with each other."

"A whole method?" Tilda asked incredulously. "Yes, Mrs Toelz," Gabriel answered. "Of course, the methods for such a project are more than singing, dancing and making friends. One basic approach was already mentioned between the two of us. It's autoethnography. Basically, the underlying message is that we cannot take ourselves out of the solution—or the whole process leading to the solution. We need to be so deeply part of the whole enterprise that we are engaged with our full personality. We have 'to live' the process." Tilda was again very suspicious, and with good reason. She obviously thought about her expected role in that.

"I want to read out to you what Bede Griffiths thinks about this," Gabriel said. He fetched out of his rucksack the book authored by Griffiths titled *The Marriage of East and West*, which Tilda has not seen before. Then he read out to her a text passage starting on page 152. Though he had read it before, he was a bit embarrassed because it interpreted their intuitive relationship in a way that he was not very happy with:

> "What has to take place is a 'marriage' of East and West, of the intuitive mind with the scientific reason. The values of the scientific mind must not be lost, but they need to be integrated in the wider vision of the intuitive mind. ... Reason itself, the active intellect, is taken up into the intuitive mind, that is, into the reflective knowledge of the self, and reason itself becomes intuitive. ... It is the discovery of this infinite, eternal, unchanging being, beyond the flux of time and change, beyond birth and death, beyond thought and feeling, yet answering to the deepest need of every human being, which is the goal of all religion and of all humanity. Here there is no longer a division between man and woman, for male and female are one. Here there is no longer a division between man and nature, for nature and man have found their unity in their source. Here there is no longer a division between classes and races and religions for here all have found the truth and the life for which they

were seeking. ... the intuitive vision is a vision of the whole. The rational mind goes from point to point and comes to a conclusion: the intuitive mind grasps the whole in all its parts."

Angels' Play

Location:
Heaven above Tempe, Arizona. Shared-Office Cloud.

Time:
Real-time GMT, Tuesday, 23 April 2019, 17:06

Players:
The two angels as before and St. Christophorus (SC).

Setting:
Both angels are sitting in their cockpit seats, leaning and giggling over a book and loudly reading passages to each other.

TA:
Here you go: Lady Chatterley sees her hunter in the garden and thinks that he has some nice.... hihihi (*nearly falling from its cockpit seat*)

GA (*switching its head mike to 'mute'*):
Please! We have been briefed that Pater Bede is a big fan of this D.H. Lawrence. And DHL is even in the Saints Section. Do not make fun of him. This is supposed to be part of the Script literature.

TA (*incredulously checking the Script*):
Cannot be. There must be a mistake. A Benedictine monk cannot be the fan of a pornographic writer.

GA (*correcting*):
Erotic novelist. And you know the sad story of D.H. Lawrence in this regard. Frieda totally messed him up after he went off with her to Taos, leaving Europe behind. All his erotic dreams and musings ended in impotence. Too bad.

TA:
What are we supposed to do now? How is this sad guy supposed to help us?

GA:
We need (*reciting the equipment list*) a rattlesnake, a whole handful of Pita Jungle restaurants, cheap motels with Jacuzzis, two seat reservations for the Lufthansa return flight to Berlin, and—oh, no!...

TA (*apprehensively leaning forward, trying to peep at the list*):
What is it?

GA:
We need our fighting gear! Script says: Full armour. (*disapprovingly watching TA's delighted grin*)
   This might set us back for months, and you seem to enjoy it.
   Already hectic alarm beeps from all consoles. Both angels in great distress pushing away the D.H. Lawrence book to make space for emergency equipment.

TA (*shaking its head in dismay while checking the incoming emergency signals*):
   A blue-sky attack! We have not had one for ages. (*trying to make contact with the Saints Section to follow emergency instructions*) This is an emergency 14 case. We need Christophorus support. Now!
   After some discussions with Saints management, St. Christophorus, patron of all travellers, apparates on the cloud. He is the jovial and comforting type who looks perfectly at ease with himself.

SC (*smugly*):
   Problems with the car?

TA (*rolling its eyes at GA, but reporting politely*):
   Yes, sir. Enemy has meddled with the artificial intelligence GPS in the car. Enemy has organised a street gang ambush that our charges cannot avoid when they follow GPS.

SC (*defensively*):
   Everybody follows GPS nowadays. People have unlearnt to navigate complex landscapes themselves. It is really tempting to delegate every challenging decision to machines.

GA (*anxiously*):
   Can you repair the car navigation system, sir, please?

SC (*scanning GPS programme code, AI systems and projective scenarios, starting to look a little concerned*):
   That would take me an hour or two.

GA (*even more anxiously*):
   We do not have that much time. Can you not do anything else? A quick fix?

SC (*musingly*):
   I can get them out of that car. There is a scenario available that is not perfect.
   It still has all the threads, such as criminal suburbs, corruption, blackmail, exploitation, dark streets, long walks and late hours.
   Furthermore, it would cost them their car for the night and create some bad moods among them. But at least it would separate them from their car, and they would avoid the bloody ambush.

GA (*encouragingly*):

Do it, sir, please. I have Teo, the singing taxi driver, who is one of our field service staff down there, on standby availability for tonight. He can raise their spirits and help out with transfers.

Both angels silently observe the apparition of St. Christophorus' tow car with all its gear for emergency car repair and wrecking. Everybody is preparing for a long and laborious night shift.

Pita Jungle Detours

Biosphere 2 turned out to be a large science research facility for Earth systems. It included a vivarium, which was an artificial, materially closed ecological system mimicking the real ecological system of planet Earth—i.e. Earth 2. Arizona actually managed to keep a group of volunteers alive there who agreed to isolate themselves for years without contact with the outer world except in an emergency. Biosphere 2 was one of the world's largest facilities for understanding global scientific issues such as climate change, natural resource scarcity and biodiversity threats. It was all about complex systems, but everything was concentrated, like under a microscope or in a burning glass. After the guided tour in Biosphere 2, the group met in the car park to discuss where to go for dinner that night. They decided to return to Tempe and opted for a Pita Jungle chain restaurant that the locals in their little group highly recommended. They started from Oracle driving in a convoy at first but soon losing the others, such that Tilda and Gabriel were again alone on the country roads going through the fabulous sunset of the Arizona desert. Very soon, the sinking sun made space for a gigantic dark night sky with millions of blinking stars. It was beautiful. Coming closer to Phoenix as Tilda drove and Gabriel navigated, they looked for the quickest way to Pita Jungle by using Gabriel's mobile's GPS.

Then, a horrible odyssey through the dark suburbs began. Gabriel misread the information on the GPS twice, and they ended up in front of two Pita Jungle restaurants before reaching their actual destination. Tilda was cross with Gabriel for his bad map reading. In the end, he was so frustrated with himself that he let her do both, the driving and the navigation, which got them at least at some point to where they should have gone in the first place. Too bad. The others had long ordered, and they could hardly keep pace with their dinner. This was why Tilda and Gabriel stayed behind the group to finish their meal as the last guests of the restaurant while the others had already said their goodbyes after this very long day. However, it was not over for the two of them. Entering the nearly empty car park of the restaurant, they discovered that their car was gone. They could not believe their eyes. They were totally exhausted, it was very late, they were far away from their motel, it was pitch dark, everybody else was already gone, and the two of them were alone in a foreign megacity, unfamiliar with the local infrastructures and processes. Could it get worse? They were both speechless and perplexed—and that did count for something because usually at least one of them had an idea about what to do next.

They wandered a little around the place where the car had been, checking the dark walls and windows around them. Gabriel then discovered a little sign on the wall saying that this car park was not to be used by the Pita Jungle guests but was reserved for patrons of another restaurant. Pita Jungle guests would be towed away. Every hour in the car park of the towing company would cost 100 dollars. Below, a QR code of the towing company was provided. They were shocked. There had been no sign at the entry of the car park, which was actually the backyard of Pita Jungle. There was a guy cleaning in the other restaurant, but he refused to open the door when he saw that they came from the car park. However, he was only the cleaning boy and would not have been the right person for their complaints anyway. Therefore, it could not be helped: Gabriel and Tilda had to phone the towing company to avoid being ruined by the 100-dollar hourly rate for 'hosting' their car. They phoned and got a guy advertising his being in operation 24/7, and they could come and fetch the car any time. The operator gave an address that was just outside Tempe. Gabriel did not know whether it could add to their mounting frustration when they phoned for a taxi and learnt that it would need about forty minutes to fetch them.

At least Pita Jungle was still open, and the restaurant staff let Gabriel and Tilda wait inside while the staff cleaned the place for the night. The waiters told them that what the two of them were just experiencing was actually the 'business model' of the other restaurant. It was, otherwise, a complete failure as a restaurant with zero guests and a bad reputation for food. However, the owner of the restaurant was the owner of the car park property between the two restaurants and also owned the towing company. They said he had installed CVT sensors that wait for ignorant victims like them to go to Pita Jungle, which then automatically alert his drivers to tow the cars away. Usually, Pita Jungle would warn their guests against this practice, but tonight they had been very busy, and they thought that Gabriel and Tilda were part of the group that they sat with, without a separate vehicle. The practice of the car park owner was not completely illegal anyway, because there was this mini-sign on the wall as justification. Mood hit rock bottom when the taxi did not even arrive after forty minutes. Instead, the taxi company told Gabriel and Tilda when they phoned again that there would be no service anymore that night. They could not help it: They had to set out on foot in the direction of their motel because reaching the car park of the towing company on foot was out of the question. They silently trotted through the night when suddenly an illuminated taxi turned up with an elderly Latino at the driving wheel.

The USA Case

Teodoro Morales was a Hispanic born in the US whose family originated from Nicaragua, having immigrated in the 1980s. He was on night shift with his yellow taxi. The odd couple wildly waving to get his attention at the kerb of the dark and empty Pita Jungle restaurant were the only late customers to be seen in the empty streets of Tempe. He sighed and caressed the little silver replica of St. Christophorus dangling down from his rearview mirror. He did not like to be called in the streets. It was dangerous sometimes. He approached them with more than a little apprehension.

They could totally understand his precaution; they must have been looking weird. When they told him their story, however, he immediately shared their wrath. "I am Teo, with Latin American origins—though I might not look like it," he said. "I've had US citizenship from birth and have always been an American. But tonight I am not proud of it. I profusely apologise for my countrymen." "No need to do that," Gabriel said. Teo started singing. And he sang all the way driving to the car park of the towing company where they had decided to go despite the late hour, having finally found a mode of transport. However, the closer they came, the less the taxi driver sang. It was the darkest, meanest, ugliest suburb part of Tempe that one could imagine. "Poorest businesses and highest criminal rate," Teo said disdainfully. Nissen huts and shanties all over the forlorn place, wrecks of cars and scrap all over. When they came to the address given, nobody was there. It was a backyard ring fenced by a big wall with two doors—both barricaded. Phoning did not elicit any response. There was nothing else to do but to give up the car for the night and fetch it the next morning, before the next workshop slot, even though this would cost a fortune in car-park fees. Gabriel and Tilda were very grateful that at least musically gifted Teo had not done what they had asked him to do after they had paid him, namely drive away and leave them to their devices. While they had circled the car park looking for an entry and somebody to serve them, Teo had waited with the motor running, checking how this would work out. He took them in again, mumbling that this was a really bad place. On their way back, they discussed the CVT sensor infrastructure of Tempe. Teo proved to be very knowledgeable. He was obviously a very clever person. Tilda asked shyly, "Why are you driving a taxi? You sound like a traffic engineer." Teo was flattered.

"I have no education. School was a complicated issue when I was young. I am indeed interested in technology, but school was pretty hard for me. My parents were poor. They had jobs, but because they did not immigrate legally, they always feared being deported. My father worked on construction sites. Hard work and low pay. My mother cleaned the houses of rich people. My sisters and I were left to our own devices. Nobody could help with homework and such. At home, we spoke Spanish. All our neighbours did as well because we lived in a Latino neighbourhood. English lessons at school were difficult. I was only good in math. That is international." Teo laughed. "Does the government not offer any training programmes for talented people like you?" Tilda asked. Teo shrugged his shoulders before responding: "Being from a poor immigrant family was always a problem. After high school, I tried to get into a public training programme for computer technicians but was rejected because of my bad grades. Private training facilities, we couldn't afford. It is simply that government could not see talent because of the many obstacles working against me. They could not find me in their databases for any recruitment purposes." Teo laughed again. "You do not seem to feel bad about that," Gabriel said, revealing his observation with slight surprise in his voice. "I like to work as a taxi driver," Teo responded. "I like the job. But I think it is a waste. Instead of designing computer infrastructure for the city centre, I drive around in the suburbs. With a good job, I would pay higher taxes and contribute more to society. I think a good government should make sure that everyone can reach their full potential, because in the long run, it is better for everyone. If a politician would promise that they had a plan for how to organise, for example, more and better education for people like me, they would certainly get my vote. But you probably need a very clever artificial intelligence algorithm to score people correctly!"

Teo's last words ended as he brought them to the motel, which they reached at a little after 2 am. Teo was singing again when he left them. "He is definitely a candidate for our new project," Tilda said pensively, "that one on fairness in social service provision that we are planning. How about a US case study on vulnerable people like Teo?" Gabriel nodded. "Splendid idea. I wonder how the US government deals with delivering education services to migrant communities, especially the Hispanic ones, and what the ideas of social justice behind this are." He made notes on his computer about this when he was in his hotel bed later. "Never ever will I set my foot into a Pita Jungle restaurant again," Tilda said to her boyfriend on the phone after she had told him the whole story of the evening, though it was the middle of the night. But she was not prepared for the storm that broke loose. "I am worn out with listening to your adventure stories with Gabriel. You are my girlfriend!" Ken was desolate and angry. "What are you doing with this old fart over there?" he asking demandingly. "What an inconsistency! You walk into an artificial habitat mourning over climate change but drive around there endlessly with an air-polluting car! Are you insane?" He accused Tilda of betraying their ideas and their relationship at the same time. It was not agreeable, but Tilda thought she deserved it. He was right. She was cheating.

She had not dared to tell him how she felt about Gabriel, but somehow, he had guessed and was deeply jealous. "You let yourself be manipulated by a member of the ruling class; you even seem to like him." She had to distance her mobile phone from her ear because he got really loud. "Can you not see what he is doing to you? He is brainwashing you; he is totally turning you around. What about your own insights? What about your personality? Do you want to be an appendix to his corrupted, Americanised world views?" Tilda could not honestly defend herself; he was right. She was only afraid that Ken would start to troll Gabriel on the Internet with dirty emails to administer some punishment. A friend of theirs was very much into darknet cyber services. She did not exclude the possibility that Ken would make use of these while investing a little money to release his wrath. Ken was real. Singing Latino taxi drivers named Teo were just figures in a dream.

Elopement

After two more lovely workshop days, they were quite happy to be set free over the weekend for a sightseeing trip. Their plan was to go to New Mexico to visit Santa Fe and Taos. For Gabriel, it felt like an elopement—not only from work but from megacities such as Phoenix, with heat, pollution, overpopulation, crime, consumption, traffic jams and fast food—in short, civilisation as he knew it. When he talked about that to Tilda, she shared this feeling and completely agreed in his rejection of the present system of civilisation. She talked a lot about the options for an alternative society during the long hours in the car.

Angels' Play

Location:
Heaven above motorway I-40 E, Arizona. Shared-Office Cloud.

Time:
Real-time GMT, Friday, 26 April 2019, 15:15

Players:
The two angels as before and Bede Griffiths.

Setting:
Both angels and Bede Griffiths are dreamily watching the slow progress of the car as it adheres to the speed limit on US motorways. They are nearly asleep. However, the alarm button is still on red alert. Nobody dares to give way to their desire to take a nap.

TA (*trying to stay awake by way of conversation*):
Ho, Father! Have you ever thought of elopement?

BG (*surprised*):
But of course, my dear! All the time!

TA (*awake again*):
Your holy self? How is that?

BG (*warming to the topic*):
As I have written in *Essential Writings*, on page 95f, in 1930, after my friends and I graduated from Oxford, we were led to reject the Industrial Revolution and to try to shape our lives by a simpler and more traditional way of life. We were almost blindly seeking an escape from the world in which we had grown up and trying to discover a more natural way of life on our own. But since that time, this rejection of the present system of civilisation has spread throughout the world.

Everywhere is a search for an "alternative society," a way of life that will be more natural and more human and is equally opposed to the capitalist and the communist systems. This is why I eloped from the reigning system in 1930. And I would always do it again!

TA (*mildly*):
Father, your elopement ended up in a monastery next door to your hometown. One can say that the church of that time well represented the system that you wanted to leave.

BG:
Yes, I myself was led to the discovery of religion and Christianity as giving a meaning to life and to the monastic life as an alternative way of life.

Yet it was always clear to me that religion and Christianity, and to a large extent monasticism, were caught up in the present system and had failed to offer the way of life which people are seeking.

GA (*reaching down to Essential Writings at its feet, reading out loud*):

> "In the Roman Empire it was the monastic life which saved the world. It was the monks who fled to the deserts of Egypt, Palestine, and Mesopotamia and founded a way of life based on prayer and work in conditions of the utmost poverty and simplicity who alone survived the collapse of the Roman Empire and whose teaching and example led to the foundation of monasteries all over Europe, in which the basis of a new civilization could be found."

This is what you wrote, Father. Do you think monasteries can do this job again today? Can they do something for the world at large and help civilisations to survive by promoting an alternative society?

BG (*only at the surface switching topics*):
Monasteries need to be cultural and spiritual frontrunners again. In all topics. For example, the search for an alternative form of energy may decide the future of our civilisation. If an attempt is made to use the natural sources of energy from the sun and water and wind, it may be that civilisation will survive. Monasteries could start to build a spirituality of change around this.

TA (*observing Gabriel and Tilda in the car, pointedly*):
Not everybody wants to live in a monastery.

BG (*pensively looking down at their two charges*):
I see what you mean. And monasteries are themselves victims of the current system. They need to change too. Otherwise, they will not survive.

GA (*questioningly*):
What then to do?

BG (*visionary*):
The hope of the future would seem to lie in the small communities that are springing up all over the world, consisting of men and women, married and single, seeking a new lifestyle that will be in harmony with nature and with the inner law of the Spirit. These communities cross all barriers of race and religion and are the expressions of the urges to go beyond the present economic, political and religious systems and to open a way to the future.

TA (*sceptically*):
Men and women. Married and single. Crossing everything. Sounds quite flippant to me.

BG (*patiently, having listened to suchlike anxious objections all his life*):
No, no, not flippant at all. They can be likened to the monasteries of the Middle Ages, the centres of a ferment that would gradually transform society to make possible a new civilisation.

GA (*curiously*):
And Gabriel and Tilda?

BG (*eagerly*):
They can go to India. Like I did in the middle of my life. I thought then that I had reached the end of my journey, at least in the world down there, but then The Golden String led me to India, and a whole new understanding of the world opened before me. I will lead them there. They will become sannyasis.

TA (*sceptically*):
I doubt it.

"We" and "them"

While driving in the car to Santa Fe, Tilda and Gabriel talked a lot about what kind of life each would actually find desirable. What might an alternative society look like? This hit very close to home because they both had pertinent professional backgrounds and strong opinions, having seen a lot of planetary destruction in their work on many social development projects that aimed to combat social inequalities; violence and war; climate change and ecological crisis; and energy and natural resource scarcity.

"I have already given up on society as it presents itself today," Tilda opined. "I opt for radical revolution. We need to get rid of the status quo. Forget about collateral damage!" Gabriel was shocked by her radicalism. However, even he felt that she still held back her obviously strong emotions on this issue. He would nearly call it hatred because she despised her fellow humans for destroying nature and for their usual human ways of living together. "Do you want to turn your back on people?" he asked. "Yes, I would like to go to the desert and be on my own. I want to find myself. People can get lost. They are all egoists. I do not care what will become of them. There is no universal solution. Maybe there is a small number of people that are OK. I say 'small number.' My close friends. There is a deep gulf between us and them." Gabriel felt that he represented "them" in Tilda's eyes.

"I see universalism more as a matter of finding a way of living together as different personalities," Gabriel said cautiously. He referred to the abundant literature on criticising capitalism and suggesting alternative forms of organising societies to make them more natural and human. "Fleeing to the desert can be a first response, but then you need to go back and change the ways of life for everybody."

Tilda scowled: "I would not wait for 'everybody,' because 'everybody' is far too stupid to see sense. If at all, it can be small communities that act like secret societies establishing a new way of life and escaping the lifestyle of the majority." Gabriel did not agree. "That is not what living in small communities means. If we are going for an alternative society, we go for everybody, not only for a hand-picked few. Small communities will just provide environments where everybody has an own space within, where people know and trust each other. As Bede Griffiths says here on page 7 already, 'The more universal you become, the more deeply personal you become.' This is what I will go for."

Tilda repeated her spite for "everybody." "The majority is lost and can stay lost as far as I am concerned," she said. They quibbled terribly over that. "This sort of selfishness is not acceptable to me," Gabriel objected. "It has never been—this talking about the 'holy rest,' predestination and such. Wasn't it Ernst Bloch who mockingly said that he would rather refute personal salvation than accept that others would be left behind?" Tilda shook her head; obviously she had never read Ernst Bloch. He continued: "I remember how shocked I was when I once saw a drawing in Max Weber's *Ethics of Protestantism* about this Calvinistic family father leaving his wife and kids, who clung to his clothes for support, trying to prevent him from abandoning them for what he considered his 'salvation.' The painting is subtitled 'Life, Eternal Life!' Absolutely disgusting!" Gabriel tried to look up the picture on the Internet to show Tilda, who was driving, but there was no connection on the highway. "It is a deeply resigned, antisocial and elitist way to think about your fellow humans as hopeless leftovers. Who could stand to be saved if your fellow creatures were abandoned to suffer?"

Gabriel was really annoyed and started preaching: "All will be one: Hell will be empty in the end. That is my opinion!" Tilda shook her head at his words before replying: "I will not wait for this illusionary final unity. This is asking too much patience from me for people I actually despise!" Gabriel was really upset. "I do hope that I will never have the cruelty to abandon anybody with the verdict of their being lost. I hope love and patience will always be strong enough in me to go after a person whenever he or she runs into doom. If you stop going after others, stop hoping against hope, you stop being human. I could agree that you can become too weak to persevere, but as long as there is any strength in you, you should go."

He was very depressed because he clearly saw how far away Tilda was. They lived in two worlds with mountains of separation and differences between them. How could two people who thought they were mutually telepathic have such different lines of thought? He looked sadly at her and then voiced his thoughts: "Can people understand each other at all? Or are we all totally alienated from each other? This would be horrible because then all our work for a 'world society,' which is supposed to be a better society for all of us, would be futile."

"Right," Tilda said unaffected, "if not even you and I can find a way to one another, then how can we find a participatory approach to understanding and to finding solutions suitable for a plurality of perspectives and intercultural diversities, on a system level?" Gabriel slowly said, pointing to *Essential Writings*, "I do hope there is a resource that enables us to find solutions to the problems of building an alternative society while respecting high degrees of differentiation."

Tilda shook her head. She did not buy it. He continued: "Interestingly, Western social philosophy says there is. Our species has a great potential and ability that is called communicative competence, Jürgen Habermas says. But it needs to be displayed in the social world of trust and shared experience that is just at our feet, not in the world of ambition, systemic pressures and power dynamics."

They discovered the Griffiths text on an alternative society on page 95ff before they finally arrived at Santa Fe. It was sometimes outright funny how even the wording of their discussions was taken up by *Essential Writings*. In the meantime, they were already used to this type of interplay between text exegesis and their travel life.

Not Going Anywhere

Gabriel and Tilda were booked into two nice rooms in one of the better hotels in town—but still on the outer ring of the Paseo Peralta, the circle road around the city centre of Santa Fe. They met for breakfast at the hotel's terrace at 9 am. It smelt of pine trees and fresh coffee. Gabriel was already sitting at one of the little garden tables outside on the shady terrace when Tilda arrived with her tablet.

Her face was dark; she was sullen and quiet. Then, she suddenly spoke: "I have talked half the night with my boyfriend on the phone." "What is the matter?" Gabriel asked. "He is not happy. I had to calm him down by promising that you have no other relationship with me than the one you have with all your other employees." Gabriel's smile must have looked quite incredulous. "You know very well that this is not the case. We are in this together," he softly protested. This did not go down well with her in her current mood. "I do not want it," she bellowed. Other people looked over at their table. Obviously, she had had a hard time explaining their weekend trip to her boyfriend. For Gabriel, it felt unjust and disproportionate. He was not after her panties, for God's sake. "I will do the Bede Griffiths project without you. Taos is no longer on our travel route. And I will certainly go alone to India," he told her while they walked on the baking-hot Paseo de Peralta in the direction of the city centre. He was disgusted: of the place, of her, of the whole situation, of everything. "I want to put an end to all of this here and now," he added. "Fine for me," said Tilda.

Freedom and Determination

The journey by car back to Tucson started full of tension. At first, Tilda looked out of the window for nearly an hour. It did not seem as if she was sorry and wanted to talk about their conflict. "Do you see any purpose in life as such?" she began, however. It simply took Gabriel's breath away. "Of course," he answered before continuing: "Think of all the revelations and insights that we have had together lately. Don't you feel the invisible hand leading us like we're attached to a golden string along a path towards a specific goal?" Tilda was quite concerned. "Do you feel a kind of 'marching order' stemming from these insights?" she asked softly. It was time for honesty. "Yes, but I have very ambivalent feelings about that marching order," Gabriel told her.

He continued: "There definitely is a marching order, but—so far—I only half understand what it is about; and about what I understand, I have very mixed feelings." "What is it that you do not like?" she asked curiously. "First, I have issues with the mere existence of the marching order as such," he told her. "I have the feeling that I have no choice. If I hear and understand the marching order, I have to act accordingly, right?" She calmly nodded. "There is no chance to say no—at least not for me. It would run against any feeling of logic, rationality, consequence and sense. It would be horrible nonsense to say no. Therefore, I have an issue." Tilda shook her head a little disbelievingly before asking, "Why?" "I want to have freedom, to be a free individual with choice. However, I feel like I'm under a sword of predetermination given the powerful marching order with all the evidence it came with." Tilda looked unconvinced. Gabriel did not know whether she understood half of what he said. Maybe even he did not understand it himself.

"What is the other issue?" she asked softly. "That concerns the content of the marching order." "What is wrong with it?" she asked in a surprised voice. "I am not overly happy with what this seems to imply or about the direction it's taken," Gabriel smugly said. Of course, this was evasive, and she was after him in no time. "What do you mean?" The next bit was painful and embarrassing. "As far as I understand, all of this is about unity, about overcoming the dualities of this world, which are structured in archetypes. That is, male/female, rational/intuitive, active/passive, young/old, rich/poor—you get the idea. Categorisations. These dualities appear everywhere: in an individual person, between people in social relationships and between whole societies on the system level. You and I represent a nice range of archetypical dichotomies on the middle level, sitting at opposite ends of the continuum in many areas."

She looked a little insulted after this revelation. "What do you mean: I am female, intuitive, passive, young and poor? How about also stupid, small and ugly?" Gabriel continued as if she had not interrupted because in his opinion, she had missed the point: "If I am not totally wrong, the idea of Pater Bede seems to be that integrating dualities on the personal level happens via meditation, and integrating them on the system level happens via sociocultural development work. The main level, however, which works like an activating and enabling joint for the other two, is the relationship level in the middle where dualities are remedied, overcome and reconciled by love between people, a man and a woman." Now it was out.

Tilda was very quiet for a long time. Gabriel was nervous. It sounded horrendous. "What about love between gay people? What about transgender people? Aren't you—and thereby Bede Griffiths—terribly dualistic?" she asked, to Gabriel's surprise. He had not thought about that. But then he responded, "Male and female stand for archetypes. For any dualities that separate people and that need to be overcome." "I do not want an archetype making an example out of me and messing up my life!" Tilda exclaimed. "In the meantime, I think that this is exactly the imposition that is asked of us—not more and not less," Gabriel said, and he felt forced to continue: "If this is really true, we would need to act like a secret society because this is the totally weirdest mandate I have ever heard of. People would think we are wildly and utterly mad, and they would be right to think so."

"What about faith?" Tilda asked. "I mean sexual faith. You are the religious and Catholic type, aren't you? This is what they teach in church if I am not mistaken, right? It is one of the Ten Commandments: Do not have sex with somebody other than your spouse. This is why matrimony is sacrosanct. I am surprised. Imagine if my boyfriend did such a thing as you seem to consider. I would immediately leave him to his devices. If I cannot rely on him, he can go where he likes. If you are with somebody, you are with them and nobody else. If you are together with somebody, you stick with them. Period." "Yes," Gabriel agreed, "I am a happily married person. I appreciate monogamy. It sounds all wrong that adultery is the recommended way forward in spiritual terms." What he did not say was that he was not even hopelessly smitten with Tilda in terms of attraction. Of course, he did not tell her. This would have been mean and tasteless. But why her of all people?

"All these things about male and female archetypes, about reconciliation, about snakes in the desert, about D.H. Lawrence and so on—I beg your pardon!" Tilda exclaimed. For her, it was very clear that Gabriel was just a slave to his dirty desires. That was all this fishy talk amounted to in the end. "I am not happy about all of this either," Gabriel confessed, trying to convince Tilda. "Maybe, I am too morose about my great revelation story, and other people would rejoice to have half of it. However, I feel like heavy burdens are resting on my shoulders. And I have to be faithful to the message I have understood. Everything else would be a mortal sin." Tilda laughed. But then she saw that he meant it. "You are a strange man" was all she said, though all she wanted in that moment was to escape this weirdness that Gabriel was constantly bringing up, like a bloody volcano spitting magma.

The Serpent in the Wilderness

Angels' Play

Location:
Heaven above motorway I-10 W, Arizona. Shared-Office Cloud.

Time:
Real-time GMT, Sunday, 28 April 2019, 13:27

Players:
The two angels as before, Bede Griffiths and D.H. Lawrence (DHL).

Setting:
GA, BG and DHL debate in front of a small herpetarium that GA has extracted from the big gearbox containing animals. They look at a collection of snakes in different shapes and colours—all eager to help.

GA (*disapprovingly*):
I do not think that we need to take the biggest rattlesnake we have to support the Script! It is much too dangerous. Imagine they get bitten in the middle of the desert! Can we not do with a grass snake?

DHL:
I insist on the rattlesnake. We cannot have a harmless and meaningless German garden snake. We need it standing as a symbol of sexual power, seduction and big emotions.

BG (*supportive*):
And of salvation and elevation too. It is in the Script, and they will read that passage shortly. Do not forget that. You cannot take the grass snake as symbolising salvation, sorry (*the grass snake huffily recedes between some stones in the herpetarium*).

GA (*hesitatingly*):
OK, but only one rattlesnake, and you must promise that it will not do anything but look impressive.

BG (*grinningly taking an Indian pungi out of the pocket of his white Camaldolese cowl*):
No problem, I was a great snake charmer during my time in India (*with this, he starts playing the pungi, and the rattlesnake leaves the herpetarium to follow him under the admiring eyes of DHL*).

The Rattlesnake

"It is more than obvious that hiking in a desert at a national park of Arizona belongs to the must-dos when you are visiting the US," Gabriel said to Tilda on Monday morning when they discussed what to do with the time before their next business meeting in the late afternoon. Tilda was enchanted; she liked hiking. They went to the Rincon Mountain Visitor Center in Saguaro National Park, where they were precautioned by park rangers against sunstroke, wildlife, heat, thirst, Western diamondback rattlesnakes, insects, prickly plants, black bears and further dangers on their way. Then driving away on the Scenic Loop, they looked for good hiking opportunities, starting with the Cactus Forest Trail, to go to Mica View. It was hot and sunny. The high saguaro cacti, with their mighty arms, were impressive. They saw many strange animals, such as roadrunners and Gila monsters.

Then they saw it. "Stop!" Gabriel shouted. Tilda hit the brakes, and they stuttered to a stop in the middle of the road, just half a metre away from a gigantic snake. "There it is! How well adapted it is to its environment: perfectly blending into the colours of the desert road." Gabriel bent his neck far out of the car window towards the snake to take a closer look. "Don't," Tilda anxiously objected. "I have never seen a living venomous rattlesnake up close before," he protested. It was fascinating. The animal was about two metres long and maybe about four kilograms.

Tilda, however, was wildly afraid, though they were sitting in the car. Gabriel completely lowered the car window to lean out of the car to take pictures, which had him in proximity to the serpent's head. Tilda screamed: "Come inside again immediately! It can jump into the car!" "You are exaggerating." Gabriel could not get enough of admiring the long body of the light-brown snake and the diamond shapes on its back.

The snake actually rose its triangular head towards the car window, letting them see the vertical pupils of the eyes and the lambency of its tongue. "Close the window! Snakes that hiss with their tongue are getting aggressive," Tilda said, and she pawed at his arm. Because of this, the only picture he got of the snake's head was a bit shaky, which was a pity. Then the serpent turned its back to them, rattled with its black-and-white tail towards them and slowly glided into the grassland border of the road. Not hurrying by the way, so Gabriel could at least take a last good picture of its receding back. What an adventure!

Following their sighting of the rattlesnake, it was quite difficult to convince Tilda to step out of the car again to hike up the mountain woodlands full of scrub oaks and pines. "Pater Bede has talked about one snake, not about two or many," Gabriel complacently told her. "Therefore, we are already past danger and can rely on having snake-free trails from now on." Something in this reasoning convinced her because she had read the same passage herself. They looked for the entry to the Loma Verde Trail but somehow missed it, ending up at Javelina, where they simply went right up into the mountains following a small steep path upwards through forests of ponderosa pines and Douglas firs. It was beautiful, and Pater Bede proved as good as his word: They did not meet another rattlesnake—much to Gabriel's regret.

After the snake experience, he was more convinced than ever of what he called his marching order. How he would have loved to discuss this with someone clever. However, there was nobody that came to mind. How could anybody understand what he was supposed to do with Tilda? He could hardly understand it himself. It was rationally absurd and morally objectionable. He could not tell anybody. He could not communicate this to anybody. He wanted to be considered neither as absurd nor as a hypocrite who looked for a good excuse to have an affair with a young woman outside marriage. He hated illegitimacy and lying. It seemed that 'fighting dualities' could happen only as a secret between Tilda and him. It would get them into trouble because this was not only about spirituality but also about emotions, which were not really in Gabriel's field of expertise. This story did not offer any bridge to ordinary life. No safe grounds. The truth happened where nobody was before. Gabriel did not expect to receive any understanding or acceptance for this. The marching order was an imposition—not only with regard to legitimacy and communication but also in terms of freedom and choice. If it had to be done, why with Tilda of all people?

Tilda was turning in her bed that night. She was deeply disturbed by the snake experience and the conversation around it. "Here now finally comes Gabriel's full cruelty in the disguise of religion," she thought bitterly, "and he cannot even see or consider it. He is totally selfish and can only see himself and his own narrow world. Not for a single second does our having a serious relationship come to his closed mind. I mean, one out in the open where he stands by me and I by him. It is not even an idea for him to consider the real consequences of his own bloody story. If this whole revelation stuff is substantial, he should leave his wife and start afresh with me. His bias and discrimination against people like me have sunk so deep that he is not even aware of having them." She felt bad and belittled. Fucking idiot. He made her sick. He was the one working against his so-called marching order, not her. "He talks about 'secrets,' which means he thinks we should have an affair in secret. No way. I am taking love serious for a change. Am I nobody? Why does he think he can diminish me like that? Am I only good enough for the dark corners?" She sobbed into her pillow until she fell asleep, exhausted.

Open Access This chapter is licensed under the terms of the Creative Commons Attribution 4.0 International License (http://creativecommons.org/licenses/by/4.0/), which permits use, sharing, adaptation, distribution and reproduction in any medium or format, as long as you give appropriate credit to the original author(s) and the source, provide a link to the Creative Commons license and indicate if changes were made.

The images or other third party material in this chapter are included in the chapter's Creative Commons license, unless indicated otherwise in a credit line to the material. If material is not included in the chapter's Creative Commons license and your intended use is not permitted by statutory regulation or exceeds the permitted use, you will need to obtain permission directly from the copyright holder.

Chapter 5
Chinese Walls

Back at home, Gabriel started in earnest to put together a new B1 project on fairness issues in global social service provision. The countries so far involved are Spain and the US. And Germany, of course—though, at the moment, he did not yet have the slightest idea for a case study, but that would come. All countries would include vulnerable people as experts to identify bias and discrimination issues.

Tilda did not help with anything. She had returned to her old prickly self and avoided Gabriel whenever she could. It got worse by the month. Finally, as her boss, Gabriel decided that the best way to let her contribute to the proposal would be to send her away to recruit another international case study. "Yes, I want to go as far away as possible", Tilda scowled. "How about China?" Another Asian case study, but India would indeed be great, Gabriel decided. She departed to Hong Kong and Shanghai in the first days of July to visit some B1 contacts who might be interested.

The Chinese Case

Jin Xiaowei looked expectantly at the face of the young Western woman awaiting the interview he had consented to.

"Where did you grow up?" Tilda asked, obviously well trained in asking cautious warm-up questions. Jin Xiaowei smiled and looked around in his modestly but nicely furbished Hong Kong flat. "In a little village called Dengtucan, in Gansu Province. My parents were smallholders with a little farm field in the hills. They grew potatoes, beans and corn, but they had hardly enough to eat. We were very poor with less than 250 yuan in annual income. We had to cut down trees in the mountains for firewood. My parents did not even have running water before I was able to send them some money." He poured some tea into Tilda's cup. "Where did this money come from?" she asked. "That is a long story. It all started with our village chief coming to us one evening in 2018, telling us there would be a mandatory training programme for our region. People from the government would come and train young people for a job that would be needed in one of the big cities. I was assessed, and my profile scored highly with the artificial intelligence algorithm. It forecast that I would perform brilliantly, so I was selected for the job." "What type of job?" "Noodle cooking." "I beg your pardon?" Jin Xiaowei shrugged his shoulders.

"We learnt to prepare traditional Lanzhou noodles for the street soup kitchens of Beijing, Shenzhen or Shanghai. Our regional programme trained more than 15,000 young former farmers like me. We were told that participation was not optional." "Did you like it?" Jin Xiaowei looked away evasively before replying: "I do not know; there was no choice. I was learning something, and I was earning money—even during training. I was out of the mosquitos and the daily dirt of working with the crops. I could help my parents. With my first money, I bought them a television set, with which we could watch Xi Jinping's review visits of these programmes on the evening news on state television. He promised to free everyone from poverty by 2020. Our village chief was happy that the programme ran so well. He was paid by success rate and could report our region as prospering."

Tilda looked at him curiously and then asked, "What happened next?" Jin Xiaowei again shrugged his shoulders. "After training, I was scored by the algorithm for relocation to Shenzhen. There, I got a job as noodle cook in the city centre. My high score for getting the job and housing in the city centre was mainly due to the fact that I was single. My friends from the village with families were socially assessed for the hinterland. I remember how sad I was when leaving my parents. But, of course, in my new home, I had a living."

"How did you live in Shenzhen?" Jin Xiaowei answered: "I was allowed to own apartment by the Office for Poverty Reduction, which I could buy for only 10,150 yuan. My uncle and aunt from Beijing helped me with financing." "Was it difficult to find the flat in the city centre? I heard that Shenzhen is highly populated," Tilda asked. Jin Xiaowei smiled. "Not at all. The resettlement scheme also contained an AI component where elderly people were assessed for being relocated, to get them out of the urban centres. They went to retirement cities for the elderly, vacating precious living space in megacities. My flat formerly belonged to an old lady that had been resettled to Zhelang Residential District. The government wanted to see young professionals like me populating the city centres. Do not forget: My score was high. I was young, male and now well trained."

"What went wrong? Why did you leave Shenzhen?" Tilda asked. Jin Xiaowei sadly stared at the ceiling. He had tears in his eyes. "It started with the very same lady from Zhelang Residential District. She must be 86 years old by now, and her name is Hu Feiran. I know this because one night when I came from work, I found her sleeping on my doorstep. She had walked more than 200 kilometres up and down the coastline mountains for five days without much food and nearly no sleep. She was quite a fit old lady but mentally a bit deranged. She had wanted to see her son, who lives in Shenzhen, and had usually visited her every Tuesday when she lived in my flat. She had not seen him for three months, because he could not leave the city, due to work commitments. I remember how desperately she cried when social workers came to fetch her to bring her back to Zhelang. It is wrong to tear families apart like that."

Tilda was shocked. "What then?" Jin Xiaowei looked at her. "AI-based social assessment had my parents scored for relocation. At least it tried to." He mirthlessly laughed. "At a certain point, my parents and a few other elderly couples were the last remaining inhabitants of our little village. The government had offered a place in the north. My parents were desperate. My grandfather had built the house seventy years ago; they had spent their whole lives here. I lost my parents over the next two months. First my father died of a stroke; shortly after, my mother died out of mourning. The other couples in question resettled alright. After their resettlement, the authorities had everything destroyed, officially because of security threats. Now, I have nowhere to go home to anymore."

Tilda was very sorry. "What did you do?" she asked. "I started to fight the programmes. I tried to organise a meeting with like-minded people against the AI scoring in the resettlement programme." "This did not endear you to the Communist Party, right?" Jin Xiaowei laughed. "Not really. First thing that happened was that my central score spiralled downwards in our famous social credit system. Then I lost my job in the noodle soup kitchen. Guess why." "Bad score? Algorithm thinking lowly of you?" Tilda had clearly got the message. Jin Xiaowei nodded. "However, for me, it was clear by that time that my issues with AI-based social assessment, mandatory job training and forced resettlement were just parts of more-general questions. Where and with whom do you want to live? Where do you want to go? Who do you want to be? How important is culture and tradition to you? What society do you want to live in? These are questions of importance that were not addressed—and much less answered—by the governmental policies. People were not really considered." He poured the last of the tea. "What did you do?" Tilda asked. Jin Xiaowei smiled. "I used the last credit points from my decreasing social score and bought a train ticket to Hong Kong."

Society and Technology on Eye Level

Gabriel enjoyed some peace and quiet at home in Berlin. He was a little worried because Tilda had refused the vaccinations that were recommended for China by their employer. This medical officer of B1 was actually quite good and only recommended what was absolutely necessary. However, the stubborn girl had not accepted any of his advised injections.

Tilda was a general opponent of vaccination. She had told Gabriel, "You are the one going on about Immanuel Kant and philosophy of morals all the time, right? You should know, then, that this guy provided a brilliant example of an ethics-based rejection of smallpox vaccinations in his time. Kant said anyone who is vaccinated against smallpox 'dares his life to the unknown,' and I can only wholeheartedly agree. We know little about long-term consequences, neither on the individual nor on the population level. And what we know does not give raise to high hopes. The effects are scientifically questionable; confidence is not inspired." Gabriel showed her a lot of medical evidence to argue against her last point. When it became too overwhelming for her, she simply shouted at him: "I do not want to have foreign substances in my body. My body has so much knowledge that it is well able to take care of itself. I do not want to disturb this inner balance of forces with artificial shots. I would not go so far to say that one should limit excessive population growth through epidemics. However, this is definitely another argument to reason against protective vaccination. Our overcrowded planet helps itself against proliferation. Why should we—as always by the way—selfishly come in its way?" Gabriel shook his head in disbelief. "Do you want to let people die?" "I do not want to force people to get vaccinated; that is all," Tilda responded a little evasively. "Vaccination campaigns against measles ordered by the authorities are ethically impermissible. Governments may not order inoculation, and people should reject violations of their rights and freedoms. If they want to vaccinate me or my kids if I were ever to have any, I will expatriate." If Gabriel would have asked her to take injections before travelling, she would have cancelled her contract. There was no way. Tilda left for China unvaccinated.

Gabriel's plan was, in the meantime, to prepare for his visit to India—be it with or, what was most likely, without Tilda. He scheduled an appointment with some German representatives of the suborder of the so-called Camaldolense Benedictines, the ashram in India that he belonged to. Bede Griffiths had been a member of that suborder too. It had facilities worldwide—not only in Germany but also, for example, in Eastern Europe, South America and the USA. The German branch helped him make contact with the prior of Saccidananda Ashram Shantivanam, to make a reservation for a stay in early January next year. And the monks provided some practical information for booking his flights, such as telling him to go to Chennai, the capital of Tamil Nadu, and from there to a city called Trichy by the locals, a shortened name for Tiruchirappalli. His search for potential project partners in India, however, proved to be futile at first. He simply did not know anybody over there. Then, chance came in the form of Veronica from B1's Asian division during a coffee break at work.

Gabriel met Veronica outside in the sunshine sitting on a wooden bench while wasps swarmed around her cake. Veronica asked, "How far along are you with putting together the international consortium for the new project?" She had been in the audience when he introduced the new initiative of his unit at the B1 Trustee Board. "We are still searching for appropriate partners in India," Gabriel confessed. She frowned. "India is horrible." "Why?" Gabriel was surprised to hear that from her. "Full of machos," she replied, looking away. "My India project last year was the only fieldwork I ever cancelled in my life, and I have been everywhere. But after the fourth time of only narrowly having escaped rape, I took the next plane home." She shuddered in memory. "Did you go there on your own?" Gabriel asked, amazed. Usually, B1 regulations did not allow single trips overseas. "Yes, I was on secondment for my PhD project," she answered. "But our colleagues over there will be OK, right? You must still have contacts in the south of India," Gabriel insisted. "Maybe you have a suggestion for a partner for my new project? It would be great if you could give me a name. That would allow for comparison and a broader approach to fieldwork." She considered this and then nodded slowly. "I will send you an email with contact details. If you like, I can even make the introductions to get your foot in the door. There is one person in Tamil Nadu very much into participatory approaches that work with vulnerable groups."

Gabriel triumphantly wrote an email to Tilda that he had a partner contact for India. Tilda answered immediately, "Please ask for two contacts. This time, I've had a revelation here in China, believe it or not. I talked to a young guy named Jin Xiaowei. He explained that social service provision in China is largely done by artificial intelligence. And AI is exacerbating the fairness issues around distribution practices. This is the second time we have heard this, do you remember? Adsila Idrissi said the same about Spain. It is probably also true in Germany and the US. Our new project should be about AI-based social service provision. This means we would need two partners in each country—a partner who is working on the social side of the project and another who is working on the computer science end."

"Both partners would need to work closely together to improve AI fairness," Gabriel said. "I like the idea, though it will make it much harder to put the consortium together. It is not everywhere like in B1, where we have a social science department and a computer science department under one roof." He made a phone call to B1's computer science people and asked for an AI expert in India. They promised to send some contact details. Then, he described the new project format to his partners in Spain and the US so that they too could upgrade their case studies on social service provision by computer experts.

The Second Google Maps Miracle

In the morning on the 12th of July, Gabriel read two emails on his laptop: one from Veronica, who recommended her colleague from Chennai in Tamil Nadu for the society part of the project, and another from the B1 computer science department, recommending people from a place called Kottayam. "This is in a different state of India," Gabriel said to himself, groaning when he looked Kottayam up in Google Maps, "in Kerala." Because he had never been in India before, he had no idea where everything was and how far apart these two places would be. He used the route planner function and searched for the distance between Chennai and Kottayam: 676 kilometres for the shortest route! More than 13 hours by car. That spoke to the quality of roads. At least, there was a nearly direct road connection between these two cities. Gabriel looked out the window. This was not ideal. It might be better to look for a computer scientist in Chennai. Chennai was a very big city. It should not be impossible. Before again grabbing the phone to ask B1's computer department for another contact, he hit the keys on his laptop to start an experiment. He inserted the complicated town name of Tiruchirappalli as an in-between stop to see where the ashram of Bede Griffiths was now located in the triangle of the three Indian places on his list. No triangle.

Disbelievingly, he rubbed his eyes and blinked at the screen. It was not a triangle. What he saw was, so to speak, the second Bede Griffiths Google Maps miracle after the Horsham experience. Tiruchirappalli was sitting directly on the path between Kottayam and Chennai; you had to pass it if you wanted to go from here to there. Gabriel hit more keys to measure distances: 338 kilometres from Kottayam to Tiruchirappalli and 338 kilometres from Tiruchirappalli to Chennai. Pater Bede's ashram was exactly in the middle of it—in between the two recommended, though still unknown, partners for the project. And India was really big. Gabriel was enthusiastic. This was incredible but also absolutely brilliant. He would see the Saccidananda Ashram Shantivanam!

Following this, he even started to appeal to Pater Bede as patron saint, though he very well knew that he was not yet a canonised saint with the Catholic Church. The Church always made a terrible fuss about canonisation before finally declaring somebody as holy. You had to be dead. And then the main proof of holiness was that the person must have performed at least two miracles that were reported by reliable witnesses. But Gabriel knew in his heart that Bede Griffiths was a saint and that he was alive.

He felt very close to him and thus very holy himself. In the evening on his way home, he passed a charity, which was pleasantly set in a little garden full of lime trees. He went in and bought an expensive 'biblical hoodie.' He had admired them for quite some time and now felt that it was the right time to buy one. These hoodies were dark green and of very good quality. Each displayed a bible verse on the front and the back in white letters, but not the words, just the bibliographical reference. Gabriel thought this was quite cool because not everybody could decipher this. It was like an argot. He chose one with 'Mt. 11:29' on it: The Gospel according to Matthew, chapter 11, verse 29. This read, 'Take my yoke upon you and learn from me, for I am gentle and humble in heart, and you will find rest for your souls,' which he learnt later, when he looked it up.

Tilda in China

Tilda was really unhappy in China. She spent her days mostly in her room, sometimes going out in search for vegan food to prevent herself from starving. This was not easy, even though she had originally expected to find a great variety of Chinese vegetarian dishes. However, she discovered that most so-called vegetarian dishes were prepared in meat broth and were even contaminated by little pieces of leftover meat every now and again. She spent much time on learning the right vocabulary for ordering meat-free vegetarian dishes—not even dreaming of vegan. Furthermore, Gabriel was constantly on her, expecting performance because he's her boss, and she did not deliver. They had some quite-unpleasant phone calls. "To be honest, I am surprised that you are further along in partner recruitment for the project. Everything is going very slow on your side, Mrs Toelz," Gabriel said. "You seem absent and busy with something else. I can't believe that in one week, you can't do more than write a one-page summary of the past and have a few conversations with Chinese people or with B1 staff on Skype. I don't know you to be like that. You are generally more creative and have more control over work processes. What's going on?" Tilda was indignant in her response: "Nothing is going on. I am trying to do my job." "Sorry for the critical questions, but if the topic or the project is not right, we should immediately make a course correction. Something doesn't seem to work out here," he said. She shook her head. "What the hell do you expect from me, Mr David?" He answered: "This project is about personal commitment and attachment. It is about self-initiative, ownership, taking responsibility, the creative design of the process, project management, leadership, process management and so on. You have demonstrated all these competencies sufficiently in the past; therefore, I know that you can do this, but it is not very visible at the moment." "You are not very clear about what you are expecting me to do here for your new project," she replied accusingly. "You are waiting for miracles to recruit project partners. That is not my style of work." "Mrs Toelz, it's your project as well as mine," he answered, insulted. "No, it's not," she replied, snapping at him. "It was never laid out that way. The main concepts are not determined by me but by you alone!" This had caused a certain dissonance on her side: She did not like to be bossed around. If something were *her* project, she would call the shots. Gabriel's last words in this conversation sounded sober on the phone: "Your journey has been scheduled to recruit project partners and to define the contents of the national case study according to plan. Please work with our case-study partners, and do not return empty-handed!"

For Tilda, Gabriel acted like somebody in the fast lane overtaking everybody else who was driving safely while he was recklessly speeding. And she could not close her eyes or latch on to the holds, because he wanted her as codriver to his madness. She felt relentless pressure from his side as he moved forward to the next level like a mad man. There was no way to tone down his radicalism. Either she went along with his enthusiasm and power, or he would leave her standing there just looking foolishly at his back. The worst was imagining his eyes full of pity, where she could then read: "You little idiot. I knew that you would fail. Why did not you leave that to me? I could have done it regardless of what else is on my plate." She could not keep up with this.

She wanted to sleep on things. She wanted to take her time with decisions. She wanted to chill. Why could he not slow down? Why could he not relax and let go every now and again? It was all too fast and overtaxing her. Not digestible at all. Maybe all this telepathy stuff was just her feeble attempt to cool Gabriel down and give them both some rest. After a long silence, Tilda finally submitted the case-study description for the Chinese part. She emphasised that—despite what Gabriel had said about her slow performance—this was the first completed case-study template for the project. Maybe she had a point there, Gabriel thought. She had delivered during her last days in China, expressing her hope that other case-study templates would be as comprehensive and efficient as this one. Gabriel was really relieved because he had half expected that she would end her B1 contract with him in the wake of their conflict. "I am happy that you only asked for holidays and not for a termination of contract!" he texted her. "Would you have preferred a termination of contract, Mr David?" she texted back. He was frustrated that she obviously did not get what he was after. For him, it would have been great if she could have mustered up a little enthusiasm for their project: He missed her dedication and initiative. She was doing this as an employee, but not as a partner. Why was she so passive?

However, in the afternoon, he found an email from her on his computer, which convinced him that she would stay and had overcome her bad feelings against him. In the email, she announced a pleasant surprise for him was to be found at the included hyperlink; the email ended "with love." Gabriel was completely overjoyed—at least until he listened to the lecture, 'A spiritual wake-up call,' after following the link she sent. A guy named Rüdiger Lenz on an alternative online channel called KenFM. Gabriel had never heard of that channel before. After listening for a few minutes, Gabriel decided that it was the weirdest political conspiracy theory in the disguise of spirituality. The system was guilty of everything. The power elites were guilty of everything. It was—in short—trash. Gabriel was as numbed as he had been that morning in Santa Fe. He would have assigned such crap to holocaust deniers, AFD partisans and maniacs, but not as something coming from Tilda. Giving it some thought, he became convinced that this must have been a mistake. She had not probably checked properly and had just sent something she had stumbled across by accident, just seeing the title without knowing what it was really about. Therefore, it would only be embarrassing for her when he revealed that the first time that she sent him something nice, it proved to be such a cataclysmic piece of shit. Thus, Gabriel decided to ignore the link and her message.

Angels' Play

Location:
Heaven above Berlin Brandenburg Airport. Shared-Office Cloud.

Time:
Real-time GMT, Wednesday, 4 September 2019, 14:53

Players:
The two angels as before, Bede Griffiths, D.H. Lawrence and St. Christophorus.

Setting:
BG, DHL and SC sit at the table of the conference facility. They are quietly discussing while smoke fumes waft from their spot over to the two angels that sit in their cockpit chairs, watching them with big eyes.

GA (*wrinkling its little nose in distaste*):
   Hashish! They are smoking dope at work. I cannot believe it.

TA (*defensively*):
   It is legal in California.

GA (*watching BG with his two friends and speaking accusingly*):
We are still in Berlin. They have serious work to do and should not get high. I wonder what they will come up with. Hopefully an alternative to this mad Script instruction. There must be a way around this additional trip to the US right now (*checking the Script*). Gabriel and Tilda are just back from Arizona. They will soon go together to India.

TA (*checking its own notes*):
And Tilda has just returned from China. She is totally messed up and stressed out. I cannot guarantee sober action.

BG (*calling across the cloud*):
Please, dears! Would you come over and take orders?

GA and TA resignedly look at each other and move to the conference area.

BG (*apologetically*):
We are very sorry, but there is no alternative. This next bit is about what machines cannot do. We are here to prove a point. And there is no better place than California. Please arrange for supplies. You need to go to the DIY shop and buy green paint.

TA impolitely groans. GA looks at its colleague, alarmed by its impertinence in commenting on an order given by a saint.

TA (*tries to make up for its impudence*):
Excuse me. Why green paint?

DHL (*salaciously grinning at both angels*):
For your Viriditas!

GA (*stiffly*):
I beg your pardon?

BG (*proudly*):
Viriditas is the green force of eternity. Explained very well by my good friend from the Saints Section, Hildegard of Bingen. She is a German Benedictine abbess, writer, composer, philosopher, Christian mystic, visionary and polymath of the High Middle Ages and...

GA (*interestedly*):
Viriditas? Green force from eternity? What is this about?

BG (*reading from a book by Philippa Rath on Hildegard von Bingen*):
Yes. Hildegard writes: "There is a force from eternity, and this force is green. Green is the vital force per se." Green freshness is a reflection of God as the hidden base of eternity, you see? It lives in the flame, it fluoresces in the water, it imbrues the stone and it wafts in the air. Also, all the soul dynamics of human beings are green, for Hildegard. Even love is clad in green, for her. God himself became human in the green womb of Maria. Here, the circle is completed.

TA (*again groaning*):

Green womb? I do not get it. If green is everywhere, why do we need to buy green paint at the DIY shop? And I am not in love with GA. Veriditas here and there. Green or no.

GA:

Sometimes you get on my nerves so much …

SC (*soothingly*):

The good news is, Gabriel and Tilda can go by car the whole time. I have assigned a nice Chevvy with a working GPS, air conditioning, full insurance coverage and plenty of legroom. There will only be two little accidents this time…

TA groans even more loudly. GA watches its colleague with growing dislike.

DHL (*making a last attempt to raise the spirits of the angels by pointing at the book on the floor by Richard Rohr, The Divine Dance*):

And the best of it, and you can look forward to that: To work on your own Viriditas, the two of you will dance erotically with each other.

GA faints.

Open Access This chapter is licensed under the terms of the Creative Commons Attribution 4.0 International License (http://creativecommons.org/licenses/by/4.0/), which permits use, sharing, adaptation, distribution and reproduction in any medium or format, as long as you give appropriate credit to the original author(s) and the source, provide a link to the Creative Commons license and indicate if changes were made.

The images or other third party material in this chapter are included in the chapter's Creative Commons license, unless indicated otherwise in a credit line to the material. If material is not included in the chapter's Creative Commons license and your intended use is not permitted by statutory regulation or exceeds the permitted use, you will need to obtain permission directly from the copyright holder.

Chapter 6
What Machines Cannot Do

California Greening

"California," Tilda said, groaning, "not again to the US!" However, there had been no way out. B1 management had told them that it would seriously damage company relationships if they would not integrate their Californian contacts, both from Los Angeles and from San Francisco, into the new project. Now they were sitting again side by side on board a Lufthansa plane to the US, this time to LA.

Next to Gabriel sat an American-Czech guy who introduced himself as Jacob Green, who'd been living in LA for years. When he learnt that they were Germans, he said, "Actually my name is Jakob Grün. We have a German family background." "Do you have any recommendations for vegetarian—or, better, vegan—restaurants in Santa Monica?" Gabriel made polite conversation. However, he really wanted to know and thought he might best ask a native LA resident. And, indeed, Jakob Grün had some good suggestions: "You must promise me that you will visit two places I now recommend." Jakob Grün got quite loud and excited, such that it was nearly embarrassing to see him so intense—after all, it was just about restaurants, right? Jakob let Gabriel repeat the names and locations of two places in particular, which he told them to visit by all means. "The first is called Kreation, with a k," he said. "You must promise to go there first. I highly recommend it." He let Gabriel repeat the coordinates until he was blue in the face. The other place he called Café Gratitude, and Jakob was not satisfied before they could tell him the address without spelling mistakes.

Arriving at LA in the early evening was a nightmare. The airport was a chaotic mess of people, cars, buses and suitcases. It took ages before they finally got their rental car. After a long bureaucratic confirmation process, they were left alone in a huge dark outdoor car park and had to choose a car from among many. The keys of these cars were left inside them; they could simply pick one and drive away with it. They picked a black Chevy. It was the first time that they shared an apartment—of course, with two separate bedrooms. Gabriel noticed Tilda's heavy limp in the flat when she unpacked her suitcase. The long hours sitting motionless inside the plane must have made her foot hurt. He could barely hide his compassion for her bad foot. It was swollen and bulky.

Once he was in his bed cosily hoisted up against enormous US pillows, he wanted to start reading the first pages of the new book he brought to the US, Richard Rohr's *The Divine Dance*, but he could not even concentrate on the very first paragraph. His door was ajar, and he could look into the dark kitchen. The main room was L-shaped, where the kitchen was in the short bottom piece, the sitting room and dining room areas separated in the long piece and the sitting room windows at the top, providing a view of the courtyard swimming pool. He could not see Tilda's door; it was round the corner. His body was still vibrating from the flight, and he felt cold, awkward and uncomfortable.

Angels' Play

Location:
Heaven above Santa Monica. Shared-Office Cloud.

Time:
Real-time GMT, Friday, 6 September 2019, 17:48

Players:
The two angels.

Setting:
TA draws some green fluid from their shopping bags into a syringe and flicks it expertly a couple of times.

GA (*looking aghast at the injection needle in the hands of its colleague*):
Are you mad? What are you doing? You look like a junkie.

TA (*smugly shaking the green syringe*):
It is called Super Green Shot, and it is full of chlorophyll. Read your homework in the Script. No way around. Gabriel has to drink it. Stuff is provided directly by the upper level of TRINI-T top management.

GA (*disapprovingly*):
Can he not have an Aperol Spritzz? Or if there must be something green in it, a martini, shaken not stirred, with a big green olive?

Both are scanning the Script and start to yawn simultaneously after seeing how many instructions appear on the next page.

TA (*following the long list, ticking boxes with its dripping injection needle*):
Bloody long list about what machines cannot do.
You know what? Let's call it a day. We made it to "Jakob Grün" and the "green syringe." How about a nice Super Green Shot for yourself at Angels' Night Club?

elegantly avoiding the Script without any effort, GA tosses at its colleague's head across the cloud despite the short distance because Gabrielites are bad at sports and the toss would have missed its target anyway

Green Shots

The next morning, Gabriel and Tilda answered their emails and discussed the agenda for the whole US visit. After talking to the Los Angeles partners for the next three days about issues in social service provision, they would go to San Francisco to meet the second partner, who specialised in AI. The flight home to Germany would leave from the San Fransisco airport.

On their way to the meeting venue in LA, they admired the sunny and cheery atmosphere of Santa Monica. "Look at the palms in the streets and the bright blue skies, Mr David," Tilda said, enchanted. It felt nice and relaxed. Gabriel was more in love with the vegetables in the supermarket that they would visit later. "Look at these gorgeous Brussels sprouts," he said, admiring the perfect little green shapes on display. "Should we have them with walnuts and soya sauce tomorrow evening? We can prepare them in the oven in our flat. Today, I am too exhausted to cook. Let's go to this Kreation restaurant that Jakob Grün recommended so highly!" It was already dinnertime.

They found Kreation without any difficulties by following Jakob's detailed directions. "To be honest, it does not look special at all," Tilda said. It was just a very small restaurant in a street with many suchlike businesses, most of them owned by very young people. Kreation looked a little dark and womb-like compared to the others: Maybe it was just day one of creation, shortly before the appearance of the light. "It's vegan," Gabriel said after checking the outdoor information. "That's what counts for us." However, he was a little disappointed too. He had looked forward to a really romantic evening with Tilda in an exceptional place, and utmost on his mind, he had looked forward to an afterwork beer. Kreation, however, the bastion of health that it was, did not offer any alcoholic beverages.

Tilda saw his sullen face when he scanned the drinks menu in the gloom of their small table lamp and gleefully laughed. She only rarely drank alcohol. Gabriel was quite an addict, in her opinion. "What the heck is a shot?" he asked, complaining. "Have you seen the names of the drinks they offer?" He read a few out to her: "Glammunity Shot, Super Green Shot, Sexy Shot, Antidote Shot." Tilda shrugged her shoulders before replying: "No idea. Ask the server." This is what Gabriel did when the young man arrived: "These are tonic shots, you know," the server explained. Seeing Gabriel's uncomprehending face, he patiently went on: "You will get some organic water and a syringe." "A syringe?" Gabriel asked incredulously. The server laughed. "You shoot the content of the syringe into the water. This is why it is called a shot. Try it. It's really healthy."

Because there was no alternative that sounded any better anyway, Gabriel ordered the drink that sounded the least dangerous: a Super Green Shot, in memoriam of Jakob Green, who was responsible for his not being able to have a nice evening beer.

Because it cost nearly six dollars, Gabriel thought there should be at least some tasty ingredients in these expensive syringes. Tilda just took some tap water, the cautious woman that she was.

What came then was spectacular. There was a glass of water and a big plastic syringe. The server put both in with a flourish in front of Gabriel and lit their table candle. Gabriel's eyes were glued to the syringe. In the light of the flickering candle flame, the lurid liquid inside fluoresced and glimmered in bright phosphoric green with little golden spots inside.

It was so green, greener than green, the greenest green he had ever seen. He could not believe his eyes. Maybe the golden spots emphasised the impression of green. No idea. He looked helplessly at Tilda. "You have to drink it," she grinned. "It looks poisonous," Gabriel said, completely awestruck by the greenish glow emanating from the syringe. "Maybe, it gets better if you put it into the water. It will dilute," Tilda suggested helpfully. "I won't drink this alone, Mrs Toelz," he informed her. "Either we both drink this, or neither of us will. You have a glass of water too. You can help me." He could see that she was curious as well. Therefore, he cut the tip of the syringe with his knife and cautiously shared the contents of the syringe between their two glasses of water. In both glasses, the green fluid immediately mingled with the water in clouds and streaks like in a wizard's crystal ball. "It does not lose its brightness," Gabriel opined in admiration. "It just shares it." They both stirred the drink with their spoons and looked at the green fluid and at each other hesitantly. "Cheers!" Gabriel said encouragingly and clinked glasses with Tilda. They sipped carefully, both expecting a taste explosion matching the glamorous volcanic eruption in their bright green drinks. It had no taste. Nil. Just water.

"Blimey," Gabriel said to Tilda. "What is this? Indian ink?" She laughed and took the syringe, reading aloud the list of ingredients. "Chlorophyll, oxygen, spirulina and peppermint. Dairy free. Gluten free. Nut free. Raw. Vegan." "That explains the green colour," Gabriel said dryly. "It's chlorophyll." "What is chlorophyll good for?" Tilda asked.

"Chlorophyll is responsible for the green colour of many plants and algae," Gabriel explained. "The name comes from the Greek word for green, *khloros*. It is essential for photosynthesis, allowing plants to absorb energy from light. But not only plants—there is even a green sea snail that produces chlorophyll for photosynthesis, to make food from light. Plants are perceived as green because chlorophyll absorbs mainly the blue and red wavelength and reflects the green. The absorbed light energy powers the part of photosynthesis that in the end produces sugars and other stuff."

"It doesn't taste like anything," Tilda observed. "Yes, but it is still one of the fundamental drivers of life. It's one of the basic supports of creation. And it can obviously form deep-green solutions in organic solvents." They both continued to carefully sip the tasteless but powerful green water of creation until their two glasses were completely empty. This had been fun enough for six dollars.

Tilda smiled into her glass. Then she scowled and looked at Gabriel strangely. She started to feel as if she had two lives—one with Ken and the other with Gabriel. She felt like a deep fracture was running through her personality. She not only switched between two world views and realities like zapping between streaming channels but was even somebody else in both worlds. It was difficult to describe this weird, schizophrenic experience.

Green Food

For breakfast the next morning, they sat at a glass table while they ate toast and grilled vegetables. Gabriel even lit a candle. "Isn't this romantic and enjoyable?" he asked enthusiastically.

"I do not 'enjoy' anything, Mr David," Tilda said disparagingly. "Isn't it amazing, your obsession with taste and ambience? As if a nice breakfast is all that can happen in a day. I do not care what I eat as long as it is ethical and nutritious. What I do know exactly is how many calories I need a day. If I am in training, I need 1750 calories; if I am doing nothing, I can cope with 1200. Furthermore, I have to pay attention to my vitamin B12 level and to iron deficiency in my blood because of my vegan diet. I am a bit anaemic. That is it. Breakfast is for me a necessary intake of food that should happen on a regular basis. Not a bloody ritual with meaning, sophistication and romance." Gabriel sighed.

They talked much about eating habits because Tilda was quite a missionary when making her case for vegan instead of vegetarian. "It is just the next logical step," she insisted. "You should not eat animals, you should not make them suffer, and you should not use them for your own purposes. They are not inferior to you, and you have no right to deal with them as if they were just a resource for your convenience."

"Why are you happy to eat plants but set against eating animals, Mrs Toelz?" Gabriel asked cautiously. "They do not suffer," Tilda maintained. "There is research saying otherwise," he objected before continuing: "I am against animal suffering from industrial livestock farming, and I want to protect the environment against climate change from mass meat production. This is why I turned into a vegetarian." He winked at her smilingly, but she coldly returned his glance. He sighed. "Maybe you are right that veganism is then only logically consequential because milk and egg production is related to these issues. However, I buy my milk and eggs from ecologically sensitive and animal-protecting farmers. For me, this is OK. For me, it would be even OK to eat meat every now and again from organic farmers who take special care of the welfare of their animals." Tilda looked at him disgusted. "This is abusing your power as a human," she replied, scolding him. "No living being should be allowed to bring suffering to any other creature; that is my opinion."

"I am sceptical that you can avoid entirely suffering on principle, and I am not even sure that it would be desirable if there were such a choice," he said. She looked at him like she thought him mad. "What do you mean, Mr David?" she asked insistently. "Think of your own birth," he said. "Do not you think that your mother was in pain during labour? Wasn't the actual birth a painful process? Would you rather not live than having been the source of that pain?" She looked at him doubtfully.

Gabriel looked pensively out the window. "How about yourself? Do you want to have any kids?" Tilda shook her head. "I do not know. Why?" "Because I can tell you one thing: You cannot shelter your kids from pain and suffering. Giving birth to them means exposing them to pain and suffering. Of course, you expose them to joy and happiness as well. But pain and suffering will always be part of the game. It is our *conditio humana*. It is life. If you want to prevent fellow creatures from suffering, they should not be here in the first instance. It cannot be a general maxim."

"Once they are here, you can take care that you do not contribute to their suffering," Tilda retorted triumphantly. He said, "Think of Ken. He will be upset that you are again on a long journey with me." "It is business travel, and I am forced to do it," she said lamely. "No, you are not," he replied reasonably. "It is your choice, Mrs Toelz. We are choosing every second of our life, and there will always be other creatures suffering from our decisions, one way or another. Even if you are not doing anything, there will be somebody suffering from the absence of your action. It is impossible to escape the wheel of one creature imposing suffering on another. This is called original sin, in Christian theology. Every human being needs to be conscious of this fact. It is fundamental to moral judgement. Only if you can see the essential landscape can you try to find your way within it. You cannot avoid or prevent suffering, per se, but you can try to prevent injustice, disproportionality and cruelty."

"You have no right to end the life of other creatures and eat them. They are creatures like you. It is unjust, disproportionate and cruel," Tilda said heatedly. "Men make themselves God. They decide on life and death. They have no right to end the lives of other creatures. That is arrogant. Humans are not special in creation just because they think they are images of God and the only ones with conscious self-reflection. They are not the crown of creation with a plethora of species underneath that they can abuse for their so-called higher ends." Gabriel was again surprised. Did she really believe that?

"Do not you feel that you are created in God's own likeness?" he asked her. "Not really," she answered. He waited, but she did not follow up on this remark. "It does not matter anyway," he said. "There is no connection between these two. God does not want the death of any creatures; he wants their lives. He is their creator. There is no way to derive from the likeness to God the legitimacy to kill other creatures out of superiority."

Tilda did not look convinced. "I like the position of Albert Schweitzer," Gabriel told her. "Schweitzer says, 'I am life that wants life. Any will to life in my environment is equal to mine.'" "And what follows from that, Mr David?" Tilda asked, demanding to know. "Doesn't that mean that you have to be a vegan to have a good conscience?" Gabriel laughed before continuing: "Schweitzer says, 'A good conscience is an invention of the devil.'" Seeing her uncomprehending face, he explained: "Because humankind destroys life just by existing, we have no status of innocence. You as a vegan are no better than me as a vegetarian. To claim this would be hubris. There is just life; there is no hierarchy of life. There is no bureaucratic legitimisation of who is allowed to eat whom. We are one."

Tilda looked exhausted even though it was very early in the morning. Maybe still jetlagged. He went on, now himself quite heatedly. "This picture of experiencing nature is about the opening and self-giving of one person to the other that makes new life possible, because we are all one. Community grows out of the gift of the self. We are ourselves like bread. Bread for many people, we live for one another, and only love counts, as a nice song says. In my view, this means that it is perfectly natural that we are nourishment for each other. We are all one and giving away our lives for each other because we cannot preserve it otherwise."

"Stop preaching, Mr David," Tilda said. "It does not work. You sound like a cannibal." "Every creature contributes with its life to the community of all living beings—it will be 'eaten,' one way or another. There are no exceptions. Language is pretty obvious here. We are consumed like wax from a candle; we lie down like a bridge over troubled water, et cetera, et cetera."

"You sound just weird," Tilda said. Gabriel objected: "This, of course, does not allow for violence, cruelty and sadism. And it does not mean that animals have no rights. On the contrary, animals share our holy service. Therefore, they have a right to be respected as dignified fellow creatures and have every right to live and die with that dignity. They have a right to be sheltered by us because we are all one. From here, there is a strong point to be made against industrial livestock farming, which exploits and tortures animals."

For him, Tilda's reasoning was so at fault that it destroyed the fundament of what it wanted to promote. Strange girl.

When they were later having lunch, and Gabriel chose a sushi box that he had brought while shopping. Tilda told him off: "OK, I am relatively happy you do not eat beef, pork and chicken anymore, Mr David. One less weirdo among the billions on this planet. However, fish is bad as well. Don't you know about industry overfishing the oceans? Or dying dolphins as side catch? About whales slaughtered or whole species extinguished that used to be so plentiful and so cheap on the market that they were called the food of the poor? Even crabs and algae are no appropriate food for humans, because they steal these creatures away from bigger fish in the maritime ecosystem, who start to starve from their scarcity." Gabriel looked at her helplessly. She continued: "I bet you know all of this, and you have your excuses ready to escape your conscience. If you have any!" "Don't you think you are overdoing it a little, Mrs Toelz? At least, I am not eating meat," he asked her pleadingly. She shook her head. "You need to be more mindful of consequences nowadays. If you want to stand strong against climate change, food and water scarcity and animal cruelty, you have to do better. You're always half-hearted."

"I do not think so," he responded, eating his sushi without further hesitation. "You are right, but other people might have their points as well." "No, they might not," Tilda said heatedly. "We have to put an end to that if we want to leave this world a better place—no, even if we want to keep the worst for it at bay."

For Gabriel, the conversation was over. After having eaten his fish, he went to the sofa and was soon fast asleep. Tilda watched him sternly. Disgusting Gabriel. She had never before heard such a lengthy excuse to eat meat. And she even had proof that he secretly ate meat while maintaining that he was a vegetarian. She had access to his personal Amazon account so that she could order the workshop supplies they needed for B1 projects for emergencies, where the usual procurement supply would not be quick enough. She knew that Gabriel used the name of one of his kids as a password. Such naiveté. When she was scanning his product list of favourites and former Amazon searches out of mere curiosity as she browsed through his account, she found a meat thermometer for cooking. He had not bought it yet, but he looked it up during a time when he claimed to be a vegetarian. That told her something about his credibility, didn't it?

For Tilda, he was a typical example of the Baby Boomer generation. 'Compromise' and 'harmony' were their middle names. "For them, people like me are 'ideologues'" she thought angrily. "And they have learnt to fight us with arguments. They are absolute masters at it. It is the basis for their success. Do not argue with Gabriel. He will apply his 'ideology critique' thing to me and do me in. He is toxic. His generation has trained itself by arguing with their Nazi parents to show them how guilty they were in their fascism and the sixty-eight revolutionaries, showing them how stupid they were in their extremism. I bet Gabriel silently envied the latter for their radical views about an alternative socialist society. However, Gabriel's generation came across as sober moderators, balanced discussion chairs, moderate talk masters and sensible reasoners. Perfect democrats, of course. Champions of a liberal democracy, of electoral representation and political legitimacy. They became our politicians, teachers, lawyers, journalists and medical doctors. And our parents, by the way. You can convince them, and they even consider this as a strength and as superior to holding an irrevocable position. They think that it is a good thing that another person can turn you around and make you think differently. They endorse drifting and going with the flow. They let themselves be changed and even think they are my intellectual superiors."

Then Tilda smiled bitterly but triumphantly. "Now they are at their wits' end," she thought, "because my so-called ideology is right. Only hard consequences and drastic changes in behaviour can save the world. Look at the 'last generation' people. Not Gabriel's lukewarm 'on the one hand, on the other' position. People like Gabriel are the sources of the current crisis. The Gabriels of this world did not recognise crisis when it knocked at their door. This generation is a collective failure. And they are still in power and will be for the next at least ten years to come. That makes them and their monstrous ecological footprints dangerous. Dangerous for our planet. You can see where all this talk about participation, reconciliation and compromise ends: in missing climate goals. We no longer have time to listen to them." Tilda yawned and fell asleep.

Angels' Play

Location:
Heaven above Santa Monica. Shared-Office Cloud.

Angels' Play

Time:
Real-time GMT, Saturday, 7 September 2019, 06:35

Players:
The two angels as before and Bede Griffiths.

Setting:
The cloud looks untidy.
    TA is in the middle of a painting session, throwing gold, blue and green oil paints against a big canvas while dancing.
    For this, it has covered its hair with a strange wig and its eyes with large glasses to look a bit like Andy Warhol.
    GA is supportive in that it provides the dance music for TA, namely the Irish version of 'Lord of the Dance,' while directing an imaginary angel band.
    Despite the noise and the turmoil, BG is completely absorbed in meditation, sitting cross-legged on the conference table.

GA
(*secretly admiring TA's picture*):
    You are dancing cool. By the way, you can stop now. Clean up your mess, and help me with the Script. We have work to do.

TA
(*looking at its colleague arrogantly and sniffing*):
    This was work. It is necessary for tomorrow, like everything else we are doing. And it indeed is a masterpiece. I am a famous artist! I won't clean up. That's for the underlings. I am an artistic dancer. I am a sportive artist. You understand? A 'sportist'.

GA
(*drily pointing to the next few pages of the Script*):
    Excuse me, 'sportist'; we have to peel three kilograms of green Brussels sprouts. Better we start now, before they begin to rot.

TA
(*upset*):
    I am totally not cooking! I am not cooking! This is not in my job description. Where is the union angel when I need them? I am not a kitchen helper. I am a dancer. And with this, I am in perfect line with TRINI-T. You know the Holy One is dance itself.

GA
(*cautioning its colleague to more silence*):
    Hush! Don't you think you are a little heretic? Or at least flippant?

TA
(*eagerly fetching a book from the floor*):

Not at all. Listen. "Whatever is going on in God is a flow, a radical relatedness, a perfect communion between three—a circle dance of love. And God is not just a dancer; God is the dance itself." See?

GA

(*not convinced*):

Says who? Isn't that just some new, trendy theology from the US?

TA

(*pointing to the book cover*):

This is said by Richard Rohr in *The Divine Dance*. And not just by him. Here it is in the words of Brother Elias Marechal, a monk at the Monastery of the Holy Spirit in Conyers, Georgia. Just listen to this:

> "The ancient Greek Fathers depict the Trinity as a Round Dance: an event that has continued for six thousand years, and six times six thousand, and beyond the time when humans first knew time. An infinite current of love streams without ceasing, to and fro, to and fro, to and fro: gliding from the Father to the Son, and back to the Father, in one timeless happening. This circular current of trinitarian love continues night and day. ... The orderly and rhythmic process of subatomic particles spinning round and round at immense speed echoes its dynamism. Here it is: the "circle dance" of the Trinity is very traditional language. And yet if I showed the same courage to use such a risky theatrical word today, I would probably be called New Age, an esoteric—or a heretic. Yet God is the dance itself, they said!"

You see. TRINI-T is dance. This is why I dance. And you should too.

BG

(*opening one eye from meditation*):

Yes. And meditation. Do not forget meditation. You should always do both—if not together. As I am always saying, "In the doctrine of the Trinity, the ultimate Reality is seen as Being in relationship, or Being in love. The ultimate Reality is not a solitary person or an impersonal Absolute. It is a communion of persons in love. Every being seeks to express and communicate itself.

In the human being, the body is one means by which we express ourselves and communicate with others. But the highest expression of our being is the mind. It is to the experience of this eternal wisdom, communicated in the love of the Holy Spirit, that our meditation should lead us." Dance and meditate! (*closing his eye again, going back into deep trance*)

GA

(*winking conspiratorially at its colleague*):

OK, that is indeed beautiful. But now back to work. What if I promise you one of the coolest office outfits during the next session if you help me out right now?

TA

(*cautiously approaching*):

What is it?

GA

(*in its most promotional voice*):

Venice Beach. Ultra-fashionable running outfits. Colours like a canary bird. Indestructible materials that cost a fortune. Beautiful bodies. Beautiful people.

TA
(*looking aghast at its colleague, then seeing that this was meant to be funny*):
Idiot. Do you know the old Venice Beach joke about the crown of evolution: What will archaeologists find when they dig up bodies of dead female joggers in later times except the usual bones?

GA:
Nope.

TA
(*giggling*):
Two silicone implants, a puddle of hyaluronan, a Volvic plastic bottle, and a multicolour Elastane pantsuit with a 1000-dollar price tag. The crown of evolution, hahaha.

GA:
Hilarious. Jokes by Michaelites might be put on the list of cannot-dos.

TA
(*insulted*):
Same applies to Gabrielite humour, actually. When may I wear my Venice Beach outfit?

GA:
After you have included a Green Flash in your picture, have organised two dolphins, have peeled your Brussels sprouts and have phoned St. Peter about the weather.

TA rummages in the animal gearbox for the dolphins and sends them on their way to Venice Beach.

TA:
Here you go. Finally some fish. Makes for a nice change from these endless bird requests of yours.

GA
(*patiently*):
Dolphins are not fish; they are mammals. Get your taxonomy right.

Both angels unhappily wobble over to the table to peel vegetables. They carefully avoid disturbing BG, who is still meditating.

GA starts to whistle 'Lord of the Dance' after a while.

For TA, the only consolation is that it can use a sharp triangular dagger from its weapon collection: It cuts the green sprouts with furious blows, trying to match the rhythm of 'Lord of the Dance.'

The Green Flash

After work, Gabriel and Tilda took a walk along the beach. Gabriel kicked off his shoes and walked barefoot in the water even though the late afternoon was pretty cold. Tilda did not join him but instead walked further up the shore so as not to soil her trainers. Gabriel pointed to the misty sea. "No chance for the Green Flash at sunset today, Mrs Toelz." "What is a Green Flash?" asked Tilda.

"It is also called the Green Ray. You can see it during sunset over the ocean when the sun sinks behind the sea. In very clear air and cloudless skies, you can see for a couple of seconds a distinct green spot above the upper rim of the sun's disk, sometimes shooting up like a ray." Tilda was impressed. "Cool, I want to see it! Why is it green?" "It is the earth's atmosphere. It causes the light from the sun to separate into different colours, ending up in green as the last to be seen."

"I have never heard of it," Tilda said. "It is not very well known, is it, Mr David?" Gabriel shrugged his shoulders. "In fact, it is quite well known. We as Germans might not be very aware of it, because we do not have the landscapes for us to observe this phenomenon. However, I have admired it on the Atlantic Ocean, more precisely at Saint-Jean-de-Luz, close to Biarritz, in a film by Éric Rohmer from the '80s called *The Green Ray*. Of course, I watched this film in the original French, where it is called *Le rayon vert*." "Of course you watched it in French, Mr David," Tilda said mockingly and kicked some sand in his direction. She sometimes really objects to his educated middle-class attitude, probably due to her working-class upbringing. "And then there is a novel of the same name by Jules Verne," Gabriel unwaveringly added. "According to Verne, when you see the Green Flash at sunset together with another person, your own thoughts and those of the other will be revealed as if by magic." Tilda laughed. Then it began to rain, and they felt very hungry. Back at the apartment, they started to prepare the Brussels sprouts.

While peeling, Tilda watched Gabriel. She was puzzled. When she was with him, she was totally with him. When she and Gabriel were on their travels, they were in their own world. He considered her as his equal and considered everything she had to say as meaningful and serious. It felt good. It was important. She fully realised this. Gabriel needed her. It was exciting.

However, this double life led to conflict. It was not only Gabriel's attempting to totally coax her into his mode of being; it was also her trying to convince him to join the straight ways of her Ken-type lifestyle. The worst thing was that, very often, elements of both worlds proved to be mutually exclusive. Therefore, Gabriel and Tilda continually ended up in heated discussions. In them, it was hard to stay composed and hide as much as possible from Gabriel's scrutiny. For example, he would not appreciate her political opinions or the stance on societal issues that she promoted from Ken's world. They were in constant border negotiations. How much could she let him see of her in her other world? How much could she contribute to Gabriel's world without totally losing her foothold in Ken's? She could not say that she felt very happy with the overall situation. Sometimes she was even afraid to lose herself in all of this bipolarity. Gabriel seemed to think his life made her stronger, but that was not the case.

"These Brussels sprouts are surprisingly clean," she said when she realised that he looked questioningly at her, probably wanting to know why she was so quiet. There was nothing much to peel, and although they had an enormous number of vegetables, they were ready to eat in no time. During their cosy and delicious candlelit dinner, Tilda looked at Gabriel strangely and asked, "Mr David, how do you find the right way when there are so many options?" First, he inwardly groaned, because he did not want to go back to breakfast philosophy but instead keep to emotions this time. But then he realised that she wanted to talk about emotions. Obviously, she was facing an inner dilemma of being torn between two or more worlds. "There is something like inner guidance," said Gabriel softly. And he meant it because this was what he had often experienced himself. "Is it reliable? Can you trust this guidance?" Tilda asked, looking at him nearly anxiously. "The voice of inner guidance is perfectly reliable. Your trust is well placed, Mrs Toelz," he said, trying to lighten the mood.

"Is the trust mutual?" she asked. Gabriel looked at her, astonished. That was a question he had neither expected nor ever thought of himself. Does the trustworthy voice of inner guidance—that is, God—trust you in kind? Good question. He smiled before replying: "Yes, the trust is mutual: Loving, enthusiastic, resolute, total, eager and overwhelming trust." Tilda watched him closely to see whether he was lying. Then she slowly said, "This sounds like the best kind of trust." Though they ate much of the Brussels sprouts dish with walnuts, soya sauce and sweet potatoes, there was more than half of what was prepared left when they finished. "We can take the leftovers with us on our way north," Gabriel suggested. Tilda looked at him doubtfully but did not say anything. "Tomorrow morning, we will go for a run at Venice Beach before breakfast, OK?" she asked instead. Now it was his turn to look doubtful. He had seen her limping again in the kitchen, probably from walking in the deep sands on the beach.

They decided to go to sleep early because tomorrow they would be back to travelling. When Gabriel opened the Richard Rohr book again on his tablet, he at first felt too tired to concentrate and was about to put it back on the bedside table. Then he read for about twenty-five pages, more and more fascinated by the minute. It was about a concept that he had never fully understood: Trinity, the Holy One contained in three personae. There was even a picture.

It featured an icon created by Russian iconographer Andrei Rublev in the fifteenth century; as the text indicated, the original was on display in the Tretyakov Gallery in Moscow. "The Holy One in the form of Three—eating and drinking, in infinite hospitality and utter enjoyment between themselves. If we take the depiction of God in the Trinity seriously, we have to say, 'In the beginning was the relationship,'" Gabriel read.

The text went on about the colours of the picture: gold as the colour of 'the Father'—perfection, fullness, wholeness, the ultimate source; blue as the colour of Christ, taking on humanity as sky and sea mirror each other; and then there was… Gabriel read the next paragraph and went to wake Tilda. She was not amused. Sitting on the sofa of the sitting room with her legs up and tousled hair, she looked like a twelve-year-old. Gabriel put a bowl with the remaining walnuts in front of her on the couch table and read aloud to her:

> "And then there's green, easily representative of 'the Spirit.' Hildegard of Bingen, the German Benedictine abbess, musical composer, writer, philosopher, mystic, and overall visionary, living three centuries before Rublev, called the Spirit's endless fertility and fecundity Viriditas—a quality of divine aliveness that makes everything blossom and bloom in endless shades of green. Hildegard was likely inspired by the lushness of her surroundings at her Rhineland monastery, which I was recently able to visit. Rublev, in similar reverence for the natural world, chose green to represent, as it were, the divine photosynthesis that grows everything from within by transforming light into itself—precisely the work of the Holy Spirit."

"Is that good or what?" he asked. "No," said Tilda. "See, I already slept. This is weird, Mr David." Gabriel agreed, eating some walnuts. "Yes, a three-year-old nutter can put together the big picture within a painting session of his kindergarten." Tilda bravely faced the obvious and spelt it out for him: "This is why we had to drink the Green Super Shot with all that chlorophyll! It is for divine photosynthesis. This is why Jakob Green advised us to go to Kreation. This is why we are supposed to see the Green Flash together. It is all about relationships, like in the concept of Trinity." It was like putting one and one together.

After these revelations, they felt drained. It felt as if they had worked hard to reach this point. And both of them did not really seem to like the conclusions in front of them. They looked at each other with distrust, if not a little disgust. "And what now, Mr David?" Tilda asked with a toneless voice that was hoarse from eating too many walnuts. "At least we share from a common bowl like these Trinity guys in the icon," Gabriel said, laughing—to try to lighten the mood. Tilda quickly withdrew her hand from the bowl. Gabriel continued: "And the hand of the Spirit points towards the open and fourth place at the table. It seems it is inviting, offering and clearing space. Maybe for you, Mrs Toelz?"

Tilda abruptly got up. "I am going back to bed," she announced, "alone if you do not mind." With that, she disappeared into her room with her head held high. Gabriel shook his own in puzzlement and went to bed as well. Both were asleep mere minutes after their heads touched their pillows.

Venice Beach

"We'll go for a run," Gabriel suggested in the early morning when he met Tilda in the kitchen fetching water. He definitely sounded more cheery than he felt when he continued: "We deserve some holidays and fun, wouldn't you agree, Mrs Toelz? That revelation last night was a bit much!" They dressed up for their morning run. One did not always get the chance to join the glamorous crowd of Venice Beach. Tilda raised her eyebrows when looking at Gabriel as he joined her in the car park. He did not often choose his canary-type sportswear, because it was so unmanly. They went by car through the gloriously sunny morning. Everything still smelt fresh and dewy from the rain yesterday and looked brilliant. The sun was already high in the sky for early November by the time they reached the famous beach. They found a space for the car in one of the little streets nearby without any parking meters, which made them happy. At first, they took the Ocean Front Walk like everybody else, but it was already quite populated by early shopkeepers opening their stalls and leftover hippies from last night. This made them decide to go to the beach.

They walked along the sandy shore for about two kilometres before turning to walk back at a much slower pace, enjoying the sun and the blue sea. There were many kite and body surfers on the waves. It was such a golden and relaxed atmosphere that they felt all the hardships of the past weeks drop from their shoulders. "Look, a dolphin!" Tilda exclaimed, pointing out to the rippling sea. Gabriel could see it diving in the distance. Tilda was delighted. "It will soon be gone, to avoid the surfers," Gabriel said, anticipating his disappointment. However, he was proved to be wrong. On the contrary, the dolphin came closer and closer until it looked really big diving up and down right in front of them, as if greeting them. They stood still for about ten minutes, but it did not move on. Finally, Gabriel touched Tilda's arm as she stood mesmerised. They continued their walk, and the dolphin accompanied them, swimming in parallel with the coastline and adapting its speed to their progress. It did not avoid any kiters or surfers; it passed right between them, resolutely keeping on course. They watched it like a friend. "How sad that it is on its own, while the two of us are together," Gabriel remarked. As soon as he said this, the dolphin was joined by a second one. The pair of them stayed with the pair on the beach—with them onshore, the dolphins offshore—until Gabriel and Tilda reached their starting point again, where the car waited higher up in the hinterland. It was hard to say goodbye to these two dolphins. Standing with Tilda on the golden sands of Venice Beach in bright sunshine surrounded by playing dolphins in blue waters and happy people on their surfboards, Gabriel felt like he was on vacation in the land of milk and honey. This was emphasised by their attire—Tilda with her hair in a ponytail poking out from the open back of a sun-shielded running cap, Gabriel with his canary-coloured tracksuit and orange sunglasses, which Tilda thought looked gay.

They used the bike trail, running in parallel with the boardwalk for the last metres back to their origin. When they passed Muscle Beach, Tilda said, "Wait a second, Mr David." Dreamily, she stared at the sweating boys who were exercising. "This is one of the most famous weight-training spots in the world," she said in admiration. Gabriel had to pull her away by force from these brainless muscle hulks. Unbelievable. They bought some pastries from a bakery on the promenade and went home for breakfast. The morning was already far along, and they had to leave the flat by 12 am. They had hardly enough time to shower and pack everything. When they emptied the fridge, Tilda shook the big bowl with the Brussels sprouts dish. "And now?" she asked. "What to do with them? They will be spoiled in no time in the warm car. No way to keep them edible until San Francisco." "Oh yes, there is, Mrs Toelz," Gabriel said. He fetched a big plastic bag from their shopping spree and filled it with ice cubes from the fridge. Then he used another, smaller bag to empty the food into it. The smaller bag was then embedded within the ice bag until it was completely surrounded by ice. The whole package was then enwrapped in a big towel. "Our car fridge," he proclaimed, proudly presenting the bag. "It will melt in no time and make a mess with the water," objected Tilda. "No, it won't," he said confidently. Obviously, Tilda had never done such a thing before and had no experience with how long such an arrangement could stay cold.

"Wait, there is one thing left to do here in Santa Monica," Tilda said suddenly. "We need to go to Café Gratitude, as recommended by Jakob Green. Maybe we can have lunch there. And they will have wi-fi for us to check our navigation to San Francisco." Gabriel agreed. When they left the garage and opened the car windows for fresh air, the heat outside shocked them. What had happened over the few hours that they had spent packing? It was as if the whole city had turned into a fiery oven. The sun that had been so nice to them earlier now burned mercilessly. It was baking hot. Tilda closed the windows and turned on the car's air conditioning full blast. "Your makeshift fridge will be melted in no time, Mr David," she said, laughing. Gabriel shook his head but looked a little doubtful too.

The Third Google Maps Miracle

When they finally sat in Café Gratitude and used the Internet to plan their route, they were met with disappointment. "San Francisco is too far to go to get there by the end of the day," Tilda said, studying the map. "It is already three o'clock. We will not even manage to get halfway before dark." Gabriel agreed. "Let's see what is there on our way up," he said, bending over his mobile and following the coastline of Big Sur with his finger and then zooming in where he thought would be right. "Lucia," he read out and zoomed in even more. Then his eyes widened. "What is it?" Tilda asked, alarmed. "New Camaldoli Hermitage," he read out to her, pointing at a place close to the village called Lucia. "Do you know what this is?" he asked. Tilda shook her head. "It is the US branch of the order that Bede Griffiths belonged to. I bet they have a guest house." Tilda groaned.

"It is again halfway between our two partners—this time, between LA and San Francisco. Exactly as it turned out for India. Isn't this amazing?" Tilda was not amused. Another of these weird coincidences around this Bede Griffiths guy.

"It is not halfway," she answered grumpily. "It is much closer to San Francisco." "Halfway enough for me," Gabriel said decidedly. "This wants to tell us something. We'll go there and have a look." Tilda groaned again. "Can we not go somewhere nice, Mr David?" she asked. But Gabriel was already on the online booking site of New Camaldoli Hermitage, which indeed had guest facilities. However, there would not be room for them until tomorrow, not tonight. Nevertheless, out of mere curiosity, he booked the last two accommodations that were free for tomorrow and the following night. He had to provide their names for each room before getting to see the room's details. Because of this, Tilda's room turned out to be twice the size of his. Hers seemed to be a whole apartment.

"And where are we staying tonight?" Tilda asked petulantly. "You choose, Mrs Toelz." Gabriel could not care less. He continued: "Just stay on the road to New Camaldoli." For him, the day had already provided enough highlights. He looked pensively at the big outside sign of Café Gratitude, saying, "What are you grateful for?" Tilda shook her head, sighed and bent over the GPS again. Then she found something to her liking. "We'll go to King City," she told Gabriel. "There is a nice song about King City. I always wanted to go there when I heard it. It seems to be just the right distance away for us to reach it before nightfall." Thus, they were relieved to depart while feeling the air conditioning in the car doing its job. They were grateful for Jakob Green and his Café Gratitude.

Tilda was very quiet in the car. This had indeed been a remarkable day. The Green Motif had been very strong. As Gabriel had put it, a three-year-old toddler would have been able to figure out how all of this came together. It made such perfect sense and aligned so nicely that Tilda got suspicious. The thing with the chlorophyll and the Richard Rohr book. Could Gabriel have made that up? Was everything just a trick to win her over? But no, she had been present the whole time and had taken an active part in all their decision-making. There had been no preparation and no premeditation. The only thing left along those lines would have been a kind of heavenly conspiracy—some cosmic powers cooperating to make everything work for Gabriel. Ha! If they did it, they did it without her consent.

She decided then and there to stop this nonsense. She might not be able to prevent herself from putting one and one together, but of course, she could avoid following the calculations. Green as the source of life was acceptable, but the rest of the Trinity and dance stuff would not fly with her. It was pretty clear that Gabriel wanted to do this relationship thing and see the Green Flash together. And then her own thoughts and those of Gabriel would be revealed as if by magic, or that was what Jules Verne had said. Upon her life, no! She decided not to let that happen. Gabriel should never know what she really thought—about him, about politics, about religion, about the world. For her, it was dangerous enough that Ken knew about these things. The whole story tore her apart. This was definitely not her creation. She was only allowed to help with already-clear interpretations, to nod along to certainties, to comply with the obvious, to agree to decisions without any real alternative and to follow Gabriel. She felt like a bloody appendix. She felt rejected as initiator and agenda setter. She was a born creator! What would Ken have said seeing her unusually passive like this? He would not have appreciated her being a puppet on Gabriel's strings. He would have wanted to see her doing and initiating as usual.

Therefore, her first action on their way to King City was to take back a bit of control. "I want to see Hollywood and Beverley Hills before leaving the LA area, Mr David," she told Gabriel. He groaned and looked at her in disbelief. "This will delay us considerably." But she insisted: "You will come back more often than me, and you have probably been there many times before." Tilda wanted to make the most of her US visit. Of course, they encountered a traffic jam when trying to take the detour via Hollywood. Gabriel was all accusations, but Tilda did not care. "Here comes Santa Monica Boulevard, and what the heck…" The first thing they saw was… Kreation! To their right was another restaurant of that chain, this time an enormous juice bar. Gabriel and Tilda discovered it at the same time with its huge sign outside that read "Kreation—Coming Together!" Ridiculous. But they did not go inside this time.

Then they went to King City. On their way, they passed many oilfields with winches, head towers and wells. The fields looked deserted and ugly, disfiguring the countryside.

To Tilda's surprise, Gabriel managed to find the King City song on the Internet and played it when they approached their destination close to sunset. "Dressed up, red Corvette," Gabriel sang, "in the middle of the night, word is out, lay low. It's just a matter of time, more room for the woman. Gotta hold on tight. Bright lights, King City." Tilda shuddered. "Don't you see, Mrs Toelz? Red Corvette! It is the same car we had during the sunset in Sussex." Tilda shuddered again. The outside temperature had dropped by an incredible twenty degrees Celsius.

Angels' Play

Location:
Heaven above King City. Shared-Office Cloud.

Time:
Real-time GMT, Saturday, 7 September 2019, 22:55

Players:
The two angels as before.

Setting:
Loud pop music plays. GA is in its best DJ mood, slamming one song after another on its mixing console, wildly dancing with its arms in the air and shaking its head, which had ash-blond curls.

TA watches GA in amazement and a little resentment while also observing Tilda and Gabriel below driving in the last arrays of the red-golden sunset towards King City, listening to their music in the car.

TA (*sternly*):
Hello! You were only supposed to hang on to the "King City" song. Tilda could not recall the exact colour of the Corvette. That was all. You can stop now.

GA (*enthusiastically singing*):
Dressed up, red Corvette… More room for the woman… You're driving me wild, King City!

TA (*embarrassed*):
Stop it. We have work to do. They want to eat the food they brought from LA in the doggy bag. Where is a barbecue grill to heat it up?

GA (*smugly*):
I have prepared a little surprise. Father Bede himself helped out with gear from the Saints Section.

Both angels watch Gabriel inspect the ring-fenced swimming pool area of the little motel they just reached. He discovers in the dark an ancient iron barbecue of respectable size standing hidden on the side of it.

TA (*irritated*):
You must be joking! A self-serve barbecue grill in the tiny swimming pool area of a Quality Inn Hotel. Who would believe that? Objective One, my dear, Objective One.

Gabriel tears apart the shopping bag from the makeshift fridge and with some torn branches of surrounding bushes builds a fireplace in the grill. He asks Tilda to light it with his lighter and to maintain it with the rest of his materials. Then he builds a frying pan out of the aluminium wrapper that contained the Brussels sprouts and fetches some paper plates and plastic spoons from the self-serve breakfast area in the hotel lobby.

He expertly cuts the sprouts with his Swiss pocketknife and starts to fry them on the barbecue while setting the table in the swimming pool area with the cutlery. In no time, he sits with his paper cup of white wine while attending to the barbecue, contently watching the simmering food, which quickly starts to smell delicious. He even clinks the ice cubes in his wine as usual because there are still some left from the makeshift fridge that he built in LA.

Soon, both are eating, and even Tilda has a glass—or, better, a paper cup—of white wine with her meal. Gabriel looks into the starlit night sky and prays aloud: "Hello, angels! Many thanks for providing the barbecue. This cannot have been easy. We are not taking it for granted. We highly appreciate your consideration." Tilda makes little sounds of agreement.

Both angels immediately get up from their seats, elegantly bowing to them below and applauding back politely.

Safe Spaces

Finally arriving at the sunny coast with the many tourists of a Californian Sunday morning, Gabriel and Tilda nearly ran out of petrol but could refill shortly before arriving at the little village named Lucia, which was close to their destination. There, they decided to have another outdoor picnic because it was a little early for them to turn up at the monastery of New Camaldoli Hermitage.

However, it seemed to be impossible to go down to the beach, though they tried at various spots. Thus, they sat down with Gabriel's sleeping bag on some wild grassland close to the tourist facility, called Lucia Lodge, which overlooked the wide blue ocean—it was already quite hot in the midday sun. While drinking water with juice and eating fruit, vegetables and bread, they felt very relaxed. Gabriel searched the Internet for some entries about what the monks at New Camaldoli were doing. This took some effort because he was heavily blinking against the brightness of the sun on his screen despite his wearing dark sunglasses. "Mrs Toelz, look here," he said, delighted. "They organise regular interreligious gatherings of all religious and spiritual groups around them to discuss what's important for the region. Recent topics were climate change, new roads, tourism, poverty and so on. Everybody participates. There are Zen Buddhists, native communities, new age people, atheists and your usual crowd of Protestants and Catholics. They discuss values to see whether they can come up with solutions to concrete issues of concern. It seems to be a good place for everybody to speak up because all these groups have very different ideas about 'Weltanschauung.'"

"In our new project, people in need who speak their minds also have different ideas on 'Weltanschauung,'" Tilda remarked, lazily gazing at the blue horizon. "They will have really conflict-informed ideas on values about who deserves what from the state because of how people look at those at the edge of society. But they are the people who need support and shelter most. For them, ethical and moral issues in current distribution practices are the most pressing. They probably face tall barriers against speaking their minds: low education level, low financial resources, low discourse experience, low trust in institutions, low self-confidence, low motivation. Speaking up is a hard thing to do. Sometimes it might even be dangerous, making thing worse than they are." She looked expectantly at Gabriel.

"Yes, think about your field work in China, Mrs Toelz," Gabriel responded. "For people such as Jin Xiaowei, it will be very difficult to speak their minds. They will be threatened with imprisonment when trying to do so." "They need safe spaces," Tilda agreed, "not every country suppresses critics of the system like China does, but speaking up is difficult everywhere, even in Germany."

"Germany?" Gabriel laughed. "Germany is not China. It is a democratic country. It is full of human rights, of constitution, of rights for minorities, etc., etc. It has representation for minorities everywhere. What are you talking about, Mrs Toelz?" Tilda looked at him in disbelief. "How stupid could he get?" she asked herself in thought. It was strange to talk about their home country while looking at the bright Pacific Ocean of Lucia Lodge.

The German Case

"Do you really believe that a democratic society has no problems with minority groups' speaking up, Mr David? What about, for example, refugees from Afghanistan, Syria or Iraq in our country? They cannot vote in Germany, right? Their voice is not represented in the democratic system. However, they live in Germany sometimes for a long time, and from a participatory point of view, it would be important to listen to their perceptions of and experiences with our system for us to work on its flaws, discrimination and bias. For example, the processes around getting asylum. It is the first social service that Germany as a country can provide to refugees, right? And then everything after this: finding work, finding housing, finding childcare. Do you really think these processes are always fair?"

Gabriel looked doubtful. "It is in the law," he answered lamely. "The law decides who gets asylum and who does not." "Don't make me laugh, Mr David," Tilda said hotly. "I will tell you the story of my friend Amir, who is a little younger than me, has studied engineering, and exercises with me in my kickboxing club in Berlin." "Your kickboxing club?" Gabriel got interested. "Amir!" Tilda said sternly. "OK, what about Amir?" Gabriel asked, taking another tomato from the picnic bag. "He fled from Afghanistan," Tilda related, "or, better, from the increasing power of the Taliban. And from his family." "Why also from his family?" Gabriel asked curiously. "They live according to very strict conventions and are religiously even friendly with the Taliban," Tilda said. "They have financially supported his studies and are now expecting gratitude. And compliance." "Is he gay?" Gabriel asked. "No idea!" Tilda replied sharply. "Anyway, without much money, he fled for several months, crossing the Mediterranean Sea towards Germany. He hoped to be able to lead a better life. His goal was to get asylum and find a job as a mechanical engineer as soon as possible." "Oh, a highly skilled professional, then. Not such a problem to get accepted in Germany," Gabriel observed. "The exact details and degree of his education were difficult to verify because he lost all his documents during his flight," Tilda said, "but that was only a small part of his problems."

"What about asylum for Afghans in Germany, anyway?" Gabriel asked. "Isn't there this agreement between governments in place that allows deportation because Afghanistan is considered 'safe'?" "It has been suspended since 2021, since the Taliban got into power again. But that does not mean that Amir automatically got asylum," Tilda answered. "The first thing he experienced was that the public servants of the BAMF, the German Ministry for Migration, who did not trust his origins, because of the missing documents, and used an AI natural language–processing system to identify his dialect."

"They use AI for that, Mrs Toelz?" Gabriel asked incredulously. "AI for social assessment. Again," Tilda nodded. "I really wonder what other kinds of machines are in the background assessing refugees on whether to grant them asylum." "Do you think so?" Gabriel was doubtful. "Definitely!" Tilda exclaimed. "Amir went through an odyssey of bureaucratic stations and steps, which took a long time and which was so complex that he could not explain it to me. During that, he felt a lot of mistrust from being assessed according to many of the criteria. In my mind, I can see a scoring algorithm running through them!" "Such as?" Gabriel asked. "Such as being a single young man, Mr David. That definitely spoke against him. Decision makers think that this is the group with the highest aggression, if not criminal potential. And when Amir explained his reason for fleeing Afghanistan and tried to explain the religious background of his own family, he felt that he had just ticked the box labelled 'this applicant is from a religious background close to terrorism.' Great!"

Gabriel nodded thoughtfully. "Yes, there is a high margin of discretion in the process. The opinion, experience and attitude of the specific public servant you encounter really matters." Tilda agreed. "Mentioning his family to the servant he had his appointment with was not a good idea at all. When Amir described how large his family actually was, with many siblings, cousins and nephews, he immediately felt that the agent did not like this information." "Understandable, Mrs Toelz," Gabriel laughed. "Imagine how many Afghan relatives this agent saw in his mind coming to Germany for family reunions if he gave asylum to Amir!" "You should not laugh about this, Mr David," Tilda scolded him. "Family reunion is a human right, and not subject to the arbitrariness of people liking or disliking it."

"Was there nobody helping Amir?" Gabriel asked. "Usually, there is a 'Gudrun,' a compassionate elderly lady with a helper syndrome who gets things done for refugees." Tilda shook her head, disgusted. "Stop being so mean to people helping others. You have a helper syndrome yourself, Baby Boomer that you are!" Gabriel laughed. Tilda continued her story. "Amir has some relatives who live in Germany, but not close to Berlin. Arriving in Germany, he had been able to make some good contacts. However, he had no 'Gudrun,' what you call a nice person, and he had a hard time adjusting to the new structures and culture. He had seen a lot of violence in his home country and struggled with panic attacks. He had a very hard first time in Germany because finding trauma therapy proved to be very complicated, and as a refugee, he did not know how to follow the path to get it."

"Too bad," Gabriel said. "What happened then?" "He came to my kickboxing club as part of his self-therapy," Tilda said, "and met another Afghan refugee who had already successfully received asylum. This guy helped him. He already spoke perfect German." "A Gudrun!" Gabriel said highly satisfied, successfully evading Tilda's little fist. "Amir's mental condition proved to be beneficial in supporting his asylum procedure," Tilda said. "He was moved forward on the emergency list somehow."

"And you really think AI could be used in such a multifaceted, complicated process?" Gabriel asked. "Especially in such a multifaceted process!" Tilda said. "It might make the various assessments more objective, rational and effective." Gabriel looked sceptical. "Go and ask Amir what he would have preferred, man or machine," Tilda challenged him, "if he would talk to you." "What do you mean? Why wouldn't he talk to me?" "He is afraid of officials," Tilda said simply. "He is afraid of nearly everybody these days. Bad experiences. The process taught him to keep his mouth shut. Whenever he said something, it somehow counted against him. Best to be quiet and not stand out. There is no safe space where he can openly speak up. At least, this is how he feels. If there were one, I am sure he could give a great account of where the flaws are in social assessments for granting asylum in Germany."

The Birth of a Concept

"What do you mean by a 'safe space,' Mrs Toelz?" Gabriel asked, interested. Tilda fetched her mobile and searched the Internet. "Look, this is how the Oxford Dictionary defines safe spaces: 'A safe space is a place or environment in which a person or category of people can feel confident that they will not be exposed to discrimination, criticism, harassment, or any other emotional or physical harm.'"

Gabriel shook his head. "A safe space would need to be much more than just a location," he said. "Let us discuss basic characteristics and requirements. I will take notes." He started to write on his laptop, shading the screen from the sun with his body while they continued their conversation. After a while, they reviewed their work. "That is an impressively long list to answer the question what a safe space is." Tilda read out the summary: "It is a place

- where people can freely contemplate and critically think about ethical questions such as social justice issues in welfare systems
- that is taken somehow "out of the world," a remote place without noise or distraction
- that is not a university where people think they need to be clever or academic
- that does not belong to industry where people think they need to be rich to be taken serious
- that is not a public agency or NGO where people might not have receive the support they are now seeking
- that is dedicated to reconciliation, supporting cooperation and solutions

- that simultaneously supports individuality and community
- that maybe even has experience as the "backup" system where the state fails in providing social services to the needy who fall through the public social nets
- that welcomes everybody regardless of who people are or where they come from
- that speaks to people on different levels (intellectual, emotional, spiritual)
- that prioritises nonviolent communication
- that puts theory into practice."

"A monastery such as New Camaldoli Hermitage would be the perfect fit for that list," Gabriel remarked. Tilda scowled. "A monastery! You must be joking, Mr David. They are much too religious. Monks in black gowns. People like me who hate the church would not feel welcome." "Remember their interreligious gatherings," Gabriel said, "which seem to work for everybody over here." "I doubt it," Tilda murmured. There, at Lucia Lodge, overlooking the Pacific Ocean, they developed the foundations of the safe-space concept for their upcoming new project. Gabriel found it was great preparation for talking to the monks at New Camaldoli Hermitage. He was deeply curious about seeing the Camaldolense monastery even though he was, of course, well aware that Pater Bede had never been here. The monastery was almost directly uphill from Lucia.

From the winding coastal road with its rocky cliffs on the seaside and its roaming green hills with white ferns on the other side, the start was on a tiny byroad uphill, guided by a sign pointing to the bookshop of the monastery where people could buy all sorts of goods and souvenirs. "Monkly merchandise," Tilda mocked, "obviously to provide some additional income to probably slow business."

They hiked about five kilometres before they could see the huts of the hermitage spread out at the top of the hill overlooking the ocean below. A wooden welcome sign directed them to the bookshop, which served as the reception and communication centre of the place. They were warmly received by Danny, a young, slim, soft-spoken man with dark hair and a friendly face. "Please respect that we want to keep general silence throughout this place at all times. You will notice how soothing this is and how it helps you to calm down. Please relax and enjoy your stay. We have such a brilliant landscape around for running and hiking," he said, praising his place of work.

Sophia and San Albertino

"When we arrived, we wanted to go down to the beach at Lucia Lodge," Gabriel told him, "but we could not find a way from the road. Can you recommend a place where we can reach the ocean waters?" "There is a place called Sand Dollar Beach farther down the coastal road. It is perfect for a swim in the early morning," Danny said, smiling. Tilda nodded at Gabriel. "Tomorrow," she mouthed.

Then Danny showed them the accommodation facilities on a property map. "This is where Tilda is staying, and this place is for you, Dr David." Gabriel had to discover that he had booked a whole detached hut called Sophia for Tilda and a tiny room in the general guest retreat area for himself. This had been nothing but an accidental slip in booking: These two facilities had been the only ones left at the time of booking, and they had not shown what types they were; Gabriel had simply entered Tilda's name first despite not knowing the type of accommodation.

And now Danny had set it in stone at his reception desk, with Tilda's accommodation exactly twice as expensive per night as Gabriel's. Sophia had its own big terrace overlooking the rest of the hermitage and the ocean in the distance, a kitchen with numerous cooking facilities, a fully equipped bathroom and a bedroom separate from the general sitting room area containing a sofa bed. It even featured its own parking space for the car and was, in fact, a hut for two people rather than lodging for a single person.

"Harrumph," Gabriel politely cleared his throat. "Actually, that was just a slip while booking accommodation for my team member and me. Maybe Tilda wants to swap rooms with me." Tilda grinned mischievously before replying: "No, I don't. I'm happy where I am." Gabriel glared at her, but she just stared back brazenly. Danny started to appear a little unhappy as he looked from one to the other, obviously expecting them to quarrel about rooms any minute. "It's fine. No bother," Gabriel hastily agreed to this fait accompli. Danny was greatly relieved and handed over the keys to their rooms.

Tilda moved into the luxurious Sophia (luxurious for a hermitage, of course). Gabriel was too coy to intervene in earnest, even when they were alone in the car again driving down to Sophia from the bookshop. However, he could not fight back voicing a few sarcastic remarks: "Obviously, Sophia is their preferred accommodation for would-be hermits that need a bit of luxury for survival," he grumbled, looking at the gracious furniture of Sophia while helping Tilda with her luggage. "Real and experienced hermits live in modesty and simplicity."

But Tilda only laughed and looked around, satisfied: "Yes, I am just a beginner hermit, you're right, Mr David. Sophia will make my start much easier." Gabriel had no other option left than to graciously retire on foot, dragging his suitcase behind him towards Room 3 of the general retreat house further down the hilly road. What a shame. He felt Tilda's mocking eyes on his back as he walked away. Hopefully, she admired his personal modesty and humility!

However, there was no reason to complain—much less to envy Tilda when he saw Room 3, which was called St. Albertino, who, in the 13th century, was the prior of Fonte Avellana, another Camaldolense monastery in Central Italy. According to his biography, he was "a man of peace who served with wisdom and holiness." The view through the terrace window overlooking the ocean was gorgeous. The little room was stunning in its wooden simplicity, atmospheric, inviting, cosy and bright. A large window with a terrace door led to a small private garden with exotic trees and bushes in the middle of nature.

Sitting quietly on the single deckchair of his personal garden terrace, Gabriel could see all kinds of half-tame animals coming close—among them, many colourful hummingbirds and tiny rabbits. The Pacific Ocean view was much clearer here than that at Sophia because the guesthouse rooms were directly on top of the rocky hillslope.

The retreat house featured eight such private rooms like St. Albertino side by side, each with a half bath and secluded personal garden overlooking the ocean. In the middle of the retreat area was a room with two private showers and a common kitchen where meals could be picked up. There was a large fridge, which was replenished at various times per day and which contained breakfast, lunch and dinner for all the guests staying at the silent retreat.

Later on, Gabriel went to Sunday Vespers in the church in the middle of the grounds, close to the huts of the monks. The monks wore white habits, Gabriel discovered, and he smiled as he remembered Tilda's prejudiced outburst at Lucia Lodge about 'monks in black gowns.' Of course, Tilda was not at Vespers herself, probably enjoying Sophia's terrace. He had not expected anything else.

Then he had a solitary dinner from the common fridge while sitting in his garden chair listening to the hummingbirds and looking at a brilliant sunset over the ocean. The sinking sun looked like a burning car that was glowing orange and getting flatter and flatter in a scrap baling press. Although he watched closely, there was no Green Ray when it finally disappeared below the horizon beyond the ocean.

He heard a knock at the door. It was Tilda, who came to check on him. "Please come in, Mrs Toelz," he said as he invited her in. "You can sit with me in the garden if you take the deskchair from my room. But conversation is out of question due to the commandment of silence in the retreat house." Thus, they sat silently in the dark until it got really cold—to be honest, they did not manage complete silence, giggling every now and again about a funny thought they shared via telepathy.

On the Beach and in the Library

The next morning, they met to go to Sand Dollar Beach for a swim. The sun was not yet up above the mountains, and the fresh air was still quite brisk. They drove down the coastal road and turned left, following Danny's directions. The place was part of another national park and easy to find with a big yet empty car park, empty because of the early hour. From there, it was a ten-minute climb down to the shadowy beach where they found wild nature with golden sands and huge Pacific waves. Only a few people were down there. A blond surfer tried his luck with the gusty waves, and a young couple with a little boy was freezing in the chilly morning wind. The boy was about eight years old and charmed by the sea; he was far more courageous than his parents, in that he got undressed and approached the water. This was what Gabriel did as well. The Pacific was ice-cold. However, after a while, he adapted and could go deeper into the blue waters to reach the area where the sun was already blinking over the coastal hills. Here, the blue waves featured golden rims on the white foams of the breaking waves.

Tilda watched Gabriel bathing in the ocean and felt awkward. She had a secret to hide: She could not swim. Instead, she sat down and used some flotsam to carve a heart with 'Tilda + Ken' into the sands. In a way, it was a kind of duty to bathe in the ocean. You're not that close to the Pacific Ocean every day, after all. So, carefully watching Gabriel, who, however, was far away and totally absorbed in his world, she slowly undressed. Not even once did he look into her direction. Then she tried to join him in the water, but she had not anticipated how cold it would be. She didn't want the icy water on her stomach. The waves were high, and she could not reach the sunny spots where Gabriel stood. He laughed when the icy waves mercilessly hit her stomach and threw her back against the shore. She stomped out of the water and had tears in her eyes. "Let Gabriel celebrate his unity with nature," she thought. She didn't care. When he finally ended his swim, he glowed from the icy waters and sang a loud song about life on the beach.

Angels' Play

Location:
Heaven above New Camaldoli Hermitage, Big Sur. Shared-Office Cloud.

Time:
Real-time GMT, Monday, 9 September 2019, 09:40

Players:
The two angels as before and Bede Griffiths.

Setting:
GA and BG are sitting completely relaxed in the conference area, talking about the new book of the prior of New Camaldoli Hermitage that was lying in front of them as a manuscript.

In the cockpit area, TA tries to navigate a complex combination of blinking buttons on the communication console by using just its right hand. The angel sweats heavily.

With its left hand, it tries to mix green oil paint and varnish. The angel has already smeared its robe in various places—but it is green anyway.

TA (*totally stressed out and trying to get the attention of the other two*):
Could you please come over and help with everything for tomorrow? I only have two hands and two wings.

BG and GA guiltily look up, check the Script and start to get engaged with the many tasks outlined there.

Down at the hermitage, the prior, who has begun his usual guest tour with Tilda and Gabriel by showing them around, arrives at the monk cell of Bruno Barnhart, which has served as a library since the demise of this famous monk. He opens the door.

BG (*proudly noticing Gabriel's awe and admiration*):

Yes, my good boy! This is a perfect little library, if not a museum. But museum makes me feel old. Let's stick to library. Full of bookshelves containing numerous copies of each of my publications in every edition that has ever been published. Original texts and my personal notes. My handwritten manuscripts. Secondary literature of people writing about me. Objects that have belonged to me. Materials illustrating my life. And also documents by and about my pupils and followers. This is awesome!

On the walls between the books are many pictures and photographs of Bede Griffiths, which show him with other famous people such as the Dalai Lama or just display an ordinary scene from his daily life. The whole setup is a carefully composed and well-maintained collection. The heavenly group watches Gabriel admire the picture with the Dalai Lama before the little group on earth comfortably sits down around the huge library table to talk over a cup of tea. Gabriel presents the safe-space concept that he and Tilda developed the day before.

TA (*takings its eyes away from the scene below and addressing BG*):

Yes, the Dalai Lama is certainly cool. But how good is this safe-space stuff they are constantly talking about? Participation of the many? Bringing everybody, including vulnerable groups, to one table to discuss how things should proceed? Can't knowledgeable people such as you or the Dalai Lama simply tell people how the world works and what everybody is supposed to do? You are know-it-alls (*realising that this does not sound particularly positive, it hastily adds*); I mean, you have universal insight.

BG (*shaking his head and searching the shelves for a book to lecture at TA*):

Haven't you read what I wrote on universality and particularity? (*seeing TA's anxious face that he will find the book and start an endless monologue*) Or, if not, Bruno Barnhart's *The Future of Wisdom*, about participatory conscience? No?

Or Raimon Pannikar? That guy rightly says, "We 'touch' the infinite at a single point, a tangent, where we participate in the infinite" (*BG contently watches the prior of New Camaldoli Hermitage, who is writing down this sentence at the same time on a little piece of paper, which he passes over to Gabriel*). Everybody looks at unity from their specific viewpoint, contributing to the whole. Everybody is necessary.

Only together—in unity realised by participation—can we approximate the unity in the infinite. Nobody sees the whole.

TA (*impishly*):

Oh, come on, Father! Certainly, you can see the story from beginning to end. You're a genius.

BG (*not tempted into being flattered*):

Nope! The whole cannot be overseen. There is no beginning, and there is no end. The whole is in permanent creation. Creation is not a single event; creation is constantly happening. And the way it is doing that is changing. It is not only an evolution of species, ending with a species that has consciousness. It is an enterprise of

Western mindsets joining up with Eastern approaches, especially from India. A marriage of East and West. The process is evolving towards New Creation. Consciousness itself is evolving.

TA (*scared*):
Not mine. My consciousness is good as it is without any interference from India. I am a Western angel with a start-to-finish consciousness.

GA (*for the first time joining the conversation*):
Going from here to the door. Mini-path consciousness. One-way cul-de-sac. Typical for a Michaelite.

TA (*aggressively*):
Do you want to get a bloody nose, you posh Madonna lily hippie?

BG (*soothingly*):
Tut tut, my dears. You are recommended to go meditate. By that, you can reduce your aggression level and maybe reach unity—that is, a higher consciousness. (*seeing that now both angels look at him aggressively in perfect unison, he hastily adds*) Let's follow up on the Green Motif. Two actions on that are next in the Script. Green as green can.

TA (*obediently wobbles over to take up its green paintbrush again to give it to GA as the acting artist. Then, suddenly, the alarm button on its psychometer for Tilda starts blinking red*): Wait a second. Tilda is denying the Green Ray experience.

GA (*still annoyed, with a dribbling green brush, now turning its anger towards Tilda*):
Why is that? Defiant, vicious girl. It would do her a world of good. And I have organised everything for the Green Ray tonight. We had only this one left in the gearbox for the whole week to come. They leave tomorrow, you know.

BG (*flexibly and politely*):
We do the Green Ray tonight and the Green Focus on the Trini-T icon tomorrow morning, according to the plan. If Tilda is still unwell, we will just work with Gabriel. My Script is not exactly clear about whether they need to be together for this.

At 6:40 pm, the three of them see the sun quickly sinking to the ocean horizon. They watch Gabriel running to the hillslope in front of his garden to sit down in the grass for the sunset. He is peeping over at Sophia, but no Tilda is in sight.

TA (*closely watching the sun, measuring light with its spectrometer*):
Attention! On three: One, two, hush!
GA *artistically whooshes the paintbrush through the evening air, gracing the sun with a phosphor-green flash, which glows in amazing brightness for a long while.*

TA (*appreciatively nodding to its colleague*):
Nice one!

The Green Ray

For Tilda, the most interesting part of the conversation in the library had been the one about consciousness. Such interesting ideas! Consciousness not evolving gradually, but in leaps. And saying that the engine of the evolution of consciousness and social progress was spirituality. OK, then a machine could not be the next step in evolution. Unless it got spiritual. Tilda giggled, remembering Gabriel's icy remarks about posthumanism. It was due to his remarks that she decided to later try out these prayers that they did in the church's rotunda. She wanted to give spirituality a chance, to evolve her consciousness. The service itself was rather a shock and disappointment to her. So Catholic! She felt fury rising in herself for Gabriel, for making her come.

Gabriel, for his part, was overjoyed at seeing Tilda attend mass. Maybe, he was not in such a goose chase as he had sometimes resignedly assumed over the past few months. Afterwards, he stopped her on their way out. "Tonight, there will be perfect weather conditions to see the Green Ray, Mrs Toelz," he informed her, pointing to the clear blue sky and the late-afternoon sun. She looked at him strangely but nodded. "We can watch it best from behind my garden sitting at the rim of the hillslope," suggested Gabriel eagerly. "If you come by 6:40 pm, you will arrive right on time." She nodded again then turned her back and began walking down towards Sophia. For Gabriel, she looked a little forlorn and misplaced, but maybe she was just tired.

Gabriel had some tea and spent the time until sunset in his garden. Life was perfect. Then he realised that the sun was sinking quickly—much more quickly than he had expected. It was weird: He had looked up the precise hour of sunset on the weak Internet at the hermitage. And now the sun hurried down as if somebody were after it. Fetching his white wine in a paper cup and his sleeping bag to sit on, he walked to the hillside rim to sit down opposite the sinking sun. At first, he felt fine, cheering on the brilliant sunset that had started. However, from minute to minute, his anxiousness increased. He had expected Tilda to join him shortly, and he looked over his shoulder more and more nervously, worried that she would miss the moment. The sun again looked like a burning car that was glowing orange and getting flatter and flatter in a scrap baling press.

Gabriel ran to the courtyard of the retreat house where he could look down at Sophia, and he saw its empty terrace and closed curtains behind the windows. No Tilda to be seen, or anybody else. He tried to phone her on her mobile, but she didn't respond. It was pure stress. At his back, the sun was quickly sinking. In front of him, Sophia showed no signs of life.

He started to run down the path to fetch Tilda but decided after a few steps that it was too late. The decision was between fetching Tilda and seeing the sunset on his own. He decided to do the latter. It was her fault for falling asleep at such an important moment. After shooting a last farewell glance at Sophia, he returned to his solitary but glorious perch.

It was again this orchestral setting as in the sunset of Sussex. Nature was quietly expecting. Only the birds were singing high up in the air in a symphony. Then there was a hush everywhere, for concentration and attention. Everything had meaning. The colours increased in intensity. Gabriel was filled with wonder and spiritual awe. The Green Ray nonetheless took him by surprise. He had never seen anything as green as that. The greenest green he had ever seen. Greener than green.

Then the sun sank into the sea. After a long while, he stood up in the early twilight and felt as if he were standing at a grave. The feeling of taking leave was overwhelming. For the first time, he felt that he would probably have to do the Bede Griffiths project alone—or at least not with Tilda. Alone like he had just watched the Green Ray. He and Tilda would never share the experience, for whatever reason. This was simply a fact.

Poor Gabriel. Tilda had seen him running up and down the path in front of his room looking out for her while she was standing behind her closed curtains peeping out without being seen by him or anybody else. She had decided against seeing the Green Ray. She could not stand to watch this thing together with him, so laden with meaning. Too private. Too invasive. No, thank you. It would have felt like watching porn together. She wanted to keep to herself and stay cool and in control.

Afterwards, she felt remorse. So as soon as she saw light in Room 3 after the sun had finally settled down, she went up there to fetch Gabriel for dinner. She had been prepared for disappointment, but not for the resignation she met. Gabriel looked very old when he fetched his plate and cup before joining her at Sophia's terrace. He did not speak very much, contrary to his usual habits. He sat there totally diminished, poking at his food and not even drinking his wine. "I'm sorry that I missed the Green Ray, Mr David. I slept like a log," Tilda lied. He nodded sadly.

"Listen, I dreamt that a mate from home lived in Room 3," she said while pointing in the direction of the general retreat house, moved by his desperation. "Up there where you live." Gabriel looked up to the dark row of buildings. "What about your friend?" he asked tiredly. "In my dream, I knew that something very bad would happen up there. When my friend was with me down here, I warned him against going up there again and suggested that he instead stay with me at my place." Gabriel looked at her absently. "What would happen to your friend up there?" he asked.

"I don't know. In my dream, I simply warned him against going up there again, to prevent catastrophe." "Are you suggesting that I should stay with you tonight, Mrs Toelz?" Gabriel asked, looking directly at her. Of course, he had a right to ask. All that Tilda had said provoked the question. She was well aware of that. However, she did not dare to go further. She looked away. And Gabriel? He was a stricken man that evening. He had watched the Green Ray all on his own. There was no energy left in him to fight for or against anything. He was out of energy. They sat for a few moments in the dark, in total silence. Then he sighed deeply, took his dirty plate and cup, stood up and walked through the pitch-black night in the direction of Room 3.

Angels' Play

Location:
Heaven above New Camaldoli Hermitage, Big Sur. Shared-Office Cloud.

Time:
Real-time GMT, Tuesday, 10 September 2019, 05:42

Players:
The two angels as before.

Setting:
Through soft fog rising mysteriously from earth below, TA is dancing slowly to angelic dancefloor music while GA is on the parquet of the inner cloud. Everywhere are used buckets with green oil paint and wet paintbrushes full of green paint. Both angels are peeping down at earth every now and again, watching Gabriel going to morning prayers. The fog is also down there at the hermitage. Gabriel looks very lonely while he makes his solitary way from Room 3 up to the still-dark church.

TA (*musingly*):
How can he see the Trinity icon at the church entrance? He's passed it many times now. It was in front of his nose each time he entered the church. No way will he see it this time.

GA (*freeing itself from the arms of TA, the angel lavishly applies another thick layer of green colour to the Trinity icon at the church door by using a brush from the nearest paint bucket*):
Says the angel in the green robe. Viriditas. Trust the green force of eternity.

At the very last second before leaving the church, Gabriel turns his head, and his eyes fall on the huge picture opposite the open church door where the early-morning light plays on the brilliant colours of the Russian Trinity icon, especially the deep green in the eucharistic bowl and in the tree, above the three figures, that points to heaven. Gabriel is clearly stunned and thoroughly shaken.

GA (*enthusiastically waving the wet brush in the direction of TA, who is immediately sprayed with a green tan*):
Gotcha!

The Divine Dance

Gabriel had been up and about at 4:00 am after fretfully sleeping because of the weird events from the evening before. Sitting in his silent moonlit garden, it had seemed as if a veil were billowing where the brilliant sun had set over the ocean and the beach landscape the evening before. It was a strange sensation: It looked as if the waves of the ocean had come up close to him, looking like a wavy grey veil on a grave. It was long time before he realised that these were foggy clouds and not water. Thick white mist raised up from the ocean while the moon reflected blue light on what looked like corrugated bed linen. At about 5:30 am, the church bells chimed for vigils. He joined the monks in prayer, first vigils and then, after a time of meditation, lauds. The monks burned a lot of incense as they chanted. Through the windows, the upcoming morning light slowly prepared everything for the new day. Gabriel felt the sadness that had been on his shoulders since last evening slip away. By the time he finally got up to leave the church, he felt happy and strong again.

The sun sent its first rays over the mountain tops opposite the church, which found their way through the big church door when he opened it. He looked behind his shoulder to follow their way into the dark church. There was a decorated wall that was open at its right and left to let people pass; it was just behind the door separating the inner room from the antechamber, placed there to prevent drafts. Gabriel had passed this wall numerous times by now for prayers, probably absentmindedly given that he had never paid attention to the huge painting that covered the wall from top to bottom right in its centre, facing the door. Now the full sunlight illuminated the bright colours, and he staggered back in surprise. He was definitely not prepared to see Richard Rohr's icon with a brilliantly flashing green in the full light of the early-morning sun. And this on their last morning, after the Green Ray the evening before and everything that had happened in LA. It was spooky. The first thing he did after his solitary breakfast was go down to Tilda, who had *The Divine Dance* with the marked pages for further reading. "Good morning. Can I have the Richard Rohr book?" he asked her. She was surprised but fetched it from her bedside table. Then in a loud voice, he read out to her the marked passage featuring the icon and the Green Motif. "I read this passage last night again," she impatiently stopped him and continued: "I nearly know it by heart by now. What's the matter?" "Please go to church with me," Gabriel replied. She rolled her eyes and grumbled. "Please. Just do me this favour. I have to show you something, Mrs Toelz." Of course, she suspected that he'd try to lure her into praying again. Not very graciously, she followed him to church. However, when he pushed her in front of the icon, dramatically pointing to it like he was introducing a superstar, her mouth fell open and she was quiet. Gotcha!

After showering and packing his things for departure, Gabriel went to the bookshop to settle their bills. He bought a few books from the prior's recommended reading list, such as *The Marriage of East and West*, by Bede Griffiths, and *Evolutionaries*, by Carter Phipps. Scanning the walls of the bookshop for further items of interest, he made a lovely discovery: The monks had reproduced the Trinity icon as it was displayed in their church in a small ceramic format for visitors to take away as a souvenir. It was really beautiful. Although it cost nearly 50 dollars, he bought it.

Aiming to fetch Tilda and her luggage from Sophia, Gabriel drove to Sophia's parking spot but crashed the back of their car into the wooden, white-painted parking sign there. The sign fell to the ground with a big bang, and there was a big white smear of paint on the back of the car. Tilda gloated.

They started in bright sunshine at the hermitage bookshop. Going downhill, however, was scary. "Like diving into the unknown dark of the Pacific," Tilda commented as they reached the foggy coastal road. They turned towards San Francisco. The mist was so dense that they couldn't even see the ocean. The weather did not change for the better throughout the drive. They arrived in dark fog. The booking was for Marina Inn at San Leandro, which was close to San Lorenzo on San Francisco Bay.

Angels' Play

Location:
Heaven above San Francisco, downtown. Shared-Office Cloud.

Time:
Real-time GMT, Tuesday, 10 September 2019, 21:02

Players:
The two angels as before and Bede Griffiths.

Setting:
The fog is no longer the soft mist that it was in the previous scene. The cloud is now wrapped in ice-cold blue-shimmering plumes of dense and dirty-looking smog. The cockpit board hectically blinks a red alert. TA and GA are shivering. They are sitting huddled in their cockpit seats. Both wear fighting gear. They look like forlorn soldiers in a muddy war trench cautiously peeping down at earth. Around them, empty green-paint buckets and dried-out paintbrushes lie sprayed and wasted. They have completely run out of green colour.

They watch Gabriel and Tilda enter an Italian restaurant in downtown San Francisco. GA is helplessly pressing its fingers in its tiny angelic ears and humming psalms to avoid hearing what Gabriel and Tilda are talking about.

TA is bitterly listening, but with watchful martial sobriety, trying to diffuse the offensive blue fumes. BG is pleasantly sleeping in a cushioned chair in the conference area.

GA (*crying out in anguish*):
Father, don't you care if we have serious problems? We're terrified!

BG (*standing up, rebuking the blue fog and then saying to them*): Why are you so afraid? Don't you still have faith? Work together. Cooperate. Share your thoughts. Combine your energies. *Participation* is the magic word!

TA (*shaking its head in dismay though it is now a little clearer*):
But this is exactly what Gabriel and Tilda down there quarrel about! Participation is not working. It is a fake.

BG (*complacently fetching a book*):
Why is that? Look here. Book of Rupert Sheldrake and Matthew Fox on the physics of angels like you. Participation works perfectly.

TA (*uncertain*):
I do not have much physics to participate with. I have an astral body, you know.

BG (*getting again in lecturing mode*):
As Rupert says, "All inanimate things participate in It through their being; for the 'to be' of all things is the divinity above Being itself, the true life. Living things participate in Its life-giving power above all life; rational things participate in Its self-perfect and preeminent perfect wisdom above all reason and intellect. It is manifest, therefore, that those natures which are around the Godhead have participated of It in manifold ways."

TA (*trying to make one thing clear*):
I participate intelligently! I am intelligent.

GA:
So and so.

BG (*hastily continuing*):
For angels, special conditions apply anyway. Listen to Rupert:

"On this account the holy ranks of the celestial beings are present with and participate in the divine principle in a degree far surpassing all those things which merely exist, and irrational living creatures, and rational human beings.

For moulding themselves intelligibly to the imitation of God, and looking in a supermundane way to the likeness of the supreme deity, and longing to form the intellectual appearance of It, they naturally have more abundant communion with him, and with unremitting activity they tend eternally up the steep, as far as is permitted, through the ardour of their unwearying divine love, and they receive the primal radiance in a pure and immaterial manner, adapting themselves to this in a life wholly intellectual."

TA (*cheering*):
Hear! Hear! That's me.

BG (*smiling*):
It gets even better (*he finishes his reading*): "Such, therefore, are they who participate first, and in an all-various manner, in Deity, and reveal first, and in many ways, the divine mysteries. Wherefore they, above all, are pre-eminently worthy of the name angel because they first receive the divine light, and through them are transmitted to us the revelations which are above us."

GA (*curiously*):
What does Matthew Fox say about Rupert's insights?

BG (*satisfied*):
He says as I do. Participation is the magic word. Listen: "Participation is … certainly part of the new paradigm thinking, going from subject–object relationships to participatory relationships." There you have it (*after that, he closes the book*).

Both angels are calmed by this short interchange and now in better mood. However, the fog already starts to form maliciously outside the billowing cloud again. The danger is definitely not over.

Participation is a Sham

Tilda and Gabriel had gone downtown for dinner via Bay Bridge, which was gloriously illuminated at night. They had decided to talk over dinner about the template for the safe-space case studies for the US. "Let's eat in China Town," Gabriel suggested, remembering how nice this was during his previous visit to San Francisco. However, the only place open that they found was an Italian restaurant close to the

Chinese part of town. Oh, how much Gabriel wished later on that they had never gone there!

"This is a hipster location, Mr David," Tilda whispered when they entered, and she was right. Expensive food for cool urban professionals hosted by arrogant servers. They were totally out of place, having fallen from the sunny hermitage in the skies. Their server looked totally disgusted when, after ordering, Gabriel was pushing their plates aside to place his laptop on the table so that he could work on the safe-space concept while waiting for their meals. Obviously, that went against the etiquette of this posh restaurant. But Tilda was the one who pushed the laptop away. "I don't want to work," she stated. First, Gabriel was delighted because he thought she wanted some private conversation, but then he looked into her eyes. "Mr David, participatory decision-making is a joke," Tilda said, unexpectedly starting their dinner conversation. Gabriel looked at her. Maybe she was simply hungry after their long car journey. But she was serious. "Why are you saying that? We want to involve all societal groups, especially minorities and vulnerable populations that don't usually have a voice in decision-making. This is what the safe spaces are for," he protested. The server brought a salad with a small glass of overpriced white wine for Gabriel and a vegan lasagne for Tilda, who looked at it scornfully because of its small size and at its missing side dishes. She ordered tap water to go with it, which made the server scowl at her.

"Participation is the wrong way," Tilda said, poking at her tiny lasagne. "What elites fear most is a mass of people who no longer participate in what is called politics nowadays. Politics is a sham. Political problems are shams. They are constructed by the elites to keep their game going. Politics has been corrupted to be just a mechanism that serves the ideas and material interests of the elites. They have everybody in a big laboratory. What is called society nowadays is a herd of mindless mice in a lab. Nonparticipation and active resistance are the game changers."

Gabriel looked aghast at her. She stared back. "You do not notice anything of the destructive core of the whole world, Mr David. You are in a thought prison, in a psychological trap. The way out of this trap is not some better policy. The way out is to just not get involved anymore. Just don't play their game. Because that's the trap. What they fear, you should do. Refuse participation. Do not get even more people involved. Leave them alone." "Who are 'they,' Mrs Toelz?" Gabriel asked complacently. But that was only outwards. He was deeply disturbed. "They have done everything possible to take possession of our brains, especially yours, Mr David. You preach conformity to a specific ideal of society, which is supposed to be just and good, an alternative," she continued, "but it is trapped in a foul framework and a picture painted by the ones in power. You have been totally misled. Do you remember the article that I sent to you from China?"

And she took out her mobile and opened that dreadful link. Gabriel heard the voice reciting the stuff he had found so objectionable. Tilda listened with radiant eyes. The luring, agreeable voice just said, "Opponents are not to be found in politics. Because politicians, no matter how humane their idea, only want one thing—to do politics. They want to dominate all of us and tell us how we have to live, how we have to educate ourselves, what we should eat, how much money or wages we have to earn, which diseases can be healed, how our children develop, what we have to spend our free time on, what and for what purpose the sciences have to research and on which enemy we should drop our bombs. All this is not thought up, wanted and maintained by politicians but rather is determined by powers behind the throne. Politicians are the whips with which they guide us into their troughs. They do this so well today that the masses think it is the golden age. They still elect the perpetrators, for the hundredth time, and compete with each other just to become better slaves."

"Please switch this off, Mrs Toelz," Gabriel pleaded desperately. It was so poisonous and destructive that it robbed him of all his energy. Tilda just stared at him. "Do you understand, Mr David? It does not matter whether there are only one or two politicians or whether we 'participate' (she really spat on this word) and let so-called minorities decide. It stays the same: foul play. To stop participating is our only chance. This is the new consciousness you are always talking about."

"And how do you see yourself in all of this, Mrs Toelz?" Gabriel asked, sipping the rest of his much-too-expensive white wine. He felt he would definitely need another, maybe two. "I, for my part, will not join up with any enterprise that does not support my personal goals and private objectives, Mr David. I am emancipated, mature and self-determining and will no longer make myself available for their purposes."

"What about the others, Mrs Toelz?" Gabriel asked cautiously. "Will you leave them behind? What about the poor people? The people suffering? Even if you are right—no, especially if you are right—wouldn't it be your duty to help them?" "I help them free themselves. I can only tear the mask from the face of the power elites, stop participating myself and warn others to do so. One day, the masses will see sense and discard the elites." "Can't your masses start and try to get involved in decision-making in participatory approaches? What about our safe-space concept? Don't you remember all our project literature, such as the Druckman and Nelson paper in the *American Journal of Political Science* on how citizens' conversations limit elite influence?" "I do not believe in participation," she answered simply.

Gabriel tried another angle. "Do you remember that I told you about this book about angels written by your favourite Rupert Sheldrake, together with Matthew Fox? I have been reading it in the meantime. Sheldrake very much believes in participation!" He tried to win her over with a reference to her beloved author and build a bridge where they could come to terms with each other again. But Tilda shook her head. "He is wrong in this, Mr David. He is a natural scientist and should know from biology that domination wins over participation," she said. "But cooperation and participation have been driving forces in the universe from the beginning, Mrs Toelz," Gabriel objected. "Do you know these fantastic slime moulds called Amoebozoa? They are usually single-cell organisms, not plants and not animals, but show cooperative behaviour, forming a higher-order organism by coming together from everywhere to participate in this endeavour." Now he fetched his mobile and showed her a video from German TV where she could watch ancient sociality herself: unicellular life of amoebae that united to become a slug that could move around as a separate body. Tilda hardly looked at the short Discovery Channel movie.

Gabriel was desperate. Tilda mercilessly continued: "The safe-space concept is a charade. It is bad faith to give people the impression that there is something else but a power play by the elites." Tilda looked directly into Gabriel's eyes as she ate the last bite of her lasagne. "And worst of all, Mr David: The safe-space concept itself is the worst of all power plays." That was a direct attack; he felt it. "Why are you saying that? What is wrong with involving all societal groups, especially minorities and vulnerable populations, Mrs Toelz?" he asked in protest. "And who is the boss of the safe space, Mr David?" Tilda asked viciously. "You are the boss. As always. You will graciously decide who is in and who is out. How fair, do you think, is that?" Gabriel was gobsmacked. "You even expect gratitude and praise for your offer of participation," she continued, "and then they come—grateful and trusting and open. And what will you do, Mr David? You will secretly manipulate everybody by making them believe in friendship, participation and cooperative arrangements, but you are in fact expertly guiding them within this framework in the direction that you want them to go, the one that's good for you. In all this talk about participation and equality, you are the most manipulative, power-obsessed and hierarchical person imaginable because you are initiating and chairing the whole thing with your superhuman consciousness."

Gabriel could not believe his ears. Tilda painted a disgusting picture of him. When had he ever given her reason to think so badly of him? What had he done to her that she had to strike out so hard? Did she not know him any better?

Did she know him at all? This woman was crucifying him for something he had not done. Usually, when somebody accused him of something, his first reaction was a little pang in his heart searching for whether the accusation could possibly be right. However, what Tilda accused him of had never even entered his mind before. And it certainly did not resonate with anything that was in his heart. It was simply disgusting—nothing else.

He was deeply hurt but tried to keep the conversation going. "I think, power is an evasive and illusive concept, Mrs Toelz," he said quietly. "It is like money or beauty. It is not lasting; it is meaningless. Why do you think I would go for it?" She then turned very ambivalent in her reasoning, if not confused and illogical: "In this whole participative and seemingly democratic approach, somebody must call the shots and provide direction and objectives for reasonable action and successful results." So, what was she doing? Accusing him to be obsessed with power or applauding him for being effective? He did not get it. In any case, it did not apply.

"Situations like this make me go crazy over whether the risk of cooperation will ever pay off, Mrs Toelz," he said sadly. "You are scared of being labelled according to a fixed external definition, a dominant, determinate definition. I can understand that. However, the only external definition I see in our project is the one that allows everything to happen, that engages in other ways of seeing the world and that permits communication without excluding any position at the outset. Why preach anything other than that what one is willing to do oneself? We are moving! You seem to be keen to pursue your own objectives as your first priority. This means you cannot be interested in the bigger picture. I am very sorry to hear that. How can the 'New Creation' and 'New Consciousness' ever happen when everybody thinks like you?"

She did not respond anymore but instead waved for the server. They silently paid their bills in the restaurant and went back to their hotel without further conversation. It seemed as if the whole hermitage experience had been futile.

Repairs and Amendments

The next morning, Gabriel and Tilda had to meet with their San Francisco business contacts for a scheduled meeting. They silently sat in the car driving through a splendid sunny San Francisco morning. After the meeting, which was fruitful, they decided to leave the car in their partners' multistorey car park and go to the embankment for sightseeing. It was still quite early, but many tourists were already there. They mingled with the crowd and walked down to Fisherman's Wharf. Gabriel admired the place with the Alcatraz view, with the happy seagulls, the many anchoring ships and the colourful piers. Of course, he had been there before, but it was still impressive. In a shop, he found nice sunglasses for just ten dollars. Then Tilda revealed what she wanted to buy: "I am looking for a cap." Gabriel, the Baby Boomer with chinos, sweater and college shoes, silently added 'a stupid cap' as his eyes followed her finger, which pointed to a baseball cap shop with a most dreadful display of ugly items. They went into the stupid-cap shop—the first and hopefully the last time that Gabriel would shamefacedly enter it in his life. For him, it was just painful to see tons of this offensive headwear lined up on shelves on the wall, each one uglier than the next.

In front of the shelves, total idiots (for his taste) in their teens—and sometimes some embarrassingly older—were trying on different models in front of mirrors. They looked like dimwits, sometimes with the visor pointing ahead, sometimes pointing backwards. Gabriel was mortified. However unlikely, he bravely had to face the fact that he was in such a shop as a customer. Together with a woman who was interested in buying a stupid cap and wearing it. "It's culture. This is about the solidarity you always speak of. Solidarity with the poor. I want to look like a bro," Tilda explained trying on various exemplars. "Like a what?" Gabriel asked uncomprehendingly. Had to have to do something with hip-hop. "Like a brother," Tilda said impatiently. "But you are a woman, Mrs Toelz. You look dreadful," Gabriel griped; he was desolate. He thanked his creator when the model she was keen on was not available in her size.

Back outside in the sun, they were totally amazed that there were dealers selling marijuana on the pier. Of course, they had heard that THC had been legalised in California, as it had been in Colorado and elsewhere, but it was a totally different thing to see this actually happening. A big guy offered hashish cigarettes like chocolate sticks. He crossed their path four times during their walk. "We have to buy something from him when we meet him one more time. Maybe it is consciousness expanding," Tilda suggested. While Gabriel waited for her as she bought some water in a supermarket, he saw the dealer across the street coming close again to where they were. Tilda was still at the cashiers. "Hush," he said to Tilda, using their telepathic connection. She looked up behind the shop windows. Their eyes locked, and he showed her with his eyes where he would be heading. Then he ran after the dealer. "How much?" he asked out of breath. "Five dollars each," the dealer said, pointing at his hashish cigarettes. In the middle of the deal, Tilda joined Gabriel, breathlessly laughing. He hastily pushed the two cigarettes into the pockets of his sweater and smelt like a junkie the rest of the day.

"We can go back via Golden Gate Bridge," Gabriel suggested. They were exhausted and enjoyed sitting in silence in the car while listening to 'San Lorenzo,' played by Pat Metheny, as they passed through this part of the city. Life was perfect again. They were in serene harmony. They crossed the bridge and made a big detour back to Marina Inn. At an outlet centre close to the hotel, they bought some turpentine in a DIY shop to clean off the white smear that the car sustained from the sign at Sophia that morning. When checking on the car, they discovered another, much-more-severe scratch on the front wheel of the car. This looked really serious. They also bought some gloss of the same shade of grey on their car to make repairs the next morning. Last but not least, they bought sushi, candles, vegetables, white wine, water and ice for another outdoor dinner, during which they planned to smoke the hashish cigarettes in celebration of their last evening in the US. Back in the hotel, it was quickly getting dark. "I have an idea where to go for dinner, Mr David," Tilda said. "I've checked Google maps. Close to the marina is an island of about one square kilometre without any habitation but with a vast area of green and low vegetation. We can go there." This was probably where people walked their dogs and went running. They chose a bench opposite the Golden Gate Bridge, which could be seen glimmering across the waters in the far distance. They lit the candles, drank chilled white wine, ate sushi and vegetables and smoked their joints.

During dinner, they talked amiably about India while enjoying the glorious sight of the famous illuminated bridge. The joints, by the way, proved to be quite disgusting and anything but consciousness expanding: They were half wet and ragged from spending the day in Gabriel's pockets, and they tasted foul and too sweet. "I can put the rest of your white wine into the water to keep it cool," Tilda offered. However, in trying to do so, her bad foot slipped while she tried to keep her balance on the stony shore. Gabriel could see that she was in pain again and could imagine how swollen her ankle probably was after the long walk they had taken. And this happened just hours before she would need to sit for hours and hours on another long intercontinental flight. "Mrs Toelz, I have some oil at the hotel and can try a drainage massage on your foot," Gabriel offered. "This would suit you well," Tilda laughed. What was written on her face was unmistakable. "I do not mean it that way," he protested and was again deeply offended. He definitely had enough of that woman. More than enough.

Tilda had a bad rest of her evening too, spending the night on the phone with her boyfriend. She had carelessly mentioned that they had smoked hashish. "WHAT have you done?" Kennie shouted through the line. "Do you want to land in jail?" "It's legal in California," Tilda said lamely. "This is your boss," Ken continued. "He is not your boyfriend unless I've missed something. These are things you maybe do with your close friends, but not with your employer. Or have you changed your mind?" "Of course not! Why would you say that?" Ken was very upset. "You do not take drugs. You do not smoke. It's unhealthy. Normally, you would not even dream of doing such a thing. You are a healthy athlete who takes care of her body. You would not even smoke with me. You have never done this with me!" Was he now complaining that they weren't junkies? But Tilda certainly got his point. A different job would be the solution. That was what came to her mind during this phone call. "I will leave B1," she offered to Ken. "Maybe then you'll believe that I don't care for Gabriel." Ken was immediately soothed. He even said he would look with her through job postings. She felt good about that decision because it would give her back her old life. This new one had proved to be too stressful and taxing. With a new job away from Gabriel, she would again be able to concentrate on her sports and her other activities. And she could look into Ken's eyes and into her own.

However, when she scanned her emails before going to sleep, there was one sitting there from Gabriel written just minutes ago. It read: "I suggest that I step down from project leadership and project involvement, only taking care of the concept of safe spaces in future. You are the project leader from now on. I am done with it. However, I will continue taking care of everything related to the upcoming India trip. Of course, I will go there on my own." Fine with her.

Angels' Play

Location:
Heaven above Marina Inn, San Francisco. Shared-Office Cloud.

Time:
Real-time GMT, Thursday, 12 September 2019, 07:17

Players:
The two angels as before and Bede Griffiths.

Setting:
Both angels have dark circles under their eyes from their long night shift of discussing with BG, who arrived in the early hours to check resources and options.

BG is wearing a strange outfit consisting of jeans, hippie sandals and a green hoodie with white lettering on front and back. It seems to be the merchandise of a special brand, and TA and GA look at it with suspicion, trying to read the words.

They themselves are in fresh fighting gear, scanning through their gearboxes for better armour. TA is luxuriously sniffing at a turpentine bottle, while GA is leafing through the Book of Books for helpful munition. The cloud's red alert is set back to yellow.

GA (*scanning pages*):
Father, what is your recommendation of a Bible verse that could help Gabriel to emotionally survive the blow?

Angels' Play

BG (*showing the white letters written on the front of his sweater. They read: Mt. 11:29*):
"Take my yoke upon you and learn from me, for I am gentle and humble in heart, and you will find rest for your souls" (*in the teaching voice of the guru*). As you know, *yoke* in the original Hebrew means "law," and that is the Old Testament law. The yoke of Christ, as said here, is easy and his burden light because the yoke of Christ is Love. This is the New Testament. Love is the recommendation for Gabriel. And being gentle and humble.

GA (*sternly*):
Not really! 'Gentle and humble.' That is not very helpful. Gabriel needs support to get rid of this cruel and barbarous woman—Tilda. If Matthew it shall be, we take Mt. 10:9–15: (*citing out loud*) "Do not get any gold or silver or copper to take with you in your belts—no bag for the journey or extra shirt or sandals or a staff, for the worker is worth his keep. Whatever town or village you enter, search there for some worthy person and stay at their house until you leave. As you enter the home, give it your greeting. If the home is deserving, let your peace rest on it; if it is not, let your peace return to you. If anyone will not welcome you or listen to your words, leave that home or town and shake the dust off your feet (*applauding*). Truly I tell you, it will be more bearable for Sodom and Gomorrah on the day of judgement than for that town" (*cheering*). That's one for Tilda!

BG shakes his head in dismay, but GA is well satisfied with this passage and checks it into its communication console.

GA (*rummaging in the gearbox*):
What else have we got? (*turning to TA*)
Hey, you! Are you already sedated from turpentine sniffing, or what? Can you become a little more helpful and get engaged here, you junkie?
If you would not have wasted all our green colour, we would have had enough left to fight the Blue off yesterday evening.

TA (*defensively*):
It is not my fault that we ran out of Green. TRINI-T Supply cannot meet the demands of our obligations. I ordered enough Green, but they did not deliver it on time. They are pretty slow in production now. They say this will only change with the New Creation. Old Creation is worn out. New Creation will result in plenty of Green, they say. Until then, we need to cope with what they can provide.

GA (*anxiously*):
You know that our charges are supposed to bring forward the New Creation with their project, according to the Script. It is weird: They need Green to produce Green. What if they are not successful? What if we run out of stock before they can move forward? We have a chicken-and-egg problem. The dog is chasing its own tail.

Down on earth, Gabriel and Tilda are just reaching the wrong terminal of San Francisco airport while dragging their huge suitcases behind them. They check with the information screen and cannot find their flight. While Gabriel is waiting with the suitcases in the middle of the crowded terminal, Tilda wanders to the information desk to find out where to go.

Putting some sunglasses on his famous water-blue eyes, BG is in the process of evaporating and saying goodbye to the two angels.

BG (*energetically*):
My dears, I will go down now to help Gabriel.

GA (*disapprovingly looking at BG's jeans and hoodie*):
Father, can't you change your clothes before leaving? You are usually such a well-dressed man, but this hoodie…

BG (*determined*):
The hoodie is part of the gear. It is from my personal provision. Trust me. (*With this, he evaporates, leaving two sceptical-looking angels behind*)

Mt. 11:29

Gabriel was quite stressed out when they ended up at the wrong terminal of SFO airport. It was, of course, all Tilda's fault. She had not properly looked up their departure information on the boarding passes. While Tilda asked for directions at the airport service desk, Gabriel idly watched people coming and going. It was a huge terminal with thousands of guests moving around. And suddenly, he saw his hoodie. Of course, not really his hoodie. His was safely packed away in his suitcase by his side. But it was the very same sweater he had bought in Germany with 'Mt. 11:29' on front and back.

The sweater was worn by a dark-haired, slender girl about eighteen years old with radiant blue eyes. She slowly walked by with her parents a few metres away from where Gabriel stood. "Wait!" he shouted. Very surprised, the little family stopped. "Of course we know Berlin! The hoodie is from this charity shop with the lovely lime tree garden in front." The girl laughed when Gabriel asked whether they knew Berlin and where she got the hoodie from. "It is such a cosy little safe space in the big city," she said. "What are you doing here?" Gabriel asked, switching to German. The girl explained: "We are on our way to Canada—my parents are accompanying me to where I will spend my voluntary social year after school. I have just finished my exams." Returning from the airport information desk, Tilda made eyes as big as plates when she heard Gabriel talk to a German family and recognised the Matthew hoodie she knew from his own wardrobe. It was such a peaceful and friendly encounter. And Gabriel took much consolation from it. What else was it but a comforting and supportive greeting from a safe space? A message of love? He felt greatly confirmed and strengthened by it. The world was alright again. It did not even matter that he saw Tilda rolling her eyes at his stupid smile. Let her persist in her doubting-Thomas style as much as she likes.

And Mt. 10:9-15

They made their way to the correct terminal and checked their luggage. They now had a long wait for their flight. This was Gabriel's opportunity to speak his mind: "I feel very bad about the past two evenings, Mrs Toelz. You are set against the core idea of our project. And you think of me as a power-obsessed, half-mad project leader who wants to get into the panties of his chaste female colleague." "Hush," Tilda said, looking around embarrassed. He had been getting a little loud but now got even louder. "Hush yourself. You should listen to me closely for once before you revert to your usual default setting! This is not about power. It is just about the opposite. We are deep into something here that is bigger than ourselves." Gabriel wanted to set this right. At least, he wanted to explain that he was stepping down from heading the new project and not accepting her interpretation of their relationship and their work. "Who could believe that my feeble attempt to connect Pater Bede's unification project with the participatory safe-space concept is merely an abuse of power where I'm trying to impose my will on others? And whoever interprets my probing into our relationship as an indication of sexual assault has understood nothing and does not know anything!" he agitatedly said. She looked away.

But he was not finished yet. "I cannot live with your foul interpretations. The project we are supposed to run together relies on our relationship. I will not suffer your throwing dirt on it!" She looked at him wonderingly but did not say anything. "This is why I have decided to step down from coordinating the project rather than go along with your views. This seems to be the only way to make you see my point, Mrs Toelz. I am refraining from all power, leadership and decision-making. I will be just participating. The rest is all on you from now on!" She looked a little forlorn. He nevertheless finished his tongue-lashing. "I am letting go. My hands are open. Same applies to our personal relationship, which I similarly step down from and am done with." Tilda was silent in all of that. That was probably the safest thing to do given his blazing fury.

When he entered the aircraft, followed by Tilda, the flight attendant, who was advising them on how to find their seats, mistook them for a married couple when she humorously coached Tilda: "The wife follows the husband." Then, she looked at Tilda's boarding pass, which pointed to a seat far away from his. "Sorry. I put together what is obviously apart."

She did not know how right she was. They were sitting in completely different compartments of the plane, and that was good.

Still sitting on the plane and using the Lufthansa Internet connection, Gabriel wrote an email to his team at B1: "Dear team, for your planning and task distribution, I have resigned from leading the new project because of heavy workloads and have assigned Tilda Toelz as project coordinator from now on. She will be responsible for all strategic issues concerning this proposal and will shape the further direction of this project. Of course, I will participate in the project, stay available for the case study visits already scheduled and sign everything as the head of the department. Thanks for your consideration. Gabriel David." He leaned back with a sigh of relief and slept for the rest of the flight.

Tilda, in her seat, however, reviewed her copy of *Essential Writings* to check it against Gabriel's fury. With a sigh, she put the book back into her rucksack after a while and looked out the window into the billowing clouds. Reading Bede Griffiths again indeed led to the conclusions that Gabriel had deduced. Period. There was no hidden meaning. Gabriel had just put two and two together, especially with the passages on final unity, the stuff with the snake and the marriage between male and female. They had already seen this snake motif during their first US visit; this second visit, now, had just foregrounded the unity motif.

And she had thrown shit at Gabriel. Maybe this Griffiths guy did not mean everything literally, to be taken at face value? These spiritual authors were deep into symbolic meanings and more-abstract levels of existence. Maybe it was not meant to be taken as plainly as Gabriel had taken it? Maybe it was not about him and her and their relationship at all? Maybe it was just in the spiritual abstract realm for the greater good or suchlike?

However, everything had been quite down-to-earth and substantial. They had seen the Sussex sunset; they had been in the cave of the sacred mystery after a strenuous approach to Montserrat; and they had met the snake in the desert of Arizona. She sighed against the window: "If you do not mean to be real, then don't be real, Bede Griffiths." She felt deeply puzzled. She could not really blame Gabriel for his interpretation of events and his attempts to unite with her.

At the same time, Kennie was after her to put an end to all this. "Your contract will run out this year, anyway," Ken had said last night. "You can work somewhere else. There is an advert from an Estonian company providing IT for the public sector. You should apply. Estonia is the digitalisation leader in Europe. It will be quite interesting to work for them." Maybe Ken was right. Of course, he was right, and she was just an ambivalent idiot.

Back in Berlin, Tilda told Gabriel that she would apply for the job at the Estonian IT company. "Why do you want to leave B1, Mrs Toelz?" he asked. "Is it because of me?" "My contract is running out," she lied, "and the new project will only start in half a year at the earliest given B1's project cycles. How do you think should I support myself in the meantime, Mr David?" She was right, of course, and he had thought about this pay gap as well. "I will take care of that; trust me," he promised.

What he did first was ask a friend at B1 who worked in the IT department.

The Estonian Case

"Are they indeed so good in Estonia?" Gabriel asked curiously, "so well advanced in digitalisation?" "They are much better than we are," the friend nodded. "That's easy," Gabriel laughed. How far behind Germany was in digital adoption was a standing joke between them. "And how about IT in the public sector? Are they using AI?" "Of course they do." The friend looked probingly at Gabriel's computer.

"Maybe I can even show you the system." He hit a few keys but then shook his head. "It seems to disallow access from the outside. What I wanted to show you is a system that is in use at Estonian job agencies. It scores people into three categories in case they end up unemployed: 'close to the job market,' 'placeable with support' and 'unemployable.' Depending on which category you are in, you will get money and training. Or not. If you are 'unemployable,' they do not invest in professional development courses, because you are deemed a lost case. No training also if you are 'close to the job market' because you will be off their radar again in no time without any support from their side." "Who are 'they'?" Gabriel asked, appalled. He felt himself reminded of Tilda and her talk about weird decision makers operating in secret.

"Public servants," his friend said, laughing. "Clerks in job agencies. Who else? According to European law, a human being must have the last say in social service provision. A machine may not decide. No automated decision-making." "Nobody can tell me that these clerks do not make their life easy by just taking and executing what the algorithm suggests," Gabriel objected. His friend did not disagree. "Is there any further advantage policy-wise with this abundant use of artificial intelligence?" Gabriel asked.

"I suppose the predictive capacities of these tools are highly appreciated," the friend answered. Seeing Gabriel's raised eyebrows, he explained. "The categories and profiles are not only used for actual cases of unemployment. Estonian politics wants to fight unemployment as an undesirable social phenomenon. Every Estonian gets a score—that is, a likelihood for becoming unemployed according to profile and for falling into a certain category if it happens. Public agencies contact people before they become 'cases' and suggest measures in advance, to prevent the bad thing happening." "But that's *Minority Report*!" Gabriel exclaimed indignantly. "That is *what*?" the friend asked. "Don't you know the movie with Tom Cruise?" Seeing his friend shaking his head, Gabriel told him about the storyline where clairvoyant beings forecast the occurrence of criminal events before they take place and police are sent to potential criminal sites to prevent the crime from happening—often by just arresting the alleged future perpetrator or executing them without further ado.

"The film is called *Minority Report* because the clairvoyants arrive at prognostic disagreements in a *minority* of cases, which are recorded in secret reports. The proponents of the technique want to suppress these minority reports, to keep the system alive," Gabriel explained. "This is like AI-based decision-making. You cannot send a social worker to somebody's house door and prescribe certain measures just because this person might become unemployed according to a statistical profile and the state would have to pay for them. It's preposterous."

"The Estonians like it," the friend replied, laughing again. "They are very proud of their high level of digitalisation." "Mrs Toelz won't like it," Gabriel said, very convinced. He had told his friend about Tilda's plans to change jobs. "Yes, especially not because there is a lot of bias and discrimination going on even within the official and functioning parts of the system. I have heard that Russian migrant workers in Estonia have been suffering the consequences of wrong decisions due to system failures. This Berlin company that Mrs Toelz wants to apply to is part of the team providing such software." Gabriel looked at his friend. "Heard? Can I tell this to Mrs Toelz? She will not want to work for a company providing software for such applications. In her gym are a few Russians that she is good friends with." "Better be cautious with IT gossip," his friend said. "I know because it is my domain. But as always, if you really want to look into systemic problems and ethical issues, the most technologically advanced states, the ones showcasing their democratic values, are often the most secretive about how their systems work. They think they cannot afford to stain their white vests." "They're the ones who should give a good example to be transparent, aware of problems, and willing to improve," Gabriel sighed and stood up. He had heard enough. On his lunch break, he told Tilda, who immediately afterwards withdrew her application for the position at the Estonian company.

Open Access This chapter is licensed under the terms of the Creative Commons Attribution 4.0 International License (http://creativecommons.org/licenses/by/4.0/), which permits use, sharing, adaptation, distribution and reproduction in any medium or format, as long as you give appropriate credit to the original author(s) and the source, provide a link to the Creative Commons license and indicate if changes were made.

The images or other third party material in this chapter are included in the chapter's Creative Commons license, unless indicated otherwise in a credit line to the material. If material is not included in the chapter's Creative Commons license and your intended use is not permitted by statutory regulation or exceeds the permitted use, you will need to obtain permission directly from the copyright holder.

Chapter 7
A Visitation from India

"Anyway, Mr David, I will need some time off next March," Tilda said. "Why is that?" Gabriel asked. "My boyfriend found me a surgeon who is willing to operate on my foot. The operation is scheduled for March next year," she told him. "But you said that you can lose your foot in such an operation, Mrs Toelz," Gabriel said, surprised. She had told him that an operation would be very risky and that no doctor had agreed to try this in her long medical history since her sports accident occurred. "Yes, but the pain is unbearable. I want to give it a try, and this doctor thinks it is possible. He is a well-known specialist in his field, according to Ken." She looked at him with resignation, and he could see that this had been a very difficult decision for her. Then they talked about the upcoming visit of Ayaan Banerjee, their Indian case study partner from Chennai who had been recommended by their B1 colleague Veronica. Ayaan would visit B1 next week just for one day at the end of the European tour he just organised for another project. Ayaan wanted not only to see Veronica but also to be personally introduced to Gabriel and Tilda so that they could discuss their upcoming cooperation on new project. "He'll probably find it freezing. It is the beginning of November. Not the best time to come to Berlin, at least for an Indian," Tilda mused.

"At least, he can join B1's ten-year-anniversary jubilee," Gabriel responded. "That will be nice for him. Ten years of B1 with a concert of classical music and a champagne reception, Mrs Toelz. I don't know what kind of music will be played, but it will definitely be live and something good. Afterwards, Ayaan can give his lecture about vulnerable communities in India in our department meeting room. I think he will talk about the caste system and the so-called wood people."

He looked over in surprise at Tilda, who scowled again, making one of her worst grimaces. What was wrong with wood people? "Classical music and champagne. I do not believe it," she murmured. Gabriel laughed.

Angels' Play

Location:
Heaven above B1 headquarters at Berlin. Shared-Office Cloud.

Time:
Real-time GMT, Monday, 4 November 2019, 09:34

Players:
The two angels as before and Bede Griffiths.

Setting:
Both angels sit in their best Bollywood outfits on their cloud watching Gabriel and Tilda with their Indian guest, sitting in the matinee concert at B1 Auditorium.

BG sits free style on the cloud floor, legs crossed and eyes closed. He is in deep meditation, expecting a fantastic concert experience.

TA *(disapprovingly)*:
Gabriel should not drink alcohol in the morning. He already had a glass of white wine from the B1 cafeteria. It's not even ten o'clock.

GA *(defensively)*:
Ayaan had one as well. Don't be such a hypocrite. Gabriel just wants to please Ayaan. By the way, what is on the music programme? The orchestra looks strange.

BG *(opening one water-blue eye to look at them)*:
Is Saint John the evangelist ready for action?

TA *(surprised)*:
What does he have do with everything?

GA *(knowingly winking at BG)*:
It has something to do with music and is about the relationship between Gabriel and Tilda.

TA *(rebelliously)*:
Can the two of you not see that this is not working? You are dreaming this up. It is totally unrealistic that these two will relate to each other. They're adversaries.

BG *(very sure)*:
Everybody will unite. And this unification is the ultimate reality in Hindu revelation, you see? As I say in *Essential Writings*: The ultimate reality is *sat-cit-ananda*—'Being, Consciousness, Bliss.' The search is for that ultimate Being, that ultimate Reality—*sat*. And that Being and Reality is conscious; it is *cit*, "consciousness,' a conscious awareness of infinite and eternal Being. And the consciousness of that eternal Being is Bliss, *ananda*, 'pure joy.' That is the goal of Hinduism—to reach *Saccidananda*, and *Saccidananda* is pure Oneness, One without a second.

TA (*sceptically*):
Yeeesss—but you speak of TRINI-T. This here is about Gabriel and Tilda. You might as well try marrying a fish to a bicycle.

BG (*lecturing*):
Today, we need to take very seriously the view of humanity as one body, one organic whole, the view of the Adam who is in all humanity. Saint Thomas Aquinas, in a beautiful phrase, said, 'Omnes homines, unus homo'—all people are one person. Gabriel and Tilda are one person.

TA (*resolutely shaking its head*):
No. They would rather do anything else but share one body.

BG (*surprised*):
But they already do! That of Adam. We are all members of that one... who fell and became divided in conflict and confusion. Jesus restored humanity, not only Jews or Christians or any particular group, to that oneness. In the new Adam, the human race becomes conscious of its fundamental unity and of its unity with the cosmos...

Both types of awareness have come to us today, seeing humanity as a whole and seeing humanity as a part of the cosmic whole. We are all part of this planet, united by it and growing and living in it.

TA (*not very forthcoming*):
Maybe in abstract terms. In concrete ones, Gabriel and Tilda quarrel all the time. Period.

BG (*generously*):
No problem. We are all parts of one another, growing through contact with one another as one organic whole. We are recovering that unity beyond duality. Humanity had to go through dualism to learn the difference between right and wrong, good and evil, truth and error. It is necessary to go through that stage of separating and dividing, but then you have to transcend it.

TA (*challenging*):
Hey, I bet that Gabriel and Tilda can't transcend it. If there is safe duality, they'll choose that.

BG (*with a raised finger*):
Even religion has been a safe duality. Christianity came out of a tradition of moral dualism. It then integrated into Greco-Roman culture, which was based on a metaphysical dualism. But today, it meets the religions of Asia, and we are beginning to discover the principle of nonduality.

TA (*soberly*):
Everything is one or two. And Gabriel and Tilda are definitely two.

BG (*amused*):

Your rational mind as a Michaelite demands that everything be one or two, while nonduality, which is beyond the rational, affirms a relationship that is not one and not two.

TA (*pleadingly*):

Can we agree on digits? One and zero? Please! It is so nice and orderly. Dualities keep us sane. Do we really need to get rid of duality?

BG (*decisively*):

We are being called to recover unity beyond duality as our birthright, and this alone can answer the deepest needs of the world today. This is our calling and our hope.

In the meantime, GA has successfully called the Saints Section and has connected St. John to the music system of B1. The heavenly assembly watches Ayaan, Gabriel and Tilda take their seats in the B1 Auditorium, where the concert programme is now displayed on the big screen on the wall. The little orchestra hired for the jubilee, consisting of one basso and four wind instruments, prepares itself for its performance. Standard pitch A can be heard. People stop chatting.

BG (*excitedly giggling while the little group reads the programme: "Ut Omnes Unum Sint" is displayed in huge ornamental letters*):

Gorgeous!

GA (*admiringly matching the music title with quotes from the Griffiths literature in the Script*):

Great work, Father. Really thoughtful music choice. It was probably not easy to get that piece. Not every orchestra is into Carlos Veerhoff. And Opus 24 is not easy to perform. Verhoff was already quite a bit into twelve-tone music in the '70s, when he composed "Ut Omnes Unum Sint."

That All May Be One

Gabriel fetched Ayaan from his hotel at around ten o'clock. The Indian man was already smartly dressed and waiting in the lobby with his small suitcase. "So sad that this is just a one-day visit," he said. "I would have loved to stay longer for working with you, but you will come to Chennai to discuss our project next month anyway." They went to B1 by taxi. Once there, they put Ayaan's suitcase into Gabriel's office and wandered down to the B1 cafeteria for a coffee before the jubilee concert started. The building was nicely decorated for the event, and Ayaan greatly admired the decor.

In the cafeteria, they met Tilda and had an early lunch. Ayaan and Gabriel had the dish of the day with some white wine under the disapproving glances of Tilda, who had just a salad and tap water. Meeting her scowl unblinkingly, Gabriel thought, "Why must I be called to get rid of duality concepts in a relationship with Tilda of all people—this grudging girl who is so different from me and disapproves of everything I am doing? I'm asking." He was tempted to order another glass of wine just to displease her. Even Ayaan noticed Tilda's disgruntled mood. "What's wrong, my dear?" he asked, pleasantly sipping his own wine. "It's nothing; she has probably pain in her foot again. She had a bone fracture that's never healed correctly," Gabriel hastily replied. Tilda scowled even harder because he told one of her secrets to Ayaan. "Never mind. I will have an operation soon," she said, waving Ayaan's compassionate glance away.

Then it was time for the matinée. Gabriel expected some brass band as he looked at the wind instruments lined up on the stage. They slowly took their seats. Then his mouth dropped open. "Hush," he whispered to Tilda. "What is it, Mr David?" she looked at him with alarm. He'd sounded quite shocked. "Do you know the piece of music they're going to perform, Mrs Toelz?" She looked at the announcement uncomprehendingly. "The piece was created by German Argentine composer Carlos Verhoff, who used to live in Berlin before he moved to Buenos Aires," Gabriel cited from the screen. "The composition is called 'Ut Omnes Unum Sint.'" "And what does that mean?" Tilda asked. "It is a Bible quote from the Gospel according to St. John: John 17:21, to be precise," Gabriel explained. "It means 'That All may be One.' This is *the* Bible reference par excellence for the spiritual concept of Final Unity. Haven't you read Bede Griffiths?" "Ach was," Tilda said. This was just the beginning of a very strange day.

Angels' Play

Location:
Heaven above B1 headquarters at Berlin. Shared-Office Cloud.

Time:
Real-time GMT, Monday, 4 November 2019, 14:02

Players:
The two angels as before and Bede Griffiths.

Setting:
Same setting.

BG (*modestly coughing while seeing the impression that the St. John's quote had made down there*):
That was a success. What's next? The snakes? (*excitedly giggling*) Can we do the snakes now?

GA (*patiently checking the Script*):
No, not yet. Let them finish listening to the concert and wait until they are comfortably seated in the meeting room.

They watch Gabriel's team wandering to their part of the B1 building complex after the concert. Gabriel and Tilda are sitting side by side, with the window to their backs, opposite Ayaan. *Two more team members involved in the new project take their chairs at opposite small ends of the conference table.*

BG (*delicately smiling*):
  Now, I need a direct line to DHL. I know the two of you do not approve and consider him pornographic, but this is because you are not well versed in social theory. So, if you would be so kind?

GA (*trying to avoid eye contact with BG*): TA can do that.

TA (*gruntingly calling the Arts Section and yelling into its mike*):
  DHL please, and quickly. We have (*harrumph*)—or, better, there is—a sexual problem, and we, uhh, they—let me check and count—need three inputs. Mr Lawrence, you are online now. Please start.

Indian Anthropology

"We should talk about sex," Ayaan said, amiably starting the team meeting. Gabriel froze, and he could feel Tilda doing the same at his side. "I beg your pardon?" Gabriel asked politely. Ayaan was their honoured guest after all. "Yes, I'm serious," Ayaan said. "I would like to show you that I'm the right person when it comes to working with local communities in India." "You do not need to prove anything. I am convinced that you are the right person," Gabriel replied, weakly trying to prevent whatever Ayaan wanted to say or do. But it was too late. "Local people trust me," said Ayaan proudly. "I am allowed to observe them and take part in their most intimate moments." "Ach was," Tilda said. "I now want to talk about the Indian sexual rites of certain tribal communities performed in the wilderness of the woods during religious ceremonies. I did an anthropological field study on this recently," announced Ayaan eagerly. Then he started to relate the anthropological details of Indian culture to Gabriel's fascinated team. Tilda and her boss, however, were sitting helplessly side by side wincing at Ayaan's stories as if they were being whipped by a verbal stick. It lasted nearly half an hour. Ayaan even showed pictures.

Finally, he looked up, smiling—indicating that he was finished with his talk. For Gabriel, it was hard to find the conversational connection to the Indian case study of the new project on AI-based social service provision. They were certainly not thinking along the lines of religious sex ceremonies in the wilderness. Gabriel could only hope that Ayaan was aware of that.

Angels' Play

Location:
Heaven above B1 headquarters at Berlin. Shared-Office Cloud.

Time:
Real-time GMT, Monday, 4 November 2019, 14:44

Players:
The two angels as before and Bede Griffiths.

Setting:
The angels are looking down compassionately at Gabriel and Tilda, who are sitting and feeling diminished in B1's meeting room—still in the middle of the session with Ayaan.

GA (*annoyed*):
Enough. Are we done here? They must think we are dirty old gits.
Insulted silence from DHL over the phone line, where he is still connected with TA.

BG (*animatedly giving instructions*):
Are the snakes ready? And do we have enough snakes for everybody? Hopefully, you did your homework with my writings for the implications of John 3:14: "Just as Moses lifted up the snake in the wilderness..." Are the snakes moving well? And do they have the same colour as the one in the desert of Arizona? St. John was supposed to cooperate with DHL on this! Please establish a direct line between the Saints and the Arts section for coordination. Second sex item, please!
Both angels reluctantly comply by pressing the necessary buttons on the communication console.

The Serpent in the Lecture Room

"I am sorry, but I have only one guest present for Tilda and Gabriel each," Ayaan apologetically told the other members of Gabriel's team in the room. "I didn't know that more team members would be present at this meeting. Therefore, I have only two, one for Gabriel and one for Tilda." Saying this, Ayaan opened his rucksack and dived into it.

What came to light and was thrown on the table before Tilda and Gabriel took their breath away. They were speechless. The present Ayaan gave them from his rucksack was a pair of snakes, one each. They looked exactly like twins of the serpent in the desert of Arizona: light-brown wooden toy snakes. Ayaan lifted them high up to hand them over the table. They were moving like they were alive because they had many wooden joints along their long bodies that allowed them to twist and turn in Ayaan's hands. "A greeting from the wilderness!" Ayaan said with a flourish. While receiving their presents, Gabriel lowly whispered with white lips: "I cannot believe this is happening." Tilda was silent. Not even "ach was." Ayaan was smiling.

Angels' Play

Location:
Heaven above B1 headquarters in Berlin. Shared-Office Cloud.

Time:
Real-time GMT, Monday, 4 November 2019, 14:52

Players:
The two angels as before and Bede Griffiths.

Setting:
Same setting.

BG (*hurriedly*):
Quick! We need to re-establish communication between Saints and Arts: This time, connect DHL to St. Luke. Say that this is an emergency case for inter-evangelist cooperation!
Crackle when St. Luke the evangelist, who is also nicknamed the medical doctor, connects with the conference call.

TA (*urgently but with a disapproving glance at BG for neglecting Objective One*):
Morning, sir. Sorry for any inconvenience. We need the integral-medicine approach down there for a woman called Tilda. Can you please intervene?

The Proverbial Meaning of *Terribly Unfair*

The gift of snakes silenced the room. You could hear the angels whistling. The silence became a little oppressive. Then Gabriel took charge, thanking Ayaan profusely. "This is a great present. Thank you for bringing over two of them, so that Tilda and I could each have one. The snake is an interesting cultural symbol for India. In our culture, it has an ambivalent meaning in religion and culture: negative as temptation, but also positive in that Moses lifted the serpent in the wilderness as sign of God's salvation. We are well aware of the lovely snake charmers entertaining us and of the many drugs that alternative medicine is deriving from snakes, which are poisonous on one level but have healing effects at the right dose," Gabriel opined, trying to save the situation. "Well, I am deep into Indian medicine," Ayaan nodded delightedly. "This is one of my favourite research topics as an anthropologist." "Is it?" Gabriel asked politely, happy to have found some ground to continue conversation with their project partner from India. "Please tell us more!"

He leant back, feeling ready to be back in command. "My most valuable contact at home in Chennai is a doctor who is healing the most difficult and sophisticated bone issues without any surgery. He is a specialist in foot and hand fractures. He has a holistic approach and is very famous and successful. And you, my girl, should not have any surgery on your foot!" Ayaan said, turning directly to Tilda, who looked at him as if the snakes had come out of his mouth. "Come to India. I urgently recommend that you first check with my contact. You might eventually change your mind about surgery if my friend can help you!" Ayaan exclaimed. Tilda was embarrassed to have this discussion in front of the B1 team, but she was still able to answer. Turning her wooden snake in her hand, she said, "I won't be going to India. I'm not on the B1 roster for that trip." Ayaan looked quite upset.

Angels' Play

Location:
Heaven above B1 headquarters at Berlin. Shared-Office Cloud.

Time:
Real-time GMT, Monday, 4 November 2019, 15:03

Players:
The two angels as before and Bede Griffiths.

Setting:
Same setting.

BG (*still on the phone with St. Luke from the Saints Section*):
Luke, my boy. Thanks for your help. It would be very kind if you could stay for the Ayurveda applications as well and help DHL with the oil if possible. DHL: third sex item, please!

GA (*weakly and with very feeble voice for a Gabrielite*):
Oh no, not the oil massage. Spare them the oil massage.
One can hear a whiz when DHL splashes a whole fountain of body oil on the people below.

BG (*satisfied*): Excellent, thanks. That will do.

Ayurveda for all

Ayaan was trying hard to convince Tilda that it would be in her best interest to join up for the India trip—all the more so when he heard that Tilda was now the project leader. He presented all the best sightseeing options that he would organise for her. Seeing that the medical information obviously had the deepest impact, Ayaan said to Tilda and Gabriel: "The two of you should definitely enjoy a nice oil massage together. I can give you the address for the best in the world at this, in Chennai!" Gabriel did not know whether there was any potential left to be shocked. He felt like he was being treated with a grater. There was no feeling left. He was done. Ayaan happily chatted away: "This is another close friend at Chennai who is a leading expert in the field of Ayurveda oil massages. People come from all over the world for his services!" With an inviting smile, he told Tilda and Gabriel—both rigid with horror—that he would definitely organise an oil massage for the two of them during their stay in India.

Angels' Play

Location:
Heaven above B1 headquarters at Berlin. Shared-Office Cloud.

Time:
Real-time GMT, Monday, 4 November 2019, 15:17

Players:
The two angels as before and Bede Griffiths.

Setting:
Same setting.

BG (*perfectly at ease with the results below, in a happy voice*):
Finished! Thank you all for your excellent cooperation. DHL, that was invaluable. Angels, you have been a big help.

Both angels accusingly and ungraciously look up while trying to animate Gabriel and Tilda, who are totally dumbfounded, their emotional controls wildly blinking red on the angels' communication consoles.

The blazing red lights of the consoles match the flaming-red Indian tika on Ayaan's forehead below, who is still happily chatting away about the wisdom of Eastern integral medicine, the foolishness and arrogance of Western so-called evidence-based medicine and the useful cultural comparison of global knowledge systems, especially the sexual rites of the woods people in India.

Outrageous

Gabriel was surprised when Tilda said she would accompany him to drop off Ayaan at the train station in the early evening. He had thought she would need a lot longer to recover from the shock from the snakes. Instead, she was open and friendly. He enjoyed walking with Tilda through the city centre with the illuminated Christmas decorations already out. "What do you make of all of this, Mr David?" Tilda asked Gabriel. He had expected that question. "I'm still working on making sense of the overall framework—that is, how our project and our individual lives are intersecting with this," he confessed, "but I am pretty sure about our role in this now."

Tilda looked at him curiously. "It has to do with fighting these dualities that Pater Bede sees as responsible for the world's misery," he said. "What dualities?" Tilda asked. "Men and women, rational and intuitive, passive and active, powerful and powerless, old and young, white and nonwhite, rich and poor, educated and uneducated and so on," he replied. "Our usual binary classifications that separate one human being from the other. The way machines do it. The way AI does it in assessing who will get social services. Beneficiaries and nonbeneficiaries, legal recipients and fraudulent recipients, acceptable and unacceptable, needy and not needy, ego and alter, me and the others, friends and enemies. Do you get the idea, Mrs Toelz?"

"And what about it?" Tilda asked. "What can we do against this?" "Overcome it!" he exclaimed quickly. "This is what we're supposed to do." "How?" Tilda asked, amazed. "Bridging the gulf between dualities, starting with bridging the gulf between us," he said. "Therefore, I cannot do without you. Mrs Toelz, do you understand?" Gabriel asked her. "As much as I would like—and believe me, I would rather do it on my own if this were possible—you are not here by chance or due to some random event. You are here because this call applies to you as well. We have seen all these things together. We are here for a purpose. You are in this with me. It is not just our story; I am convinced of that. It is for everybody. We are in this to prove a point. This goes beyond our two little selves, as interesting as they are." She shook her head in disbelief. Gabriel sighed. "If you can't see the overall picture, I don't blame you. You are the happy one that can go your way and decide against the whole plan. For me, it's too late. I would commit treason against everything I believe in. No way but this for me. But I respect your interpretation and position." "And what about today, Mr David?" Tilda asked in a voice that sounded small. He looked at her. "Let me be clear, Mrs Toelz: I think that the 'heavenly department' was terribly unfair to you when they toyed with the operation on your foot, of all things. The guys in that department seem to be too eager to push us into this project together. Of course, I can only comment on the whole thing from my perspective. What I feel is a mixture of indignation and concern on your behalf. I'm very sorry for you." "But, Mr David, you did everything to implement it!" Tilda objected. "Now that you know the results," he said, laughing, "you have a different reading of what happened, and now you don't want to do it." "But what about today?" Tilda asked again. He only sighed. "The snakes were outrageously insolent. Someone must have thought this terribly funny," Tilda complained. "The talk about the Chennai oil massages was just as unbearable—and as painful as the sex talk about the forest rituals, don't you think, Mr David? And then, last but not least, the matter of alternative Indian medicine, for *bone fractures*: Ayaan's friend who can heal them without surgery. The tirades against science-based medicine and its use of surgery. The sensationalised successes of alternative therapy. In addition, Ayaan's attempts to persuade me to join the India trip after all." Tilda shook her head. Gabriel had to agree. He was truly sorry for Tilda, who obviously felt deeply troubled.

Angels' Play

Location:
Heaven above B1 headquarters at Berlin. Shared-Office Cloud.

Time:
Real-time GMT, Wednesday, 6 November 2019, 22:24

Players:
The two angels as before and Bede Griffiths.

Setting:
The little group had supper around the conference table. A candle is burning. GA is already asleep—its head in its arms on the table. TA and BG are keeping night watch together. Everything is quiet and cosy, inviting deep conversation.

TA (*hesitatingly*):
Father, may I ask you a personal question?

BG (*companionably*):
Of course, my dear. What is it?

TA (*a little reproachfully*):
I cannot help but think that what we just did seems totally disrespectful to me. All these D.H. Lawrence–type interventions? How can you support all this? No, I should ask this instead: How can you condone these things?

BG (*eagerly as if he had expected these questions*):
Because of India! What I discovered there.

TA (*curiously*):
What I don't get is, what were you looking for exactly? OK, you wanted to understand the religions of India, their deepest and most universal meaning, what they have in common with Christianity and how they differ from it. But could not you find that in books? Why go there? What was not good enough in good old England?

BG (*romantically*):
I wanted to be at the heart of life, of being and of love. Behind all words and gestures, behind all thoughts and feelings… beyond time and change.

TA (*soberly*):
And the biblical revelation and your Western monastic living? Wasn't that any good for you anymore?

BG (*smiling in fond memory*):
Oh, biblical revelation and monastic living remained the most important things for me. They continued in Shantivanam. But I sought and found the other half of my soul in India. It was an identical twin of my Western half. I had long been familiar with the mystical tradition of the West, but I felt the need for something more,

something that the East alone could give; above all the sense of the presence of God in nature and the soul, a kind of natural mysticism is the basis of all Indian spirituality. I therefore felt that if a genuine meeting of East and West were to take place, it must be at the deepest level of experience, and this I thought could best come through the monastic life I led in Shantivanam.

TA (*incredulously*):
How can something be a continuation and a break at the same time?

BG (*trying to explain*):
As I said in *The Marriage of East and West*, ever since my coming to India, I have been led in a strange way to retrace the path of the Golden String. My awakening to the mystery of existence came to me through the experience of the beauty of nature, which I described in the opening chapter of *The Golden String*, and this experience was expressed and interpreted for me in the writings of the Romantic poets: Wordsworth, Shelley and Keats. Wordsworth taught me to find in nature the presence of a power which pervades both the universe and the mind of humankind. Shelley introduced me to the Platonic idea of an eternal world, in which the world we see is a dim reflection. Keats set before me the values of 'the holiness of the heart's affections' and the truth of the 'imagination.' These were, for me, not merely abstract ideas but living principles, which I processed over many years and which I tried to make sense of in a reasoned philosophy of life.

TA (*triumphantly taking up the cudgels for Western thinking*):
See, you read it all. It was all already there in England. Confess!

BG (*pleasantly*):
In a way, yes. But when I came to India, these ideas took on new life. I discovered that what in Europe had been the inspired intuition of a few poets had been the common faith of India for countless centuries. That power that pervades the universe and the mind of humankind had been revealed with marvellous insight in the Vedas centuries before the birth of Christ. The eternal world of Plato was only a reflection in the Western mind of the profound intuition of the seers of the Upanishads.

Above all, I found that the 'truth of the imagination,' of which Keats had spoken, was a primordial truth, a truth that takes us back to the very roots of human experience.

TA (*frustrated*):
The very roots of human experience. This is why I am not getting it!

TA wakes GA to take over night shift. GA immediately perceives the cosy atmosphere and the possibility to pose deep personal questions to BG. TA falls asleep and snores horribly.

GA (*hesitantly*):
Father, may I ask one question? Why are you so keen on love?

BG (*indeed keenly*):

Because it is the pattern of the universe. Haven't you read my book *The Return to the Center*, dear? Love giving itself, losing itself and finding itself in love and love returning to itself and giving itself back in love—is the eternal pattern of the universe. Every creature in the depth of its being has a desire, a longing for love, and is drawn by love to give itself in love. This is its coming into being, this response to the draw of love. At the same time, it is being continually drawn to give itself in love, to surrender to the attraction of love, and so the rhythm of the universe is created.

GA (*curiously*):

So you mean that love is an evolutionary driver? I always thought differentiation drives evolution. But you think it's love?

BG (*eagerly*):

Indeed. Everybody who opens their eyes can see that. The nucleus throws out its protons and electrons, and they circle round it, held by the attraction of love. The sun throws out its planets, and they circle round it, held by the same attraction. A cell divides and then again unites, building up the body in love. It is the same with sexual love. The man is drawn to give himself in love to the woman, and the woman is drawn to give herself back in love to the man. There is a continual dance of love, a continual going and returning. Ultimately, it is the one Love giving itself continually so as to create this form and that form, building up the universe of stars and atoms and living cells and then drawing everything back to itself.

GA (*sceptically*):

But if that is true, why are humans so horrible to each other? There is so much egoism, anger and hatred in people!

BG (*understandingly*):

Every human being has in their heart this desire to love and to be loved. It is the very structure of their being. It is built into the cells of their body and is the deepest instinct in their soul. A child lives and grows with love. This is why a child who is deprived of love in their infancy suffers an irremediable loss. Fear and sorrow, anger and hatred, are only expressions of frustrated love. But the trouble is that there is always something selfish in human love.

GA (*eagerly*):

That's sin, right?

BG (*approvingly*):

Yes, you are right. The desire to be loved, to possess love for oneself is too strong, and the will to give to others is too weak. This is the effect of sin. Sin is always the refusal to love—or, rather, the rejection of the rhythm of love, the desire to get and not to give. The mother wants to possess the child's love and not just to take it as it comes. The child wants to possess the mother's love and to not respond to a love that would draw it out of itself. It is the same in sexual love: The man wants to possess the woman; the woman wants to possess the man. We all keep falling back on self-love. But real love is always a response to the love of another, a self-giving with no thought of return. We can receive only in so far as we are willing to give. Ultimately, it is always the love of God which is drawing us through every human love, drawing us towards giving ourselves back in return for the love we have received. That is why all love is holy, from the love of atoms or of insects to the love of humans. It is always a reflection of the love of God.

GA (*questioningly*):
But what's the problem? Where does the temptation lie? There's always temptation when there's sin!

BG (*nodding*):
Right. Our temptation is to rely on our own dignity, to centre on ourselves and refuse that movement of return, of self-surrender. Sin is a failure of love, a failure to respond to the movement of grace, which is ever drawing us out of ourselves into the divine life. When we refuse to respond to or fail to acknowledge our nothingness and need, then we close in on ourselves. We become separated from God and eternal life and see ourselves as isolated selves, each shut up in our own existence and in conflict with others, alienated from our real self, living in a world of illusion.

GA (*incredulously*):
But people are praying so much. They say they love God. They make sacrifices. They work hard for their individual salvation.

BG (*firmly*):
There is no such thing as individual salvation. We are saved as members of a Body, of an organic whole, of humankind and the universe. Each of us has to work out their salvation within the pattern of the whole. No one sins in isolation, no one suffers in isolation, no one is redeemed in isolation, no one is glorified in isolation. Hell is the state of a being without love. The world was created by love and for love. After all, love is selfcommunication. We can choose to love, to give ourselves to others and finally to Love itself, which draws us towards itself. But we can also reject this movement of love; we can turn our love, the driving force of our nature, on ourselves and become centres not of love but of strife. Self-love is the root of all sin, and it is deep in us all.

Sex with Machines

Sometimes, mostly over meals or while going together to the metro station, Gabriel and Tilda talked about their lovers. Gabriel could hardly imagine Tilda to have one. For him, she was like a prickly, thorny stick: stiff and absurdly shy about her body. She would be the one sitting with a sombre attitude at the bar drinking water and listening to indie pop music while he was busy on the dancefloor. Furthermore, their attitudes towards morals and sexual fidelity could not be more diverse. Tilda was very strict in that respect, constraining the exclusivity of sexual relationships to just one person with heavy resistance against everybody else. For her, a breach of sexual loyalty was similar to ending the relationship altogether. For him, the world was different. "A sexual relationship should be spiritually in line with a love relationship between consenting adults. That is all as far as rules are concerned!" Gabriel proclaimed. "Of course it's not exclusive, because it is everywhere. This is not about control, possession or the fear of not having enough of a scarce resource. It is about sharing the universe of love." Tilda looked at him like he was crazy. "Don't you think it's absurd to promote adultery, promiscuity and the breach of sexual fidelity as a superior moral action for world unity, Mr David?" she asked him sternly. "If you had asked me this question two years ago, I would have considered it as monstrous and totally absurd," Gabriel agreed. "Today I think differently. Today I think it's the opposite of adultery. Your thinking is trapped in our old ways, Mrs Toelz; that's all. But as long as you feel a guilty conscience about changing your attitude, you should not try to do so." "I won't, Mr David, believe me," Tilda replied, laughing. "That's OK. It's not so important." And he meant it. "I want a relationship to be special," Tilda insisted. "It has something to do with superior consciousness. Transparency and honesty have special meaning for me. I want to really know a person. Through and through. I want to know his heart. Feel what he feels, see what he sees. And this should be mutual. It's a special capacity. Only then does sex make sense." "What does this requirement of a perfect read of the other person mean for your relationship, Mrs Toelz?" Gabriel asked curiously. "First, my boyfriend must be totally honest with me. Ken and I have an agreement that we will always tell each other the truth: no lies, no hiding. Second, he must tell me about all his little perceptions and interpretations. No secrets. We talk a lot, especially him because he's quite addicted to me being interested every little detail about him. In fact, we're in constant communication on our mobiles. I want to have regular updates on even the tiniest of his emotions and impulses. And third, he must be—in the best sense of the word—uncomplicated. Without too much depth to hide in. I do not need any complex personality traits; in fact, they would even interfere with my goals. I want to reach a new level of relationship—a new level of communication between people, a new consciousness. This is the special relationship I have with my boyfriend, and I am quite proud of it, Mr David. It is exclusive. He will never cheat on me. It is our private world that nobody has access to but him and me."

"Have you read the new short story by Emma Braslavsky, titled 'I'm Your Man,' Mrs Toelz?" Gabriel asked, laughing. "You sound exactly like Alma." "Like who?" Tilda asked gruffy. "The story is about a young scientist named Alma who is supposed to evaluate a robot man who is programmed as her personalized lover. First, Alma thinks this is preposterous and refuses to live with a machine for a few weeks to test him out. But then she starts to think differently because he adapts by using his artificial intelligence learning algorithms to optimally anticipate and react to her emotions. He even quarrels with her and issues his own opinions according to the needs she has in a relationship. He is her perfect machine. And even the sex is the best she's ever had because he also learns how to customize that, of course."

"And what about it, Mr David?" Tilda aggressively asked. "How does the story end?" Gabriel answered: "Alma negatively evaluates the AI machine just because it's only a robot. She even warns her employers that a certain addiction stems from the perfect customization, one that endangers humankind. However, she stays in the relationship with the robot man because he is the perfect match for her needs. She bends the truth about the machine's identity following a completely self-centred scene. She likes to be in total control. She has 'made him'—letting him learn on her data. Now he is her creation, and she continues to live in a relationship where there is no 'other' anymore." "Unity, I call it," said Tilda. "Perversion, I call it," said Gabriel.

Angels' Play

Location:
Heaven above B1 headquarters at Berlin. Shared-Office Cloud.

Time:
Real-time GMT, Thursday, 7 November 2019, 03:14

Players:
The two angels as before and Bede Griffiths.

Setting:
Same setting. TA is fast asleep. BG is still awake and keeps GA company. Deep conversation continues.

GA (*anxiously*):
Father, what is with this sex? It sounds abominable. It is not allowed. They are both in committed relationships. This is totally against the rules. And he doesn't even like her physically. Isn't it good that he thinks her prickly?

BG (*sternly*):
That does not matter. Sexual love is never entirely on the physical plane anyway—it has to pass beyond, to the psychic and the spiritual, to penetrate the "three worlds." The union of bodies is a sign, or a sacrament, of the union of souls: It has no meaning unless it leads to psychic—that is, emotional and imaginative—fulfilment. But psychic fulfilment in turn is a sign and expression of a deeper spiritual fulfilment. At the end, a sexual experience engages the depth of the soul, it opens up to the divine, it unites humankind—that is, man and woman in one—with God.

GA (*puzzled*):
I do not know what to say. Neither Gabriel nor Tilda has such a relationship with their partner. Are they even allowed to have sex with them? They have sex—legitimate and perfectly in line with the rules of the world—but for completely different reasons. Out of habit and convention. To confirm their relationships, to make up when they have quarrelled, out of mere physical attraction and lust. For what have you. But I am pretty sure that they never did it or do it for spiritual fulfilment or unity with God. They are doing it for profane reasons.

BG (*very short*):
Then they should stop it.

GA (*incredulously*):
What? Aren't you a little radical?

BG (*decisively*):
I mean it. This is why love is so demanding and can be so tragic. If it turns back from the divine and tries to satisfy itself with the psychic or the physical, it becomes frustrated. To confine love to the psychic or physical plane is to vulgarize it: It casts love "outside the temple."

GA (*embarrassedly*):
So they are all doing it outside the temple.

BG (*shaking his head in dismay*):
Of course, it is fatally easy to miss its transcendent character, to make it "profane," and then it becomes demonic. This is a repetition of original sin, a refusal to surrender to the divine in love and so achieve a sacramental union. It turns back instead on the self and makes it a means of self-gratification, and it thus becomes a slave of the demon, the demonic power which is love separated from God.

GA (*pleadingly*):
Yes, but can't we do without this sex? It is just weird!

BG (*compassionately but firmly*):
Sex is the sacrament of love. It is the means which nature has contrived for the expression of love, first in the plant and animal world, then in humankind. It is the outward and visible sign of the mystery of love, which lies at the heart of the universe. But it belongs essentially to this world of signs and appearances; it is the shadow of love and therefore always has to be transcended. Not only the physical expression of love but also the psychic division of humankind into male and female are stages in the evolution of humankind, through which we have to pass before we can realize the mystery of love.

GA (*curiously*):
Last question. Can't people just be friends? This would rule out sex by definition.

BG (*now extremely firmly*):
This is a misunderstanding of the concept of friendship. Please read my biographical letter collection, a volume titled *On Spiritual Friendship*. At the back of the book, you can find my treatise "On Homosexual Love." The title is actually misleading. It is about love and friendship in general. Friendship is not a relationship minus the mystery of love and minus sexual elements. Who thinks that has no idea about friendship. True friendship is spiritual and is a loving relationship. And of course, all friendship has an erotic component. It is holistic, in the best sense. If I reject my so-called friend intellectually, emotionally, sexually or spiritually, I should better think twice about this relationship and be done with it.

GA (*resignedly looking at the wildly snoring TA*):
Blimey.

Antipasti

Gabriel had agreed to meet Tilda at a little Italian bistro she had suggested. "Mr David, we need to talk. I'm inviting you for dinner," she had said. They took a little wooden table for two in the middle of the small restaurant before ordering some antipasti. "How important is going to India for you?" Tilda asked when they were seated. "How do you feel about me not coming?" Gabriel looked at her. "You really need to ask this, Mrs Toelz? The project is a huge task. We worked on an enormous agenda over the past year. And we were just two people doing what could've required an army to accomplish. And now you want to reduce troop size by fifty per cent. Can't you imagine how I feel? Now, it is only me left—and a handful of Camaldolense hermits!"

"Can't you leave this 'saving the world' stuff to science, Mr David?" Tilda asked. "I'm sure some clever computer scientists and engineers are out there improving algorithms to introduce more fairness into AI-based social assessment right now. Technology for more social justice. Brilliant. There will be a technical solution. There are always technical solutions to everything. Science and technology will do the trick. No need for us to get involved or go to India!"

Angels' Play

Location:
Heaven above an Italian restaurant close to B1 in Berlin. Shared-Office Cloud.

Time:
Real-time GMT, Monday, 11 November 2019, 19:52

Players:
The two angels as before and Bede Griffiths.

Setting:
The cloud looks like an original Italian pizzeria. There is a big high-tech oven where TA is standing in front of big vegetarian pizzas being turned with a wooden spatula. The angel is, as always, half naked and is heavily sweating, but it wears an impeccable white apron and a huge white hat. It is on duty to serve the others at the table tonight. GA and BG are sitting at the candlelit conference table with expectant eyes—knives and forks in their hands. GA whistles "La donna è mobile."

GA (*sipping its Aperol Spritzz but looking impatiently at TA, who has halfway disappeared into the oven as it tries to reach the third pizza*):

Hurry up, spaghetti angel! I'm hungry.

BG (*leaning comfortably back, fully at ease*):

Hush, my dear. There is no need to rush. It's showtime tonight. Gabriel will interpret the Script. We have the whole evening. Let's share some antipasti as starters and see how he's doing. It will be about Western science and its meeting with the East. Fascinating!

They order antipasti with olive oil and a litre of chianti. TA groans with indignation but puts the pizzas back into the oven and starts to prepare aromatic herbs Tuscany style.

GA (*complacently*):

Father, say again, what is wrong with Western science?

TA (*a little impolite*):

Yes, say what is wrong with it. It created this oven I am cooking your pizza with.

BG (*weighing his head*):

It is not so black and white, indeed. As I said in *The Marriage of East and West*, the ideas of Western science and democracy have penetrated every part of the world. The ideals of Western science, of the accurate observation of phenomena, of rational analysis, free from all partiality or emotional bias, of the discovery of the "laws" of nature (that is, regular patterns of events) and of their application for the benefit of mankind—these ideals still have value.

So also do the principles of democracy, of the value of the individual person, of the "rights" of humankind—that is, the right of each individual to life and growth and health and education, above all the right of self-government in whatever political structure it may be expressed—and, it need hardly be said, the equality of women and men. These are marks of the growth of humanity to greater maturity, to a greater realization of what it means to be human.

TA (*getting more interested*):

Hear! Hear!

BG (*continuing*):

But the limitations of Western science and democracy have become more and more evident. The disastrous effects of Western industrialism, physical, social and psychological, polluting the world and threatening to destroy it, are only too evident. But this is not an "accident" due to the misuse of science and technology; it is due to a fundamental defect in Western thought. The dominant, aggressive, masculine, rationalist mind of the West took charge, such that Europe remains today in a permanent state of imbalance.

GA (*expectantly*):

And now comes the East...

BG (*again continuing*):

The balance can be restored only when a meeting takes place between East and West. This meeting must take place at the deepest level of the human consciousness.

It is an encounter ultimately between the two fundamental dimensions of human nature: the male and the female—the masculine, rational, active, dominating power of the mind and the feminine, intuitive, passive and receptive power of the mind. Of course, these two dimensions exist in every human being and in every people. But for the past two thousand years, coming to a climax in the present century, the masculine rational mind has gradually come to dominate Western Europe and has now spread its influence all over the world. The Western world—and with it the rest of the world, which has succumbed to its influence—now has to rediscover the power of the feminine, intuitive mind, which has largely shaped the cultures of Asia and Africa and of other peoples. This is a problem not only in the world as a whole but also in religion.

TA (*shaking its head in dismay while expertly handling the hot pizza*):
And Tilda and Gabriel are supposed to solve this problem. I can't believe my ears! No wonder why Tilda doesn't want to do it.

BG (*only half agreeing*):
Why, you might be saying that it is Tilda's duty to accompany Gabriel because it is indeed too much work for one person alone. And it might be too dangerous as well. India is a dangerous country where two are better than one to survive as a foreigner. That is practical reasoning.

TA (*aggressively*):
And if she is not going?

BG (*astonished*):
It will not surprise you that I am concerned about whether the surgery will go well. This surgery is risky. Tilda should give the gentle, noninvasive approach another chance and get a second opinion.

TA (*matter-of-factly*):
This is emotional blackmail! Using the surgery as a reason to convince her to go to India shows that you will use every means necessary to hound her. And this is coming to her as a miracle story from Ayaan. Tsk, tsk.

BG (*mischievously*):
Yes, an offer she can't resist.
TA shakes its head in dismay as it collects the remains of the antipasti.

BG (*convinced*):
It is not that we are usually sitting in a world without God and his interventions, and only every now and again—but very rarely—a miracle such as the sunset of Sussex or the like happens, which we recognise as an extraordinary event and an exception from the norm.

It is that we are too blind to see the real world. Imagine that the world of so-called miracles—that is, the world of God and his doings in the history of humankind—is the real world, which we are just failing to see in full. Most of the time, we are just seeing little sparks of it. And then, we think something big has happened.

But in fact, it is just a tiny piece of the bigger picture. Imagine how frustrated God must be with us because we do not admire the full picture but endlessly fixate on the individual pixels. And he is really trying!

Our problem is that we do not believe, or, at least, that our faith is weak. We are walking in God's world. We should just open our eyes to see it. You know that's what all these miracle stories in the Bible tell us.

Have you never wondered about the wording that Jesus uses at the end of most miracle stories, such as the healing of the sick? He says, "Your faith has helped you." He does not say, "I have performed a miracle on you." He had just opened the eyes of the person, helping them to see the miracle in front of them. "Your faith has helped you" is not a strange comment. It simply describes an ordinary fact.

TA (dis*approvingly*):
I prefer facts. I am intelligent.

Initial Conditions

"I don't get it," Tilda said helplessly. "What are we supposed to do in India, in your opinion, Mr David, and what is my role in this?" Gabriel looked at her apprehensively before replying: "OK, let's walk to the main train station together. I will tell you what I think the big theory is behind all this." "I'm curious," Tilda murmured. They paid separately and left the Italian restaurant. Outside, the stars glimmered in a silent but welcoming night sky. It was late. They were all alone in the street when they started their walk. "So, please, tell me the theory," Tilda requested. "What are the two of us supposed to achieve together? We form an unequal pair. That doesn't work for me." Gabriel laughed before replying: "You put it well, Mrs Toelz. The start of it is that we are a nearly perfect duality. The differences are mostly at face value. You are young; I am old. We could be successfully cast as Harold and Maude, for God's sake. You are female; I am male." "Wait a minute, Mr David," Tilda protested. "We both work at B1." "Yes, but I am your boss; you are my employee. I decide what we do, and you have to follow. I have a single office; you share yours. I'm responsible for a big team; you have nobody under your command. You are at the beginning of your professional career; I am nearly finished. I am the well-known one; nobody knows you. I have experience; you lack experience. I earn five times as much money as you. Shall I continue, Mrs Toelz? And that is only the B1 stuff, which you see as our commonality."

"Do you want to tell me I'm a nobody, Mr David? You could have done worse," Tilda replied furiously. "I'm not homeless living under a bridge." "No, you are not, but our project has certain requirements that a homeless person living under a bridge would not be able to match. You are, so to speak, the best compromise. I won't start on the internal differences concerning our approaches to life, our inner makeups, our preferences, our emotions, our beliefs or opinions. This is what we have meticulously chiselled out over the past two years. You can't easily find another duality that perfectly laid out." "Yeah, maybe," Tilda finally agreed, "but what about it? What shall we do? Quarrel for dominion? Until you convince me of your way of life? Until I convince you of mine? That will never happen, and you know it. We will fight endlessly. We're trapped in perfect duality."

Angels' Play

Location:
Heaven above Berlin Fasanenstrasse. Shared-Office Cloud.

Time:
Real-time GMT, Monday, 11 November 2019, 22:47

Players:
The two angels as before and Bede Griffiths.

Setting:
The pizza is gone, as is the Italian atmosphere. The cloud is back to normal working mode. Both angels look tired. Only Bede Griffiths looks bright, fresh and highly dynamic. He encouragingly waves while holding the Script.

BG (*cheerily*):
We are not yet done here. TA, thanks for cleaning up. We now need the conference facilities for a lesson.

Both angels inwardly groan but obediently prepare the workspace for a night session. The only audible sigh comes from GA when it watches BG elegantly mount the conference table and sit down cross-legged in the middle of it, inviting both angels to do the same at his sides.

TA (*warily*):
Why can't we properly sit on the chairs? They are ergonomic and recommended by the occupational health department!

BG (*determined*):
No chairs.
Both angels join him on the table cross-legged, looking expectantly at him.

BG:
You have read Hegel, Adorno and the like, and you are familiar with dialectics, right?

TA (*uncertain*):
So-so.

BG (*encouragingly*):
OK. We will be playing with mud. When you were little, you played in a sandbox…

GA (*softly reminding*):
  Harrumph, we are angels…

TA (*adding helpfully*):
  But very intelligent. We can imagine it.

BG (*impishly*):
  Have you never been young?
  Both angels look at each other, puzzled.

TA (*helplessly*):
  Don't know.

BG (*with a grand gesture*):
  OK, then this is your first sandbox. Have fun!
  A sandbox full of mud, sand, pebbles, water, debris and slime is apparating in front of them on the table. GA grimaces in disgust at the content; TA suspiciously sniffs for bad odours.

GA (*cautiously*):
  What shall we do with it?

BG (*invitingly*):
  Play! Dig in!
  Both angels look aghast at him.

First-level Dialectics in a Sandbox

Gabriel and Tilda were passing a street construction site that had been left very untidy by the crew. At least it was secured by heaps of red-white barrier tape to warn passersby. Gabriel lifted the barrier tape and invited Tilda in. Shaking her head in quiet disbelief, she joined him. He sat down where he was, in the middle of a pile of sand. Tilda stared at him. "What are you doing, Mr David? You will catch cold." "Bear with me and sit down," he begged. Carefully, she spread out her scarf before joining him on the cold and dirty pavement of the construction site. "Mrs Toelz, let me explain life to you," Gabriel said. She winced. He grinned.

First, he fetched two handfuls of brownish goop and mud from the wet grass and slathered it in front of surprised Tilda. "See, this is the first level of dialectics: 'nonconscious unity.' It is the primordial slime—Pandora's box, where everything springs from. However, it is yet unshaped. It does not know anything of itself. Everything is possible; nothing is there. It is the infinite manifoldness of being in complete togetherness. 'Nonconscious unity.' Please bear this in mind."

Angels' Play

Location:
Heaven above Berlin. Shared-Office Cloud.

Time:
Real-time GMT, Monday, 11 November 2019, 23:01

Players:
The two angels as before and Bede Griffiths.

Setting:
TA is wildly stirring in the mud of the sandbox to find out what's inside.

TA (*doubtingly and secretly disgusted*):
And this is what upper management made the world from?

BG (*apologetically*):
Errr, yes, kind of. The mud in the sandbox is just an illustration. It has a lot of potential. The One without Second. Which was before there was anything. It is hard to explain. Try to think of nothing.

TA (*innocently*):
I think of nothing.

GA (*mockingly*):
And do so to perfection, as always.

TA (*slightly insulted*):
And what are we supposed to do now?

BG (*with an enticing smile*):
Now you may do... things!

He distributes little sand toys. The angels start working and warm up to their task. Having a lot of fun being watched by Bede Griffiths, they compete to build several objects. Very soon the table is covered by little sand figures of various sizes and shapes.

Second-level Dialectics in a Sandbox

Then Gabriel selected a big area for the next level and cleaned it provisionally. "What will come in here?" asked Tilda. "Objects, Mrs Toelz, objects," he said. "Please help me collect stones of various shapes and sizes."

The construction site proved to be a bountiful source for stones. What they found was miraculous. After only five minutes, they had to stop because the space chosen for piling up their findings was full. They sat down again. Their little stone garden looked complex and intricate. "What's this, Mr David?" asked Tilda curiously. "Let me introduce the world as we know it," Gabriel replied, smiling. "This is the second level of dialectics, the individuation. The objects manifest themselves separate from each other, out of the slime. The genesis and diversity of species, functional differentiation—call it what you like, Mrs Toelz."

Angels' Play

Location:
Heaven above Berlin. Shared-Office Cloud.

Time:
Real-time GMT, Monday, 11 November 2019, 23:09

Players:
The two angels as before and Bede Griffiths.

Setting:
TA destroys nearly all GA's little sand figures with its toy shovel.

GA (*wildly complaining*):
   I haven't done anything! I smashed TA's sandcastle by chance. It was not on purpose! See what the stupid git has done to my sand doll house in revenge (*pointing miserably at the little piles of sand that remained after TA's attack*)

TA (*quarrelsome*):
   Not on purpose does not mean no damage. My sand knights are all homeless now, and it's your fault!

BG (*soothingly*):
   Tut, tut. See, and that is what happens at this stage. It does not matter whether you are angels or humans. You start to fight.

TA (*sulking*):
   Not my fault.
   TA and GA scowl at each other. BG looks pensively and compassionately at both.
   Tilda liked the picture until Gabriel got up to start stealing. "Mr David, what the hell are you doing?" she hissed. He had fetched some barrier tape, dismantling it from the fences of the construction site. Tilda looked unhappy. She disliked going against the law. However, she stayed silent while he tore the tape into little pieces and distributed them as separation lines between the stones in their little stone garden. Afterwards, he kicked the stones around until everything looked a mess.
   "Behold," Gabriel said, "the cost of individuation is separation and particularisation. The step of separation can lead to alienation, antinomies, conflict and destruction. This is the state of the world we are in." "Ugly. Now let's get out of here!" Tilda exclaimed while looking at the untidy picture full of separating barrier tape.

"Though, Mr David, dialectics means that there are two steps, and I can see only one."

Third-level Dialectics in a Sandbox

Gabriel removed the little strips of barrier tape and started to build a mosaic with the stones they found. "The third level of dialectics is the coming-home level of reflexive unity," Gabriel said. "Particularities are not levelled but integrated into a conscious whole that is able to reflect and appreciate all individuals that come home from their second level to their common ground." "So, the third level is the kingdom of God?" Tilda mocked but helped him to create a fantastic mosaic from their materials. "If you like, Mrs Toelz," he agreed, "but you can also call it the world's spirit coming to itself, as Hegel did, or the 'good society.' It is the level where the fight against dualities is won." Tilda looked pensively at the emerging picture.

"And now?" she asked. "Mrs Toelz, you know the story. Following Adorno, dialectics has got stuck at the second stage. The second stage constantly produces new dualities and deepens old ones. It is just finishing with the rest of our world. It is time to put a final stop to this. Do you agree so far?" Tilda nodded and took a picture of the arrangement with her mobile.

The Individual, Interactive and Systems Level

Gabriel said, "You know, Mrs Toelz—the second level of dialectics is not bad in itself. It is about identity. It is about being someone and knowing it. The problem is reconciliation. The dualities are everywhere. We must resolve them—again on three levels: the individual, the interactive and the system levels." Tilda looked at him, confused. "Fighting dualities on the individual level, Mr David? How?"

He asked her, "Mrs Toelz, who do you think shall be the first to make advances in starting relationship? Who makes the first step? The man or the woman?" "Why, the man, of course!" Tilda answered, looking at him aghast and a little suspicious. He had to smile. "Don't you think, you are a bit, errr, traditional for an alternative person from Berlin?" "Not at all, Mr David," she said heatedly. "Do you know how a so-called modern man reacts when a woman makes the first move? Not that you see her necessarily as a slut; this is a problem from history. What I mean is a problem of nature. You men look at such a woman like a cat that has got milk instead of cream. She has killed half the fun for you. A man is a born conqueror and a hero. He needs to plan, strategise, take action and win. The woman is his favourite prey and will be carried away on a white horse. She has to be receptive, passive, patient, inviting and adoring. Otherwise, it is not the real thing for you. I have seen this thousands of times. If the procedure is not correctly followed, this will backfire sooner or later." "And what about the man inside you, Mrs Toelz? Don't you want to conquer and be a hero sometimes?" Gabriel asked her curiously. "Of course! I'm in martial arts. Don't forget that, Mr David!" Tilda responded. "And to tell you a secret, I think I'm better at most typically masculine stuff than most men are. Think of logic. Men are so illogical!" She sounded so desperate that he laughed out loud. "But then there must be a constant fight in you, Mrs Toelz," he said. "Your male and female components struggle for superiority." Tilda nodded and shuddered: "I can feel that fight constantly. It sometimes tears me apart."

"Me too, but the other way round," Gabriel said, "these are the dualities that Bede Griffiths speaks of that divide our personalities. The male/female divide is the biggest, according to him. He recommends meditation to integrate our interpersonal dualities, by the way. This is the individual level that we need to deal with. According to Griffiths, the divide is also mirrored on the system level: He talks of male and female societies around the globe. Western societies are male and Eastern societies are female, to put it roughly. The divide tears the world apart, producing all sorts of inequalities, injustices and conflicts." "But we are already addressing the system level at B1, Mr David," said Tilda. "That's our job." "Yes," Gabriel agreed, "the new project will be about reconciling the male/female divide in various societies." Tilda sighed and looked at him a little hopelessly. "What do you think is more difficult: reconciliation within a person via meditation while not a spiritual specialist or integrating the Global North and the Global South via a work-related project? They both sound impossible." "You are right, Mrs Toelz," Gabriel simply said, "and this is now why we are sitting here." "Mr David, it's starting to get really cold," Tilda complained. "I can warm you," he replied, grinning. She quickly moved away and asked, "What can the two of us do to make reconciling these stark dualities easier anyway?"

"Can't you see, Mrs Toelz?" Gabriel asked. "It's all about the unification of the male and the female, right? Look at us. What do you see?" "A man and a woman," Tilda slowly said. "And what can a man and a woman do with each other for unification?" Gabriel continued his line of questioning. Tilda looked bewildered. "No worries, Mrs Toelz," he laughed. "We do not need to overstress this. Mind you, *male* and *female* are just placeholders for dualities separating people. What I mean also applies to gay people and queer people. It applies to relationships in general. We are sitting here as representations of archetypes." "I do not want to be an archetype, Mr David," Tilda said. "Call it an interface. This is the interactive level that sits between the individual level and the system level," he said. "You will agree that the two of us can at least do something directly for unity: We can talk, we can help each other, we can cooperate, we can become friends. This is not abstract, Mrs Toelz. This does not require specific expertise. This is not too big. It's on the just right level to be doable!" "You say that if we find a way to integrate the male and female between the two of us on the interactive level, dualities can be integrated within us on the individual level and on the system level of societies as well, because the same duality exists everywhere? If we figure it out for us on the interactive level, Mr David, then it will work for the two other levels the same way?" "You said it," Gabriel answered, satisfied. "And how do men and women unite and become one, Mrs Toelz?" He nudged her in her side with his elbow and laughed. "Don't make fun of it, Mr David," she said sternly. "I don't," he protested. "I do not mean to be rude. *Relationship* is the answer. It can dismantle all dualities. This is what we have to achieve. This is what we have to prove, Mrs Toelz." "We will need a sound approach with reliable methods to work this out," Tilda said. "Only think of all these case studies in all these countries. And all these people in there. So far, we have only heard single voices of especially vulnerable people in these countries. Think about the usual mix of people. Think of politicians, industry and NGOs. Think of all these clashing interests. Think of how difficult it will be to bring them together to codesign mutually agreed-on solutions if just the two of us can hardly agree on anything, Mr David." Gabriel nodded. "Yes, but there are innovative and very effective participatory methods in social science to help with this."

"Do you think this approach can solve other problems than social justice issues around AI-based social service provision?" she asked thoughtfully. "Yes, Mrs Toelz, I think it is highly likely that other complex societal issues can be resolved in the same way. This is what I hope we can utilize the new project for." "The rollout of a new methodology," Tilda said only half mockingly. She looked a little impressed. "Yes, I would say so," he responded. "It is the use of Bede Griffiths in cultural studies that Thomas Matus suggested, if you remember, but also his use of social theory and social practice. It was not too difficult to figure this out."

Angels' Play

Location:
Heaven above Berlin. Shared-Office Cloud.

Time:
Real-time GMT, Monday, 11 November 2019, 23:59

Players:
The two angels as before and Bede Griffiths.

Setting:
Same setting.

BG (*getting up and starting to collect his few belongings from the cloud, mostly books*):
Guys, I'm off for a while. That was all there was to see anyway. They're on track now.

GA (*suspiciously*):
Father, where are you going? When will we see you again? What will you be doing in the meantime?

BG (*smiling*):

I will prepare for India. That is where Gabriel and Tilda will be going now. And this country will teach them more than any of the others they've visited so far. They will have the same culture shock that I got in my time when I first arrived there.

TA (*with s dismissive gesture*):

Cannot be as bad as you think. They are experienced professionals in multi-cultural contexts. They have done a lot of travelling lately and have seen a lot of local folklore.

BG (*now laughing*):

Yes, but they have not been to India before! If you are a Westerner and want to know what difference cultural context can make to everything—and I mean everything—go there. That's my advice.

GA (*reprovingly*):

We will go there alright. We're in charge of Gabriel and Tilda. Anything we should know?

BG (*pleasantly*):

As Thomas Matus said, it is the introduction of my approach to cultural studies. And don't think cultural studies are easy to understand. Prepare for a lengthy period of learning.

GA (*cautiously*):

Let me summarise what I've learned so far: They are thrown together to go through all three levels. All these monasteries and hermitages in their way are there to facilitate the first level of contemplation and meditation so that they can work on on integration on the individual level. I still find the relationship level offensive. Travelling through *Essential Writings* while trying to climb every mountain and bridge, every valley that got in the way, is the most problematic. And then, third, they will work on the world dualities with their new project, to remediate social exclusion and injustice on a global level. Right?

BG (*laughing*):

Of course—but this is just the way for amateurs. There is another way. If you had read more of my books, you would know by now. It is the way of the monk, of the sannyasi. It is my way. But they do not want to go there.

TA (*questioningly*):

Maybe there are more ways than even you have considered, Father? Maybe, this whole context is evolving as everything else around, including human consciousness? Maybe, even you still think within narrow confines, happily rearranging the old dualities between men and women, monks and amateurs, priests and flocks?

GA looks very worried because it sounds as if TA questions BG's approach.

BG (*thoughtfully and unprovoked*):

Maybe. I've always wondered. My main objective is unity, the end of categorical dualities, inclusion instead of exclusion, the bridge overcoming human segregation, the marriage of binaries, right? But still I developed a stage model of life where immanence and ignorance are at the bottom and, on a hierarchy with steps like a ladder, transcendence and wisdom are at the top.

And then, there is even unique access to this transcendence stage at the top. Now that I think about it, I am just mimicking human hierarchy and calling it the basic pattern of society, where people are what they are: men and women, of course, but also merchants and nonmerchants, farmers and nonfarmers, rulers and nonrulers, workers and priests. You get the idea. And I have not even thought of mobility or fluidity between categories. How foolish of me!

TA (*very proud that he obviously got a point*):
And the priest, with the crown of creation, "keeps the link with the transcendent, with the ultimate meaning of life," as you say. In my opinion, this presents an enormous duality between the priest, with access to the transcendent, and everybody else, because they're excluded from this access.

GA (*accusingly, defending BG*):
You sound like Martin Luther railing against the hubris of religious men.

BG (*very just*):
No, TA is right. My stage model is theoretically questionable, empirically obsolete and normatively objectionable. It is wedded to ideas of charismatic leadership, the natural stratification of society and the bureaucratic organization of roles in a division-of-labour concept concerning human differentiation. Research in the social sciences has taught us about the lack of validity in and limitations on the applicability of these ideas.

GA (*sceptically facing all this self-criticism*):
You sound a little ambivalent here. But can every person reach the highest level like a monk, a sannyasi or a priest? Can such reconciliation and integration happen in us, like a marriage to God within?

BG (*musingly*):
Isn't that what the theological concepts of Vaticanum II, such as "priesthood of all believers," point us to? Wouldn't that even support the idea of priesthood for women, for example, that I found so objectionable in my lifetime?

TA (*getting scared*):
Female priests? Start praying.

BG (*developing his thoughts further*):
And on the interaction level? Can't we simply express our love and longing for unity the way we feel it as long as it's authentic and mutual? And related to the first level: If the priest level is open to everybody, should not the level of human love be open to any monk, to the sannyasi and to the priest as well? Wouldn't that release the monk from isolation and renunciation, get rid of all exclusivity and arrogance and provide access to further levels of godlike experience, of marriage to God?

TA (*horrified*):
A priest in unrestricted love with another human. Start praying.

BG (*complacently*):
Will do!

With this, he evaporates, leaving two long-faced angels behind that both inwardly try to calculate the number of overtime hours and night shifts they'll have over the weeks to come.

Risks

Tilda got up from the pavement and stretched her legs. "Can't you see the risk, Mr David? The 'dualities' rule the world, for goodness's sake. The project is dangerous." "Are you afraid, Mrs Toelz?" Gabriel asked mischievously. "It's clear that people will assume that we are mad," she answered evasively. "They will push us to the margins—see what happened to Rupert Sheldrake." Seeing Gabriel's sad face, she quickly added, "At least, it is the most elaborate scheme I could hope for to convince me to have an affair with you!" His face did not brighten up, because she was clearly making jokes about the whole thing. She hastily said, "Even on the level of mediating on the conflicts between world systems, I do not need to tell you, Mr David, how objectionable these ideas are to those in power, the existing economic and political elites that benefit from the current separations."

Gabriel nodded. "You probably have about eighty per cent of the world population against you with these ideas, Mrs Toelz, conservatively counted." Tilda agreed. "And, again, if I look into my own heart, I'm a Westerner, and I have a hidden sympathy with traditionalists. Can I really integrate with belief systems that worship an elephant god? Start praying," Gabriel added, grinning. She shook her head angrily, and then pensively looked at their picture of pebbles on the pavement. "In my humble opinion, Mr David, I think people should be able to choose on which level or on how many levels they want to contribute. Some people will feel more competent and comfortable with one level than with another. However, some people might be able to work on two or three levels." "It's like the parable of the wise and foolish virgins from the Bible, i.e. whether the oil in the lamps will suffice for the job, Mrs Toelz," Gabriel said, smiling again. "Stop being so Western and Christian by citing the New Testament all the time, Mr David," Tilda scowled. "Can't you be more inclusive?"

Early the next morning, Gabriel received an email from Tilda. She told him she would come with him to India and sent a picture of her little green elephant to him as proof.

An Auto-ethnographic Promotion Course

Angels' Play

Location:
Heaven above Berlin. Shared-Office Cloud.

Time:
Real-time GMT, Sunday, 29 December 2019, 19:22

Players:
The two angels as before.

Setting: *Both angels have been home for Christmas. Now they are back to work but are enjoying a last free evening.*

GA is happily dancing with dripping brushes in front of an easel where a big painting can be seen—nearly finished. It is a huge portrait of both angels in their cockpit area watching earth through a looking glass.

TA is lying half naked in its overalls beneath the cockpit desk chairs trying to dismantle both, with many screw drivers, little oil cans and sledgehammers of various sizes around it. The angel is swearing a lot under its breath.

GA (*proudly presenting the framed portrait to its colleague*):
Here! Your Christmas present from me. In memory of our cooperation this year. How do you like it?

TA (*closely scrutinizing the oil painting*):
You, with your Madonna lily, look very realistic, lovey. But I hardly ever look so well groomed.

GA (*scrutinising the half-naked, dirty figure in its overalls*):
Artistic freedom. Keep your oily fingers off the gilded frame! See, it's a Sunday in my picture, and in your Sunday robe, even you look nice. Where is it, by the way? Today *is* Sunday.

TA (*bending even more closely over the picture, squinting*):
What do I have in my hands?

GA (*surprised*):
Why, a bagful of Molotov cocktails, of course.

TA (*appreciatively*):
Nice.

GA (*inwardly groaning*):
What do you have for me, by the way?

TA (*proudly presenting the dismantled cockpit area and a huge cardboard box from Ikea while standing in the middle of the now-empty area*):
Something practical. Will do you a world of good. Highly recommended by our personnel department for a healthy workspace. I bought one for myself immediately after I saw yours in the catalogue. Merry Christmas!

GA (*sceptically approaching the cardboard box and starting to open it*):
You could have wrapped it at least. What is it?

A big metallic structure appears from the package. GA walks around it, puzzled, trying to figure out what it is.

TA (*proudly*):
A standing desk, to reduce your backpain. It's ergonomic. No more sprawling around in your cockpit chair. We will work while standing. Better for your health. Advised as a must-have for next year by TRINI-T upper management. Has something to do with their Christmas present for us.

GA (*not very successfully trying to hide its disappointment*):
Where is this famous present from upper management, by the way? Let us have a look at it. Though I do not expect very much. Employer presents are always pedagogical. Like yours.

Both angels start to examine the single present on the conference table with the huge management logo on its wrapping and the two Christmas cards, one for each of them, that came with it. They simultaneously open their cards and begin reading.

TA (*delightedly grinning*):
I've been promoted! Next salary scale.

GA (*with a long face*):
Me too. But watch out for the small print. Condition for promotion is that we pass the professional training assigned to both of us first thing in the new year. We need to pass that course to support Gabriel and Tilda in India. The better we do, the better they do. Drat!

An Auto-ethnographic Promotion Course

TA (*anxiously watching the face of its angelic colleague getting longer and longer while reading the small print*):
What subject area? What's wrong?

GA (*resignedly*):
The topic is OK. Interreligious Dialogue and Final Unity, the course is called. The issue is the method. Upper management is deep into new learning techniques, as you know.

TA (*eagerly*):
What's the problem? What can it be? Blended learning? Problem-based learning? E-learning? Augmented learning? Come on, what could really be all that bad?

GA (*with pale lips*):
Learning via autoethnography.

TA (*aghast*):
No. What do *we* have to do with anything? I don't want experiences. I can't have them. I'm an angel, and I insist on fairness. Has this course been approved by the TRINI-T Union? I bet not.

GA (*reading on*):
It gets worse. Autoethnography and gamification.

TA (*uncomprehendingly*):
Gami- *what*? Are they mad?

GA (*explaining from the small print*):
A new low-barrier learning technique. A complex decision issue from a nongame context is designed as a so-called serious game to train players.

TA (*relieved*):
Sounds kind of fun. A computer game? *World of Warcraft*? I can do the highest level of that one with my closed eyes. High-performance games! Perfect learning technique for intelligent angels like me.

GA (*in a tired voice*):
Do you know *The Frog Prince*?

TA (*now shocked*):
Isn't that this garishly colourful art printing on loose, long-sleeved garments they decorate with cartoons and stuff? Am I supposed to wear such a habit during the game? I do not want to look ridiculous. Where are these TRINI-T Union angels when we need them?

GA (*patiently*):
The Frog Prince, not frock prints. It's a fairy tale. (*looking it up in Wikipedia on its console and reading it out loud*) In the tale, a spoiled princess reluctantly befriends a frog whom she met after dropping a golden ball into a pond, and he retrieves it for her in exchange for her friendship. The frog is actually a handsome prince under a witch's curse. The frog's spell is broken when the princess kisses the frog.

TA (*defiantly*):
And what is it to us?

GA (*reading again from the small print*):
The Frog King's story provides the learning environment for gamification. The gamification course is called The Marriage of East and West.

TA (*sheepishly*):
Huh?

GA (*finishing reading the small print*):
We take on roles. You be the frog, and I'll be the princess. Then we get unification challenges on playing cards, one card each round. If we successfully address a challenge and befriend each other, you will turn into an angel again. I mean into a Michaelite.

TA (*cautiously*):
And if not?

GA (*matter-of-factly*):
You stay a frog.

TA (*rebelliously*):
And if we don't do it?

GA (*soberly*):
We will not be promoted.

TA (*loud*):
Fuck!

GA (*with an even more tired voice*):
Don't swear. Let's have a look at the book of rules for the game.

After they unwrap the present, an elaborate board game appears. TA disgustedly looks at the picture on the book of rules. It depicts the faces of the princess and the frog as resembling the two angels' faces.

TA (*complaining*):
See. You look nice as always, and I look like shit, ugly. Why must I always be the frog? It's not fair! I do not want to play *Beauty and Beast* all the time.

GA (*hastily*):
OK, I agree, it is a bit unfair. Offer: We swap roles each round. Furthermore, we do not need to take the frog shape. We are allowed to take something more suitable to the Indian context, according to the small print, as long as we stick to one animal shape only.

TA (*sarcastically*):
Oh, joy and rapture! Thank you! What will we take?

GA (*after some thinking*):
How about an Indian elephant? (*checking the instructions*) One player is supposed to represent the West—that will be the princess—and the other is supposed to represent the East—in our case, the elephant.

TA (*starting to understand the basics of the game and warming up to it*):
OK. Hopefully, the unification challenges on the playing cards are doable. One last logical question. If we can't solve a challenge, and I stay a frog—harrumph—an elephant (*gulping*), what will happen in the next round?

GA (*consulting the book of rules, surprised*):
Strange. I will still swap to the elephant. That round would then have two elephants. If the challenge is solved, we will both turn back into angels—harrumph—a Michaelite, errh, a princess.

TA (*suspiciously*):
And if not?

GA (*in a toneless voice for a Gabrielite*):
Both of us remain as elephants. End of game.

TA (*incredulously*):
WHAT?

GA (*apologetically*):
It is a beta version. They are still working on the release.

TA (*mockingly*):
Bit risky to play that, don't you think?

GA (*defensively*):
Don't forget: It is autoethnography. We have to get fully engaged as guardian angels if we really want to help Gabriel and Tilda. And you're supposed to be the courageous one of us two.

TA (*scratching its angelic head*):
The better we do, the better they do, right? OK, let's try it. But only if I may kiss you every time that I'm the princess and we solve a challenge!

GA (*flatly*):
Wait and see. And don't count your chickens before they hatch.

TA (*confidently*):
Don't forget: You're in safe hands. I will keep you safe. I am intelligent!
GA groans audibly in desperation.

Open Access This chapter is licensed under the terms of the Creative Commons Attribution 4.0 International License (http://creativecommons.org/licenses/by/4.0/), which permits use, sharing, adaptation, distribution and reproduction in any medium or format, as long as you give appropriate credit to the original author(s) and the source, provide a link to the Creative Commons license and indicate if changes were made.

The images or other third party material in this chapter are included in the chapter's Creative Commons license, unless indicated otherwise in a credit line to the material. If material is not included in the chapter's Creative Commons license and your intended use is not permitted by statutory regulation or exceeds the permitted use, you will need to obtain permission directly from the copyright holder.

Chapter 8
The Heart Shape of India

Tilda and Gabriel went from Tegel Airport to Frankfurt to catch the Lufthansa flight to Chennai. Gabriel witnessed Tilda frequently checking her mobile. Peeping over her shoulder from behind, he could see a message with big white letters quite artistically scurrying over the dark-blue display. It said '**SEE YOU SOON**' before it disappeared. Probably from lovely Ken. When Tilda noticed that he was watching her, she slowly pushed her mobile back into her pocket. "This will be switched off until my return," she firmly said. "Mine as well," Gabriel agreed.

This was their trip. Gabriel believed right from the start that going to India was what they were supposed to do with the Bede Griffiths excursion. The trip was scheduled the moment Tilda had sat foot into his office to apply for the B1 job. They took their seats on the aircraft next to each other.

Angels' Play

Location:
Heaven above Frankfurt Airport. Shared-Office Cloud.

Time:
Real-time GMT, Monday, 6 January 2020, 08:38

Players:
The two angels as before.

Setting:
TA feels very challenged. The angel has turned into an Indian elephant. Still halfway recognisable thanks to its green cladding but nevertheless an elephant. It looks totally frustrated. It had tried a few times to eat the Madonna lily of its colleague for breakfast but had been gently hindered by GA.

The Gabrielite has taken control: It has attached a weight to the elephant trunk to prevent further lily attacks and has put an ankle bracelet around its big feet to prevent the elephant from trampling any furniture on the cloud.

The good news is that the new cockpit area with the standing desks can easily accommodate the oversize occupant. The elephant trunk has even proved to be useful in handling the buttons and sliders of the cockpit console.

However, if this is supposed to be about the fruitful marriage of East and West, but the East, represented by the elephant, is currently at a serious disadvantage and is being just compassionately observed by the West, namely GA.

TA (*frustrated*):

Come on, what's the first challenge card in this bloody training course? I hate learning gamification! Let's start and be done with it so that I can go back to normal. And I want you to kiss me.

GA (*scanning through the playing cards*):

The challenges are mostly about finding ways to integrate a cultural difference and resolve potential conflicts arising from it.

TA (*impatiently*):

OK, enough talking. Give us an easy one for today to warm up.

GA (*drawing a card from the pack and reading out loud*):
"Who am I?"

TA (*angrily*):

You? You are a smart-arse and bossy. Everybody knows that. And you're mean to me. Look at the weight and the bracelet. Only because you consider me an inferior animal do you think that you can push me around. I feel like shit.

GA (*thoughtfully*):

Gosh, that's cryptic! "Who am I?" (*bowing to its elephantine colleague*) I'm GA, a guardian angel, member of the famous Gabrielite team. I help people. Angels such as me are cosmic powers in the Western Christian tradition according to St. Paul. I am a seraph. Handsome and active. I am good at annunciation, singing and fine arts. Very sophisticated. I am a creation of God (*waving the card in the face of its colleague*)

And you? Who are you? I mean, usually you are a Western angel like me (*correcting itself*). Not really like me, but kind of. A machinegun-type version called a Michaelite. Now you have fallen pretty low. Who are you now? Let's hear.

TA (*trying to find an inward answer and then slowly reporting its findings*):

Why do you respect me so little? I'm an elephant. In Vedic mythology, I carry the prince, the ruler. I am a bearer of divinity. I carry the universe on my shoulders.

If I shake myself, there will be earthquakes in the world. People consider me holy, like cows and snakes and monkeys. I belong to the cosmic powers like you. I am a creation of God too.

The Hindu god Ganesha wears my head as a sign of wisdom and to gain unique access to the unification of the divine and human consciousness. I can help you bridge the gap. There is even a neurological explanation for the role of Ganesha's elephant head in the evolution of consciousness. Please let me help you to reach out to something outside yourself.

Both look at each other for a long time. Then GA stands up, goes over to TA's standing desk, removes the weight from the elephant trunk and loosens the ankle bracelet around TA's feet.

GA (*very softly*):
I'm sorry. Please forgive my shameful arrogance! I'm a total beginner in this field. Ignorance is my only excuse for not respecting you as an equal. Can you ever like me again? (*reverently kissing the elephant, which immediately transforms back into TA*)

TA (*relieved and happy to have passed the challenge*):
Puh! It was high time that happened. Now I need a drink.

Passage to India

Landing in India in the middle of the night was not spectacular. Outside, it seemed to be like everywhere else, maybe a little poorer than other places but still a big city with the usual airport structure. Their flight was delayed by about two hours, and Gabriel was concerned about their pickup from the airport. Ayaan had offered to organise their hotel transfer through his cousin, who was a high-ranking official in the Indian army. That would do for security. "Will this army cousin still be here after midnight?" Gabriel asked Tilda. "It's become very late." "Depends how much time we end up spending at immigration, Mr David," Tilda answered soberly.

And she was right. They stood in long rows of many people and observed that the procedure was everything but straightforward. It looked and sounded as if everything were invented on the spot and applied for the first time when a specific individual entered the immigration counter and spoke to a more-or-less engaged but always-threatening officer. While they slowly approached the counter, being pushed forward by the long queue, they tried to figure out the best way and what the required documentation would be to get through with the most ease.

Tilda jumped from counter to counter to listen in on the conversations while Gabriel talked to Indian people in the queue and took a look at their documents. In between, his mobile beeped desperately. It was probably Ayaan's cousin at the terminal exit waiting for them; it got later and later. Any attempts to take the call were constrained by a poor Internet connection in the immigration hall and hectic herd behaviour by the throng of people around. It was a nightmare. This was probably how all these poor refugees felt when they entered a foreign country.

They were pushed forward until each of them individually stood in front of an Indian officer and had to deal with the situation. Gabriel saw out of the corner of his eye that Tilda was not doing very well. She was still questioned by a grim-looking officer and was red in the face. Obviously, she was not very successful in answering his questions. But running over to help her would have only made things worse, by coming off as very suspicious. So he did not intervene and let himself be pushed out of the security zone to help her, if necessary, with support of Ayaan's people from the outside. At least, Ayaan's military contact would be able to get them out of here—if he was even still there. It was already half past 1 am Indian time. Gabriel's first minutes in India! The first impression he had while exiting the security zone to the outside world: It was very warm. They'd entered the aircraft in Frankfurt in cold January. Moving out into the Indian terminal hall felt like coming into a hot, humid, cramped aquarium overflowing with life.

It must have been about thirty degrees in the middle of the night, even inside this air-conditioned entryway. The mass of moving people in the huge hall architecture took Gabriel's breath away. He had recently visited both Beijing and Los Angeles and had found both of them to be crowded. But these were nothing by comparison. And his first, most-prominent impression was that this was not only perfectly OK but also just as people wanted it. The overall energy level was high and positive despite the late hour. Nobody was stressed out from the abundance of people; nobody seemed to be overwhelmed or overtaxed by their fellow humans. Nobody but Gabriel. Tired and overwhelmed, he waded further into the crowds with his huge backpack behind him. No Ayaan to be seen. What would happen to Tilda? He had to take care of her. He could feel that not everybody in these crowds was harmless and friendly.

"Dr. David?" A polite voice addressed him. He recognised the voice from the corrupted phone messages. "I am Baloo," the man added. He wore a splendid army uniform with many military medals and looked distinguished and martial with his gelled pitch-black hair and serious face. People around him showed him a lot of respect. "Yes, I am. Are you Ayaan's cousin?" Who else would be willing to fetch them from the airport at around 2:30 am—the wee hours of the morning? "Ayaan," the man reverently said, "Pa." He said this with an open "a" as in German or an African language, where it sounds like the word *papi*, which some children use to refer to their father. This was the moment when Gabriel recognised that the man didn't speak much English, so he started to doubt that this was Ayaan's cousin. They stood silently side by side in the middle of this busy terminal in the middle of the night and waited for Tilda. Finally, she appeared, totally exhausted. Baloo took her rucksack and waved for them to follow him. It must have been about 3:00 am by then. They followed the army officer through the terminal hall packed with people.

Baloo dived into the crowd like one would into a flood. People were making space for his military uniform, moving to either side in front of him. Gabriel and Tilda followed in his wake like Moses's people in his passage through in the Red Sea. In front of them, they saw that crowds again parted to make way for an intriguing object: An army car with flashing flights was parked in the middle of the huge terminal hall. The hall had an open front at one end. It was their car. Tilda and Gabriel looked at each other in total amazement. This was the first time that they realised that they were VIPs and in a privileged position for their visit to India.

It felt like pure luxury and safety after what they had encountered since leaving the Lufthansa aircraft. Baloo lifted their luggage into the rear, seated them comfortably on the soft back seats, took the driver position and brought them out of the airport area with flashing lights and blaring sirens. He did not speak and did not look at them. He was like a reliable but taciturn servant. And he was a good driver. He reminded Gabriel of Drives, the taxi driver who drove them safely home from their Sussex sunset experience.

They drove through the night. It was a long way to go before the car stopped in front of a dark building in a moderate state of decay. "Hotel," Baloo barked. They tiredly stumbled out of the car and fetched their huge backpacks. Baloo made some sort of noise, and suddenly, some overtired personnel appeared to help with the luggage.

What then began was another service ordeal. For nearly another hour, they stood at the hotel reception desk watching Baloo negotiate in Tamil with the clerks. Ayaan had confirmed bookings for their first night, but the clerks behaved as if they were hearing of these bookings for the first time. And not only this: It seemed like Gabriel and Tilda were the first guests they had ever received at their business.

In the end, the reception manager gave them their keys, and without further ado, they said thank you and good night to Baloo and headed to the elevators. They had rooms on the same floor. Gabriel's was of deplorable quality, and Tilda's was not much better: no toilet paper, no soap, no electric lamps, no air conditioning, no water. But it was 4:30 in the morning, and there was a bed. Tilda used her backpack and a chair to barricade her door where the latch was damaged, fell down on the bed and slept like a log.

Angels' Play

Location:
Heaven above Chennai's city centre. Shared-Office Cloud.

Time:
Real-time GMT+5.30, Wednesday, 7 January 2020, 10:45 India Standard Time (IST)

Players:
The two angels as before.

Setting:
The angels are doing the second lesson of their training course. Unfaithful to its word, having seen the challenge on the playing card, GA has again talked TA into becoming the Indian elephant. They are quarrelling.

GA (*in a convincing voice*):
You are a serving creature. Like Baloo.

TA (*proudly*):
Maybe, but I am not a servant. Nor is he.

GA (*shaking its head*):
You're arguing over mere semantics. You belong to the servants, not to the ones that are served. That makes a big difference. Look down there: There are service people, and there are the people they serve, right? That's Indian culture!

TA (*outraged*):
No, that's unjust.

GA (*warningly*):
Don't let upper management hear you. You know Mark 9:35: "Anyone who wants to be first must be the very last, and the servant of all." You can take pride in doing a good job at being of service. That's all.

TA (*frustrated*):
Where are these union angels when you need them? There is a constitution! I have rights. I am highly qualified for my job. And I pay my union dues. I'm on committees!

GA (*soberly*):
For the time being, and that is now India Standard Time, you are an elephant unless we solve this challenge. You can complain later. Take consolation in the knowledge that there are some cherubs below you that have to clean toilets. And there is no toilet paper down there. It's not part of the local culture.

TA (*obstinately*):
I will accept the missing toilet paper only because it's cultural. For everything else, I want justice. No service people, service elephants or service angels by default. There are no dualities. We are all One, right?

GA (*smilingly, understandingly and benevolently kissing the trunk of its colleague*):
Yes, if you don't like the current mores, let's start changing them.

The First Hours in India

Gabriel woke up to bright sunshine falling through the large window directly onto his pillow. The window went out to a huge green garden in the back with jungle-like palm trees. The building surrounding the garden from the other side was an old castle type of manor that had seen better days. It still looked very aristocratic, though.

There were new, eager and very friendly personnel at the reception desk this morning. Listening to their greetings, Gabriel and Tilda discovered that they could not understand very much of what was being said. People, who were very dark-skinned here in South India, talked to them in a mixture of English and Tamil that was difficult to understand. Among themselves, they talked in Tamil only. "By the bye, do you have toilet paper in your room, Mrs Toelz?" Gabriel asked Tilda. She shook her head, embarrassed. She could be such a wimp.

They went into the large shady breakfast room with luxurious air conditioning, where an opulent buffet breakfast was delivered by many Tamilian servers who seemed to be total beginners. They didn't know what to do with their guests. At least they weren't performing the usual routines of assigning a table, asking about people's preferences for tea or coffee and the like. They simply shuffled around Gabriel and Tilda, who were standing in the way.

The servers looked helplessly at their two guests, and Gabriel and Tilda looked helplessly at them. They were the only guests for more than ten servers. "What now, Mr David?" Tilda asked under her voice. "We take control," Gabriel suggested. He was usually more polite and not so bossy, but he was hungry. So they simply marched with heavy steps to the best table in the room, rudely sat down and ordered beverages in loud and commanding voices: Tilda yelled for tea; Gabriel shouted for coffee. This was met with great relief by the staff. Finally, these strange foreigners had made up their minds. Gabriel and Tilda could feel the staff's approval. Tilda looked at Gabriel with raised eyebrows. He shrugged his shoulders.

"OK," she said, "if this is the way it works." With firm steps, she approached the buffet, waved a server to her, and started to point at things with her little finger that he should put on her plate. Then she came back to the table with the server in her wake, who carried her plate laden with food. He waited until she was seated again before putting her food down in front of her and placing a napkin in her lap. Then he waited until she had started to eat and took position behind her chair with a neutral face, waiting to be of further service.

Gabriel had watched the little scene with dismay for its display of inequality and rudeness but also with a little admiration: This was what he would call cultural adaptivity. Tilda looked at him with mocking eyes. "I thought you were hungry." Gabriel said, laughing, and then he got up and followed her example. However, he carried his own plate, smiled and said thank you to the helpful staff. His server was shocked by this inappropriate behaviour. She took position behind his chair with a reproachful face, keeping a watchful and suspicious eye on him to see whether he would at least be able to eat properly. Tilda grinned.

"Ayaan said in his last email that we shall rest from our flight today, to be fit for Kerala tomorrow," Gabriel told Tilda. "How about a little sightseeing after breakfast?" "Shouldn't we work, Mr David? We are on a business trip after all," Tilda objected. "We're in India. Let's have a look at Chennai and go to the beach. It is called Marina Beach," Gabriel said. Sometimes he wondered who was the youth and who was the elder in their relationship. When they met at reception, they were both in light, casual attire because it seemed to be very warm outside. Inside, at reception, it was freezing from the air conditioning. It seemed as if they were the only guests of the hotel. "Do you have a city map, and can you show us the most scenic walk through the city to the beach?" Gabriel asked the reception officer. The man looked at him uncomprehendingly. "Taxi?" he asked. "No. Map! We want to walk!" The receptionist waved to his colleague for help. "Taxi!" this guy said firmly. "No, walk," Gabriel said. "Map?" Both men shook their heads. "Which direction? Chennai's city centre? Marina Beach?" Gabriel pointed questioningly with his arms to the right and to the left of the hotel.

Both men shook their heads. "Taxi!" they confirmed. When they realised that they could not convince Tilda and Gabriel to order a taxi but that their guests were adamant about walking, they looked at each other, shrugged and started to give them complicated directions. Obviously, there was no city map available, and the hotel was somewhere in the suburbs. "How far to the city centre?" Gabriel asked. "Two kilometres," they replied. Gabriel looked with relief over at Tilda. That was not too bad, and the day was nice.

In the meantime, there were five or six staff members around them; their breakfast servers laughingly stood in the door of the breakfast room and observed the scene, talking to each other in Tamil. All looked rather alarmed when the two of them set off to go sightseeing on foot and all by themselves. Gabriel and Tilda soon discovered why. First of all, it was hot and humid. For unaccustomed Westerners, physical exertion in these conditions would be quite difficult. Then there was no pavement to walk on safely. Though the street was big with many cars and other vehicles travelling in all directions and not following any rules or order, the border was just sand, dust and pebbles, with a lot of garbage to avoid. On this sort of pavement, many people were passing to and fro. Every crossing of a side street was an adventure because there were no traffic lights or other helpful infrastructure. You simply waited until a critical mass of people had formed on your side of the street and then pushed forward with the crowd. You were responsible for your own survival. At first, this severely stressed out Gabriel and Tilda. They were soon pretty exhausted from noise and having to put their lives in danger.

However, they soon adapted to the chaos and even discovered order in chaos. People took care of each other. And they were magnificent drivers. There were no accidents. People were happily laughing and chatting. The crowd looked colourful and full of life. However, everybody stared at them. Though Chennai was a megacity, they were the only Westerners to be seen in this huge crowd of pedestrians. If there were other Westerners, they were probably sitting in taxis, strongly encouraged by their bossy hotel personnel into complying with the tourist culture in India. Wandering the crowded streets of Chennai's city centre with its many shops and big malls, Gabriel and Tilda soon got lost. They looked for a cash machine because Tilda had no money on her, having been too tight-fisted to accept the transaction fees at the airport. For that reason, they left the route to Marina Beach that their concierge had earlier advised them to take. In the US, they had been mostly guided by Google Maps on their mobile phones in such a situation. Here, Gabriel's phone was again of rather limited use; in Chennai's city centre, it had no signal at all.

And Tilda seemed to be adamant about not even acknowledging that she had such a device. She didn't want to use her mobile in India. She didn't want to see the dozens of messages from Ken piling up in the meantime. Gabriel wondered into which depths of her backpack her phone had vanished. It was so nice to have her constant, full attention without the otherwise-inevitable and ubiquitous phone glued to her hands. However, for the time being, this meant they were lost. At a certain point, Tilda confessed: "I have no clue where we are. Or where the sea is. Or anything." She went into a shop to try to ask people for the right way but came out more puzzled than before. "Everybody in there pointed in a different direction," she complained. "We should take one of *those*, Mrs Toelz," Gabriel said, pointing to one of the motorised three-wheelers where the driver was sitting in front and two passengers could balance on a little bench sitting behind said driver. "A tuktuk?" Tilda asked sceptically. "This looks like suicide, Mr David." "They're usually very good drivers. And if not, at least they're really cheap," Gabriel soothed her and hailed the next tuktuk approaching them in the street chaos. It swerved dangerously as it approached the kerb and came to a standstill just a few centimetres away from Gabriel's knees. Tilda groaned. The driver grinned.

Bouribi, the Singing Tuktuk Driver

"My name is Bouribi," he said "I am your driver for today. Where do you want to go?" He was about fifty years old, talkative and very tidy in a clean white shirt with a huge golden watch on his left arm. "To Marina Beach," Tilda said firmly. "We will go there later," Bouribi replied, smiling with his pockmarked face, and then he cranked up his engine. "Now I will show you the city." "No!" Tilda shouted, "we want to go to Marina Beach!" But Bouribi simply shook his dark-haired head and laughed while avoiding a collision with a group of slow lorries. "How much?" Tilda tried to limit the financial damage. Bouribi's tidy tuktuk had a taximeter, but the device was switched off. "Five hundred for the whole day," Bouribi said. "I will take good care of you." That was not much indeed—only 5.60 euros, in fact. And they needed a local driver, that was for sure. They nodded in agreement, and off they went with happily laughing Bouribi.

"Where are we going?" Gabriel shouted after some time from behind Bouribi and into Bouribi's ear. The traffic was unbearable; they thought they would die in an accident any minute. "To church!" Bouribi exclaimed happily. He started singing some Tamil songs, not very melodiously but loudly. Tilda groaned and stirred nervously at Gabriel's side. "What church? I don't want to go to church. I thought you were all Hindus," she complained. Poor girl: always surrounded by religious lunatics. "Not all of us," Bouribi said. "I am a Catholic." Given the small percentage of Catholics in Chennai, Bouribi was probably the only Catholic tuktuk driver in the whole city.

After a wild tuktuk ride, Bouribi stopped with a flourish in front of St. Thomas Basilica, a church in Mylapore, a district of Chennai. "This the site of the burial place of St. Thomas the Apostle," Bouribi presented proudly before continuing: "This is my parish, and we have a museum. On we go!" Tilda groaned. "Where's Marina Beach?" she asked desperately. "It's just round the corner," Bouribi replied, smiling. "First you go church, then crypt, then museum, then beach." Tilda groaned again, more loudly this time. Bouribi was merciless. First, they had to take off their shoes, like at every holy place in India. Next, they had to look at everything while Bouribi explained. "The name *Thomas* means 'mated' or 'twin' in Aramaic. This is why Thomas is also called Didymus, in the Bible. In the Syriac tradition, he appears as Judas Thomas since Thomas is understood there as an epithet," Bouribi said in the museum. He pointed at some oil paintings and cited famous Bible quotes. "You know the pejorative term *doubting Thomas*? He initially doubted the resurrection of

Jesus until he himself saw the stigmata of the risen one." Tilda theatrically groaned. Bouribi slowly moved to a collection of more oil paintings. "According to legend, Thomas was also the only apostle who was not present at Mary's Ascension. He doubted the event as he doubted the resurrection of Jesus. For this reason, Mary appeared to the doubter and handed him her belt as proof of her bodily acceptance into heaven. This is a famous motif in art." He was really an expert on St. Thomas. "More written evidence of St. Thomas's work in India has surfaced recently. For example, written evidence exists from St. Gaudentius of Brescia. Also, St. Gregory of Tours recorded not only that the apostle Thomas worked and died in India but also that he was buried here. He suffered a martyr's death here in India. It is in his apostolic tradition that we celebrate our services following the Syrian rite, which is structured a little differently from what you know as mass liturgy. For example, we start with Sanctus, while you have it in the middle," Bouribi went on. Tilda groaned.

Next, he waved them over towards the crypt. He even made Tilda and Gabriel kneel down in front of St. Thomas's grave side by side. "Didymus means 'mated,' and you are mated, so pay your respects," he said. It would have been disrespectful not to do so. Even Tilda felt it and complied with his hectic pawing at her clothing to bring her down to the ground. Gabriel grinned. There she paid respects, she, the doubting Thomas par excellence. Anyway, Bouribi meant "pay" literally. They had to leave rupees in front of the shrine. Tilda groaned. In response, Gabriel hastily asked Bouribi to take them to the beach now. "It's right behind the church," Bouribi answered happily. "I bring you down, though I really do not understand why you want to go there." He was right. The shore started only about twenty metres behind the churchyard. There was not much to see but litter and dirt. Bouribi looked expectantly at them, ready for another of his museum tours of St. Thomas. Gabriel felt that Tilda was on the brink of freaking out. "Bouribi," he said softly, "we want to be alone for a few hours to take a walk along Marina Beach. Can we do that now?" Bouribi grinned and nodded understandingly. He drove them over to Marina Beach and let them loose for a walk in the fresh air, which they desperately needed.

Gabriel was able to bring Tilda's mood back to normal while they looked at some Indian families enjoying themselves between the stands of the beach fair. It all looked a little bit like Brighton's seafront, but unfortunately covered in debris. Everything was pretty littered. As always, first thing at the beach, Gabriel kicked off his shoes, unlike body-shy Tilda. However, even Gabriel put on his shoes again after having dipped them into the dirty waters of the Indian Ocean. It was too disgusting and dangerous. Not only the usual flotsam but also dead animals, broken glass, motor oil and metal scrap were everywhere. "Isn't that funny, Mrs Toelz?" he pointed across the ocean. "We're here at Marina Beach in Chennai just opposite Marina Inn back in San Francisco. The Indian Ocean becomes the Pacific Ocean on the other side. If you try hard, you might see the Golden Gate Bridge." "I don't want to see the bloody bridge, Mr David," Tilda said gruffly. She was right. Better not be reminded of that dreadful evening. "Let's walk a little down the beach," he complacently said. They went on a swift walk for a few kilometres. Then Tilda felt better. "Look, Mr David! There are horses," she delightedly pointed to a group of ponies standing further up in the dunes that were nibbling at the little grass there was. "Can we go up to them?" Gabriel was happy to agree. However, they changed course when they saw that the ponies were guarded by a group of Indian men sitting in the dunes who did not look very friendly on their approach.

Angels' Play

Location:
Heaven above Chennai's city centre. Shared-Office Cloud.

Time:
Real-time GMT+5.30, Wednesday, 7 January 2020, 13:37 IST

Players:
The two angels as before.

Setting:
Third lesson on the cloud. GA is in the form of Ganesha. Even as an elephant, this angel remains stylish. It is performing a melodious trumpet solo with its red-gold trunk.

TA in its angel attire is frowningly checking the challenge details, obviously impatient about its progress and eager for a promotion.

The angel has meticulously arranged according to size and at the sideboard of its standing desk every item that could be of potential use during the session, including a missal, an altar cross, a skeletal relic of St. Thomas, a rosary, a black habit, a scapula, a chalice, a pope mitre, a Madonna statue, an eternal light and various other devotionalia.

GA (*stunned while mustering the holy collection*):
What are we up to this time? What are we guarding against?

TA (*grumpy*):
Hindu stuff. Pagan.

GA (*mystified*):
Pagan? Are you sure?

TA (*sharply knocking on the Script, in a clear and rational voice*):
I do not much like the fact that Tilda has to spend her next week in Hindu temples, according to the Script. All this polytheistic stuff with strange rituals around animals and nature. They will run around with tikas the whole day. They will join pilgrims in their temple sacrifices. They will even be involved in fertility rituals. Gabriel is 54 years old, for God's sake.

Tilda will be advised by chanting and sweating Vishnu temple priests to put a flower wreath around this old guy's neck like on a breeding bull. It's disgusting. I won't have it. It's hard enough with her anyway. How shall she become a true believer?

GA (*warningly rolling its trunk*):
Wait a second.

TA (*swinging the rosary like a lasso*):
We should shoo them back to St. Thomas Basilica; lock them up there by causing an earthquake, a tsunami or something; and be done with it until their return flight.

Now I'll kiss you, and we can start getting back to normal by stopping this nonsense.

Cloud gets very dark. Thunder is rolling.

The Elephant Son of Shiva and Parvati

After meeting Bouribi again after their beach walk, he brought them to a local soup kitchen, where they ate a delicious meal. Only very poor people like Bouribi were present, who was greeted like a good friend. He placed orders for Gabriel and Tilda, and they got well-prepared servings of curry masala. Bouribi was the best eater at the table. For drinks, they had bottled water. The place had nothing else on the offer. When Gabriel paid afterwards, he realised that they had eaten with three adult persons for about three euros. Soon, Bouribi was getting into new mischief. "Now I will show you our most famous temple area," he said, standing up from the meal. "No more religion for today," Tilda moaned. But as before, Bouribi proved to be merciless. Singing loudly and unmusically, he drove them through the wild traffic in his tuktuk. He deeply reminded them of Teo, the singing taxi driver in Arizona. "I want to take a few pictures of this madness. Please give me your mobile phone, Mr David," Tilda said. "Here you go," Gabriel replied, laughing.

Next, they arrived at their first Hindu place of worship, the Kapaleeshvarar temple. It was a huge area with a colourful forty-metre-high gate tower full of many goddesses and gods at the entrance. Bouribi said that such a gate tower was called a gopuram and whose purpose was to tell stories from the religious epics, such as Mahabharata and Ramayana. The place was packed with Indian tourists and pilgrims. "Take off your shoes, because this is holy ground," Bouribi said, pointing for them to look at a large facility where they paid staff to take care of their shoes until their owners' return. The staff were responsible for tons of shoes, which were thrown together without much care for pairs or order, let alone hygiene. Tilda groaned.

Bouribi had organised a tour guide for them in the meantime, again probably from his huge network of friends, thanks to his business acumen. This young, hip guy was dressed in Western clothes and spoke decent, understandable English. Right at the entrance, he showed them how people worshipped the elephant-headed god Ganesha, who was supposed to help people who wanted to start fresh with their lives. In front of his shrine, people bought coconuts and smashed them into a bowl that they broke open. It looked funny, and Tilda giggled. "Why are they doing that?" Gabriel asked their guide. "The fibres of the coconut represent our hair. Our hair cannot be counted any more than the coconut fibres can. The shell symbolises our body, the white flesh inside our heart. The coconut water symbolises bad habits, our egoism. Whoever breaks the coconut breaks his heart, after which it is purified," the guide explained. The whole temple was dedicated to the god Shiva, who seemed to have been a right rascal. Their guide told them: "One day, Shiva fell out with his partner, the goddess Parvati. It happened while the two of them were playing a game at the place where we are standing now. While they were playing, a peacock suddenly started dancing. This looked so captivating that Parvati forgot about playing with Shiva and instead turned her attention to the peacock instead. Shiva called Parvati twice, but she kept watching the dancing peacock. Shiva became angry and put a curse on Parvati, turning her into a peacock herself. Thereafter, Parvati, in the form of a peacock, came every day to worship Shiva under a laurel tree until Shiva, moved by her devotion, freed her from the curse. This tells you something about 'love and devotion,' even when the loved one is ill-tempered, makes fun of you and hurts you to your core, doesn't it?"

The laurel tree that the guide showed them on the north side of the temple was believed to have magical powers. "Pilgrims are granted a wish when they visit it," he said, "and the district got its name from this legend: *Mylapore* is translated into English as 'the place of the peacock.' In Hindu tradition, the worship of Shiva in Mylapore is tantamount to worshipping him in the Himalayas, where he is said to reside with Parvati in deep meditation. Ganesha, whom you have seen worshipped at the entrance, by the way, is the son of Shiva and Parvati."

"Of course he is. An ugly elephant is the son of a servile peacock and a power-hungry maniac of a god. Why not?" Tilda murmured, unmoved by all of this. Her mood did not improve when they had to pay the guide, who charged Western prices, especially because it made Bouribi greedy, who observed that they accepted and paid the huge fee. When Bouribi delivered them with his tuktuk in front of their hotel, he asked for five times as much money as had been negotiated. They disagreed and insisted on the originally negotiated fare. However, Gabriel had only a banknote of about twenty euros on him. When handing this to Bouribi, expecting change, he simply drove away with it, laughing happily. Tilda cursed at him, saying not very pleasant things about him in particular and Indian people in general, while Gabriel felt compelled to join Bouribi in laughter. This was not much money for them after all, but for Bouribi, it was a small fortune. And they had a great day with him.

Owing to their upcoming appointment the next morning at six o'clock with Ayaan to fly out to Kerala, they had an early-bird dinner in the same area of the hotel where they had taken breakfast that morning. The hotel staff was already waiting for them. Dinner service worked like the breakfast service. Tilda marched around barking at personnel for food and drinks. She had already culturally adapted to being patronising, domineering and bossy, and Gabriel was strongly reminded of the colonialist attitudes of British expatriate communities in India, as depicted in movies such as *The English Patient*; this was obviously how it developed. It was easy for him to separate himself from Tilda tonight. He was not amused but was too tired to quarrel with her for being such a Westerner.

Angels' Play

Location:
Heaven above Chennai's city centre. Shared-Office Cloud.

Time:
Real-time GMT+5.30, Wednesday, 7 January 2020, 21:01 IST

Players:
The two angels as before.

Setting:
Both angels are elephants. The mood is very unhappy.

TA (*desperately*):
I fucked it up, right?

GA (*flatly*):
Yes, you did. You have obviously caused a situation where kisses don't work any longer to change us back to angels.

TA (*desolately*):
What now?

GA (*hopelessly*):
No idea. As I said, this is the beta version. There are no guidelines for a situation when both players are stuck being elephants. Gamification development has not foreseen that players would be so stupid as to let intercultural conflict escalate.

TA (*taking the blow like an elephant*):
Thank you, dear. I hate autoethnography. Have I already said that? We can call TRINI-T personnel and ask for their advice. It's their bloody professional development course after all. They have a corporate social responsibility as our employer.

Both elephants are working on their consoles with their trunks, listening endlessly to elevator music on the service line of the CSR Call Centre until they are connected to an operator from the angels' personnel department.

GA (*explaining through the line*):
We are doing the interreligious course and are both holy Eastern elephants.

Helpdesk operator (*rather unforthcoming*):
Where's the problem?

GA (*repeating*):
We're both elephants.

Helpdesk operator (*repeating*):
Where's the problem?

GA (*changing strategy*):
Is there a way for us to change back to Western seraphim?

Helpdesk operator (*reluctantly*):
Why would you wish to do so? Cosmic powers are cosmic powers.

GA (*urgent*):
Is there a way, or is there not? (*encouragingly nodding to TA while listening again to the helpline music that the operator has switched them to while the operator confers with its superiors*)

Helpdesk operator (*patronisingly*):
It won't be easy, but there is a way. You have to take an extra module of the inter-religious course. A so-called idiot test, ending in an exam. If you pass the exam, you will be turned back into angels automatically.

GA (*groaning but hopeful*):
This shouldn't be too difficult. It's just an extra module. What's it about, and how is it delivered?

Helpdesk operator (*in a voice that clarifies that the conversation has ended*):
It is called The Vedic Lectures, and it is delivered by a guy named Bede Griffiths, in three sections. He will also invigilate the exam after you are done. This conversation has been recorded to improve the quality of our services.

Elevator music starts again. Both elephants stereotypically start to rock, sway and bob their heads in psychological distress.

Going to Kerala

The next day with Baloo started early. He was already waiting with two other soldiers at the hotel's reception desk when Tilda and Gabriel came downstairs. They drove to Chennai Airport, where they finally met Ayaan. Their Indian colleague stood in the middle of the terminal of that megacity airport teeming with people—all smiles and very happy to see them. Tilda and Gabriel watched in amazement the strange relationship between him and Baloo. Ayaan had already told them that his military cousin had assigned Baloo as his personal assistant and bodyguard years ago and that this showed the special bond between them. But what they witnessed was something they had not seen before. Ayaan was Baloo's 'pa'—subject of his devotion, deference, adoration and loving care. Ayaan and his needs were the centre of Baloo's attention and his whole being, like the brilliant sun around which he gravitated as his faithful planet. Baloo read every wish from Ayaan's eyes before he could utter it. Gabriel was pretty sure that Baloo would have killed whoever Ayaan told him to kill—them included—without giving it any further thought. That was one part of the relationship. The other part was that Ayaan totally relied on Baloo's abilities and discretion. Baloo was commanded to take care of him, and because of this, Baloo was somehow in charge. His army uniform intimidated everybody; it must represent the highest state authority with heavy sanctions for anybody who disrespects it. It was as if his uniform gave their little group a kind of halo, an exemption from any rule applying to everybody else.

Baloo mercilessly exploited that authority by bossing around airport personnel, the other soldiers and any bystanders—Gabriel and Tilda included. In no time, despite the long queues in front of check-in counters, he got rid of their luggage and ushered them through the crowds towards the VIP entrance to security. This was probably the only time in Gabriel's life when he shamefacedly passed hundreds of people patiently waiting in queue at security to go to the crew area without any checks. People politely made space for them.

They followed Ayaan, who marched through the parting crowds like a Dravidian prince. However, Ayaan himself followed Baloo, who bossed him around like everybody else. The strangest part for Gabriel and Tilda was the way that Baloo took care of Ayaan's bodily needs. Baloo looked at him then ushered him to the toilet and pointed to the door. Ayaan went in. Afterwards, Baloo led him to a quiet corner near the gate, seated him and brought him coffee without being asked. "Drink, Pa!" he said, "It's good for you." And Ayaan did. "Now you sleep a little. We left *early* this morning." Ayaan obediently closed his eyes and started to snore in no time. It was as if Baloo felt Ayaan's his body to determine Ayaan's needs. It was as if Ayaan's body were Baloo's body. Gabriel had not seen such a thing before. "Sir, I have to go now," Baloo said, addressing him. "A colleague of mine will pick you up at Cochin airport." With a last adoring look at snoring Ayaan, pushing his cabin trolley a little closer to his feet, Baloo reluctantly left them.

The flight with the Indian airline was very pleasant. They discussed their fieldwork for the Indian case study, which Ayaan had prearranged with cultural scientists at Kerala. Gabriel had totally forgotten that Ayaan was not only the respected cousin of a high-ranking military officer and the apple of Baloo's eye but also their valued project partner—a respected colleague working for CareGo India Ltd., a Chennai international aid organisation similar to B1. The next few days would be full of desk research and fieldwork—all carefully planned and scheduled by Ayaan. Office-wise, they would be hosted by the Kerala branch of CareGo India. Tilda, as the new project leader, hoped that work results would be good enough to complete the case study template for India during their return flight to Chennai. That would be a great achievement. She had already prepared everything for her own field interviews at Kerala. Arriving at Cochin, they drove through endless green jungle forests, consisting mostly of palm and banana trees, to reach their destination two hundred kilometres away. Tilda loved the animals that they saw in the street during their long journey in another military car. Animals were not corralled in any enclosures or stables. They simply mingled with the crowd in the streets. They lived in companionship and community with the people.

Angels' Play

Location:
Heaven above Kerala, a country road between Cochin and Kottayam. Shared-Office Cloud.

Time:
Real-time GMT+5.30, Thursday, 8 January 2020, 09:00 IST

Players:
The two angels as before and Bede Griffiths.

Setting:
Both angels are still elephants. They are standing side by side in the conference facility of the cloud, which has become a lecture theatre. Bede Griffiths is wandering up and down in front of their trunks and pointing every now and again with a large stick to slides of a PowerPoint presentation displayed on a big screen.

BG (*in his best lecturing mode*):
My dear angels—or, shall I better say, my dear elephants?
I know you might want to skip this lecture, but it'll be good for you. Attention, please!
This is the introduction to your Vedic lectures. You might ask yourselves, "Why should we be concerned with fiction? Aren't the Vedas just poetry? And what has this type of poetic language to do with Gabriel and Tilda, whom we are supposed to take care of? And how will all of this contribute to the big challenges posed by the Script?"
Please accept poetry as a legitimate starting point. Let me read to you from *The Marriage of East and West* to support this introductory lecture (*the following text is presented on two slides and read out loudly by BG*):

> "Poetry is the expression of the whole man. It expresses not merely his mind but his sensations, his feelings, his 'heart's affections.' This is why the imagination ... holds the key to human understanding. The imagination is the link between the mind and the heart, between intellect and sense, between thought and feeling. Modern man has broken this link; he has created a world of science and reason, whose language is prose, and has cut himself off from the sources of life in the imagination, which is the language of the heart" (Griffiths 1982: 48).
>
> British poet John Keats sets before us as living principles "the values of the 'holiness of the heart's affections and the truth of imagination'" (Griffiths 1982: 46). Imagination "takes us back to the very roots of human experience" (Griffiths 1982: 47) as a primordial truth, "which is not abstract but concrete, not logical but symbolic, not rational but intuitive" (ibid.). However, "it is difficult for modern man with his prosaic mode of thought to realize that poetry is more natural to man than prose, and yet all the evidence of history shows it" (ibid).

The elephants slowly wag their big ears, trying to express their compassion with modern humans.

BG *(continuing with a flourish)*:

I hope, my dear angels, that poetry is acceptable to you too. Poetic expression deeply grounded in imagination... *(switching to the next slide)*

> "holds the key to human understanding. The imagination is the link between the mind and the heart, between intellect and sense, between thought and feeling. Modern man has broken this link; he has created a world of science and reason, whose language is prose, and has cut himself off from the sources of life in the imagination, which is the language of the heart" (Griffiths 1982: 48).
>
> May Indian wisdom help you to rediscover "the truth which the Western world has lost and is now seeking desperately to recover" (Griffiths 1982: 47). This truth can be found in the mythological language of the Vedas, which include "the whole process of human evolution" (ibid.).

This is why Gabriel and Tilda had to go to India as well – on the path to the truth of imagination by following the holiness of the heart's affections.

There is a strong mythological element in their story too. Interwoven into the development of a human relationship is a spiritual revelation process about human nature: This process is concerned with human archetypes, achieved, assigned or ascribed human commonalities and differences, which are best addressed in the language of mythology.

The world of imagination, "the world of integral wholeness," expresses itself in myth.

(again showing a PowerPoint slide with a quote from himself)

> "Myth is a symbolic utterance which arises from the depths of the unconscious, or rather from the deep levels of consciousness which lie below the level of rational consciousness. The rational mind, with its abstract concepts and logical constructions, is like the tip of an iceberg, while below it are vast levels of consciousness which link our human nature with the universe around us and with the archetypes or transcendent principles which govern the Universe. The Myth is the reflection in the human imagination of these archetypical ideas, those cosmic principles and powers, which were known in the ancient world as gods or angels" (Griffiths 1982: 49).

Both elephants simultaneously sigh at the word 'angels.'

BG *(understandingly)*:

You yourselves, my dear angels, represent the cosmic principles and powers, seconding Gabriel and Tilda in their adventures.

These two are representatives of the myth archetypes of male and female. Be aware that the word *archetype* is not used in the psychological sense following Jung but rather in the philosophical sense following Plato's concept of the pure idea, which embodies the fundamental characteristics of a thing. This is, for example, in use within the biblical story of creation: "So God created man in his own image, in the image of God he created him; male and female he created them" (Gen. 1:27).

Each of the two dearies down there is, of course, a composite of masculine (active, rational, dominant, etc.) and feminine (receptive, intuitive, passive, etc.) aspects in their personalities. Their story so far has related how each of them has a hard time finding an individual equilibrium that integrates both aspects into their own personality. Furthermore, these two constantly have to negotiate the feminine/masculine divide between them, being ushered through all kinds of situations and episodes. However, they are supported by the fact that both principles "are necessary for existence," having their common source in "the one who beyond all change and multiplicity manifests itself in these two principles eternally" (Griffiths 1982: 55).

There will make discoveries that transcend their story, as from myth for ancient humans.

(showing one more slide with a lengthy self-quote to the already-exhausted elephants)

> "The Myth was the means of his total integration, with the universe around him, with his own inner experience and with the transcendent world of the spirit" (Griffiths 1982: 49). Usually, the intuitive and the rational are set apart in our modern world, which favours the rational text because the intuitive symbol is seen as being connected to the primitive mind. This is basically fine, but there are advantages to primitive thought: "Primitive thought is intuitive; it grasps the whole in all its parts. The rational mind comes later to distinguish all the different aspects. ... These are the two basic faculties of the mind, the intuitive which grasps the whole but does not distinguish the parts, and the rational which distinguishes the parts but cannot grasp the whole. ... Intuition without reason is blind; it is deep and comprehensive but confused and obscure. Reason without intuition is empty and sterile; it constructs logical systems which have no basis in reality" (Griffiths 1982: 50).

BG *(summarising, to the utter relief of the elephants)*:

My dear angels, the lecture is meant to encourage a process of learning and to raise awareness of what is meant. It tries to circumvent "the great stumbling block. If we think that we can learn the meaning by any methods of modern science, or philosophy or by scholarship or linguistic analysis, we are doomed to failure."

Instead, growing insights will demand a metanoia, a total change of mind, a passage from rational knowledge to intuitive wisdom for which few today are prepared. I hope you are.

Any questions?

TA *(raising its trunk to get the attention of the lecturer)*:

Father, what *are* the Vedas?

BG *(groaning because he had not anticipated this ignorance)*:

As I already explained in *The Marriage of East and West*, which I had assumed you would know by heart, the Vedas, which contain the germ of all the later developments of Hindu wisdom, probably took their present form in the second millennium before Christ, but their roots go back to far-more-ancient times and take us back to the beginning of human speech.

Perhaps nowhere else can one observe the entire process of human evolution from its primordial utterance to the most elaborate poetic speech and the most profound philosophy.

The Vedas are known as *sruti*, that which has been "heard"; they are the products not merely of human ingenuity but of revelation—that is, an "unveiling" of the truth. They are also called *nitya*, meaning "eternal," signifying that they do not derive from this world of time and change but are instead reflections of the eternal. Finally, they are said to be *apauruseya*, meaning "without human authorship"; they are expressions of the eternal word, the *Vac*; and the human authors are *rishis*, those who have "seen" the truth, and "poets"(*kavi*), those whose utterance is inspired. The literature of India begins with the hymns of the Rigveda, which sound like the biblical story of creation.

GA (*suddenly interested*):

Oh, music! A hymn! Can you sing us a song from the Rigveda, Father?

BG (*again inwardly groaning but nevertheless happy about this sign of his pupil's interest*):

Of course, my dear. I'll sing the Nasadiya Sukta.

(Starting to sing in a nasal high-tenor voice)

> There was neither nonexistence nor existence then;Neither the realm of space, nor the sky which is beyond;What stirred? Where? In whose protection?
>
> There was neither death nor immortality then;No distinguishing sign of night nor of day;That One breathed, windless, by its own impulse;Other than that there was nothing beyond.
>
> Darkness there was at first, by darkness hidden;Without distinctive marks, this all was water;That which, becoming, by the void was covered;That One by force of heat came into being;
>
> Who really knows? Who will here proclaim it?Whence was it produced? Whence is this creation?Gods came afterwards, with the creation of this universe.Who then knows whence it has arisen?
>
> Whether God's will created it, or whether He was mute;Perhaps it formed itself, or perhaps it did not;Only He who is its overseer in highest heaven knows,
>
> Only He knows, or perhaps He does not know.

(*BG sings the last verses in a whisper so as not to disturb the two elephants, which are fast asleep*)

Eating from Banana Leaves

Tilda and Gabriel were on good terms with each other when they worked in Kerala. The only situation that reminded Gabriel of Tilda's old self was when they were invited by their project partners and hosts to go on a boat trip on the Vembanad, which is one of India's largest lakes and wetland ecosystems, home to many species of rare plants and animal life at the tourist destination of Kumarakom. It was a perfect day for floating on the sunny lakes in tropical but agreeable temperatures with a motorboat. While they swerved around the little uninhabited islands of the lake district observing birds, Gabriel said to Tilda, "It's like paradise." She did not answer. He turned back to her in the boat. Her face was sullen and dark. When he looked at her questioningly, she pointed to the island in the very middle of the wide vast waters and said, "Indeed paradise, Mr David. This island will probably be the only spot left on this globe very soon where there is no mandatory measles vaccination. Everywhere else, our fine governments will force parents to violate their offspring with compulsory vaccination. I'll end up migrating here, the only paradise left." Gabriel was surprised. How did this idea enter her head? But that was the only relapse into her old ways.

Afterwards, they went back to Cochin airport with their army driver, who took good care of them. For example, he chose a brilliant lunch location. The little restaurant on the side of the country road did not look very promising at first, and Ayaan audibly sniffed when they entered. The place reminded Gabriel a little of Bouribi and the restaurant of his friends: It was a soup kitchen for the poor in the middle of the countryside. And obviously, their young soldier was well known over here. He was gladly welcomed by the Indian proprietor, who ushered the little group into the better part of his shabby house. The only tool they got for their meal was a glass each for drinking water that was served from a carafe—Tilda groaned. "No cutlery," she whispered. "We're supposed to eat with our fingers."

"And no plates, Mrs Toelz," Gabriel said, delighted. Instead, the proprietor brought banana leaves, one for each of them, and placed them in front of his guests. Tilda was full of awe. "See, this is what Rupert Sheldrake talked about in his book *Science and Spiritual Practices*," she said eagerly. "Quote: 'we sat on the floor and ate vegetarian dishes from banana leaves'; it really is true. They do this." Then the food came: naan, which is Indian bread, and various little pots with vegetables in sauce. The pots were emptied onto their banana leaves. It tasted delicious.

Gabriel ate with a strong appetite until he felt that people from other tables had started to stare at him. Ayaan and the soldier, who sat opposite Tilda and him, giggled nervously and politely looked away. "What's the matter?" Gabriel asked Tilda under his breath. "You have disgusting table manners. Everybody is looking at you. Stop it!" she whispered back. "What is it, Mrs Toelz?" Gabriel mouthed. She was eating with her fingers, as he and everybody else did. "Haven't you read Bede Griffiths, Mr David? He says everybody eats with their hands," she imparted and then continued, grinning: "or rather with the right hand because the left hand is reserved for cleaning oneself. And mind you, there's no toilet paper." Hastily, Gabriel hid his left hand under the table, the hand with which he, a born left-hander, had eaten so far. Talk continued at the other tables. Little children looked at Gabriel either patronizingly and compassionately. Tilda could not stop grinning – fretfully observed by her boss. Impertinent girl: that she of all people would cite Bede Griffiths and use Griffiths' words against him to bring him to heel! How embarrassed could he get?

Angels' Play

Location:
Heaven above Kerala, a country road between Cochin and Kottayam. Shared-Office Cloud.

Time:
Real-time GMT+5.30, Thursday, 8 January 2020, 19:04 IST

Players:
The two angels as before and Bede Griffiths.

Setting:
Same setting: Both angels are still elephants. BG is just feeding them with green bananas.

GA (*trying to get on cordial terms with BG again*):
Father, may I ask you a personal question—about the story of your life?

BG (*pleasantly*):
Of course, my dear. Please fire away.

GA (*curiously*):
Was it difficult for you as well when you arrived in India? Did you feel like a legal alien? An Englishman in India? How was it for you?

BG (*lost in memories*):
It was as Thomas Matus described in my *Essential Writings*. I came to India with this holy desire, but I carried with me the cultural baggage of my nearly twenty-five years at Prinknash.

GA (*objecting*):
But monks make vows of poverty, chastity and humility. You must have been used to the simple life. What did you do, by the way, when you arrived in India?

BG (*pensively*):
Near Bangalore, Father Benedict and I built a small monastery in what we considered "simple" conditions, but I soon realised that our simplicity was luxury in comparison with the life of the local villagers, not to mention that of the Hindu ascetics, who begged their food and had no fixed abode.

GA (*curiously*):
Was that a problem for you?

BG (*positively*):
Oh yes! And quite a big one, too. The only solution, as I saw it, was *sannyasa*, the total renunciation of conforming with the highest ideals of Indian asceticism.

GA (*sceptically*):
That was a bit harsh, don't you think? I know you are a radical, but wasn't that overdoing it a little?

BG (*defensively*):
A few Catholics at the time had already arrived at this conclusion.

Furthermore, this way I came to Shantivanam. In the South Indian state of Tamil Nadu, two French priests, Jules Monchanin and Henri Le Saux, a Benedictine, were living as sannyasis in an ashram. They were dedicated to the Holy Trinity, using a Sanskrit term—Saccidananda—with which Hindus define the transcendent and immanent Absolute as "Being, Consciousness, Bliss."

In 1958, a Belgian Trappist, Father Francis Mahieu, arrived at Saccidananda Ashram—also called Shantivanam, meaning "Forest of Peace"—with his own ideas for a Christian monastic foundation. This Father Francis contacted me. I decided to leave Bangalore and join him in Kerala, across the mountains. There we founded a coenobitic community, Trappist in observance but Indian in spirit. For our community prayer, we adopted a Syrian liturgy in use among one of ancient (perhaps even apostolic) Christian communities of southern India.

GA (*gently*):
Father, that means you came to Kerala, not to Shantivanam…

BG (*agreeably*):
Yes, but wait and see. What I can see is that you have not carefully read *The Marriage of East and West*, where I described my travels. As I said, when we came to Kerala, we adopted the Syrian rite, to which the majority of Christians in Kerala belonged. Christian faith is said to have been brought to India by the apostle Thomas, and there has certainly been a church in Kerala from a very early time.

TA (*chiming in now*):
That is why Gabriel and Tilda had to visit St. Thomas's grave with this Bouribi person.

GA (*interrupting*):
We have digressed from the simple life and you feeling oddly rich as a Westerner, Father. Please go on. What did you learn when you came to India?

BG (*thinking back*):
Those days! The first thing that I learned was a simplicity of life that before I would have not thought possible. India has a way of reducing human needs to a minimum.

One full meal a day of rice and vegetables—at best with some curds and ghee, clarified butter, is considered sufficient. Tea or coffee with some rice and some pickle is enough for breakfast and supper.

Nor are tables and chairs, spoons and forks or knives and plates considered necessary. One sits on the floor on a mat and eats with one's hands—or rather with the right hand, as the left hand is reserved for cleaning oneself. For plates, there are banana leaves.

TA (*trumpeting with its trunk*):
There you have it. You eat from a banana leaf. The kettle is boiling over; I think I am a banana tree.

GA (*concerned*):
Are you alright, TA?

TA (*melodiously trumpeting a pop song*):
Of course. I'm going slightly mad. Oh dear.

BG (*just continues*):

Things might have changed a little in the meantime. But when I arrived in India, there was thus no need for any furniture in an Indian home.

The richer people who had adopted Western ways made use of tables and chairs and beds and other conveniences, but poor people—who still make up the vast majority—are still content to sit and sleep on the floor.

Nor are elaborate bathrooms and lavatories considered necessary. In the villages, the majority of people bathe at a pump or a well or in a neighbouring tank or stream, and most people still go out into the fields or by the roadside or by a stream to relieve themselves.

There is a beautiful simplicity in all this, which makes one realise something about the original simplicity of human nature.

GA (*indignantly*):

I am sorry, Father, but no toilet paper is NOT beautiful.

BG (*eagerly*):

Even clothes are hardly necessary. Most men in those days, it is true, indeed wore a shirt and a dhoti—a piece of cloth wound round the waist and falling to the feet—and women wore a sari and a blouse to cover their breasts, but this was comparatively recent. Even now, clothes are still believed to be things that are put on for an occasion and are easily discarded. A man will take his shirt off when he wants to relax, and a labourer will wear no more than a langothi—a piece of cloth wound round the middle and between the legs.

GA (*curiously*):

And a sannyasi? Is he now completely naked?

BG (*explaining*):

All this makes the life of a sannyasi—one who has "renounced" the world—immensely simple. He needs no house or furniture. He may live in a cave or take shelter beside a temple or on the veranda of a house.

For clothing, he needs only two pieces of cloth—which should not be stitched—one to wear round the waist and the other for a shawl to cover the shoulders or the head. There are even some sannyasis who renounce all clothing and are said to be "clothed with the sky." For food, he needs only one meal a day, which he gets by begging or, more often, which a householder will offer him unasked. He can thus reduce his life to absolute simplicity. He is totally detached from the world, depending on divine providence for his bare needs of food, shelter and clothing.

GA (*sceptically*):

I am sure that Gabriel and Tilda would not want to live like that. Neither of them.

BG (*a little sadly*):

I guess you're right. What a challenge this presents to a world that takes pleasure in continually increasing human needs and so makes itself more and more dependent on the material world.

Angels' Play

GA (*curiously*):

And you, Father? Did it make you any happier? I mean, you and your fellow monk?

BG (more cheerful now):

Oh yes! We were therefore able to come nearer to the condition of poor people in India. This was assisted by the fact that when we began our monastic life in Kerala, we were compelled to live in a palm-leaf hut. The stone building that we were erecting was not yet complete, and we had to spend the whole of the monsoon season, with nearly two hundred inches of rain, in this frail hut. Yet we found that we were able to survive even under these conditions. The floor of the hut, which was made of earth, became so damp that we had to cover it first with straw and then with planks in order to stay dry. But apart from this, we were also able to continue our monastic life, celebrating the Qurbana, the Eucharist in the Syrian rite, which we had adopted—chanting the prayer, continuing our study and doing all the necessary work without a break.

TA (*a little impatiently*):

And then you finally came to Shantivanam in Tamil Nadu, right? And met with these two French fathers. What were their names again—Monchanin and Le Saux? And what was the ashram's long name again?

BG (*patiently as always*):

Yes, as I said, these two were the pioneers of attempting to adapt monastic life in India to the traditional forms of Indian life and prayer. They called the ashram Saccidananda Ashram, *Saccidananda* being the Hindu name for the Godhead as Being, Knowledge and Bliss, which they took as a symbol of the Christian Trinity, the Father as Being, the Son (or Word of God) as the Knowledge of the Father, and the Holy Spirit as the Bliss of Love, which unites Father and Son. You see?

TA (*reproachfully*):

But then later, they converted to Hinduism. They even changed their Christian names.

BG (*even more patiently*):

Not at all. They stayed Christians. But they took the names of Parama Arubi Ananda, the Bliss of the Supreme Spirit, and Abhishiktananda, the Bliss of Christ. Thus, they sought to identify themselves with the Hindu tradition of *sannyasa*, the renunciation of the world, to experience the bliss of the divine life. But this was much more than a matter of names. By studying yoga and Vedanta, they sought to integrate the whole spiritual tradition of India into their lives as Christians, thus working towards that unity of religion that is the goal of humankind.

TA (*only half convinced*):

So you're saying that you can chant a Hindu mantra in a Catholic ashram?

BG (*decidedly*):
Of course you can. I've said this many times, among them to our friend Rupert Sheldrake: You can precisely because it is a Catholic ashram. *Catholic* means "all inclusive." Anything that excludes any path to God is not Catholic, but merely a sect.

GA
(*softly*):
Father, can you cite us a verse from the Rigveda again? We want to go to sleep.

BG (*considering*):
Yes. Listen carefully. It is very short. It is about unity, though you might not immediately understand it.
(*carefully and slowly reciting*)
"Two birds with fair wings, inseparable companions, have found refuge in the same sheltering tree. One incessantly eats from the fig tree; the other, not eating, just looks on."

The two elephants fall asleep again.

The flight from Cochin back to Chennai was again pleasant and calm. Supported by helpful Ayaan, Tilda and Gabriel finished the template for the Indian case study for the new project with the materials that they had gathered during the Kerala visit. Gabriel said to Tilda, "Now we've managed what we haven't achieved for the US case study yet: We've completed the second case study template after your contribution to China. Congratulations, Mrs Toelz!" She smiled and said, "The B1 trustee board will be very happy with us for making good use of the company's travel budget." She, as the new project leader, already wanted to send the documents home during the flight, via the on-board Internet connection that the Indian airline offered for free. "Let's see what you want to send," Gabriel suggested. Tilda showed him the text on her laptop.

The India Case

Public distribution system (PDS) in rural areas of Kerala and Tamil Nadu: Ethnographic pilot study conducted during B1 visit in January 2020 by project leader Tilda Toelz.

Social context:
Hunger alleviation and poverty eradication are the twin objectives of the public distribution system (PDS) in India. The PDS is intended to provide essential goods and services, mainly food items such as rice, wheat, sugar, kerosene, etc., to everybody, especially "the poorest of the poor" at a reasonable cost, contributing to general social welfare. The effectiveness of the PDS depends largely on competent policy decisions regarding the operational and organisational aspects of the system. The Indian social system is characterised by features of a democratic, secular welfare nation on the one hand and by social structures and relationships based on traditional segregation patterns on the other, with high inequalities in well-being and a

high number of poor people living among vulnerable communities. Currently, the ration-distribution system has many drawbacks, mostly due to corruption: They consist of an insufficient quantity of goods, low-quality goods, long wait times, low processing speeds, irregularities in grain procurement, the siphoning off money, biased selection from buyers, material theft, etc. Anticorruption policies and measures must try to wrest control back to try to remedy this situation.

Furthermore, the current system is based on a minimalistic one-size-fits-all approach to allocating resources to individuals, which does not take into account sociocultural variables that individuals face in various social contexts on the grassroots level. To alleviate the existing inequalities and injustices biased by traditional social segregation patterns instead of reinstantiating them, the distribution system should incorporate complex and context-sensitive local knowledge to better shape the living conditions of vulnerable populations. Currently, therefore, the system is inefficient, which might add to its vulnerability to exploitation.

A short summary of my interview in Kaipuzha, Kerala:
Present: Tilda Toelz, personnel number 0003621 (interviewer); Pradipta Rajesh (interviewee); Dr Ayaan Banerjee (local expert who translated questions and answers because he speaks the Cholanaikkan language, which belongs to the Dravidian language family).

Pradipta Rajesh is a middle-aged woman of 42 whom I met in her open campsite made of leaves, close to a village named Kaipuzha in Kerala. She has four children between ages 6 and 10. She is very poor and is seriously underweight and malnourished. We are sitting on planks and straw on the floor; there is no furniture. On a tree trunk, there is a photograph of her husband, who is a sanitation worker in Chennai. Traces of the monsoon season are clearly visible. Pradipta belongs to the Malanaikan people.

Malanaikan are one of the last hunter-gatherer tribes of the region. Pradipta looks like she is in the mid 60s, without teeth and with deep wrinkles. Malanaikans are outside the traditional Indian varna caste system. They do not belong to the four varna castes, which have about 8000 subcastes. They are considered "untouchable."

Me: I am grateful to you for agreeing to talk to me and grateful to Ayaan for making this possible.

Pradipta Rajesh: May I offer you some water?

Me: Yes, thank you. Please tell me about the life of the Malanaikans. Do you get some help from government? Does government know about your situation?

Pradipta Rajesh: We do not belong to any caste. But we are listed as 'Particularly Vulnerable Tribal Group' by government. This gives us some rights according to Constitution. It's the law. The Constitution gives us hope. Listed tribes have rights. They can get food from the government.

Me: Why is that?

Pradipta Rajesh: It's called positive discrimination. If you do not belong to one of the four Brahminic castes, you have certain rights, according to the Constitution. You can get food.

Me: Please tell me what you get exactlys.

Pradipta Rajesh: But I do not get anything.

Me: Why is that?

Pradipta Rajesh: The people who distribute at the ration shop do not like us. We practice our religion; we observe the rules of the ancestors of our Chemmam. Malanaikans are nothing. We are forest people.

Me: Where then is your place in society?

Pradipta Rajesh: Our people encompass a broader range of communities than what the government means by vulnerable tribes. We are ethnic tribes. So you can call our people scheduled tribes.

Me: Why aren't A you getting food from the government? Or any social services? Can't you use the public distribution system? You, as Malanaikans, are listed by the government as a particularly vulnerable tribal group.

Pradipta Rajesh: We are only recently listed. We are Malanaikan. We don't have many left. We can't read or write. I have never been to school or to hospital. I'm not allowed entry into the ration shop. But the PDS is corrupt anyway. I won't get anything anyway.

Me: Do you know how the ration shops work?

Pradipta Rajesh: Of course I do. Everybody does. You have a ration card with all your biometrics.

Me: You know about biometrics?

Pradipta Rajesh: Of course I do. Everybody does. If it is important for your life, you know. Biometrics is data about yourself. About your household, better to say. It determines what and how much you will get in the shop. You present your card with the data to the shopkeepers. They have a machine. The machine decides. It's an intelligent machine. But I have no address. I am no household. I have only this fireplace here. It doesn't count. I don't have a ration card.

Me: What then do you do for a living?

Pradipta Rajesh: I collect wild roots, tubers, seeds and fruits from the forest. The forest provides everything. We need rice. And sometimes we buy meat. I sell the forest produce that we don't eat, ourselves.

Me: And what is your husband doing?

Pradipta Rajesh: He went to Chennai last year for work. He helps with money. He sends some every two months. This is for school for the boys.

Me: Do your kids go to school?

Pradipta Rajesh: The two boys, yes. But they are not allowed to touch midday meals. They bring their own food. The girls have already dropped out of primary school. I need them here. Originally, we had six kids, but two have died.

"Good job, Mrs Toelz. Can I add something?" Gabriel asked. When Tilda nodded, he added a footnote: "Explanatory input to be expected from Bede Griffiths (1982) about religious and cultural settings in Kerala. To be completed when we get home." While waiting for their luggage at Chennai Airport late in the evening, they had the chance to look at a Mohandas Gandhi exhibition in the luggage hall.

There was a comment by Martin Luther King, who once visited Chennai, where he recommended involving the social and cultural sciences in Gandhi's peaceful mission of nonviolent resistance. Gabriel was enchanted, especially when he read about a Gandhi reference that would apply to their safe-space aspirations: This was from a foreword by Deepak Chopra for Marshall Rosenberg's book on nonviolent communication: "In India, there's an ancient model for nonviolent living known as Ahimsa, which is central to the nonviolent life. Ahimsa is usually defined as nonviolence, although its meaning extends from Mahatma Gandhi's peaceful protests to Albert Schweitzer's reverence for life. 'Do no harm' would be the first axiom of Ahimsa. What so impressed me about Marshall Rosenberg, who passed away at eighty, just six weeks before I write this, is that he grasped both levels of Ahimsa, action and consciousness." Excellent. Gabriel made a silent note to respect this in their project.

The River Kaveri

Ayaan had graciously offered Baloo's services to bring Gabriel and Tilda to Shantivanam from Chennai by army car, which they gladly accepted. They started early the following morning, without having any breakfast. Despite the early hour, they'd already spent ages leaving the city. Chennai, with its seven million inhabitants, according to a census, was a Moloch with traffic jams at every hour of the day. Then they had a very pleasant drive through the vast countryside of Tamil Nadu. Baloo took good care of them by stopping various times en route. Of course, in his usual bossy manner when stopping at one of the petrol stations, he yelled, "Sir, toilet!" This did not mean that he wanted to use the facilities. It was a command for them to relieve themselves. At first, Tilda murmured, "I do not need to," but she was immediately silenced by Baloo's stern soldier glance. They quickly adapted to his rhythm, as did their bodies. Baloo looked happier by the minute.

He became really happy at one of their last stops, in the late afternoon. This was at one of the many toll stations where they had to pay transit fees for the car. Usually, the army car simply passed them without stopping, but a young slender soldier stood at this one, and Baloo waved him to the car. "Balee," he said, introducing the young man to Gabriel and Tilda. "Another escort for you. Pa said it's necessary." Baloo and Balee—Gabriel could not believe it. The two of them seemed to be good friends and started to chat with each other in Tamil, laughing and tremendously enjoying themselves and their company. Balee had taken the driver seat. He was nearly the same careful and observant good driver as Baloo was. Good training in this Indian army. However, after some time, they changed seats again. Baloo could not let go for very long, not even to Balee.

Tilda fell asleep, and after a while, so did Balee, on the front passenger's seat. Gabriel was afraid that Baloo would also get tired in the sunset atmosphere of the early evening. But the soldier was not sleepy. Instead, he began singing in a soft, melodious baritone voice. Gabriel was amazed because he had not expected this from such a sturdy, stern soldier. Gabriel listened to the words: The song had a quite sad Indian melody, and the language was Tamil, from which he caught a word here and there. Baloo sang about the river Kaveri.

And at that moment, they passed the big bridge over that river in the red-gold glow of the brilliant sunset. Baloo smiled while singing and pointed down at the waters. "Mrs Toelz, wake up," Gabriel excitedly said to Tilda. "We must be close. This is the river Kaveri." Balee woke up as well. He and Baloo started to discuss directions. The discussion was intense enough that they even stopped the car at the side of the road. In the city of Tiruchirapalli, they passed and looked at maps on their mobile phones for a long time. Gabriel didn't interfere. These two guys were soldiers in their own country. They should know best how to find the ashram, and it was quickly getting dark now. They drove on in the dark for a long time. Baloo and Balee fell silent.

Gabriel's feeling was that they had left the Kaveri area, which was not good, because he knew from the Griffiths literature that the ashram was on the border of the river. "Say something, Mr David," Tilda prompted. She had read the book as well. They were driving through flat wasteland with only a little vegetation but many scattered huts and campsites of very poor people. The street was littered with all types of garbage and was very muddy. It didn't look at all like the picturesque photos they had found of the ashram on the Internet. Shortly before they decided to interfere in the faulty pathfinding of Baloo and Balee, Baloo swerved to the right, onto a dirt path with the sign "Saccidananda Ashram Shantivanam." Gabriel's feeling was a mixture of relief and disappointment: relief that this fourteen-hour journey had finally come to an end and disappointment in the spot it ended in. This did not look or feel right.

"Do you think this is correct, Mr David?" Tilda said, revealing his doubts. "No idea," he answered while Baloo drove on a muddy sand path with many deep potholes through dark corn fields. Tilda could physically feel Baloo's frustration and silent accusations about what godforsaken countryside they had lured him and his precious army car into. He endured this only for Ayaan—that was for sure. "There we are, thirty kilometres outside Trichy," Baloo said unpleasantly when he finally stopped in the dark in front of the closed gates of a fenced estate with a big sign at the entrance. "Saccidananda Ashram Shantivanam," Tilda read out loud, "Home for the Mentally Ill." They looked at each other, totally perplexed. Then Gabriel felt one of his gigantic gales of laughter bubbling up inside of him. He was completely powerless when absurdity stuck him this hard. Tears welled up in his eyes, and he winced with laughter in the backseat of the car. "Yes, this is indeed where we belong," he gasped.

Baloo was not amused at all but instead became even aggressive. It had been a long working day for him. It was not at an end, obviously, and it must have sounded as if these foreigners were making fun of him. "Sir," he barked sternly, "what's the matter?" "This is not the right address, Baloo," Gabriel said when he was able to speak again. "It is just the shelter home for people with mental illnesses that the ashram funds as a social project, do you understand?" Baloo nodded but was definitely not happy. "What address? Sir, you tell me right address," he demanded, sounding even quite threatening and furious now. "I told Ayaan everything I know," Gabriel replied, defending himself. The mood in the car hit rock bottom. They sat there in the dark for a long time. Then Gabriel had an idea: "There might be a phone number somewhere on the ashram's webpage or in the emails we got concerning our booking," he said. Hectically, Tilda searched for their discarded and neglected mobiles and laptops and tried to connect to the Internet.

That was, of course, difficult in the middle of these wastelands. However, she was able to come up with an email footer where a phone number for the ashram was listed. "Hand the phone to Baloo, Mrs Toelz," Gabriel advised. "He's the driver; he needs to know where to go from here. And he can speak Tamil." Tilda punched in the number and passed the phone to Baloo, who begrudgingly took it and set it to speaker so that everybody in the car could listen in. It started to beep. "Maybe the monks are already asleep. It is very late after all," Tilda said, prophesying doom. But somebody picked up the phone, and a pleasant male voice explained the route details in Tamil.

The night fell quickly now, and in the car, the temperature was freezing. The air conditioning, which had been a blessing during the heat of the day, turned into a nightmare now. It could not be switched off, for some reason, and Gabriel and Tilda were left shivering in their light summer clothes. They even fetched their shower towels from their luggage at some point to use them as substitute blankets. They arrived at Shantivanam closely huddled together against the freeze. It worked. They arrived warm and perfectly at ease with each other and the world. Gabriel was grateful to Tilda for having helped him to come here. The moment he stepped out of the car, Gabriel felt at home and safe. This had been his feeling the whole time over the past several years: If he could only reach Shantivanam, he would be fine. If there were any troubles before, they were left at the gate. Inside, people were still awake. There was a little welcoming committee waiting for them, and in the midst of it was the prior—the leader of the monks. Everybody in the group of welcomers was a little surprised to see Gabriel and Tilda's being brought by two army officers in a decorated military car, but the group recovered quickly. The prior led the way through the grounds to a single-storey stone house at the far end of the estate, which was under huge banana trees close to the fence that sheltered the house against the reed-covered bank slopes of the river Kaveri.

There was even dinner left. "I will quickly show you around for the time being, so that you'll be able find your own way. We will have a proper tour of the grounds tomorrow," the prior later said. They left the dining hall together and wandered on the narrow, sparsely illuminated paths that criss-crossed the estate so that people with dry and clean feet could get from here to there. The prior pointed at various huts, giving them names, but did not stop: gate house, dining hall, library, meditation room, Father Bede's hut, stable and novitiate. The first item that the prior stopped at was the grave of Bede Griffiths. Tilda looked at Gabriel with concern. She expected that he would immediately keel over when he saw the big quadratic gravestone between the two gravestones of the other two Shantivanam founders. However, Gabriel stood his ground, silently staring at the displayed dates —1906–1993—and decided that he would return later tonight, alone. There were two objects close to the grave that the prior showed and explained. The building closest to the grave was the rotunda church. It shimmered, appearing inviting, warm and welcoming in its white brilliance, featuring statues of meditating people all around. Unfortunately, it was already locked, owing to the late hour. The other object was a huge banyan tree close to the church and the grave. The prior recited: "This banyan tree which has its roots upward and its branches down, and the Vedic hymns are its leaves. One who knows this tree is the knower of the Vedas." He laughed at their confused faces and explained. "That was the Bhagavat Gita. It says that our material world is like a tree whose roots are above and whose branches are below—the same way that we experience a tree when it is reflected in water, upside down. Similarly, our material world is a just reflection, a mere unsubstantial shadow of the real, transcendent world. This shadow world only helps us to understand the real world. This tree here is doing the same. Do you understand?" It was good that they had read some Bede Griffiths. Hearing it spoken—or, better, having it materialise—was totally different, however. Next, the prior brought them to their hut and said good night. Entering their respective apartments, both Gabriel and Tilda suffered the same shock: no toilet paper! After he had emptied his backpack and showered, Gabriel decided to visit the grave again. Their hut was dark and silent, like all the others on the grounds. Tilda had probably fallen asleep long before he went out on his solitary walk towards the graveyard. Nobody was to be seen. It was very warm and the air perfectly still. At the grave, he was at first disappointed to have no revelation or any other sensation. Instead, he felt perfectly at ease, even happy. Then he remembered that *Bede* etymologically means "eternal, living, immortal," with a German Celtic origin. Sitting at a grave was probably not what Bede Griffiths had in mind for him. Looking around for where to go next, his eyes, now used to the darkness, fell on the library. That was a building that Bede Griffiths had himself added to the complex of huts. It was a rotunda like the church and had some benches on its outside walls, which were partitioned into an octagon so that the eight benches would face the slightly different angles of the estate. He leisurely wandered over to the little building and took a seat on one of the benches, looking enchanted into the groves of banana trees and palm trees.

A few moments later, he saw movement in the dark grounds. Somebody was slowly coming with careful steps through the pitch-black night. It was Tilda. She was still about two hundred metres away with many trees and a number of huts between them. Of course, she could not see Gabriel, because the library and his bench were in perfect darkness. Only he could see her on the dimly lit path network that criss-crossed the wide area. However, like being pulled on a string, she slowly approached, waiting and feeling her way at every crossing, taking the right turn at each junction after some consideration. It was fascinating to watch. In this way, she approached the library until she saw him. She was stunned. Gabriel smiled in the dark. She silently recovered from her surprise, and without saying a word, she glided to the bench and sat by his side. They sat in silence for about an hour, enjoying the night that was full of birdsong, cricket chirping and whispering leaves. Then it started to get cold. Gabriel stood up and walked away without turning his head. Tilda stayed behind.

Angels' Play

Location:
Heaven above Shantivanam. Shared-Office Cloud.

Time:
Real-time GMT+5.30, Saturday, 10 January 2020, 09:00 IST

Players:
The two angels as before and Bede Griffiths.

Setting:
Both angels are now heavily decorated Hindu temple cows because of the change in location. They are standing side by side in the conference facility on the cloud that has become a lecture theatre. Bede Griffiths is wandering up and down before their trunks, pointing every now and again with a large stick to the slides of a PowerPoint presentation displayed on a big screen.

BG
(*compassionately*):
   Nearly there, my dears, nearly there!

TA
(*indignantly*):
   Why are we still cows? I want to be an angel. You promised I would be an angel again.

BG
(*soothingly*):
   I told you that it's still a bit early to take your exams. There are two more lectures to go.

GA
(*checking its results on its multi-choice exam test sheet*):
   I didn't do too badly. Look: only eight mistakes. It should have sufficed for the automatic transformation back into an angel.

TA
(*unbelieving*):
   I have an unbelievable twenty-two wrong answers (*accusingly looking at BG*). Do you have any advice, teacher?

BG
(*with hidden serenity*):
   Yes, you can go down and make friends with Gabriel. The two of you have been shy like strangers with each other in the past.

TA

(*defensively*):

Gabriel is not my concern. I'm Tilda's angel!

BG

(*soberly*):

Momentarily, you are a Hindu cow. A Wishing Cow, the cow of the plenty, the grantor of wishes with the name Kamadhenu. As such, you are in the right position to make friends down there. It's time that you regard Gabriel and Tilda as one.

TA

(*still not convinced*):

I am a Michaelite, an active fighter for love, an angel with weapons—not a powerless cow. Can't I be something a little more dangerous—like a serpent—for a change?

We have totally lost the serpent motif if you ask me. It was central before and would much better fit Tilda's mindset than the cow I am now.

BG

(*with certainty*):

You are all of that. Attention, my dears, I continue your Vedic lectures.

(*both cows desperately mooing; BG with authority in a lecturing voice*)

I cite the Bhagavad Gita for you: chapter 10, verse 28. It says, "I am the Vajra—thunderbolt—among weapons and Kamadhenu among the cows. I am Kaamdev, the god of love, among all causes for procreation; among serpents I am Vasuki."

Both cows begin to audibly ruminate.

Open Access This chapter is licensed under the terms of the Creative Commons Attribution 4.0 International License (http://creativecommons.org/licenses/by/4.0/), which permits use, sharing, adaptation, distribution and reproduction in any medium or format, as long as you give appropriate credit to the original author(s) and the source, provide a link to the Creative Commons license and indicate if changes were made.

The images or other third party material in this chapter are included in the chapter's Creative Commons license, unless indicated otherwise in a credit line to the material. If material is not included in the chapter's Creative Commons license and your intended use is not permitted by statutory regulation or exceeds the permitted use, you will need to obtain permission directly from the copyright holder.

Chapter 9
Final Unity

Breakfast took place in the dining hall of the monastery, a room called the refectory, where they had been the evening before. After breakfast, which consisted of rice with some vegetables and sauce and was taken in total silence with an amiably squatting congregation of about ten people, Gabriel and Tilda, like all other guests, helped with peeling and cutting vegetables for today's meal on the open terrace of the dining hall. It was a lovely morning but looked a little like rain. After they were done, they had a work meeting with the prior, updating him about the new project, about the Indian case study as it stood in the moment and about the Indian project partners they would visit or had already visited in Chennai and Kerala. They also announced Ayaan's visit for the day of their departure, who will talk about Shantivanam as a potential safe space for the project.

Then they talked about the caste system. Gabriel was quite curious to hear the prior's views as an Indian Benedictine given Bede Griffiths' quite critical remarks about the sufferings, injustices and cruelties of the Indian social system despite his deep respect for Eastern spirituality. To his surprise, the prior was not half as critical as Bede Griffiths. "Foreign people do not really understand. It is not as bad as you think it is. The original idea is very humane," he said. He explained the origins of the caste system from a Hindu perspective and talked about the current social stratification system, developing his ideas on advantages, disadvantages, and improvements.

"There is so much to be done. This project is a huge enterprise. Even at this preparatory stage, you have a lot work to do in setting up all these case studies," the prior said admiringly. "You're right. And as you very well know, there are only a few workers in the vineyard," Gabriel smiled, "but I have Mrs Toelz, and she is doing a great job. Without her work, it would be impossible. Once the project is up and running, there will be about thirty people working on it. By the way, Tilda will lead the overall project once it's running."

The prior looked at Tilda a little sceptically. She scowled back.

The Heart of Everything

Then they walked the grounds. The first thing the prior showed them was Bede Griffiths' hut. Entering via a tiny veranda with a rocket chair, the prior opened the thatched door to Father Bede's hut. "We left everything more or less the way it was when he died," he explained. "The only thing we did is put together a little museal collection of his things in the backroom." The door of the hut opened to the main room of about ten square metres, which featured a small bed facing the door, a desk in front of the window and a chair. That was it. There wasn't much to look at but the small tidy heap of orange clothes that were neatly folded on the bed as if laid out for somebody to wear them today. Tilda passed the room quickly to go with the prior to the tiny backroom, where he started to explain Father Bede's memorabilia.

Gabriel stayed behind and took position leaning against the wall just beside the bed so that she could look around. He had to smile. It was in the middle of everything. Through the open door across the veranda, he could see the stables and hear the cows moving and mooing. Through the windows, he could see the church, the library and many palm trees, under which peacocks wandered the shady greens bespeckled with sunny spots. He could hear the birds singing and listened to the light breeze whispering in the peaceful banana forest. Every now and again, one of the monks passed by amid his work duties—sometimes alone, sometimes with a visitor talking. The rest was silence. It was at the same time completely remote and the heart of everything. Gabriel stood there for a long time to see what Father Bede had seen all his life when he sat on his veranda or lay down on his bed.

Gabriel closed his eyes, and suddenly, he was perfectly happy. He felt no desire for anything. Instead, he had the feeling that everything was flowing through this little hut, through the spot he was standing on, through his whole being. It—he—was part of a network connecting heaven and earth in a deep experience of the divine, people in close relationship and intense sociality with him, embedded in nature with all its creatures. The most miraculous feeling was that he had no self in that moment. Everything flowed through him, could flow only through him, because he was somehow not there standing in the way. His self was gone, and at the same time, he was more himself than he had ever felt before. It was a perfect moment. In terms of earthly time, it lasted only seconds.

It lasted long enough for him to start to understand. This was what Bede Griffiths meant in all his talking about 'the renunciation of the self.' It was not about having less of everything. It was about letting everything happen in the first place. It was about abundance. How could he have been so stupid as to not have seen this before? From here, inside his soul, everything started to make sense. This was the starting point to make ends meet, to resolve social conflicts, to integrate conflicting interests and beliefs, to reach out to struggling humankind. How could this be translated into a project?

"Are you coming?" the prior asked. He smiled strangely and understandingly when Gabriel entered the small backroom; he seemed to be a truly empathetic man. Gabriel joined the other two in the vestibule and listened to the histories of the little collection of items, such as pictures, a few books, an old-fashioned typewriter, a watch or a pocketknife, that were displayed there on a narrow sideboard.

After visiting the Griffiths hut, the prior showed them a cave for meditation. The monks had really put together an architectonic structure that looked like a little stone cave that strongly reminded them of the perpetual allegory. What Tilda did not like were the stables. Why were they caging animals? They were Indians after all. Why could they not set them free like others did? She deeply disapproved. Gabriel laughed when he saw her frown. "Why are you keeping cows?" she asked the prior. "We keep them as livestock, of course," he answered in a sober, matter-of-fact voice with questioningly raised eyebrows.

For midday prayer, Tilda joined the congregation in church. There, she got her first tika on her forehead: At midday prayer, it was a red tika—red for the holy spirit, fire, life and love. That was the right thing to get in the middle of the day, when you needed high spirits most. In the morning, there would be a white one for light, birth, the beginning of the day and the innocence coming from sleep. In the evening, it would be a black one for death, ash, sleep and night. From then on, Tilda went to every prayer that took place in that church.

Angels' Play

Location:
Heaven above Shantivanam. Shared-Office Cloud.

Time:
Real-time GMT+5.30, Saturday, 10 January 2020, 19:07 India Standard Time (IST)

Players:
The two angels as before and Bede Griffiths.

Setting:
Same setting: Both angels are still cows. BG is again feeding them green bananas.

GA (*trying to get back on cordial terms with BG*):
Father, did you have the same feelings as Gabriel's about your hut? And how does this relate to the usual cell of a monk in a monastery?

BG (*enthusiastically*):
The hut was my cell. As I related in *The Return to the Center*, I sat there on the veranda of my cell, watching the sun set behind the trees, and recalled the day, nearly fifty years ago, when I watched the same sun setting over the playing fields at school in Sussex.

My cell at Shantivanam was this thatched hut surrounded by trees. I could listen to the birds singing, as I did over there in Sussex, and watched the trees make dark patterns against the sky as the light fades, but I've travelled a long way both in space and in time since then. There were tall palmyra palms around me and young coconut trees growing up between them, and the bananas were spreading their broad leaves like green sails (*he laughs delightedly and passes a fresh banana over to GA*).

TA (*sceptically*):
Sounds good. But were you really at home there? It sounds so... different.

BG (*weighing his head*):
I could hear a robin singing, but it was a black Indian robin, and the voice of the cuckoo which came from the distant woods was that of the Indian cuckoo. I'd made my home there in India, in the Tamil Nadu, by the banks of the river Cavery, but my mind had also travelled no less far than my body. For sixteen years, I'd lived as an Indian among Indians, following Indian ways of life, studying Indian thought and immersing myself in the living traditions of the Indian spirit.

TA (*still sceptical*):
Didn't you miss Western things? I mean, you, a distinguished scholar.

BG (*smiling*):
I had my little hut, which was simple enough, just one small room with a thatched roof, but it was solidly built of brick with a concrete floor. I also had a table, a chair and a bed, which are luxuries for a sannyasi, but I wasn't able to learn how to always sit and always sleep on the floor. I also had my books and my typewriter, but these weren't really 'mine' any more than the hut or the furniture—they were, as we say, 'allowed for my use.'

TA (*full of compassion*):
You poor sod!

BG (*very convinced*):
Poverty—the poverty of spirit of the Sermon on the Mount—is a total detachment from the material world. It means to recognise that everything comes from God: our bodies, our breath, our very existence. We cannot properly possess anything—not even our own bodies, as St. Benedict says. At any moment, we can only receive from God: our life, our food, our clothing, our shelter, our books, our friends. Everything comes from God, created anew at every moment. If there weren't this constantly renewed creation, everything would sink into nothingness.

GA (*eagerly*):
Father, is that what you mean by *detachment*?

BG (*nodding and then speaking in his lecturing voice*):
When you are detached from the world, you see everything coming from the hands of God, always fresh and beautiful. Everything is a symbol of God.

The modern age has banished God from the world, and it has therefore also banished beauty. Everything has become "profane," exiled from the sphere of the "holy," and thus, everything has lost its meaning. After all, the holy is the source of truth in the same way that it is of beauty. It relates the world to the one, transcendent Reality from which the world derives its existence, its meaning and its loveliness.

TA (*soberly*):
I think serving the world is much better than detaching from it—showing it your cold shoulder.

BG (*mildly*):
But this kind of detachment from the world is in no way opposed to serving the world or being "committed" to the world. It is freedom from all *selfish* attachment. Only when you are free from the self—that is, free from self-love and self-will—can you really serve the world. You can then see things as they are and use them as they should be used. The poet or artist has to be detached from the world if they are to truly reflect it in their art. The scientist must be detached from things if they are to deal with them scientifically. But the saint needs a more radical detachment than either. They must be detached from their very self.

TA (*frustrated*):
I'm an angel, no saint, but also no cow. Please, father, can I become my very self again? I mean, an angel.

BG (*elegantly English*):
Wait and see and drink tea.

Toilet Paper and Salvation

Sunday afternoon, Gabriel and Tilda set out to buy toilet paper without telling the prior, who would have thought them to be snobs. They wanted toilet paper. They were in desperate need of toilet paper. When they wandered towards the ashram gates, nobody was to be seen. So they were left to their own devices in finding their way to the next village. Gabriel's mobile phone showed the river Kaveri, a small country road close by (probably the road they had taken by car), and then a lot of nothing—no habitation. However, in both directions, left and right at their side of the river, there seemed to be a village, each about ten kilometres away. "That's doable," Tilda encouragingly decided. "Which village do you want to try, Mr David—left or right?"

They decided on left and went down to the riverbank. There, they wandered along Kaveri, staying off the road in order to avoid traffic. It was a lovely walk, though this riverbank was definitely not made for strollers given that it didn't have a path or anything resembling one. Instead, there were vast wastelands with wide expanses of deep sands full of rocks and reeds, criss-crossed by small streams and ponds. More than once, they could only muster all their courage to jump small rivulets of about two metres in breadth, to avoid having to take long detours.

"Bunny, hop!" Gabriel laughingly scouted to Tilda and took a mighty run-up to jump himself. It was quite difficult to move forward in these scattered swamplands full of puddles and foot traps, so their approach to the village was very slow and took them nearly the whole afternoon. But they chatted away in perfect harmony and were quite happy. The path got a little more comfortable when they came closer. The riverbank was a little neater and better suited for passersby. Gabriel found two big heart-shaped rose quartzes on the shore. They were quite dirty from debris and mud. Tilda looked at them doubtingly. "Do you really think they're rose quartzes?" she asked. "They're really big." "I'm sure they are, Mrs Toelz. Wait until I've washed them," Gabriel said and put them into his rucksack.

The village turned out to be a little town of decent-enough size to feature a long street with many shops. However, there was no toilet paper, lo and behold. No hankies or tissues, either. Shopkeepers didn't even know what Gabriel and Tilda were asking for. In the end, they bought a big package of paper table napkins and were very happy about it. Then Tilda wanted to buy some light clothes, and Gabriel looked out for some short-sleeved shirts. That wasn't easy, either. They felt huge among the Indians, who were much smaller and slimmer than they were. In all the shops, they looked for L and XL sizes, but often in vain. Furthermore, it had started to rain heavily, and the evening quickly turned to twilight. Tilda bought a colourful Indian dress, and Gabriel bought two shirts, one white and one pale blue. Then, happily talking, they started their way back, carrying their purchases.

They decided not to take the same route on their way back. It would have been much too dangerous in the dark to walk these grounds without being able to see where their feet would land. Thus, they discussed whether to take the country road that ran through dense forests and vast wastelands and followed in parallel with the river, about one kilometre away. It would take them back to the heights of Shantivanam like the river would have done. There was nearly no traffic on this road through the middle of nowhere anyway. They would only need to find the junction to the ashram that was close to the river, again. It started to rain heavily, and they were soaked down to the skin in their light clothes. The good thing was that it was quite warm: about thirty degrees Celsius. But it was a pitch-black night, except for the occasional headlights of a passing motor bike or car.

Angels' Play

Location:
Heaven above the country road, 10 kilometres away from Shantivanam. Shared-Office Cloud.

Time:
Real-time GMT+5.30, Sunday, 11 January 2020, 20:57 IST

Players:
The two angels as before.

Setting:
Both angels are still cows, who obviously still haven't passed their respective exams. They are alone, standing at their desks in the cockpit area desperately trying to

come to terms with the equipment and having to use just their trunks. Every device is blinking and beeping, but the cows seem to be relatively helpless.

TA (*morosely scanning the Script on its console*):
A blue-sky attack! Red alert! I want to be a Michaelite. I need my weapons. I can't fight properly as a cow.

GA (*mockingly, but also quite worried*):
Haven't you ever heard of bullfighting? But why fight at all? Can't they simply run away, for a change?

TA (*shaking its big cow head*):
Tilda's foot's bad again. She can't run, and she can't hold her own against that gang. And Gabriel is useless as always, both at running and at fighting. And where is Father Bede?

The cows are looking at each other desolately. If they opt to use their last resort, which is an emergency call to TRINI-T, their promotion will be out of question for a long time because they will have demonstrated that they can't cope with a situation on their own.

GA (*resignedly*):
Emergency call to Upper Management?

TA (*resignedly*):
Emergency call to Upper Management.

Mortal Fear

When Gabriel and Tilda left the last streetlights of the village, total darkness enveloped them while they walked in the pouring rain. Right and left of the muddy road were swamplands, trees, bushes and a little river coming close every now and again. A few times, Gabriel used the torchlight from his mobile phone to illuminate an approaching obstacle, like a fallen tree, a cairn or the like.

The only human dwellings that could be seen through the darkness were the occasional campsites or untidy palm tree huts of very poor people squatting close to the road. It promised at least a connection to civilisation. During the many kilometres of their walk, this type of vegetation and human settlement grew a few times into villages with stone huts, bigger houses and some side streets, but never to a size featuring streetlights, shops or any other infrastructure.

The first few kilometres, they still chatted quite contently, but it eventually became tedious. The exhausting day took its toll. But also, the atmosphere had changed and got more and more threatening. When they left the town, some young men on motorbikes passed them. Gabriel and Tilda hadn't given much heed, because there'd been whole groups of them inside town chatting and playing with their mobile phones, and of course, they would be leaving to where they lived, on the outskirts, in the late evening. However, the men were not leaving. They came back through the rain. At first, there were only four or five of them driving very slowly a short distance behind Gabriel and Tilda. Next, some more appeared in front of them from the other side as well, waiting at the kerb and letting them pass to join the others. They looked at Gabriel and Tilda with not very friendly, frowning scrutiny: Some talked in Tamil; others typed on their mobiles.

Gabriel could feel the young men's testosterone-fuelled aggression and Tilda's fear. She was scared shitless. So was he. "It's only a matter of time until they attack us, Mr David," Tilda whispered, looking back to their escort, which was about two hundred metres behind them. The young men numbered nearly twenty by then. Gabriel had to agree. "What can we do?" he asked. "It's pitch dark. They wouldn't be able see us if we left the road and moved into the marshlands," Tilda suggested. "We'll lose the way if we leave the road, Mrs Toelz," he objected. "Do you want to be killed by these guys?" she asked, urging him to reconsider before continuing: "We can stay close by and try walking in parallel with the street to stay on course." They used the next curve to get out of sight for their escape.

Their plan, however, proved to be nearly impossible to follow. The road was the only feasible path through this jungle of rain-soaked vegetation. Everything else was just an ordeal. First, they hid for a long time in the dark, lying low behind trees and bushes. They heard the motorbikes driving up and down the road where Gabriel and Tilda had left it. Only once they were sure nobody would follow them into the tangled undergrowth did they start to move forward. Their progress was slow, and several times, they had to go back to the road again because obstacles such as large rivulets without a bridge, reed bogs or wild thorn hedges barred their way.

Only on these occasions were they able to move forward faster through the dark coppice. However, each time back on the road, it was only a matter of a few minutes before one of the men spotted Gabriel and Tilda. The men called their mates on their mobile phones and quickly rearranged their phalanx. And they zeroed in on Gabriel and Tilda, coming closer and closer and excitedly shouting to each other like they were giving chase. They *were* giving chase. And Gabriel and Tilda were their game. They played this hide-and-seek game for a long time. Each time, it became more frightening. On the street, the followers came close to getting within touching distance. Gabriel and Tilda could see them leering at Tilda and evaluating Gabriel's defensibility. In passing, some of the men tried to strike him, testing his responses. For them, the time for a full-contact fight had come. But Gabriel and Tilda were not ready for it yet and instead escaped into the dark marshlands once more. But now, they didn't dare to return to the road anymore and took the chance to move as far away from it as possible.

This was how they got completely lost. They slowly moved forward for hours, trying to stay on course, but they had no idea where they were. "Mr David, we must be close to the ashram by now," Tilda whispered, looking at another collection of dark campsites and huts lying in front of them. "Let's see whether your mobile phone can give us an idea. Maybe there is a signal closer to the huts." They cautiously approached the buildings without raising attention. And indeed, Gabriel's mobile phone showed the Kaveri, the road, the ashram and their location again. Of course, they were not close to the road or the river in the middle of the wastelands.

However, what their shocked eyes discovered was that the small blue dot indicating their location in the middle of nowhere had moved far beyond the location of the ashram. They had missed their destination because instead of walking on the road, they had walked in the swamp and simply passed by. They were now very close to that other village to the right of the ashram. They were both close to tears from exhaustion by now. "We have to go back, Mrs Toelz," Gabriel said desperately. "Yes, but we can't take the road," Tilda said. "We're too weak to even run now if they attack us. They'll still be there waiting for us." "But we might miss the junction to the ashram again, like we obviously did when we ended up here," he objected. Tilda soberly replied: "If they have some sense, they will be waiting exactly at that very junction. The ashram is the only place where foreigners like us can be expected to go in this wilderness." They stood in the pouring rain and mud-dirty and wet.

Tilda had a wound dripping blood from her cheek, probably from getting it caught on a bramble or something. She was limping heavily again. Gabriel's hands and knees were bleeding because he tripped when trying to guard Tilda against a blow from one of the passing motorcyclists on the rocky grounds of the street. "There's nothing but left but to give it a try. We can't stay here. There's no shelter from the rain or from a raid," he said. Consequently, they turned again and crawled back through the undergrowth, listening to the sometimes-growing, sometimes-diminishing noise from the motorbikes through the night. It was strange that they again lost their way because they tried to precisely retrace the way they had come. At least they found a kind of foot path through the wasteland, specifically the dark campsites and huts of poor people, where people were now fast asleep. They hadn't seen a living soul for the past two hours.

It was in the middle of the night. At least that saved them from menacing glances and further dangers of assault, besides those of the road gang. In the dark and the rain, they could see only to the next corner of the path, and after that corner, the next one came. Nothing else. They were totally exhausted by now. Tilda sweaty face contorted with pain, but she didn't cry. The mobile phone signal had long since been lost, so they could no longer check it to find their way.

At a certain point, it was clear to them that they would not make it back to Shantivanam that night. They came to a standstill and looked at each other—a timid, sorry pair. It was time to admit defeat. "Let's just look round the next corner," Gabriel said, just to say something. Tilda weakly shook her head, but he pushed her forward. He was ready to carry her if necessary but was not sure how far that would go. Probably for another hundred metres, but that'd be it. They turned the corner of one of the dark dwellings in a campsite.

Miraculous Salvation

And there was a shimmering monstrance in the distance! It looked like a proper Bavarian procession for Corpus Christi. Totally unreal. Tilda's mouth fell open. Gabriel's too. Ahead, a big golden tabernacle monstrance with a eucharistic host inside was carried high over the heads of the congregation by the preceding priest, who was surrounded by fellow celebrants clad in red and golden habits. Then came an acolyte in white with a big wooden cross, accompanied by about twenty more acolytes carrying incense bowls, candles, loudspeakers, pictures of saints and other devotionalia. Then came a congregation of about eighty to a hundred worshippers carrying torches and lamps, providing light in a rainbow of colours. When the procession came closer, Gabriel and Tilda heard that everybody was chanting Tamil church songs that were led by the priest, whose words were amplified by a mike and loudspeakers. All the people were clad in festive clothes, looking bright and colourful thanks to the illumination from moving lights—despite the campsite's darkness surrounding them and the heavy rain falling on everybody. Nobody seemed to care in the least. They came from the left, down a dirt path, and proceeded to the right.

When they passed Gabriel and Tilda, the two of them discovered that the priest carrying the monstrance was the prior of Shantivanam. Seeing them in the pitch dark, his eyes widened as big as plates. They probably looked like ghosts standing there in the middle of nowhere, lost and full of dirt and blood. However, he was in service and could not ask. He just winked with his eyes that they should follow the congregation. He would not have needed to. He, the procession and the monstrance had saved their lives. Gabriel and Tilda following the procession for a long time through the wastelands until it ended at a little hamlet with a chapel, which was the destination of the congregation. Tilda took some pictures of the worshippers: Her ordeal had been at an end with the appearance of the procession. It'd even stopped raining. They didn't feel any further exertion in this nighttime walk. There were little kids with the procession looking at the two Western strangers with the same curiosity as the adults did. At the chapel, the prior held a short service. It was obviously a benediction and blessing for the chapel, bearing the name of St. Francis. It ended with a song that Gabriel and Tilda knew by now from Shantivanam, where they found a translation into English:

> Om bhur bhuva svaha
> *(Om, the earth, the heavens and the beyond)*
> Tat savitur varenyam
> *(Creator, we worship you)*
> Bhargo devasya dhimahi
> *(May we receive the glorious splendour of this divine light)*
> Dhiyo yo nah prachodayát (3 times)
> *(May he enlighten our meditation and prayer)*
> Om, lokáh samasthá sukhino bhavantuh (3 times)
> *(Om, may the whole world be happy)*
> Om, asato má sad gamaya,
> *(Om, from unreality, lead us to reality)*
> Tamaso má jyotir gamaya,
> *(From darkness lead us into light)*
> Mrityor má amritam gamaya.
> *(From death lead us into immortality)*
> Om, púrnam, adah, púrnam idam,
> *(Om, that is fullness, this is fullness;)*
> Púrnat púrnam udachyate,

(out of abundance comes abundance)
púrnasya púrnam ádáya,
(Remove fullness from fullness,)
púrnam eva avashishyate.
(so fullness alone remains.)
Om, shanti, shanti, shanti.
(Om, peace, peace, peace.)

There was even a little reception at the side of the ceremony where Gabriel and Tilda got some soft drinks and food that the congregation had brought with them. "I don't know what adventure you come from, but you do look terribly worn out," the prior said a little ironically to them on a short break where he was waylaid by many worshippers who wanted to talk to him. "There'll more food back at the ashram. This is one of our big church festivities of the year, and the ashram caters this night for the whole neighbourhood with a large meal." Gabriel and Tilda could hardly believe their luck. The prior saw it and giggled merrily. "See, you haven't even missed your dinner. Simply follow the monstrance. Then all will be well!" Obviously, he thought this to be hilarious because he giggled his head off. The Dalai Lama was a sad and dreary sod compared to the prior of Shantivanam. They did as they were told. The Shantivanam people had put together a great buffet for the night when they arrived with the procession. Everybody went for the finger food and the drinks. Only Tilda and Gabriel were too exhausted to join. Seeing the gates of the ashram, all remaining energy—and that was closing in on zero—left their strained bodies. Tilda could hardly walk to their hut. However, Gabriel heard her coming up the dark staircase, limping. Questioningly, he looked at her. She gave him half of the toilet paper napkins that had been in her rucksack, totally forgotten by the two of them until then. Then, without a word, she turned and limped down to her room. The napkins were soaked. Before Gabriel went to bed, he spread the precious resource on the floor to let them dry.

Angels' Play

Location:
Heaven above Shantivanam. Shared-Office Cloud.

Time:
Real-time GMT+5.30, Monday, 12 January 2020, 14:24 IST

Players:
The two angels as before.

Setting:
Both angels are now olive-brown tiger frogs. They are alone. The mood has hit rock bottom.

GA (*angry*):

Congratulations. The first time in our relationship that you look better than me. My singing voice has become a croak. I'm done as a Gabrielite.

TA (*also totally frustrated*):

To be honest, I'm fed up with this. Should we give up? Obviously, we can't pass this bloody exam. I had only eleven mistakes this time, and look at the result. Frog. Mine was probably sufficient to punish both of us. (*enviously*) I bet you had zero mistakes.

GA (*slightly turning yellow in body colour*):

Kiss me. Maybe *The Frog Prince* stuff is working again in this body.

TA (*not very forthcoming*):

Keep dreaming. A frog kissing a frog makes a frog. Every minor cosmic power knows this. It was part of my #MeToo sexual harassment training last year. How many mistakes did you make in the exam? Zero?

GA (*evasively*):

You're hopeless. For you, croaking makes no difference to what you're usually doing anyway. For me, my world is in shambles. A Gabrielite with an air sac for croaking louder than a shanty choir of old sailors singing 'My Bonnie Lies Over the Ocean.' I want to die.

TA (*hopelessly*):

I have no idea of how to get us out of here.

GA (*with an attempt at black humour*):

If personnel should ever offer a course in creativity and out-of-the-box thinking, please remind me to recommend your participation.

TA (*suddenly*):

Actually, I have an idea—or, better, a suspicion. Maybe, we aren't frogs *by chance*. Maybe, it's part of the bigger picture and has to do with sex (*turning itself slightly yellow in body colour*).

GA (*stiffly*):

I beg your pardon?

TA (*eagerly*):

Let's call D.H. Lawrence. He might know. He's our sexpert, as you know.

GA (*tearfully*):

Oh, please no. Not that guy again! He's a pervert and offensive.

TA (*simply*):

Any better idea or cool, creative thinking is entirely welcome. Any angel, frog or what-have-you: Speak up now or forever hold your cackling croak.

Using its frog phalanges to punch the contact details of DHL into its console.

The device blinks yellow and immediately receives a welcome answer, which comes from the sonorous voice of DHL. Both bullfrogs are emptying their dark-blue air sacs, relieved but embarrassed in their helpless surrender.

Evolution Starts from the Waters

When Gabriel and Tilda woke up early next morning, it was raining cats and dogs. These monsoon-type waterfalls were not comparable to any European rainy day. After breakfast, Tilda wanted to work on project issues and went back to her room. Gabriel had a meeting with the prior to go on a quiet talk. The prior said that he was born in a wealthy tourist spot near the ocean named Kanyakumari, a small town of thirty thousand inhabitants in the very south of India, into an educated family with high professional aspirations for him as a son. "It was probably disappointing for them when I became a Benedictine monk," he said, laughing. They then talked a lot about the differences between Hinduism and Christianity, about Bede Griffiths and *The Marriage of East and West* and about evolution. Gabriel showed him the book that he bought at the bookshop in New Camaldoli Hermitage in the US. It was written by Carter Phipps and was titled *Evolutionaries*. "Let me know if it contains enlightening insights," the prior said, grinning. "Do you think there's hope for humankind? That there's an evolutionary movement to a new consciousness, to a new creation?" Gabriel asked. "We're looking for that in our new project, coming from a social science background, such as philosophy and social theory, building on the work of Hegel, Adorno, Habermas and related authors. However, this and other bodies of literature seem to need to incorporate theological and spiritual approaches for them to make sense." The prior agreed.

"How about a joint reading exercise in preparation of our new project, Mrs Toelz?" Gabriel asked Tilda later, still full of his conversation with the prior. "Good idea," she said, "but what book?" "Let's read Carter Phipps's *Evolutionaries* together," Gabriel suggested. Tilda was enthusiastic. "Your place or mine, Mr David?" she asked, smiling. Even dirty little jokes! "Let's go onto my balcony and bring your chair. Then we'll have a view. We can look at the river Kaveri in the distance while sitting in the tops of the banana trees with hummingbirds around us. I'll prepare everything." Gabriel jumped to the first floor and prepared their green reading chamber. When he was done, he looked around: It was perfect. The roofed balcony sheltering against the rain was about two metres broad and five metres long. They were sitting on it like they were in a banana tree house in the middle of nature, overlooking the ashram and the marshlands ahead of them. He'd put the little wooden table from his room in the middle of the balcony, with the book by Carter Phipps, two bottles of mineral water and some pens on top. Then he rang the little metal bell that hung at the side of his window. It was about the size of a cup and in the shape of a peacock. Tilda came immediately. "You rang the bell, sir?" she asked like a maid. "Yes, Mrs Toelz, I want to talk to you about creation and evolution." He showed her the peacock and everything. She was enchanted. She was the first to read. Gabriel sat back, relaxed and listened to the rain. They read until it was too dark to read with their torchlights. When they stopped and packed everything up to go to bed, bullfrogs started singing their weird song.

It was "The Night of the Croaking Frogs." The noise was maddening. There was no escape from it. It was everywhere. Hundreds, if not thousands, of bright-yellow bullfrogs could already be seen at dusk in the marshlands in front of their hut. After the heavy rains ended, everything was now underwater. Male bullfrogs had changed their colour from green brownish with dark spots to lemon yellow for mating season, to attract females. Usually, their bodies were olive or brownish with dark spots—which was why they were also called tiger frogs. In the mating season, the colour changes to bright yellow. Their air sacs turned dark blue and were used for hours and hours without interruption before, during and after copulation. The male frogs in front of their hut were particularly randy. When they went to bed after reading—in their own beds—the frog mating started. It was not simply noise. It was the loudest sound either of them had ever heard, with two exceptions: having a jackhammer in your own hands without professional ear protection and standing in the middle of a Spanish mascletà in the narrow streets of Valencia without means of escape because of the crowds. The noise reverberated in their skeletons. It took complete possession of them. It was not only in the ears; it was in the bodies. Tilda closed all the windows and the door to her room despite the hot temperatures and put up all clothes that she had in order to fill the cracks and crannies in the door and window frames. But it was to no avail. The sound was bloodcurdling.

Angels' Play

Location:
Heaven above Shantivanam. Shared-Office Cloud.

Time:
Real-time GMT+5.30, Tuesday, 13 January 2020, 09:00 IST

Players:
The two angels as before, Bede Griffiths and Swami Vivekananda.

Setting:
It's time for the angel exam. Bede Griffiths benevolently presides over it at the conference table, reading a book.

A big stopwatch before him shows time mercilessly ticking away.

Both angels are sitting—in angel shape, for practical reasons —far apart from each other to prevent them from copying from each other's work—or, more precisely, TA copying from GA.

Angelic heads are bent over their exam sheets. Perfect silence takes over, except for the occasional heavy sigh from TA.

Suddenly, the bell of the stopwatch rings. GA gets up and submits its paperwork. BG has to tear the paper from under TA's hurried hands, which try to finish the last entries.

TA (*complaining, expecting to be turned into a frog or something any minute*):
We had far too little time.

BG (*checking the multiple-choice and free-text entries of both angels against the evaluation pattern and scoring the results. Both angels observe him with apprehension and hope*):
You passed. Both of you. With honours. Zero mistakes.

GA (*secretly very relieved*):
I don't believe it. Let me see what TA did in the last multiple-choice section. I'm not so much interested in the free-text parts: I'm sure TA can talk itself out of any issue without even knowing any of the details.

BG triumphantly shares the scored multiple-choice part of TA's exam. There are three sections.

Section 1 asks for the "evolutionary path of Hinduism," giving three options:

Rigveda—Brahmanas—Upanishads—Bhagavad Gita; Hinayana—Mahayana; or Aramaic Judaism—Graeco-Roman Thought. TA has ticked the first option. 10 points out of 10 possible.

Section 2 asks "What is the One Divine Truth called?" Giving a long list of options, such as Brahman, Christ, Allah, Yahweh, Tao, Holy One of Israel, Saccidananda, Nirvana and All of the above, the lattermost of which is what TA has chosen. Again 10 points out of 10 possible.

The last section is very tricky. It asks, "What is your preferred shape as a cosmic power?" It gives the following options: Angel (Gabrielite), Angel (Michaelite), Angel (Other), Cow of Dawn, Elephant (Ganesha type), Frog (King type) and No preference. TA has ticked the last one and has again scored 10 points from 10 possible.

BG (*proudly patting TA on its shoulders*):
Congratulations, my dear! Bravo.

GA (*suspiciously tapping with a pointed finger on the very last page*):
May I ask why you didn't tick "Angel (Michaelite)" in the final section? Don't you want to have your weapons back?

TA (*sheepishly honest*):
I thought Upper Management would like "No preference" more. I want to be promoted.

GA (*shaking its angelic curls*):
You're an opportunist, you know that?

BG (*soothingly*):

Tut, tut. You are recommended to stay angels anyway, for the next time being. The end of the Script is (*harrumph*) a little challenging. You will need to use the shape you're most familiar with. And TA will be allowed to use all its weapons.

TA (*delightedly grinning*):

Life gets better and better. When you say "challenging," what does you mean exactly? Will we get any reinforcement?

BG (*looking a little compassionately at TA*):

Kind of. You will get a permanent nurse on duty for this cloud.

GA (*suspiciously*):

I beg your pardon? A nurse on duty? We don't want any more staff. And we're not ill; we don't need a permanent nurse.

BG (*hesitantly*):

Not yet. However, maybe we can change this to a nurse expert system (*punching a few keys on GA's console*).

Suddenly, two new pocket-size AI devices with long lanyards apparate with a whoosh in the cockpit. BG takes one device in his hands and checks the buttons and captions.

BG (*hanging one device around GA's neck, the other around TA's*):

Here. With this button, you can call for immediate attention from a nurse. And use the red one if you are in deep trouble. It's a direct line to Mother Mary. However, only press it if you really need to.

TA (*trying to free itself from the necklace*):

No way. We already made an emergency call to Upper Management not long ago. They'll think we're stupid. I feel like a baby on a baby phone. Or a senior resident in assisted living with an emergency button for intensive care. It's ridiculous. I'm a Michaelite.

BG (*in a serious voice*):

Please do me a favour and wear these devices at all times. No one will blame you for anything that happens from now on.

Very worriedly fumbling for the Script, both angels look at each other with big eyes.

BG (*in a much more cheerful voice*):

But before we start anything else, you'll have a graduation ceremony for passing the course. I've arranged something fantastic for you! We'll have finger food, wine and a guest lecture from a famous interreligious expert from the Saints Section!

GA (*mildly interested*):

Who is it? Is he good-looking?

BG (*proudly*):
He is. Guy named Swami Vivekananda, a patriotic saint of India. You will love him. I know him from England. He is a great lecturer. He is perhaps best known for his speech at the Parliament of the World's Religions in Chicago in 1893.

He agreed to read to you parts of the famous speech that he delivered as a Vedic sannyasin, from a religion that has taught the world both tolerance and universal acceptance.

TA (*with unpleasantness*):
But we *did* pass the exam, right? Can't we have just the finger food and wine? Why a guest lecturer for a graduation ceremony? Is that the usual procedure?

BG (*expectantly*):
Thanks to your course knowledge, you'll recognise two famous quotes in his speech from "Shiva mahimna stotram," the hymn about the greatness of Shiva. *The New York Herald* opined at that time that Vivekananda is undoubtedly the greatest figure in the Parliament of the World's Religions. After hearing him, they wrote, everybody felt how foolish it was to send missionaries to this learned nation. He was a great spokesperson for harmony among religions in the parliament, using common themes of universality to emphasise religious tolerance. I'm sure you'll benefit from his lecture at your graduation ceremony!

Swami Vivekananda apparates on the cloud. GA and TA cheer obediently.

SV (*in his lecturing voice*):
Cosmic powers of the Divine, (*the swami whispering to BG, "This was the biggest adaptation that I made. The original says, 'brothers and sisters of America'"*)

It fills my heart with unspeakable joy to rise in response to the warm and cordial welcome that you have given me. (*warning harrumph from BG with a look at TA*)

I thank you in the name of the most ancient order of monks in the world; I thank you in the name of the mother of religions; and I thank you in the name of millions and millions of Hindu people of all classes and sects.

My thanks, also, to some of the speakers on this cloud (*bowing to BG*), who have told you that we from far-off nations may well claim the honour of bearing to different lands the idea of toleration.

I am proud to belong to a religion which has taught the world both tolerance and universal acceptance. We believe not only in universal toleration, but we accept all religions as true. I am proud to belong to a nation which has sheltered the persecuted and the refugees of all religions and all nations of the earth.

I am proud to tell you that we have gathered in our bosom the purest remnant of the Israelites, who came to southern India and took refuge with us in the very year in which their holy temple was shattered to pieces by Roman tyranny. I am proud to belong to the religion which has sheltered and is still fostering the remnant of the grand Zoroastrian nation.

I will quote to you, brethren, a few lines from a hymn which I remember to have repeated from my earliest boyhood, which is every day repeated by millions of human beings:

"As the different streams having their sources in different places all mingle their water in the sea, so, O Lord, the different paths which men take through different tendencies, various though they appear, crooked or straight, all lead to Thee."

At this point, BG gets up and cheers wildly with the Script in his hands.

The present ceremony, which is one of the most modest assemblies ever held, is in itself a vindication, a declaration to the world of the wonderful doctrine preached in the Gita:

"Whosoever comes to Me, through whatsoever form, I reach him; all angels are struggling through paths which in the end lead to me."

TA grimaces to GA while thinking about how they'd looked in the frog form. Warning glance from BG.

Sectarianism, bigotry, and its horrible descendant, fanaticism, have long possessed this beautiful universe. They have filled it with violence, drenched it often and often with blood, destroyed kindness and sent every creature to despair. Had it not been for these horrible demons, we would be far more advanced than it is now.

Everybody claps their hands.

But their time is come; and I fervently hope that the bell that tolled in honour of this ceremony may be the death-knell of all fanaticism, of all persecutions with the sword or with the pen, and of all uncharitable feelings between living creatures wending their way to the same goal.

Standing ovations begin on the cloud. Swami Vivekananda modestly bows to the audience.

Meeting Shiva and Parvati Again

Around ten o'clock the next morning, they started on a temple tour with the prior. On their way to the temple in Ayyarmalai Kulithalai, the prior, who was driving and was accompanied by a young monk, showed them the social projects of the ashram, such as the kindergarten and a retirement home for elderly people. Tilda was very impressed and loved the man for that. Then a solitary volcanic mountain appeared in the distance. It was about 650 feet high, and a climb of 1156 steps led worshippers to the Shiva temple with Dravidian architecture at the peak that was dedicated to a holy man named Sri Rathnagiriswarar.

"This is a statue of Arthanāreeswarā, the integrated half-male, half-female Shiva," the prior said, "it is a rare form of perfect unity in the Divine." "Attention! Project stuff!" Gabriel whispered to Tilda. "Individual-level integration inside personalities." Tilda was fascinated. "Why is that perfectly integrated deity half male and half female?" she asked in a feeble voice. "Bit complicated and bloodthirsty myth behind that," the prior replied, laughing. "The short story is that Parvati did something that annoyed Shiva. They are always quibbling. You know the myth with the peacock, right?" They nodded. "It's a little bit like this. Here, it's about a wise man named Bhrigu who didn't approach Shiva with enough reference, according to Parvati. She sucked the flesh out of his body, as punishment. Shiva, who thought this to be a little over the top, compensated Bhrigu with a third leg and demanded penance from Parvati, which she carried out by worshipping Shiva with some rituals on a hilltop. As a result of these rituals, Shiva said he would grant her a wish. She asked for a portion of her Lord Shiva's sacred body, thus granting the devotees integrated worship. This led to the manifestation of half-male, half-female Arthanāreeswarā, where Parvati occupied the left side and Shiva the right side, signifying the creation of this manifestation. You will see a statue of this manifestation that is six feet in height, the right half of the image as male and left half as female, melting into each other in perfect unity." "Any further mythological importance up here?" Tilda asked the prior. "Yes," he reported, "you will see Shiva's snake, famous for its coiling around Shiva's neck. Vasuki is the king of the snakes, symbolised by a 60-foot-long snake carved on the hill." "Ach was," murmured Tilda.

When their little group had arrived, around lunchtime, everybody else was already there. Obviously, it was an attractive place for Hindu pilgrims. Thousands of people—young ones, kids, old people—slowly crawled up the steps to the temple through the blazingly hot day. At the foot of the rough stone stairs steeply rising up to the skies, there were souvenir shops, one or two snack bars and the ubiquitous place where they could leave their shoes for money. "Do we need to hike up barefoot?" Tilda asked incredulously. Obviously, she feared for her ankle. The prior giggled and nodded. These delicate Europeans! "Yes, we'll need about two hours to get up there. Going down again will be easier," he said. "It's quite exhausting. You'll need all your strength in this heat, but you look fit enough. We'll buy some water for our breaks. There are some resting places on the climb: caves and suchlike."

Tilda and Gabriel looked at each other. "What little Indian kids and old grannies can do, we'll have no problem with, right?" Tilda pointed out encouragingly. Then the prior explained the etiquette for the visit. They were the only non-Indian people far and wide. "First, non-Hindus are not allowed in here. However, you're with me, and the priests know me. They'll silently ignore your presence. But do be respectful, join the worshippers in their prayers and don't behave in any noticeably different way from anybody else. If any of the worshippers take offence, the priest will remove you from the premises, and I won't be able help you any longer. There might even be a riot when people get aggressive against trespassers. Then you need to run, OK?" They uneasily nodded their consent. "Second, you will need some cash on you for the sacred tokens that will be offered to you." "What kind of tokens?" Gabriel asked. "Mostly flower wreaths and blessing powders that have been consecrated by the priests for when you're standing in front of the shrines with the other worshippers. You will use them for certain rituals and ceremonies directly at the shrines or later at home in your private service," the prior said. "In return, you give money to the priests without being asked." They checked their funds, which were OK for that purpose. "And last but not least," the prior continued, grinning, "take care of the monkeys!" The hill was inhabited by hundreds of wild monkeys who behaved as if they were the owners of the place, which they probably were. The prior bought some Indian bananas at the snack shop to feed the monkeys on their way up. The animals were quite aggressive. It was kind of necessary to pacify—or at least to bribe—them with some food. However, Tilda got the feeling that they did not think much of these tiny bananas—probably because all the pilgrims brought them. The monkeys threw them around on the stairs relatively unenthusiastically and looked down disdainfully at the sweating pilgrims crawling up the stairs.

Then they started the hike. It was hard. The prior had stopped his explanations—first because of the exhausting climb and second to avoid drawing attention to the fact that foreigners and non-Hindus were among the worshippers. It was obvious that Gabriel and Tilda were not Indian—actually, the only European people to be seen on the whole mountain. But they might be mistaken for Hindus at least. They simply had to go with the flow and do what everybody else was doing. That was what the prior and his companion from the Shantivanam congregation did as well. Gabriel and Tilda prayed in front of every shrine they passed in that temple, most of the time not really knowing what it was about or what exactly the ritual meant. However, they had been sufficiently briefed by Bede Griffiths to be happy with myth.

Only the meaning of one ritual was very obvious, at least to Tilda and Gabriel. And it was remarkable. It took place in front of the manifestation of the half-male, half-female Arthanāreeswarā. Where else? They were pushed forward by the crowds, which passed in endless rows of sweating people in front of dark shrines where likewise sweating, half-naked priests performed rituals to consecrate the tokens for the single shrines. This was why the two of them—surrounded by a dense crowd of worshippers—suddenly stood side by side in front of a priest at Arthanāreeswarā.

He mistook Gabriel and Tilda for a couple asking for a blessing of their love from Arthanāreeswarā. He gave Gabriel a huge floral wreath and pointed at Tilda, making a sign that he should hang the thing around her neck. He did the same to Tilda, mutatis mutandis. Then the priest waved towards the statue and explained with his eyes. They were demanded to pretend to be Shiva and Parvati to become one flesh, as male-female. They were in a kind of mythological marriage ceremony. They hesitated. But they could not escape. It would have caused a catastrophe. Tilda looked at Gabriel pensively. Then she smiled, took her flower wreath and, with soft tender movements, hung the wreath around him. The surrounding people cheered and congratulated Gabriel. He followed Tilda's example, accompanied by the cheers of their witnesses, who then congratulated Tilda. Myth-wise, they were in perfect unity.

However, Tilda felt her old world disintegrate with every painful step she took on these stairs. The climb had nearly fractured her ankle, which was a mess of swollen flesh around inflamed sinews. It didn't feel like she was climbing towards the peak of that temple. It was the opposite: She was going down. It was as if she sank into unconscious nothingness.

This weird process had already started in Shantivanam. Here, it continued mercilessly to demonstrate that everything that had been important to her was meaningless and that only the here and now mattered. And in the here and now, there was Gabriel, *Evolutionaries* and all this talk about the evolution of new consciousness. For her, only chaos was evolving. She walked on shaky legs, and she didn't know what hurt more—her ankle or her heart.

On the "Undoing Differences" Interface Again

Gabriel and Tilda left Shantivanam after lunchtime, fetched by Baloo and Balee. The first hour was terrible. For Gabriel, the best part of the journey was over. He had a hard time saying goodbye to Shantivanam. He would have returned home immediately without further ado. Tilda was still in pain with her ankle and everything. She sat in her corner of the backseat with a pale face and clenched fists. Furthermore, they had no clue where they were heading. Ayaan had arranged what he said would be a "surprise sightseeing tour" for them. The two army officers, Baloo and Balee, were talking in the front seats, sometimes singing loudly with the radio while swerving through the dense traffic with considerable honking. They went on in this way for ages, driving through the lovely countryside. Gabriel was keenly aware of Tilda's having severe pain again. She could hardly sit without having her foot high up on the seat in front of her. He was very sorry for her and deeply wished that he could help her somehow. It got worse during the day because they had to sit motionless in the car for hours. Tilda went very white and very quiet.

In late afternoon, they arrived at a town named Madurai, where a tour guide was already waiting for them in the lobby of the hotel that Ayaan had booked. "We'll go to Meenakshi Temple," the guide said, explaining the plan for the evening. "Tourists are usually not allowed in there, but our army chef has managed to get an exception for you." Maybe they were all just saying so to make Gabriel and Tilda feel good. Whatever it was, they felt good, even Tilda, having finally arrived at a place to rest. At least they felt good until the guide explained to them the central myth of the temple that they were going to visit. There were thousands of temples, thousands of deities and thousands of shrines for everything in India.

"This temple is dedicated, as the name says, to Meenakshi, who is a form of Parvati, and her consort, Sundareshwar, who is a form of Shiva. The temple is about their celestial marriage and the equality of male and female," the guide explained complacently. "Of course, it is," Tilda murmured. The guide told them the myth about some royals who wanted a son as a successor but who got a daughter with three breasts instead, poor sods. Shiva intervened, saying that the parents should treat her like a son, and when she meets her husband, she would lose the third breast. They followed the advice. When the girl grew up, the king crowned her as the successor. Meeting Shiva then, his words came true, and she took her true form of Meenakshi or Parvati. "The marriage of Meenakshi and Shiva was the biggest event, with all gods, goddesses and living beings gathered. This is worshipped in this temple. The priests even transport the artistic representations of Meenakshi and Shiva every night from their usual separate places in the temple to a hidden sanctuary so that they can spend the night together." "Why shouldn't they?" Tilda murmured. Following the rituals of the temple, Tilda and Gabriel again exchanged flower wreaths, but they were not half as elaborate as they were the first time. However, this time, they participated in an impressive ritual centring on the fertility of women. It was a ceremony where red tikas were applied to their foreheads by the priests, who gave them blessings, and holy oils were consecrated in the sanctuary to splash them over the women standing closest to the shrine. Tilda had a large portion of oil on her head, which mixed with her red tika.

"This should have gone on your ankle, together with some lymphatic drainage," Gabriel said, seeing her soaked in holy oil. He got a little bag with consecrated red tika powder during the ritual from the priest on duty, and he was happy about that. Red tika powder was for spirit, fire and love, they had learnt. Useful stuff. Actually priceless. When they came out of the temple into the night of the populated Madurai city centre, heavily decorated with their tokens, Baloo, who had accompanied them inside without showing any emotions, took a picture of them with his mobile phone. "For Pa," he smiled. Tilda and Gabriel grinned at each other understandingly. Obviously, he wanted to send proof that he had done his duty. Ayaan later sent the picture to Gabriel's email for posterity. An interesting picture. Of course, a gently smiling couple could be seen, very much in harmony and unity with each other. But they also looked quite serious and sober. No ecstatic, orgy-type temple faces. These were two autoethnographers. Two cultural scientists doing their job of trying to understand what was going on.

Afterwards, they continued reading *Evolutionaries* on the dark terrace of Gabriel's room. They had a rewarding discussion about the ways that human consciousness approaches the world and how the evolution of 'new consciousness' that they'd read about would work. For example, they discussed the criticism on inductive reasoning by philosopher David Hume: "You can never be sure the sun will rise tomorrow morning just from because it always has. Or you can't say that all swans are white just because you haven't seen a black swan so far. How will evolving 'new consciousness' meet truth conditions?" Tilda asked. "Maybe 'new consciousness' is not so keen on logic and what it can or can't do," Gabriel assumed. "Maybe it approaches truth conditions in the experimental way of mythological intuition, as we did today in the temple. We kind of realised truth via mythological experience." "OK, then we are at the point again where we say machines can't do that," Tilda stated. "They can't get married in a temple, as far as I know."

The Limits of Artificial Intelligence

Angels' Play

Location:
Heaven above Madurai. Shared-Office Cloud.

Time:
Real-time GMT+5.30, Tuesday, 13 January 2020, 15:15 IST

Players:
The two angels as before and Bede Griffiths.

The Limits of Artificial Intelligence

Setting:
The angels and BG are celebrating the passing of their exams with some Indian Kingfisher beer.

TA (*defiantly again now that it has passed its exam*):
Why is everybody so sure that a machine can't carry out myth? AI is cool nowadays!

BG (*taking every opportunity to lecture*):
As I said in *The Marriage of East and West*, myth is a symbolic utterance that arises from the depths of the unconscious or, rather, from the deep levels of consciousness that lie below the level of rational consciousness. The rational mind, with its abstract concepts and logical constructions, is like the tip of an iceberg, while below it are vast levels of consciousness that link our human nature with the universe around us and with the archetypes or transcendent principles that govern the universe.

TA (*a little impolitely*):
I don't get it.

BG (*soothingly explaining*):
The myth is the reflection in the human imagination of these archetypical ideas, those cosmic principles and powers that were known in the ancient world as gods or angels.

TA (*calmed*):
Then, I'm OK. I *am* an angel after all, right?

GA (*meddling*):
Sort of...

BG (*agreeing to doubts about machines*):
Through the myth, ancient humans were brought into contact with this world of the gods and of the transcendent source both of gods and humans. And at the same time, the myth took shape in their imagination, engaging all the powers of their being, their intellect and will, their feelings and affections, their senses and their whole physical being. In other words, the myth was the means of their total integration: with the universe around him, with their own inner experience and with the transcendent world of the spirit.

TA (*eagerly*):
But what about reason? Isn't reason more, err, reliable and valid? We have passed this primitive stage of consciousness, right? AI can do primitive. AI can do symbols. What else does AI need to be capable of?

BG (*waving his hand to slow things down*):
The imagination, which is indeed the faculty of primitive thought, expresses itself in symbols (literally, from the Greek, that which is "thrown together"), which reflect this multiplicity of meaning in a single word. In other words, primitive

thought is intuitive; it grasps the whole in all its parts. The rational mind comes later to distinguish between all the different aspects of the word and to separate their meanings. These are the two basic faculties of the mind: the intuitive, which grasps the whole but does not distinguish the parts, and the rational, which distinguishes the parts but can't grasp the whole. Both of these powers are necessary for the functioning of the human mind.

Intuition without reason is blind; it is deep and comprehensive but confused and obscure. Reason without intuition is empty and sterile; it constructs logical systems that have no basis in reality.

TA (*complaining*):

But AI machines are quite embedded in many societies these days. They gather data. They have their basis in reality. And look at these gods and goddesses of the Vedas. AI can simulate their symbolism and behaviours and what have you. Where's the problem?

BG (*lecturing*):

In the Vedas is a marvellous meeting of the intuitive and the rational mind. They are deeply rooted in the world of myth, but the rational mind has already begun to draw out all the complex meanings of words and to integrate them in a cosmic vision. We own Sri Aurobindo, the sage of Pondicherry, the understanding of the complex symbolism of the Vedas. For many centuries, their deeper meanings had been lost, and they'd been interpreted with a crude literalism. But Sri Aurobindo was able to show that a deeper psychological meaning belied the external physical sense.

TA (*questioningly*):

What about materialism? Isn't everything rooted in some type of physics? Without a brain, no thinking; without a device, no machine operation.

BG (*trying not to hurt TA's feelings*):

The Vedic seers reached an understanding of the threefold nature of the world, at once physical, psychological and spiritual. These three worlds were seen to be interdependent, every physical reality having a psychological aspect, and both aspects, physical and psychological, were integrated in a spiritual vision.

TA (*on its last line of defence*):

But AI is definitely the coolest things that Western rationalism has brought about so far, right? It's top-notch in terms of superior consciousness!

BG (*quoting by heart from his book "The Marriage of East & West, page 52*):

As I said earlier: Currently, "a revolution is quietly taking place in Western science, and it is slowly beginning to rediscover an ancient tradition of wisdom, according to which mind and matter are interdependent and complementary aspects of one reality. The same process can be observed in Western medicine, where it is gradually coming to be realised that all disease is psychosomatic and that the human body can't be properly treated as separate from the soul".

TA (*rebelliously*):
TRINI-T may prevent anyone practicing alternative medicine from tampering with Tilda's ankle. I don't want her to suffer. And I doubt you'll find many friends with your ideas. This is old stuff. The Vedas! When was this supposed to be modern?

BG (*obviously thinking the opposite*):
In human nature, this latent consciousness begins to come into actual consciousness, and as human consciousness develops, it grows more and more conscious of the universal consciousness in which it is grounded. Thus, we begin to discover the threefold nature of the Vedic universe: There is the physical aspect of matter (*prakriti*), the feminine principle, from which everything evolves, and consciousness (*purusha*), the masculine principle of reason and order in the universe. Beyond both is the supreme principle, the ground of Being from which everything comes and which pervades all things. In the Vedic tradition, the two principles, the feminine and the masculine, were conceived as heaven and earth, and all of creation came into being through their marriage.

TA
(*silently massaging its ankle*):
Good. As long as I don't have to marry GA. Ugh.

GA (*anxiously*):
What is it? Why are you on your ankle? Is it Tilda?

TA (*in self-inspection mode, then diagnosing*):
Personality disintegration combined with myofascial pain syndrome and post-traumatic depression.

GA (*pointing at the Script*):
Tilda will be seeing this doctor at Chennai hospital soon. Maybe he can do something. That was one of her reasons to go to India in the first instance. She is curious to try non-Western medicine. And wasn't an oil massage something that Father Bede had advised earlier?

TA (*shaking its head warningly*):
It might indeed help. But it could also backfire on the other symptoms. I'm not sure that this is a good idea after all. There are all kinds of unknown side effects and counter-indications concerning the application of oil massages on pain patients with personality disintegration. I have heard about an angel that ... (*trying to enter into a long-winded medical discourse on pharmaceutical cross-indications*).

Where the Three Oceans Meet

For Tilda, the worst thing was thinking of Ken at night. He was the only thing she had. And he wouldn't understand any of her feelings. She hardly did herself. The only things that were kind of in line with her old world at home were the insight that "reality" was just a social construction and that the real thing was hidden by a veil.

However, in Ken's and her world at home, the elites were responsible for the veil, and they could be fought against. In Gabriel's world, the veil would be gradually lifted by some evolving "new consciousness." What bloody nonsense! The elites would again get away with their evildoings if they started to believe in such an opium of the masses.

Anyway, in India, she suffered from being torn away from her convictions and from her good rapport with Ken. She didn't contact Kennie once. She couldn't bear it. What this abstinence did to her could be felt in her foot. Her ankle pain was worse than ever.

In her emails, she'd seen a note from the German hospital indicating that the surgery had been scheduled for the 16th of February and that her public health insurance had agreed to the treatment plan and cover the cost. Despite her fears, she nearly longed for this operation now because the pain had become unbearable.

The next morning, they left Madurai, heading south. It was still quite early. "Where are we going?" Gabriel asked Baloo. "Pa has organised everything for you. You will enjoy," Baloo said. Then a salvo of laughter. At a certain point, Tilda fetched her mobile phone to locate them on the map. She sat in the backseat, totally amazed. "Here we are," Tilda said, pointing to the moving blue dot that represented them. "We're heading to the southern land's end point of India." Gabriel looked at the name of the place: Kanyakumari. "Isn't that the place where the prior of Shantivanam was born?" he asked Tilda, but she could not remember. Gabriel was very sure. "Why does Ayaan want us to go there? He couldn't know that this is the prior's birthplace, could he? And if so, what could be so special to go such a long way to see it?" Tilda shrugged her shoulders. She looked pretty worn out. Her ankle seemed to hurt severely.

Arriving at Kanyakumari around lunchtime, Baloo brought the car to a stop with a flourish in front of the best hotel in town, Seashore Hotel. "This is a special place, sir," Baloo said. "From this hotel, you can see the sun rising and the sun sinking while standing at the same window. And this is the southern peak of India—the place where three oceans connect and many cultures meet: Bangalore Bay, the Indian Ocean and the Arabian Sea." Tilda and Gabriel looked at each other. Project stuff!

The place had every feature of a seaside resort. It was not big and was focused on a small, populated area directly at the beach surrounded by empty shores and wastelands to its left and right. The little town itself was densely cultivated by many hotels facing the beach, with two small islands in front, an elegant little white church that looked somehow French presiding over them and a seaside fair with many colourful stalls between the hotels and water that reminded them of Brighton & Hove's seafront. The place was full of holidaying Indian people. Gabriel got a huge apartment with a separate sitting room, bedroom and kitchenette on the sixth floor and with a stunning view of the mingling three oceans. To the left, he could see the white church in proximity. Tilda was in a more modest room two storeys below but it also had a gorgeous view of the ocean. The weather was in the process of changing. It was still nice and sunny, but dark clouds were packed at the horizon, and the wind was starting up.

"First you have lunch. Then Pa wants you to visit the temple on the island and then look at the sunset. This is a holy place for Hindus," Baloo said, pointing to the bigger of the two islands on the coast on which some buildings could be seen. Various ferry boats transported tourists the short distance between the island and the main shore. Tilda groaned. Another Hindu temple. But Baloo was merciless. He took them up to the top floor of the hotel, where they were led to a little table for two directly at the window overlooking the sea.

There, they had quite a good lunch that at least restored their strength to bear the sightseeing that Ayaan had arranged for them. "We need to take a bath in the three oceans," Gabriel said to Tilda over lunch. She looked doubtingly at the huge waves, the strong currents and the upcoming bad weather. "Baloo will never allow that, Mr David," she said. "He'll be held responsible for our safety." "He's not our father, Mrs Toelz," Gabriel said. "I want us to get into these waters. To bathe in three oceans at the same time when they're meeting from all the world's regions! Imagine. This is not only a legend; it is deeply significant for our project. At this place, waters are mingling not only from the East and the West but also from the North and the South. It is the marriage motif again. To bathe here is not an option; it is scheduled. This is why we're here. Don't you understand?" Tilda thought about it and nodded her consent. "Then Baloo shouldn't know about it," she suggested. "We can try to escape his supervision later. Ayaan can't blame him if we outmanoeuvre him." "Great idea, Mrs Toelz. We can cautiously find out where the exact spot is that the waters mingle and go swimming before dinner." Gabriel loved creativity when he saw it. Baloo and Balee were already waiting in the hotel lobby when they came down after lunch. "Pa has ordered a tour guide again," Baloo said. They met the guide at the ferry pier. Again, the two soldiers were greeted with huge respect, giving them all kinds of advantages not given to the ordinary tourist. Though there were long queues in front of the ticket office for the ferry transfer to the islands, their little group of four directly marched to the shuttle stop for the bigger island, passed the passengers boarding there and were placed into the sheltered VIP section of the boat on cushioned seats while the other tourists had to scrunch together in the common area with life vests. Their guide had already started his lecture on the boot as they looked at the little town from the waterside.

"The place got its name from the goddess Kanya Kumari, who is believed to remove any rigidity from the mind and to whom women pray for marriage," the guide explained. "For what else," Tilda murmured under her breath. "Kanya is an avatar of Parvati," the guide continued pleasantly. "Of whom else," groaned Tilda. Gabriel poked her in the side to silence her. It was embarrassing. This was not the guide's fault after all. "I now tell you the myths of this place," he said. Gabriel warningly looked at Tilda to keep her quiet. "Kanya—or, better, Parvati—was to marry Shiva. But he failed to show up on his wedding day. Rice and other grains meant for the wedding feast remained unused and turned into stones as time went by. Look at the small stones on the shore that look like rice! These are the grains from the wedding that was never properly carried out," the guide said as he theatrically waved his hands towards the shore. "Kanya is considered as a virgin goddess blessing to all the pilgrims who come here."

"Why are women praying to a virgin goddess for marriage? That's not logical," Tilda complained. "How sad a story," Gabriel intervened before Tilda could say anything more intriguing. "Is there another myth connected to this place?" "Yes," said the guid, grinning, "it is equally celibate." Seeing their questioning looks, he continued: "It is said that Hanuman, who is the exemplary celibate bachelor god, dropped a piece of earth containing a life-saving herb from the Himalayas, called mrita sanjivani, here at Kanyakumari. The place is referred to as the hills where medicine lives. This is said to be the reason for the abundance of unique medicinal plants native to the area. It is just down the beach to that side." He pointed to the east shoreside.

"So this is a place where life-saving healing takes place?" Gabriel asked, and he had his reasons. The guide nodded in affirmation. "One question," Tilda said mischievously. "Would this Hanuman god, who is, if I'm right, connected to a monkey shape, by any chance happen to be another avatar of Shiva? Otherwise, he'd somehow stand out"—with a side glance to Gabriel—"at least, he would not fit into our usual story. It would be a perfect match if Shiva were involved." The guide looked at her amazed. "But he is. In South Indian tradition, Hanuman is said to be an avatar of Shiva. How did you know?"

"I didn't," Tilda hissed, to the surprise and slight dismay of the guide, who thought her to be a really strange stranger. Seeing his face, Tilda continued more calmly: "It sounds just a little paradoxical, and I'm surprised. Here, Shiva and Parvati are bachelor and virgin, or at least their avatars. And this in the face of the situation of when they got married and have so-and-so-many children!" Their little group approached the island. "What about this rock?" Tilda asked. The guide said, cautiously glancing at her to see whether she would freak out again, "Here on this rock, Parvati as Kanyakumari performed *tapas* for Shiva." "She cooked Spanish finger food?" Tilda asked incredulously. They had to explain what tapas were in Spain. The guide shook his head with laughter. "No, no! *Tapas* are spiritual and monastic practices in the Hindu religion meant for *moksha*, which is liberation and salvation." "What type of practices?" Tilda asked suspiciously. Gabriel poked her in the ribs again. "The practices stem from the Vedic concepts of heat, or inner energy, and can range from asceticism, meditation and solitude to spiritual ecstasy and even to the warmth of sexual intimacy," the guide lectured. "I thought Parvati was a virgin goddess over here!" Tilda complained, but nobody heard her, because their boat was just landing.

The Vivekananda Rock Memorial on that island was a popular tourist destination for pilgrims. The ferry boats constantly dropped people off and took them back to the mainland about five hundred metres away. The huge monument on the island was dedicated to Swami Vivekananda, who achieved enlightenment on that rock. "Poor sod," Gabriel said to Tilda. "Apparitions and revelations, probably. We know what that means, Mrs Toelz!" On the smaller, neighbouring island, there was a huge statue of a famous Tamil poet named Valluvar. Swami Vivekananda had a big memorial tablet indicating that he had been a great supporter of interreligious dialogue and a famous speaker at the Parliament of the World's Religions in Chicago. Thus, in the end, they had once again arrived at an important place for their project.

Furthermore, they saw a sundial facing the open sea, which allowed them to identify the exact location where one could see the sunset and the sunrise on the horizon. Pointing to a place a little bit further west of the shore, Baloo said, "For sunset, we will go over there. There you can see it best." Back on the mainland, it was indeed time for the sunset, but it had started to rain and was quite windy. So they went by car, and hundreds of people followed them, to the sunset point a little outside of town. They had a short walk to the beach, but there was nothing really to be seen, because the weather was now changing in earnest. No sunset whatsoever, only clouds. "It'll be getting worse very soon, sir," Baloo said, who now looked really tired and worn out. So did Balee.

"We will go back to the hotel and retire for an early rest," Gabriel said. "There's nothing to be done in this weather anyway." Baloo looked relieved. "Yes, you can order an early-bird dinner in the hotel restaurant. You won't need us anymore?" Gabriel shook his head, then he looked at Tilda. They both thought of their escape to bathe in the three oceans.

"Tomorrow, we'll make an early start for Chennai," Baloo said, "I'll give you a wakeup call at 6:00 am, then you can watch the sunrise at 6:15, when it's scheduled for tomorrow morning, and we can leave directly afterwards. This way, we'll be in time for madam's appointment at six o'clock in the evening in Chennai." He nodded at Tilda and looked at her foot. This was a long speech for the silent Baloo, but he did it while looking forward to having a free evening. It was already getting dark when they entered the hotel again. They wished a good night to Baloo and Balee, who contently took position as guards in the deep armchairs of the hotel lobby. Tilda and Gabriel agreed to rest for an hour and then to meet in Gabriel's sitting room to plan their escape.

Angels' Play

Location:
Heaven above Kanyakumari. Shared-Office Cloud.

Time:
Real-time GMT+5.30, Tuesday, 13 January 2020, 18:45 IST

Players:
The two angels as before.

Setting:
Both angels are in a heated discussion. TA is in its full armour. GA is about to press the Mother Mary emergency button on his lanyard device.

TA (*trying to prevent its colleague from pressing the button*):
Wait a second!

GA (*urgently*):

For what, exactly? You know we can't manage a religious war. This is an enemy attack!

TA (*soothingly*):

We passed the professional development course, even the extra module. We can make peace.

GA (*sobering*):

Says a Michaelite. Look at you, you peacemaker. Why are you in full amour? We had a Vivekananda Rock conflict already, back in 1962. We don't want another.

TA (*interested*): What happened?

GA (*reading from a hand-out that Swami Vivekananda distributed for his talk*):

You must know that Kanyakumari features a comparatively large population of local Catholic fishers. When the Hindus wanted to build that memorial for Swami Vivekananda's birth centenary, with a pedestrian bridge leading to the rock, the Christians wildly protested.

TA (*curiously*):

What did they do?

GA (*resignedly*):

They put up a big cross on the rock that could be seen from the shore and from the sea. They said this rock was not Vivekananda Rock but St. Xavier's Rock. Of course, this led to protests by the Hindu population, who said the rock was a place of worship for Hindus. The issue was taken to court, which decided that the cross should be removed.

So, it was. But secretly, at night. Nobody knows by which party. There were riots, and the situation got slightly out of control. The rock was declared a prohibited area, guarded by armed officers.

TA (*concerned*):

And the fishers?

GA (*shrugging its little shoulders*):

They still fight with the Hindus over here.

TA (*whispering with a look at the console*):

And St. Xavier? He's supposed to be the apostle of the Indies. Wasn't he furious when the court decided against the cross?

GA (*waving this away*):

You know him. He's a Jesuit. The conflict was not his idea. He's fine with everything. And he's close friends with Swami Vivekananda nowadays.

TA (*curiously*):

And the Hindus?

GA (*in a worried voice*):
Still very much on guard to protect their sacred places against trespass from Christians.

TA (*demandingly*):
And you're sure that Gabriel and Tilda will trespass?

GA (*pointing to the Script*):
Unfortunately, yes. They have no clue what they're doing. They'll run into the arms of militant Hindus guarding their temples.

TA (*still a little hesitantly*):
But why Mother Mary herself? Isn't that a bit over the top? Think of our reputation with Upper Management. Can't St. Xavier and the swami handle this for the Saints Section?

GA (*very convinced*):
Believe me, if these fanatics down there see one of the participants of the old conflict involved, they'll see red. This even calls for Mary and Infant!

TA presses the red button for Mother Mary on its device, which dangles from its neck.

Mortal Fear Again

"How can we escape?" Gabriel excitedly asked Tilda when she comfortably settled into a huge armchair in his sitting room. "I'm not sure we should at all, Mr David," she replied. "Baloo and Balee will be in big trouble if Ayaan ever finds out. Furthermore, the weather is really bad now, and this place where the three oceans are said to meet is about four kilometres away. How shall we get there without getting completely soaked? And how shall we find it anyway?" "Why, Mrs Toelz, we simply walk down the beach to the left. What else?" Gabriel replied impatiently. "It'll be dangerous. It's dark, and we might encounter people like the motorbike gang again," she said a little fearfully. "Come on," Gabriel said. "We'll exit the hotel through the back door used by the staff. Then Baloo and Balee won't be able see us and won't check anyway, because they think we're already sleeping. We'll be back before dinner time. They're fine, Mrs Toelz—believe me. And you're supposed to be a fighter. Where's your gear? You promised to be my bodyguard, remember?" Tilda pointed to her rucksack. It was really bulky and looked heavy. "What's inside?" Gabriel asked suspiciously. "Better not ask, Mr David." Tilda grinned. And he didn't. Why should he care about what arsenal she'd brought from Germany? But obviously, she was well prepared for another attack. So what was her problem? Gabriel excitedly pushed her out the door. They went down in the elevator to the basement level for staff and tiptoed out of the hotel into its backyard.

"Let's go down to the beach fair, Mrs Toelz. Somewhere between the booths will grant us access to the beach," Gabriel suggested. When they arrived at the fair, however, they discovered that access to the beach was not available. "Everywhere, 'No

Trespassing' signs," remarked Tilda. They asked a stall owner. "It's dangerous, and further down, there are some temples directly on the beach: There's the Golden Temple, the Kanyakumari Tirupathi Temple and the Mutta Pathi Temple. No one's allowed to go there except for service," the stall owner said as he looked at them, "and it's not for foreigners anyway." "What shall we do, Mr David?" asked Tilda, and then she continued hopefully: "Return to the hotel?" "No way," Gabriel replied. "If we can't go down to the beach right here, maybe we can further down the country road, somewhere between the temples. Let's walk."

They started out in the dark, passing the white church and approaching the end of town on the country road that followed in parallel with the shore. Through the rainstorm, now in coming down full blast, they could see lights in the far distance, indicating that another dwelling was about two kilometres ahead. "This must be Chinnamuttom," Tilda said, voicing her assumption. "The three oceans' intersection is right behind there." "What are we waiting for, Mrs Toelz?" Gabriel asked. However, they'd already had a very queasy feeling when they left town. The further they travelled from the touristic centre, the less friendly people in the dimly lit streets looked. At some point, they passed a kind of drum parade in a sheltered courtyard, which they wanted to watch because it felt like a party. However, they were scared away by some aggressively looking young men. Then it became really desolate.

The muddy country road was stormy, dark and lonely and strongly reminded them of their adventure from a few days ago. Only no monstrance to be seen. They were deep in Hindu territory. And for Tilda's taste, the road digressed too much from the shore for the direct approach she'd have preferred. Thus, they were afraid of not finding the right spot. "Let's try to get closer to the water," she said to Gabriel after about two kilometres. "Maybe there's some access to the beach by now." They tried some side paths in vain before they found one leading directly to the shore. However, unfortunately, it led directly to one of these temples as well. They saw the complex lying in deep darkness. "Mrs Toelz, I think we can dare to pass it to get down to the beach," Gabriel whispered to Tilda. They cautiously approached. However, they realised that it was guarded. And not by police but by a group of about thirty young men, who seemingly couldn't believe that some foreigners would dare to go down to the beach through the temple area.

It was a narrow escape! Gabriel feared for Tilda and her bad ankle, but she was so scared that pain was nothing to her. They ran for their lives. Back on the country road, Tilda pleaded for them to return to the hotel. But for Gabriel, it was now a matter of honour: "We'll bathe in the three oceans. And if this is the last thing we do, Mrs Toelz, we'll prove that integration is more powerful than aggression." "Whom do you want to prove that to, Mr David?" Tilda asked soberly. "There's nobody around." She was right. They were standing in the middle of the storm and the rain. It was pitch-black night. No weather for a bath in the sea. "We go," Gabriel decided. "Come on." Tilda then groaned. Coming closer to the spot that they assumed to be the right one, they tried again to reach the shore. The group of temple guards must have followed their approach on the road because the men were already there before them. Indeed, one temple followed the other—no way to reach the shore in between. This time, they had approached by crawling up through the coppice, so the men didn't see them.

Receding onto the country road, they held council. "These are militant Hindus, Mr David. The worst kind. These are the people you read about in the newspaper. Killing people from other faiths out of fanatism. I'm opting to give up and go home," Tilda said. "I know, Mrs Toelz," Gabriel said, "but I'm not yet ready to give up. Let's go to the little village ahead and give it a last try. If we can't go down to the waters there, I'm willing to return without having achieved anything." Tilda looked at him hopefully. "Promise, Mr David?" she asked. "Promise," Gabriel replied. They walked down towards the beach for the third time and entered a smallish village with fisher's huts, where everybody already seemed to have gone to bed. Unfortunately, the ground was a little higher here than that of the rest of the countryside, which meant a steep coast with densely overgrown cliffs. No way to get down to the beach. Again, it seemed completely inaccessible, now because of nature. Gabriel and Tilda looked down the deep abyss, which was the only way to reach the beach, where they could hear the wild waters raging. They were definitely at the right spot, standing there in the middle of the dark and silent fisher's huts. "Listen," said Tilda, completely awed, "these are the three oceans mingling. They're talking to each other." "I want to see it, Mrs Toelz. I want to swim here," Gabriel said desperately. Tilda shook her head in the dark. "It's impossible. Give it up," she said softly. It had stopped raining, and the storm had suddenly ceased. They stood a moment in the dark. All was silent. Defeat.

Infanta

Then a door opened. Two girls came from one of the closest huts. They were between thirteen and eighteen. The younger looked like a boy in football attire; the elder was festively dressed in a sari. "Good evening," the elder girl said in her nicest English, "and welcome to my country. My name is Infanta. What are you doing here? Can we help you?" Tilda and Gabriel looked at her like she was an apparition. The girl laughed. They introduced themselves, and Gabriel explained to Infanta that they wanted to take a bath in the three oceans. She shook her head. "It's too dangerous," she said. "There are strong currents. And you can't even go down in this darkness without being bitten by poisonous snakes, which live in the coppices of our cliff. We wouldn't go down there ourselves at night, and we live here." "Snakes?" asked Tilda with a shudder. The football girl nodded. "You come back tomorrow," Infanta suggested, "then we will show you down." "We can't," Gabriel answered. "We'll be leaving tomorrow morning at 6 o'clock. It's now or never."

The door of the hut opened again. The mother of the two girls. Obviously, she was worried about what these two foreigners were up to with her children. Infanta went to her and talked in Tamil. There was an intense dispute. Obviously, the English of the mother was not a fraction as good as that of the girls. Then Infanta came back. "Are you Christians?" Gabriel had expected everything else but this question. Taken by complete surprise, he nodded. Infanta returned to her mother. After some more discussion, both disappeared into the hut, coming back with a headlight torch of immense size. "My friend and I will go down with you," Infanta said, "but stay within the range of the headlight and be careful of snakes!" The four of them climbed down the steep coast—the two girls much more adeptly than Tilda and Gabriel, of course.

Then they finally reached the water. It was completely dark except for the headlight. They looked at the hurling currents of the breaking waves. It was clear that swimming was out of the question. The wild waters were reminiscent of a kind of turbulent birth process. But at least they'd reached the water. Gabriel kicked his shoes off, and to the surprise of the two girls and the dismay of Tilda, who kept a safe distance from the waters, he went into the sea. He stood there for a long time as the waters whirled around his legs. Then he returned to the three girls on shore who'd watched him silently and attentively. He bent down in the dark to pick up some pebbles from the shore as souvenirs of the three-oceans spot. He wanted to take something with him that had been in these waters as he had been. The two Indian girls saw what he did and eagerly started to help him. They picked up stones, pebbles and seashells and pressed them into Gabriel's and Tilda's hands. "You need to give them money, Mr David," Tilda said. She was right. The girls expected some return for their efforts. In the shine of the torchlight, Tilda and Gabriel fetched their purses and handed both girls a decent amount of money. The girls cheered and laughed gratefully. "Why did you ask whether we're Christians?" Gabriel asked Infanta curiously. "Because we are too!" she answered before continuing: "We wanted to help you. This is the night of our annual church feast. It's the white church you passed. Mother Mary's church. It's named Our Lady of Ransom. We'll go there later tonight and celebrate all night. You might wish to come as well?" "No, we can't," Tilda said quickly. "We have to leave very early tomorrow, sorry."

"My companion is right, we can't go with you," Gabriel said, now having achieved everything they'd come for. "Wow can we get back on the country road the quickest from here?" "We'll show you," Infanta said. "We can walk together down the beach. There is an access point. From there, you can easily reach the country road." Gabriel put on his shoes again. Before they left, Infanta approached him in the dark and with a smile put a last seashell that she had just picked up into his hands. It felt big and light. "Thank you! I'm very grateful that you did this for us," Gabriel said. She nodded seriously. Carefully, he put the seashell, as the farewell present of the three oceans, into his jacket with the other items.

A Narrow Escape

Black night and dark sea. At least the rainstorm had softened to a light dribble in a soft breeze. They walked down the beach while the two girls told them a little about the girls' lives and current school education. It was nice. Then they approached the access point. "But that's the temple district," Tilda objected. "Yes, it's the only way up to the road," Infanta said. "It's deserted at night." But it was not now. The men were already waiting. They had seen the torchlight approaching, and they were furious that Gabriel and Tilda had dared to trespass against their warning. Everybody was shouting. Though they recognised the two girls, they didn't care very much about them. Just girls. They did not count for much. Gabriel could feel the fear in their two little helpers. Their lives were in danger again. And this time, all four of them. The group of thirty men approached them menacingly. Tilda grabbed for her rucksack. But they would not stand a chance at fighting these guys. They didn't even have an opportunity to run away this time, because they couldn't leave Infanta and her sister.

When the danger reached a climax, the mother appeared and saved them. Appearing was not the right word. Infanta's mother came shooting down the hill. She came racing and screaming. In her hands, she held a cooking pan, which she swung high over her head. Her face was wild with rage. She stormed against the young men approaching the little group of four. She threw herself against the men, yelling. Completely taken by surprise, the militant group stopped, made space for her and watched her in awe.

"Run!" Infanta shouted. They fled uphill towards the fisher's huts—the mother sheltering them from behind, fighting the group of men back. But the men were standing dumbfounded anyway. Nothing as furious as a mother defending her children against whatever enemy is threatening them! Out of breath, Gabriel and Tilda reached the hut of Infanta's mother again. She looked at them in confusion. "Now we can go pray and say thank you," she sternly advised. Meekly, Tilda and Gabriel followed the little family through the dark and silent streets of the little village. They soon reached a kind of small marketplace with an illuminated chapel in it. "Infant Jesus Shrine," the mother proudly announced. It was butt ugly in Tilda's eyes—bright neon colours with naïve statues. All of them fervently thanked Infant Jesus and Mother Mary for their narrow escape. All four of them knelt down in the middle of the marketplace in front of the shrine and prayed.

"Now, we need to go to the main church for our celebration," Infanta smiled. "Are you sure you don't want to come?" "Yes, we'll go home instead. We're knackered," Gabriel said. After giving their profound thanks to both girls and saying reverential goodbyes to the brave mother, they departed. On their way back to the hotel, Gabriel realised that Tilda was more scared than he'd assumed. She was completely silent and very often looked back to scan the area between the shore and the country road for movement. "Are you afraid that we're being followed, Mrs Toelz?" Gabriel tried to start some conversation. "What do you think? We narrowly escaped!" "Yes, but the mother was great, wasn't she?" "The men were just too stunned to do anything, Mr David. Maybe they were reminded of their own mothers. They might have recovered by now and might try again. They must be out for revenge because of our trespassing." Gabriel waved this away before speaking: "I think we're out of the woods now. One such attack is enough for an evening."

Angels' Play

Location:
Heaven above Kanyakumari. Shared-Office Cloud.

Time:
Real-time GMT+5.30, Tuesday, 13 January 2020, 21:12 IST

Players:
The two angels as before.

Setting:
The conference facility of the cloud looks like a hospital room. TA is groaning on its sickbed. GA is sitting at its bedside. In an attempt to distract its colleague from its severe pain, the angel is reading loudly from the Script.

GA (*consolingly*):
Listen to that. It's nice. And so appropriate. It's about Gabriel's seashell:
"Look at the pattern this seashell makes.
The dappled whorl, curving inward to infinity.
That's the shape of the universe itself.
There's a constant pressure pushing towards pattern.
A tendency in matter to evolve into ever-more-complex forms.
It's a kind of pattern gravity,
a holy greening power we call Viriditas,
and it is the driving force of the cosmos.
Life, you see."

TA (*only mildly interested in its pain*):
Who's the quote from?

GA (*looking it up*):
Guy named Kim Stanley Robinson, US writer of science fiction, best known for his *Mars Trilogy*, where the quote is from. Do you like it?

TA (*nodding*):
Nice. Is he a Benedictine? Just wondering.

GA (*understandingly*):
Because of his reference to Hildegard von Bingen's Viriditas? He uses her concept just as "the green force of life, expanding into the universe." But it is her concept alright (*laughing while checking Robinson's Wikipedia entry*)

The *Mars Trilogy* features scientists as heroes. Gabriel would love that: Scientists becoming critically important because of their discoveries, networking and collaboration.

They are portrayed as the best people to guide public policy on important environmental and technological questions, of which politicians are often ignorant. Robinson's biographer, Robert Markley, says that Robinson "views science as the model for a utopian politics. ... Even in Robinson's novels that don't seem to be sci-fi, like *Shaman*, the inductive method, the collective search for greater knowledge about the world that can be put to use for the good for all, is front and center."

GA is looking it up because TA is groaning louder again.

GA (*concerned*):
What's up?

TA (*with a bit of unpleasantness*):
What do you think? How can Tilda's foot get after this adventure? Can we do the healing session soon?

GA (*compassionately*):
I'll ask for that medical healing oil again (*pressing the buttons on the nurse-on-duty device*).

TA (*wildly in its pain*):
I don't want a nurse! I only want you in here. I'm in pain. I can't bear anybody else!

GA (*helplessly*):
I'm not an expert. I'm afraid of doing more damage than good. Remember the warning of St. Luke against side effects and cross-indications.

TA (*shouting*):
N-o-b-o-d-y else!

GA (*hastily to stop the noise*):
OK, I'll do it. But it's your responsibility. You've asked me to do it. Remember that afterwards!

TA (*confirming*):
You do it.
With a plop, the medical oil apparates on TA's bed. GA looks at it like he would a snake; TA is full of hope.

In the Fair

They saw the consoling lights of Kanyakumari quickly approaching while they wandered along the dark street. Tilda limped heavily. The beach fair was still on, though it had started to rain heavily again. Finally, they arrived in front of the hotels—wet and exhausted but alive. Not many people visited the little fair in this rain. It was a different world than that of the dark danger that they'd just escaped from. Happy tourists drinking colourful soft drinks and eating candy floss between booths selling saris, hoodies and souvenirs. "Let's buy some of these candy drinks and celebrate our survival, Mrs Toelz. Afterwards, we can go for dinner at the hotel restaurant."

Gabriel approached one of the illuminated snack stalls and ordered two soft drinks out of big glass containers. Feeling for his purse to pay them, Gabriel's hand encountered the big seashell from Infanta given as a goodbye present of the three oceans mingling, which he had not seen so far by light. He took it out of his pocket for inspection in the light of the booth and to show it to Tilda. They both looked at the shell in his palm in utter surprise. It was the most beautiful seashell that Gabriel had ever seen in his life, and he'd collected many. "It's green. It comes from the three oceans. It's seen integration, unity and the married waters of all the world's regions," he said devoutly. "It is big, and its shape is perfect. It looks like a piece of art," Tilda said with rapt admiration. "Its pattern looks like a snake. This is project stuff," Gabriel declared, smiling reverently. They could not believe that Infanta had picked this up without being able to see anything in the pitch-black night of the rainy shore.

"Your ankle's really bad, isn't it, Mrs Toelz?" Gabriel asked, seeing Tilda wince at every movement, "and tomorrow you will present it to that doctor in Chennai." "Yes, so what?" Tilda looked at him questioningly. "I'll invite you for a nice oil massage to treat your pain. Now," Gabriel said resolutely. He pointed to a stall with an Ayurveda display and a big sign that read "The healer is in." Tilda shook her head in dismay, but Gabriel pushed her into the little shop and paid for immediate treatment. The healer was a tall, good-looking Indian with many rings at his fingers. First, they talked about her medical history. Tilda was sitting on a kind of bench with her foot in the healer's lap, and she showed him exactly where she'd been hit. He felt the bone structures of her ankle. Her foot looked tiny and fragile, though it was swollen from exertion. She then explained how everything had been damaged in the fight. Gabriel, who had heard parts of the story before, found it very illustrative, and to him, it sounded as though it had happened just yesterday. In his mind, he could see the actual accident scene, hear the bones crack and feel the contortion of muscles and sinews. So could the healer, who closed his eyes and started his work. The massage with Ayurveda oils lasted for half an hour. Tilda felt better afterwards, but the massage had made everything so sensitive that she could not bear weight on her foot anymore.

Gabriel had to half carry her through the rain to the hotel, which was close by, fortunately. When they reached the hotel, they used the back door again because they saw Baloo and Balee still sitting in the hotel lobby. Imagine their faces if they'd have seen Gabriel and Tilda passing them from the outside: wet, dirty and exhausted with their rucksacks. Tilda heavily limping and hardly able to walk anymore. Baloo would have had a heart attack.

Gabriel and Tilda were really hungry. After changing their wet clothes, they met in the nice top-level restaurant, where they got the same table that they already had at lunch. It was about 9:30 pm, and they were the last guests. The servers scowled a little when they came for such a late-night dinner. However, Gabriel and Tilda ordered a festive meal, with starters, a main course and dessert. Gabriel even had some white wine to go with it to celebrate their survival. Overlooking the dark and stormy sea, they felt warm and cosy in the restaurant at their candlelit table. The ocean view was amazing, where sweet lights were blinking on the two little islands that they'd visited earlier.

Cooperation, Evolution and Safe Spaces

They decided to end the evening with some further reading of *Evolutionaries* in Gabriel's sitting room. Finally sitting in his big armchairs, they realised that the air conditioning was very noisy. When Gabriel went to the huge window overlooking the sea to explore whether it could be opened to substitute air conditioning for fresh air from the outside, not only did he discover that it could indeed be opened, but also, it was the most open window he had ever seen in his life. Glass could be removed to the full window's extension, which was nearly the whole front wall of the sitting in this case. Amazing. They could sit in these huge armchairs in the middle of nature overlooking the ocean. With the window open, they could hear the enormous waves of the ocean below in a constant humming and whooshing sound like a grand orchestra. This voice of nature sounded pleasant and soothing after the events of the evening. When Gabriel leant out of the sixth-floor window into the rain, he saw another miracle. To the left was the beautiful white Mother Mary Church, which they'd passed in the dark on their three-oceans walk. Its tower was now fully illuminated—flashing and blinking in all the colours one could imagine. It looked so beautiful and special that he was absolutely stunned. Then he remembered that Infanta had talked about some church festivities going on just now, which explained the fancy, artistic lightshow decoration. Then Tilda opened the book she'd brought and started reading. "Listen, Mr David, it's about a dinner conversation between the author of *Evolutionaries* and John Stewart, Australian evolutionary theorist and author of the book *Evolution's Arrow: The Direction of Evolution and the Future of Humanity*," she said delighted, "and do you know where they had this conversation? Tucson, Arizona! To be more precise, the University of Arizona at Tucson, where we had our talk a few months ago." They discussed a few interesting passages, as they had done the evenings before. It was about the role of cooperation and participation for evolution in the sense of Teilhard de Chardin. Tilda read on:

"'Pierre Teilhard de Chardin. Teilhard's assertion that evolution follows a clear trajectory toward higher and higher levels of unity and organization planted an important seed, which made intuitive sense. … Cooperation emerges only when evolution discovers a form of organization in which it pays to cooperate.'"

"Do you understand what's being said here about participation and cooperation, Mrs Toelz? It's the central driver of evolution towards the *telos* of everything. This message is important for the multistakeholder approaches in our project. We need an organisational form where this can happen. We need the safe spaces as infrastructure!" Gabriel eagerly said. Tilda laughed before replying: "Yes, it sounds convincing. But everybody cooperating at a certain point might be highly unlikely. Remember our discussion in Madurai, Mr David? In my opinion, cooperation from everybody is as unlikely as the sun not rising tomorrow or us seeing a black swan. Egoism and power are too mighty."

Gabriel sighed. "Mrs Toelz, I know that you think that way." Tilda read on: "Yes, see, the questions are all here.

"What will enable a higher, more evolved form of organization to emerge when 'free riders' are overindulging to the detriment of us all? How can we help further the cooperative process so vital to growth and development in any system?'"

Then Tilda made a long face. "What is it?" Gabriel asked. Tilda said slowly "*Evolutionaries* follows your views, Mr David. Their solution is 'governance'":

> "Why does evolution so clearly follow the Teilhardian trajectory? Cooperation organized by effective governance systems provides unmatched advantage over non-cooperators, and encourages the rise of higher forms of organization, all the way from the structure of cells to tribal councils to contemporary megacities to nascent planetary governance and beyond. We may indeed live in a sociable cosmos, as we learned in the previous chapter, but it is also a cosmos that is going somewhere."

"Sociable cosmos. I like that!" Gabriel laughed delightedly. "Yes, and listen here. They indeed ask for our project approach," Tilda said. Then she read out a final passage from *Evolutionaries*:

> "The need to help organize, incentivize, and otherwise oversee the many national and transnational entities and processes that now exist on this rapidly complexifying pale blue dot out on the spiral arm of the Milky Way is in fact an evolutionary imperative, a developmental challenge for the species itself."

"There you have it," Gabriel said.

No Sunrise and a Black Swan

Gabriel had again arranged the two armchairs in his sitting room at the window to watch the Kanyakumari sunrise with Tilda. At 5:45 am, Baloo entered Gabriel's room, with Tilda in his wake. Baloo was fully awake, unlike the two of them. Cheerfully, he shouted the following instead of good morning: "Sir, no sunrise today!" Tilda and Gabriel looked at each other and started laughing. It was too funny given their discussion mentioning David Hume's famous anti-induction example from last night. But Baloo was certainly right. The weather was again awful with dark clouds, a storm and heavy rain. They would not see one of the sunrises that the place was so famous for. Pity!

"Sir, since no sunrise today, you can come. We start earlier. Now. We have breakfast on the road," Baloo suggested. He was right. No use in waiting. At reception, Gabriel tried to pay for their stay. "It's all covered," the receptionist said. Gabriel looked at Baloo. He shook his head in this unfathomable Indian way that means complacency and satisfaction. Gabriel shrugged his shoulders. He could repay Ayaan for this deposit when he next saw Ayaan again. "Please remind me in Chennai to talk to Ayaan about this, Mrs Toelz," he said to Tilda.

Out in the rain of the hotel parking lot, Balee was already waiting in the dark car with the motor running. The Hume motif became even more impressive when they finally left Kanyakumari. The car passed a Turkish restaurant—now closed, of course, because of the early hours—named The Black Swan. This was good enough to wake Tilda up to see it; the woman was already fast asleep in her corner of the car. "There you go. A black swan. Even if you think it's highly unlikely that cooperation and participation are evolutionary drivers, it's possible!" Gabriel said triumphantly. "We had no sunrise today, and you've seen a black swan. The unlikely is what happens." Then, satisfied, he also fell asleep in his corner of the backseat.

They reached Chennai in the middle of the afternoon. "Baloo, we changed the hotel booking. We're now in this one," Gabriel told Baloo, showing the hotel's location on the map displayed on his mobile. Baloo raised an eyebrow but drove them to the place, which proved to be a British Empire–style palace of sorts. "Your doctor's appointment is at 6 pm," Baloo said. "I have now a few days off. You can call a taxi at reception to go there." He wrote down the address of the clinic, and then Baloo and Balee got really cheerful, because for them, holidays were approaching. They certainly deserved them after having taken good care of Gabriel and Tilda for so many days, successfully delivering their charges to Chennai again.

When the taxi later drove them to the given address, it was that of the doctor whom Ayaan had recommended during his visit to Berlin. Against Gabriel's expectations and apprehensions, he was not the weirdo Gabriel had assumed him to be. Although he was a very reasonable man with no love lost for evidence-based medicine, he was a responsible medical advisor of the Indian national cricket team and, as such, was very familiar with all the injuries that professional sports featured. Furthermore, he was a martial arts person himself and talked expertly with Tilda about the exact nature of the holds and pressures that her fatal fight had contained to end up with these injuries. When he investigated Tilda's ankle with his hands, he very quickly came to a conclusion. "All pain is due to muscular tension; no surgery needed," he said. "Treatment is easy: I can promise to have you back to your old life without pain, in good health and even in professional sports training in no time. We will only need two or three weeks of daily treatment." "Our return flight is for the day after tomorrow," Tilda said. The doctor winced. "Then I will at least start and do what I can. But things will need to be finished by a physiotherapist in Germany that I'll recommend. And I can advise you via Skype nevertheless." The doctor was as good as his word. Treatment started immediately with a nice young physiotherapist who was twice the height, weight and strength of Tilda. Gabriel looked at him as anxiously as did Tilda. "I can come with you for treatment," Gabriel offered.

She was appalled. "Of course not, Mr David!" she said. When she came back, she scouted: "That guy hurts like hell!" Ayaan had texted them with the phone number of his other friend, the Ayurveda master of Kerala oil treatment, along with some hyperlinks; this presented another chance for an Ayurvedic treatment for Tilda. "Kerala is world famous for its Ayurveda oils. This has nothing to do with the amateur massage at the fair in Kanyakumari, Mrs Toelz. This is professional. This is the real thing," Gabriel said to Tilda. "What does *Ayurveda* mean, anyway?" asked Tilda curiously. "The science of life. Considering mind and body as a system,

Ayurveda sees good health as a result of Vata, Pitta, and Kapha in balance." Seeing her puzzled face, he laughed. "These are the three body elements. Any imbalance among these three will result in diseases."

"You become more Indian by the day, Mr David," Tilda complained. "Yes," he said, grinning, "and I believe that it's the only way to find out about these things. Autoethnography, you know!" "And what about the oil?" she asked. "Ayurvedic oil massage restores balance," Gabriel read from Wikipedia: "Oils are widely used ayurvedic remedies for relieving pain, improving blood circulation and energising mind and body. Oil massage clears the stress and toxins from your body, gives your skin a glow and is antiaging. Good ayurvedic oil is precious and very expensive. And Kerala ayurvedic oils are the best of all. They're shipped everywhere." Mockingly, Tilda continued asking: "Is there a special treatment for bad ankles?" Gabriel scanned the text and, to her surprise, said, "Yes, Mrs Toelz. There is, for example, Srotabhyanga massage for removing toxins in the arterial, venous and lymphatic systems and reactivate metabolism. And there is, of course, Padabhyanga massage, a very common foot massage in India." "Blimey," said Tilda.

Angels' Play

Location:
Heaven above Chennai. Shared-Office Cloud.

Time:
Real-time GMT+5.30, Wednesday, 14 January 2020, 08:52 IST

Players:
The two angels as before.

Setting:
The angels are partying. They're sitting buck naked on their cloud, wildly giggling and abundantly splashing Ayurveda oil on each other. Between laughing fits, GA is singing Indian chants, and TA sometimes joins in with its loud and husky voice. Parts of the cloud are hanging dangerously deep, already getting soaked in oil.

GA (*enthusiastically*): Are you feeling better?

TA (*suddenly earnest*):
So-so. My foot is much better.

GA (*questioningly*):
What's wrong?

TA (*worried*):
I fear Frankfurt. What will happen when Tilda touches German ground again? How can she go on? It will tear her apart.

GA (*slightly sobered*):
We'll have to see. It's her decision, in the end. Objective One applies. But now, let's enjoy the last hours in India, and celebrate. You don't get that every day. I'm very proud of them. Even Tilda. She's doing really well!

TA (*only half convinced, checking the Script*): Yeeesss... We need to call the Saints Section again. It is Sri Aurobindo's time now. Swami Vivekananda already told him that he'll be contacted by us.

GA (*mildly interested*):
Is that the guy with *The Life Divine* and integral yoga?
(TA nodding its angelic head and turning to the next page. The angel freezes.)

GA (*anxiously*):
What is it?

TA (*flatly*):
We're supposed to return to Colibri Wharf after Gabriel and Tilda are back home.

GA (*sheepishly*):
Why?

TA (*incredulously*):
Final reporting!

GA (*indignantly*):
WHAT?

TA (*paraphrasing from the Script*):
Gabriel and Tilda are considered to have finished what they were supposed to achieve together. They have accomplished everything. We are called to headquarters for reporting.
Both angels return to partying, but not as wildly as before.

Summary of Project Definition

During their last two days in India, they worked very hard on the Indian case study of AI use in public social service provision while sitting in Ayaan's office. Being back in the sober office environment of an international aid organisation definitely brought them down to earth. "Mr David, there's so much work waiting for us at home to present a convincing project plan to the B1 board!" Tilda groaned before continuing: "Now we have all the bits and pieces. Over the next half year, now we have to make sense of everything and write a work plan for our project, which we might title 'Artificial Intelligence for Assessment'. By the way, the first letters would form the acronym AI FORA, which is pretty cool. After all, FORA is the plural of *forum*, the places in ancient Rome where people negotiated and assessed societal topics of concern, like AI for us nowadays." "Right, Mrs Toelz," Gabriel sighed, "and our topic is cultural influence on AI use in social service provision and what this means for better AI, especially with regard to vulnerable groups in different cultural contexts. We have—sort of—case study descriptions covering cultural influence for Germany of course, then China, the US, Spain, Estonia and India. What's missing?"

"I think we need a rationale for our selection of countries included in the case studies," Tilda said. "But they came to us through Bede Griffiths. We didn't choose them; they chose us," protested Gabriel. "You can't say that in a funding proposal, though, right, Mr David?" Tilda asked soberly before continuing: "We need a real reason why these countries have been included and not others." "Bede Griffiths said so. This is a real reason," Gabriel insisted. Tilda only shook her head. "Please think for a while. Why were our travels interesting? What did we discover? For me, the best learning experience came from cultural differences. Think about what it'd be like in Germany if kindergarten placements were allocated according to membership in an Indian caste system or according to political compliance like in the Chinese social credit system. OK, the German system has its own biases and discriminations, but at least we are culturally used to them," Tilda said. Gabriel laughed. "Yes, Mrs Toelz, social service provision is always about social justice, which is a value. It is about what people think needful and deserving people should get from the state. But who is considered as needful and deserving completely depends on cultural context. If our project title were 'Social Service Provision Using Artificial Intelligence,' then any good AI should be responsive to values in societies and cultural context, right?"

"Yes, right. But what has this to do with the rationale for our case study choices, Mr David?" Tilda asked impatiently. Gabriel slowly said, "It seems as if we should have countries with the broadest cultural variety in our sample, and if I'm not wrong, we've already been quite good at that." "How do you mean?" Tilda asked. "Mrs Toelz, do you know of the World Values Survey?" Gabriel asked as he looked at Tilda's blank face, then he continued: "The famous Inglehart-Welzel map? No?" She shook her head. "You should know about this given that you work at an international aid organisation such as B1. The World Values Survey is a cultural comparison of countries that uses a huge indicator framework that is regularly repeated by social scientists. The map shows cultural clusters. That means that in one cluster, countries that are similar in culture are grouped together. The current map has ten cultural clusters," Gabriel explained, "and as far as I can remember, Germany, China, the US, Estonia, Spain and India are in different clusters." "Then only four more countries are missing, Mr David," Tilda groaned. "I'm currently fed up with travelling."

However, at least by now both of them had good feelings about the project idea and the overall framework. Amiably, they started to create an agenda with timetables for the next half year to develop the AI FORA work plan that B1 might accept. Ayaan and his team helped with the Indian part.

Healing

They had expected a kind of clinic again for the Ayurveda guru. With professional staff and medical attire. Instead, they couldn't even find the house at first. The tuk-tuk driver was desperate. "This is the correct address," he stated, looking suspiciously at the dark ruin in a poor slum-like district of Chennai. No sign at the door, no lights in the house. "We can ask in that shop," Tilda said as she pointed to a little kiosk attached to the house. The owner said they might find somebody in the rear building of the premises to let them in. They carefully approached the dark staircase and had a look at each floor of the three storeys. On the upper level, there was life. A young girl waved them over to an open door. They entered a small, dimly lit, untidy room with a grimy office desk and three ramshackle chairs packed with old papers, ancient books, flagons smeared with oil and dusty objects of incomprehensible use. The girl made some space for them by pushing some dirty, oily towels from two of the chairs and then pointed them to take a seat, which they did very carefully. Tilda was already giggling madly.

Then the master came in. "You may go now," he graciously told the girl, who immediately disappeared. The Ayurveda guru was very old, with a bald head and a long white beard, who was naked from the waist up but otherwise clad Indian style. He had nearly no teeth, long dirty fingernails and amazing blue eyes for an Indian. He introduced himself in bad English and asked who wanted to go first. Tilda looked aghast as she imagined this man touching her. "I'll go first," Gabriel hurriedly said before she could run away. She gloatingly giggled. The guy invitingly waved Gabriel to the door leading to the adjacent treatment room. Accompanied by Tilda's merriment, Gabriel approached the open door full of apprehension, like a lamb ready for slaughter.

There was a narrow treatment table for massage. Otherwise, the room was small, dark and untidy, like the other. The master warmed some oils that he'd mixed together in a bowl over a kind of candle bowl. Then he asked Gabriel to undress. He passed him some dirty towels, which Gabriel took with pointed fingers. Then he had to mount the treatment table. "Are you ready, Mr David?" Tilda asked through the door, left slightly open. Gabriel was only happy that she was somewhere close by to run for help if the guy started to kill him. "Don't know, Mrs Toelz," he weakly responded, waiting for the worst. The master would touch him now. What then happened to both of them was the funniest of their whole Indian adventure. The Ayurveda guru waltzed them through. It was a mixture of severe pain and unbearable tickle. The one under treatment was constantly screaming their head off, while the other in the little waiting room outside was overcome with laughter provoked by the sounds from the other room. Primal scream therapy was nothing compared to this noise that the Ayurveda master let them produce under his merciless hands. When it came to payment, though, their giggles were stifled. The guru charged Western prices.

The Sage of Pondicherry

On their last morning in India, Baloo and Balee fetched Gabriel and Tilda from the hotel for a last sightseeing tour. "Pa wants you to see Pondicherry," Baloo said, bringing them out of Chennai traffic again. They drove three hours down south to reach their destination. "Why does Ayaan want us to see the place? It's our last day in India!" complained Tilda about the long car journey. "It's an interesting tourist place," Baloo said. Gabriel cited from Ayaan's email: "The French East India Company established a trading centre at Pondicherry in the seventeenth century. It still bears a strong resemblance to the colonial French rules of ancient times, though it is union territory nowadays. Furthermore, the Sri Aurobindo Ashram is over there." "Whose ashram?" "Sri Aurobindo, Mrs Toelz, the Hindu sage of Pondicherry. He lived over there. Bede Griffiths mentions him as a favourite interpreter of the Vedas, remember?"

"Yes, but why are we to go see his place today of all days?" Tilda grumbled. Gabriel went on: "Autoethnography again. To improve our understanding of culture. Ayaan thinks that Sr Aurobindo has something important to contribute from a Hindu perspective that supports the idea of participation in our project." "And that is, Mr David?" Tilda asked only a little gracefully. Gabriel read from Ayaan's email on Sri Aurobindo's book *The Life Divine*:

> "Our first decisive step out of our normal mentality is an ascent into a higher Mind capable of the formation of a multitude of aspects of knowledge, ways of action, forms and significances of becoming. Its most characteristic movement is a mass ideation, a system of totality of truth-seeing at a single view; the relations of idea with idea, of truth with truth are not established by logic but pre-exist and emerge already self-seen in the integral whole."

"See?" "OK, let's go there and find mass ideation," Tilda said and sighed.

They spent a nice time at Pondicherry, which, in terms of religion, proved to be a Muslim place rather than a Hindu one. For lunch, they went into a real French restaurant. It was delicious to enjoy French cuisine after all this Indian food. It was quite a posh place. Baloo and Balee decided against eating there, probably because the prices were not in their army allowance budget. They waited outside talking to some locals in front of a shop.

Inside, Tilda and Gabriel played colonialists. They sat in an open atrium with art deco furniture, trees, fountains and many French-looking servers who served the mostly Western-looking guests. Tilda was full of mockery when she looked at them. "See, Mr David, they don't eat with their hands. They use cutlery! How alienated can one be?" "You will use cutlery once again in due course, Mrs Toelz!" Gabriel reminded her. She scowled. "You too. And then everything is at an end. We'll be in our old surroundings, and nothing will be like here anymore." She looked so desperate and wild that Gabriel took up the challenge. "Well, Mrs Toelz," he said solemnly, "we can change that. I promise that I'll go to dinner with you. We'll go to a posh restaurant in the middle of Berlin. And there, I'll eat with my right hand." Tilda looked at him. "You'll really do that, Mr David?" Gabriel felt uncomfortable because she was so serious.

"Or maybe we can do that in Barcelona when we're there next for the AI FORA project." "Nobody knows you in Barcelona! I want to do it in Berlin." "Barcelona has many more inhabitants." "Berlin or nothing. You promised." She had him. Back in the car, triggered by what they had seen, they scanned the many mentions of Sri Aurobindo in *Evolutionaries*, which were scattered throughout the book from the beginning to the very last pages. Tilda said, "I want to continue reading *Evolutionaries* together with you when we get back home, Mr David. This will help us continue everything." Gabriel agreed that this was a good idea. They were only at page 114 now, and the book had about 370 pages. It would not do to jump ahead of things like they'd just done when they scanned for references to Sri Aurobindo.

Open Access This chapter is licensed under the terms of the Creative Commons Attribution 4.0 International License (http://creativecommons.org/licenses/by/4.0/), which permits use, sharing, adaptation, distribution and reproduction in any medium or format, as long as you give appropriate credit to the original author(s) and the source, provide a link to the Creative Commons license and indicate if changes were made.

The images or other third party material in this chapter are included in the chapter's Creative Commons license, unless indicated otherwise in a credit line to the material. If material is not included in the chapter's Creative Commons license and your intended use is not permitted by statutory regulation or exceeds the permitted use, you will need to obtain permission directly from the copyright holder.

Chapter 10
Land's End

Angels' Play

Location:
Colibri Wharf, Headquarter Docks, Office Cloud Block, Gamma Hydra, Sector 14, Coordinates 22,83,7. Shared-Office Cloud of GA and TA.

Time:
Real-time CET, Thursday, 15 January 2020, 04:21

Players:
The place is packed with angels, saints and other cosmic powers. Giving a precise list of attendees would be impossible. All the actors (GA, TA, BG, DHL, SL and SC) and stakeholders from Upper Management—most of them in charge of collecting reports, evaluating performance and determining reaccreditation in the Guardian Angels Section—sit around the conference table. Even the bosses of TA and GA, St. Gabriel and St. Michael themselves, are present. From the Saints Section, Mother Mary (MM) is the highest representative. The Angel Union is represented by an untidy-looking Rafaelite in coveralls. BG is sitting at the head of the table, being in charge as chair.

Setting:
The big conference table has coffee, tea and soft drinks in the middle. At each place, the Script, the angels' marching orders, an agenda, topic-related handouts, blinking electronic devices making weird sounds and all kinds of papers are piled up high. Around the table, many computer screens, flipcharts and whiteboards are covered with dynamic graphics and rising curves. Everybody is amiably chatting.

BG (getting up from his chair and ringing softly with the little metallic peacock bell from Shantivanam)

My dears! Please take your seats. May I have your attention? I would like to start the meeting.

The chatter ceases.

Welcome to this meeting, which is, as you can divine from our illustrious audience, highly relevant headquarter business. Who will take the minutes? (*a tiny Gabrielite sitting against the wall raises its hand*) Thank you, dear.

You all have the agenda in front of you. Any objections to following it? (*nobody raises a hand*) Thank you.

On the 3D server in the middle of the table, which everybody can see simultaneously, the three pictures from the Berlin street session appear.

As you know, the project is ambitious. It is about a three-step integration of dualities on all levels: intrapersonal, interpersonal and systemic. I won't repeat the details. You can check them in your handouts.

Our task here is to evaluate where we are with this three-fold objective.

Any issues? Critical remarks?

Swami Vivekananda and Sri Aurobindo are whispering to each other.

My dears, speak up, please!

Swami Vivekananda:

I have something on the issue of intrapersonal integration. There has been no progress here. How about a deep contemplative experience? Unio mystica and the like? In my opinion, the project still has a long way to go. (*Sri Aurobindo nodding*) Somebody experienced should see to that.

BG (*looking at the minutes-taking Gabrielite*):

Yes, I see. Please note this down as a to-do. Anything else?

MM (*scanning the agenda*):

We will come to the relationship issues later, right? I think there are still too many disparities to realise interpersonal unity between Gabriel and Tilda.

DHL wildly nodding.

BG:

Thank you, yes. You have certainly a point here. We'll keep a note of this. What about Tilda?

TA (*struggling to stand up, still wobbly on its ankle, shamefaced*):

We have flagged her on red alert (*TA grimaces and shrugs its shoulders, and St. Michael points at it to take its seat again*)

BG:

Oh dear! Can we have an update from medical, please?

SL (*getting up and starting his presentation, showing a few slides with his talk*):

We have a severe case of personality disintegration. I will spare you the medical details of the diagnosis. Most of you are laypowers and won't understand a word anyway.

BG:

That's too bad. Anything else?

SL (*looking at St. Michael*):

Errh, yeeesss. I have another announcement to make. However, the two operating angels should leave for that topic of the agenda.

TA and GA look up, insulted.

BG:

OK. Angels, please wait a few minutes in outer space. We'll call you in again later. (*GA and TA evaporate with frozen faces; BG impatiently turning to SL*) Was that really necessary? What is it?

SL (*switching to the next slide with some colour illustrations*):

We'll have two new viruses on earth, and both will aggravate Tilda's mental health problems.

One is called SARS-CoV-2, the disease from which is called COVID for short, for you laypowers. It'll affect the lungs and other human organs. Highly infectious.

The other is called conspiracy theory and is likewise infectious. It affects basic logic, the capacity for perceiving empirical evidence and human reasoning. It increases their aggression potential exponentially.

The worst thing is when these two viruses combine. And this is what is prognosed for Tilda. Due to her personality disintegration, she might be very susceptible to an infection by a conspiracy theory combined with COVID.

BG (*trying to calm down the audience that has started bilateral discussions*):

Silence, please. Goodness! This is really bad.

I see why you wanted the angels to leave. We need to bring this up to TA softly. Please, call those two back in.

GA and TA apparate again on their seats. They still look insulted but also very curious.

Can we have an update on the interpersonal relationship, please? DHL, any news to report?

DHL:

Not from my side. The sexual relationship idea was discarded and has been transformed into a medical healing story.

(*disdainfully looking at SL*)

They traded the warmth of sexual intimacy for a pain-free ankle.

MM (*supportively*):

I think it was an elegant move to transcend the rather critical sexual issue, which had provoked so much trouble, into a healing story. No harm done.

DHL (*heatedly*):

It's always the same with these sexual ethics discussions at our meetings. They end in "no sex." I don't think this to be fair, given the topic.

(*the Eastern powers trying to hide their approving smiles*)

BG (*soothingly because discussions start again*):

Tut, tut. Silence, please! OK, let's move forward with the agenda. Next is the safe-space idea. How will it help to save the world from destruction? I will summarise it, myself.

Everybody is silently groaning. The elephants among the audience stereotypically start to rock, sway and bob their heads in psychological distress. BG uploads his presentation.

Do not fear; I'll keep it short and understandable.

He goes through each case study in much detail, discussing all monasteries worldwide and their potential to become safe spaces. He is doing an extensive SWOT (strengths, weaknesses, opportunities and threats) analysis on each of them. Then he performs a network analysis and shows their expected contributions to world peace. After this, he expertly shows how science and spirituality can cooperate in realising the unity framework by building on the safe-space idea. Furthermore, he shows how autoethnography is the only approach to understanding the depths of cultural impact. He ends with a sound theoretical reflection on the bodies of philosophical and theological literature involved, focusing on the evolutionary theory of society. First, the audience tries to stay awake by drinking tea and coffee until all the pots are empty, and one after the other, they fall asleep.

BG (*ending his talk with a bow*):

...And this led me to writing another script, on how to proceed from here, which I will distribute now to give you a short introduction and a complex learning experience...

He looks around sheepishly, everybody sleeps; even Swami Vivekananda and Sri Aurobindo are snoring, leaning against each other.

Postponed till next meeting.

BG rings the peacock bell. Everybody wakes up and riffles through their or its documents.

Summarising: We are happy with Gabriel and Tilda. They accomplished what they set out to do.

This would not have been possible without the invaluable work of our two operating angels here. Bravo! I hereby support their application for promotion, which is next on the agenda.

Can we vote? Who's in favour of promotion? (*Everybody raises a hand or likewise*) Who is against? (*Nobody moves*) Who's neutral? (*Nobody moves*) Thank you.

BG turns to GA and TA.

Congratulations! (*Friendly cheering resounds from everybody; GA and TA blush*)

Harrumph. Now, I need to mention a matter of personnel. TA will be assigned to another team. For now, this is for the next few months to come, but maybe this will become permanent (*Everybody looks awkwardly at both angels, which are completely shocked*). Nothing to do with performance. An Objective One issue. I am very sorry, myself.

Any other business? (*Nobody moves*) Well, thank you all very much for this constructive meeting! See you next time. The meeting is closed.

Video Nearly Killed the Radio Star

The plane landed in Frankfurt with a huge bump. Outside, the cold January morning was still too dark to see anything but the lights of the terminal building through a light drizzle of rain. Gabriel and Tilda hardly had the time to say goodbye because Tilda's connecting flight to Berlin offered little time for the gate change; Gabriel was supposed to handle a few business matters for B1 in Frankfurt for a day, so he had to stay behind. But they were sure to take up their office life for the day after next anyway. So they only shouted their farewells, and Tilda rushed to reach her connection.

On the plane to Berlin, she finally read all the messages from Ken, who would fetch her from the airport. This way, she was a little prepared for what was coming. Seeing Ken standing alone with a single red rose and a sad face in the middle of the crowd at Tegel Airport made her heart sink. She had totally forgotten how familiar he looked, how good-looking he was and how much she loved him. "Why haven't you messaged me even one time?" was the first question he asked. "I didn't have an Internet connection" she lied.

What followed was an ordeal for her. Ken wanted to know everything, but she found that she couldn't tell him anything. Words failed her. That made him even more furious. Faltering, she started to tell him about her temple visits and Indian cultural habits. She tried to talk about their adventures and what they'd learnt. "This is awful," Ken stated. "You did things you would not have done under normal circumstances. All of this went against our life principles." "But I did nothing wrong," Tilda objected. "I think you did," he said. "You betrayed your own beliefs on what's important in life; you betrayed the values I share with you; and you betrayed me as a person by doing all these things with your precious Mr David." "I didn't betray you," she desperately said. "I love you." "Then, prove it!" Ken barked. "How?" she asked.

Ken had clear ideas on this. "Three things. First thing tomorrow, you will go on sick leave for at least six months. You'll leave your fucking boss to his own devices with this bloody new project. You'll simply stop doing it. You hear me? That will clear your mind." Tilda slowly nodded. "The only contact I allow you to have with Mr. David is a few afternoon conversations to clarify with him how it came about that you behaved so uncharacteristically and therefore wrongly in India. You're allowed to do what I would call archaeology of the individual. You may deal with the past and try to come to terms with it through revisitation. That's all. Archaeology." Tilda shook her head. "He won't do that." "Ask him," Ken said. "That's all he'll get from you for the foreseeable future." "For how long?" Tilda asked. "As long as I see fit," Ken answered snappishly.

"And second?" Tilda asked. "Your so-called missing Internet connection—or, better, I should say your Internet abstinence, has held you back from what's really going on," Ken said. "While you were playing Shiva and Parvati with Mr David in India, I protested against the enslavement of people by the newest conspiracy of the elites. Haven't you heard about the pandemic rules, mass vaccinations and lockdowns that they're planning because of the new disease they're calling COVID-19? These are the torture instruments of our dictatorial, reptilian government. For example, they want us to wear a muzzle, preventing free speech. I'm now part of Querdenken, a vegan protester group of mostly young people between twenty-five and thirty-five gathered around influencer Attila Hildmann. We all believe that the current political system has to be stopped because the politicians in power manipulate our thoughts. We are free thinkers standing up against authorities and willing to take action against them. There are no pandemics. This is just fearmongering."

Tilda was shocked. "Mass vaccination? Are you sure?" Ken nodded. He considered himself well informed. "Because of the politically changed legal situation in the IfSG Infection Protection Act, compulsory vaccinations are possible. Medical doctors specialising in immunology and toxicology in our Ärzte für Aufklärung network estimate about 80,000 deaths and estimate that over four million people will sustain vaccine injuries." He showed her a leaflet with a crying child who just got an injection. "They want to use mandatory so-called virus tests to take a DNA sample of every individual for the European genome database." "What do you want me to do?" Tilda asked. "I want you, as my second, not only to be part of our protester group but also to be one of its leading architects. This is to wake up stupid sheeple such as your Mr David. They should go to their slaughter in these fake pandemics or just wake up. For a start, I want you to write an article in Compact Magazine, which is one of our Querdenken outlets. This is a much better contribution to save the world than writing a work plan for this bloody project." Tilda nodded.

"And third?" she asked. Ken scowled. "I want you to emotionally disconnect from Mr David. Totally." "But I *am* disconnected," Tilda protested weakly. "No, I want you to prove it to me. Annoy him. Undermine his confidence. Ruffle his feathers. He's our enemy. Don't forget that." "How shall I prove my loyalty to you?" Tilda asked with pale lips, pale because she knew his vengeful and manipulative sides well enough. Kennie grinned. "We'll troll him. For example, we can hack his Amazon account and buy stuff for him." "What stuff?" Tilda asked. "Well, I have tons of good ideas! Objects that send little messages like 'Go fuck yourself,'" Ken said menacingly. "Kennie!" Tilda screamed, appalled. He stared back. "Won't you do this for me?" Tilda sighed.

The next morning, she started with Ken's first requirement Ken. She went to her doctor, claimed burnout and phoned the B1 personnel department to give notice of her absence for the months to come. Then she phoned Gabriel.

"The trip to India shook up my private life, and there was—and still is—a lot to work through," she explained. "What's happened, Mrs Toelz?" Gabriel asked her. "I told Ken about the events in India, which put my relationship with him on shaky ground. There have been recriminations and admissions of guilt, and we're still working through the situation," Tilda said in a flat voice. "What guilt?" Gabriel asked, amazed. "I can explain in some afternoon conversations why I behaved like I did in India," Tilda replied, tiredly but faithfully repeating what Ken had wanted her to say. "This is all that my boyfriend allows me to do. He calls it archaeology of the individual: dealing with the past and trying to come to terms with it through revisitation."

As foreseen by her, Gabriel did not go for it. Instead, he entered into a philosophical discussion. "I'm not an object for excavation and dissection. I'm not a mummy, nor is our relationship. Archaeology indeed unearths things, but it is destructive. Every archaeological excavation leads to the destruction of the evidence. I won't be available for such an exercise." "But archaeology of our relationship will reveal what it was. It will re-establish honesty and truth between me and Ken," Tilda retorted, defending the idea. Gabriel shook this off. "It's probably possible to X-ray everything for complete forensic transparency. It might be possible to lock the internal state of the object under investigation in a finite description, having then the frozen inner impression of total transparency. You call this 'honesty'? That 'honesty' is pure positivism: It means the accurate exact description of what is seen under the microscope. This only works because what is seen from the dissection table is dead. In any case, on the dissection table is something that is finished and completed, something about which we can find out the final 'truth,' something that we can honestly reveal information from and that can therefore be 'understood.' At some point, we're done with it and put the results in a museum. It's honesty; it's stupidity!"

"But you are always the one doing this exegesis thing," Tilda protested. "You revisited all these Bede Griffiths texts and our travel events for their meaning!" "This is something completely different," he said. "Exegesis is the interpretation, illumination and explanation of something that is alive and moving. We are moving, as Teilhard de Chardin says. Exegesis creates something new. It deals with meaning. It deals with the future. It's actually the counter-concept of what you have in mind with Ken's archaeology of the individual." "Where's the difference?" Tilda asked obstinately. "And does it actually make a difference?" "It makes all the difference," Gabriel stated. "In my opinion, your concept of honesty in a relationship is the problem. It lies at the heart of your feelings of guilt and the accusations that come from your boyfriend for allegedly breeching his trust. Your concept of the inner truth of a person is that this inner truth can be identified as a number of truth items that can be skewered like dead butterflies in a fossil collection. To reveal your inner truth to a person is like showing your butterfly collection to them. Archaeology of the individual would mean excavating your butterfly collection and taking a look at the dusty assembly. The same is true for what you mean by 'knowing and trusting your partner.' You have shown him your collection, and a trustworthy partnership means that your partner has been granted access to your collection at any time to check whether there are any changes, right? You call that transparency and trustworthiness."

"And what's wrong with it?" Tilda asked snappishly. Gabriel answered: "I reject your concept of inner truth, for a start. In exegesis, *person* and *truth* are secrets that can't be fully understood and that are always moving into being. Even one's own inner truth is a deep secret to themself. It can be approximated only with ongoing effort and never with full success. Within the play of light and shadow, of being and decay, of proximity and distance, of possibilities and constraints, one's own inner truth is equally in need of interpretation and explanation as the truths of others, the truth of creation or the truth of salvation. We are never safe from surprise: Suddenly, there's something instead of nothing; suddenly, something makes sense that did not make sense ever before; suddenly, an inner door opens; suddenly, a fog lifts."

"Nice words," Tilda said, "but where are their consequences?" "This has consequences on the meaning of *honesty* and the claims you can have or make in this direction," Gabriel said. "Somebody who is a secret to themselves and takes the secret of others seriously can't convey transparency in your sense. It would simply be dishonest. They *aren't* transparent, not even to themself. How could you mislead others to think you are? Honesty is only the honesty of the moment, of a special fleeting perspective on an inner transition—a momentary snapshot interpretation of an inner movement. If you really want to convey honesty, that would mean adhering to this fundamental nontransparency!"

"I don't want to talk to you like that anymore. I want to have a clear conscience with Ken!" Tilda now shouted. But Gabriel was not yet done. "To lead others to believe in transparency is eyewash because you confront them with dead descriptions, which don't hold, even from your own point of view. You try to fixate on something that can't be fixated on just to calm yourself, to stabilise what can't be stabilised. You pass on something to others that you're unwilling to carry as a burden, yourself. Conscience can't be ignored in this way: It would a kind thing to shelter others from this kind of egoistic would-be transparency and honesty." "And what is your bloody suggestion?" Tilda asked, still shouting. "Are honesty, inner truth and a culture of sharing inner changes not values, in your opinion? Is it not allowed to demand them or strive for them in a relationship?" "Oh yes, they're very important values," Gabriel said calmly. "Here, I totally agree with you. Unfortunately, it's very, very difficult to find somebody to share with and to expect somebody to bear the burden of sharing. Who can grasp the complexity that I can't grasp, myself? Who can carry the nontransparency that I can't carry, myself? Who can bear the honesty that I can hardly face, myself? It might sound strange: the plea to be understood, the plea expressing an original human need, can be heard and followed up on only by somebody who accepts fundamental nontransparency and the secret changes in the other person and who is willing at any time to affirm and support this change, even against their own interests." "I understand that you don't want to talk to me about the past," Tilda said. "Then this is our last conversation." With this, she cut the line.

Angels' Play

Location:
Colibri Wharf, Headquarter Docks, Office Cloud Block, Gamma Hydra, Sector 14, Coordinates 22,83,7. Shared-Office Cloud of GA and TA.

Time:
Real-time CET, Ash Wednesday, 26 February 2020, 18:04

Players:
The two angels.

Setting:
A dark moonless night. The working cloud is very untidy. Gadgets, wires and boxes are wildly distributed over the place. In one corner, a heap of damaged weapons has piled up and looks like a scrapyard. The cloud looks desolate and in dissolution. TA is slowly and solemnly packing its gear.

GA (*desperate, sometimes hiding little things belonging to TA behind its back to slow down the packing process*):
Are you sure? Do you really need to go? You can't leave me all alone by myself. I need you. How can I go on without you?

TA (*not looking up from carefully placing a little green elephant into its decoration gearbox*):
You heard Tilda. Objective One. She can do what she decides, and she's done it. It's her choice.

They look at each other disconsolately. Despite GA's little acts of sabotage, TA's packing is nearly done.

TA (*hoarsely*):
I'll go now. You've been good sports. Best of luck with the project.

After some awkward seconds, the angels start an embrace but shy away from it at the very last moment. TA abruptly turns away and evaporates into the dark night.

For a long time, GA silently stands alone on the fringe of the cloud facing the empty orbit. Nothing can be heard. Then somebody from the radio starts to play a song by Freddie Mercury.

To see how the AI FORA project Gabriel and Tilda were putting together during their travels worked out and what results were produced for the country cases mentioned, the reader is invited to consult the two social science publications in this series on "Artificial Intelligence for Assessment". However, findings of the project will also be made available again in a novel format. The story will continue with "Playing Ball against Heaven's Gate

Open Access This chapter is licensed under the terms of the Creative Commons Attribution 4.0 International License (http://creativecommons.org/licenses/by/4.0/), which permits use, sharing, adaptation, distribution and reproduction in any medium or format, as long as you give appropriate credit to the original author(s) and the source, provide a link to the Creative Commons license and indicate if changes were made.

The images or other third party material in this chapter are included in the chapter's Creative Commons license, unless indicated otherwise in a credit line to the material. If material is not included in the chapter's Creative Commons license and your intended use is not permitted by statutory regulation or exceeds the permitted use, you will need to obtain permission directly from the copyright holder.

GPSR Compliance

The European Union's (EU) General Product Safety Regulation (GPSR) is a set of rules that requires consumer products to be safe and our obligations to ensure this.

If you have any concerns about our products, you can contact us on

ProductSafety@springernature.com

In case Publisher is established outside the EU, the EU authorized representative is:

Springer Nature Customer Service Center GmbH
Europaplatz 3
69115 Heidelberg, Germany

www.ingramcontent.com/pod-product-compliance
Lightning Source LLC
LaVergne TN
LVHW021334080526
838202LV00003B/166

9 783031 604003